P9-CMS-732

COMPLETE
HANDBOOK OF
BUSINESS ENGLISH

COMPLETE
HANDBOOK OF
BUSINESS ENGLISH

William Repp

Prentice-Hall, Inc.
Englewood Cliffs, New Jersey

Prentice-Hall International, Inc., *London*
Prentice-Hall of Australia, Pty. Ltd., *Sydney*
Prentice-Hall of Canada, Ltd., *Toronto*
Prentice-Hall of India Private Ltd., *New Delhi*
Prentice-Hall of Japan, Inc., *Tokyo*
Prentice-Hall of Southeast Asia Pte. Ltd. *Singapore*
Whitehall Books, Ltd., *Wellington, New Zealand*

Library of Congress Cataloging in Publication Data

Repp, William
  Complete handbook of business English.
  Includes index.
  1. English language—Business English. I. Title.
PE1115.R45   808′.066651021   82-485
ISBN 0-13-160960-2   AACR2

Printed in the United States of America

Dedication

To my special joys—

Rick, Steve, and Michelle

...and Cindy

What This Book Can Do for You

This instant reference book will help you solve just about any problems you might have with using English correctly and effectively. It will help you locate the answers to many questions of business English usage you face each day, without the bother of last-minute searches through book after book of wordy reference material.

You're busy. Most successful executives juggle 10, 20, or 30 projects at once. But you still have to get things done through people—using the English language.

Yet, look what can happen on the managerial firing line each day:

- You find yourself writing a proposal to a key government official to get a major contract and you're suddenly not sure how to address him or her;
- Your crackerjack secretary, who's an expert at spelling, is out with the flu and you have to send a memo to the chief executive officer. There's one word in the copy that *looks* misspelled, but you're not absolutely sure, and you can't find the dictionary.
- The production division has already begun to convert to metric units, but all your previous correspondence has been in the traditional units. Obviously, you can't ask someone from production to help you convert the old units into new ones.
- The vice president of finance has just asked you to give the committee an overview of your department—at 9 a.m. tomorrow morning. You haven't given more than three presentations in five years, so you need a refresher in good presentation techniques—fast.

This convenient *Complete Handbook of Business English* will help you solve each of these problems *in seconds*. It can help you:

- *Put* punch into your sentences and reports simply, with the right choice of punctuation.
- *Grab* your reader's attention—right from the start!
- *Show* you how to dictate letters and memos without wasting your time.

- *Tell* you, in everyday language, the meaning of business terms, scientific words, foreign phrases, and common word roots to help you quickly determine word meanings without having to resort to a dictionary all the time.
- *Decipher* expressions peculiar to publishing, marketing, real estate, finance, and business law.
- *Make* the parts of speech work *for* you, instead of against you.
- *Know* what the initials of major organizations and associations actually mean.
- *Master* the techniques of leading an effective meeting, with only a few minutes of preparation!
- *Decipher* the meaning of idioms, clichés, and jargon, and guide you toward which words and phrases you can and can't use.
- *Write* powerful reports that will cause people to sit up and take note of your ideas.
- *Guide* you to using charts, facts, figures, and statistics ... in powerful, persuasive ways.
- *Check* any piece of writing and measure its clarity, simplicity, and degree of personal touch.

In short, the *Complete Handbook of Business English* summarizes and organizes nearly every reference related to the use of good English and puts them into a single book for fast and easy access.

For example, you often encounter acronyms for business and governmental organizations, because using acronyms saves time and space. But if you're not familiar with them, they can present a hopeless maze of hidden meanings.

Knowing common abbreviations for military and government organizations is also important as business people seek to work more and more closely with federal, state, and local departments and organizations that use short-cut word references as a way of life. This book locates all the most common abbreviations and acronyms you'll encounter in business—over 3,000 of them—in just one volume.

Important executive directives—letters, memos, notices, reminders, and advisories—are always put into writing. Knowing *how* to put those directives into writing, without having to ask a secretary or subordinate for advice, can be a valuable time-saver. This book will show you how to handle those directives clearly, concisely, and quickly.

Sometimes the mountain of business and technical jargon can cause an executive to waste precious time searching for clarification of a strange word stuck in the middle of a sentence. This time is better spent in other executive duties. The *Complete Handbook of Business English* puts the meaning of jargon and idioms, as well as business, computer, and scientific terms, and even foreign words and phrases, within easy reach.

No matter how articulate you are, from time to time you want to refer to the time-tested principles of good grammar. The *Complete Handbook of Business English* summarizes the basic rules of grammar so concisely that a thorough briefing takes only a few seconds. Spelling, punctuation, pronunciation, and the correct use of each of the parts of speech can be checked easily and quickly for accuracy with this comprehensive guide.

Thus, when a major report, letter, or memo is ready for final typing, you can add the finishing touches to its impressiveness by checking the *Complete Handbook of Business English* to assure that the order of presentation is logical, that you've followed the principles of good business communication, and, as a result, have put your ideas in the most favorable light possible.

When you think about it, isn't the goal of any executive to sell good ideas by putting them in the best light possible?

There are few executive training or management development programs that don't stress the importance of clear, concise communication. And every executive quickly learns that his major job is to get things done—through people.

Too often we forget, however, that it's only through words, written or spoken, that we can accomplish anything.

An executive's memo that shows poor grammar, misspelling, or punctuation errors that muddle the meaning of a sentence, says something devastating about that executive's ability to communicate well enough to get things done effectively.

Unfortunately, few executive training programs can afford the time to review English usage in detail. The exploding technology that must be learned and reviewed in a bewildering variety of fields each year by anyone in a managerial position is staggering. What's needed is a one-volume reference of English usage that can stand alongside a dictionary as a companion communications tool—the *Complete Handbook of Business English*. The dictionary tells *which* word to use; the *Handbook* tells *how* to use those words and phrases, and *how* to put them together in sentences that move people to action.

Today's executive has no time for intensive study of the rules of English usage such as a pronoun reference or verb agreement. Each day—each hour—decisions must be made, communicated quickly and efficiently, and, most of all, effectively. This single volume contains the most important tools of English usage, listed in the briefest possible way. It invites a warm welcome into the executive suite.

William Repp

Contents

COMPLETE
HANDBOOK OF
BUSINESS ENGLISH

PART I

Putting Good English to Work

---

1. THE FIVE MOST IMPORTANT RULES OF GRAMMAR

Grammar describes the way our language works. It is a system of rules that tells us how to use the parts of speech correctly. Once you know the key rules, writing and speaking correctly is relatively simple. First, let's review the parts of speech, and how we use them:

Nouns	name people, places, things
Adjectives	tell the kind of noun; limit, or modify nouns
Pronouns	stand in for nouns (his, her, my, your, etc.)
Verbs	say something is being done
Adverbs	say how something is done
Conjunctions	join words together (and, for)
Interjections	show surprise (Oh!)
Prepositions	relate nouns or pronouns to other words in the sentence (in, through, before)

Next, here are a few key observations on the English sentence.

A sentence is a group of words that express a complete thought. It is grammatically independent and complete, and it's marked with a period at the end (those that end in a question mark or exclamation point simply show tone of voice).

The simplest, clearest word order for any sentence is

Subject	Verb	Object
The man	bought	a typewriter.

Some verbs don't show action, but link a subject with other words that describe the subject. These are called *linking* verbs, and the explanatory words are called *complements*, because they complete the meaning of the verb.

Subject	Linking Verb	Complement
The manager	was	careful.
The department	seems	efficient.

Rule 1   Make sure the subject and verb agree in person and number. A singular person must have a singular verb.

Example

Subject		Verb
Each	of the managers	*makes* more than $15.00.
All	the managers	*make* more than $15.00.

Two or more singular nouns linked by *and* need a plural verb.

John and Mary won the award.

Two or more singular nouns linked by *or* need a singular *verb.*

Either John or Mary deserves the award.

If the nouns linked by *or* are different in number, the verb should agree with the nearest noun. Put the plural noun next to the verb.

Either John or the other managers are wrong.

If a noun refers to an entire class, as a whole (a "collection" noun), give it a singular verb and pronoun.

His group *is* large; *it* keeps him busy trying to manage it.

If a noun refers to the members of that class, give it a plural verb and pronoun.

The employees *have* a right to give *their* opinions.

Don't use both a noun and its pronoun as subjects of the same verb.

Incorrect:	My boss, who works upstairs, he is underpaid.
Correct:	My boss, who works upstairs, is underpaid.

Rule 2   A noun and its pronoun must agree, in person and number, whether they act as subject, object, or possessor—the different *cases* of pronouns. Cases of personal pronouns:

	Singular	**Plural**
Subject	I, you, he, she, it	we, they
Object	me, you, him her, it	us, them
Possessor	mine, your(s), his, hers, its	ours, theirs

Cases of the relative pronoun *who*:

Subject	who	(Ask the manager who knows)
Object	whom	(Whom are you thinking of?)
Possessor	whose	(Whose book is this?)

If a pronoun is the subject of an *infinitive*, use the objective case.

We waited for *him*   to make   the decision.
                              (infinitive)

If a pronoun comes before a gerund, use the possessive case.

Nobody liked *his*   acting   that way.
                              (gerund)

Rule 3   Keep a verb consistent in tense, voice, and mood. Tense shows the time of the action expressed by the verb. Voice shows whether the subject acts (active voice) or is acted upon (passive voice). Mood is the form of the verb that shows how the action is viewed by the writer or speaker.

Voice

Active voice: I decided.
Passive voice: The decision was made.

Mood

The indicative mood states a fact or asks a question.

The manager *is* here.
Is the manager here?

The imperative mood expresses a command or makes a request.

Please *let* us know your address.
Report to Personnel at once.

The subjunctive mood expresses doubt, supposition, probability, a condition contrary to fact, a regret, or a wish.

The managers look as though they *were* sure of themselves.
I wish that he *were* more prompt.

Tense

Present tense	shows a present or habitual action
	He is *deciding* the issue.
	He *decides* the issue.
Past tense	shows an action that was completed in the past
	He *decided* the issue yesterday.
Future tense	shows an action yet to come.
	He *will decide* the issue tomorrow.
Present perfect tense	shows a past action extending into the present that is not necessarily completed.
	He *has discussed* the issue every day.

Past perfect tense	shows a past action completed before some other past action
	Today I saw the manager who had made the decision last month.
Future perfect tense	shows an action that will be completed before some future time.
	We will have decided the issue before tomorrow noon.

Active Voice

	Simple Form	Progressive Form
		(shows that the action of the main verb is continuing at the time shown by the auxiliaries.)
Present	I drive	I am driving
Past	I drove	I was driving
Future	I will drive	I will be driving
Present perfect	I have driven	I have been driving
Past perfect	I had driven	I had been driving
Future perfect	I will have driven	I will have been driving

Passive Voice

	Simple Form	Progressive Form
Present	I am driven	I am being driven
Past	I was driven	I was being driven
Future	I will be driven	I will be being driven
Present perfect	I have been driven	I have been being driven
Past perfect	I had been driven	I had been being driven
Future perfect	I will have been driven	I will have been being driven

Rule 4   Make sure that modifiers are clear. Modifiers (words, clauses, phrases) describe, limit, elaborate, or in some way change the meaning of the subject. Keep the modifier close to the word it modifies so their relationship will be clear.

Modifiers shouldn't *dangle*. They dangle when they're not clearly linked to the word they're supposed to modify, or when there's no word in the sentence for it to modify.

Incorrect: Walking down the aisle, the typewriter caught his eye.

Correct: Walking down the aisle, he spotted the typewriter.

Modifiers shouldn't be misplaced or so widely separated from the words they modify that they confuse the reader.

Incorrect: He had marked on the floor the machines needed in red pencil.

Correct: He had marked in red pencil on the floor the machines needed.

Rule 5 Use adjectives to modify nouns or pronouns and adverbs to modify verbs, adjectives or other adverbs.

Incorrect: He drives careless (adjective).

Correct: He drives carelessly (adverb).

Incorrect: He works considerable (adjective) faster than she does.

Correct: He works considerably (adverb) faster than she does.

2. HOW TO USE THE PARTS OF SPEECH EFFECTIVELY

Words are your tools for communicating; they are what you use to get things done through people. Grammar tells you what each kind of tool is used for and how to use it correctly.

You have eight different tools to choose from—the eight parts of speech:

Nouns

These name *people, places, things, or qualities.* If the noun names something you can see, smell, feel, touch, hear, or taste, we call it a *concrete* noun. If the noun names a mental idea, like love, hate, faith, or joy, we call it an *abstract* noun.

If the noun names something official, or a special person, place, or thing, it's a *proper* noun. The other nouns, which name the class or kind, are called *common* nouns.

Example: On his trip to Buffalo, John ran into trouble when his car overheated.
      car = common noun (concrete)
      Buffalo, John = proper nouns (concrete)
      trip, trouble = common nouns (abstract)

HOW TO USE NOUNS

Concrete Nouns	These are especially important, because they help you name specific items accurately. Use concrete nouns to identify any person, place, or thing with the senses: touch, taste, hear, feel, see.
	Examples: man, woman, desk, typewriter, blackboard, chart.
Abstract Nouns	When you have to identify a quality or an idea, use an abstract noun. We call it "abstract" because we abstract or remove the quality from a number of concrete nouns and come up with only the essence of the idea or quality.
	Examples: hope, failure, success, fear, happiness, kindness.
Proper Nouns	When you want to name specific persons, places, and things, use a proper noun. You'll identify it by its initial capital letter.

	Examples: President, Miriam, Christmas, New York, James.
Collective Nouns:	Use a collective noun that has a single rather than a plural form to name a group. When you think of the group as a single unit, use a singular verb to accompany it. When you want the noun to mean all the people, places, or things in the group, use a plural verb.
	Example: The department has a good production record. (The collective noun, *department*, is considered as one unit, so we use the singular verb, *has*.)
	Most decide to begin work at 8 a.m. (The collective noun, *most*, is considered as the people in the group, so we use the plural verb, *decide*.)

Pronouns

These take the place of nouns. They are like stand-ins. Use a pronoun when you get tired of using the same noun or long name over and over again. And just as there are many different kinds of wrenches in a tool set, there are different kinds of pronouns:

Personal:	I, you, he, she, it, they, we, them (*they* refers to people)
Demonstrative:	this, that, these, those (they demonstrate or point something out)
Relative:	who, which, what, that, whoever, whomever, whatever, whichever (they relate someone or something to someone or something else)
Interrogative:	who, which, what (they ask a question)
Indefinite:	one, none, some, any, anyone, anybody, someone, somebody, no one, nobody, each, everyone, everybody, either, neither, both

HOW TO USE PRONOUNS

There are different ways to use pronouns, depending on the work they do in sentences. We use them in *three* different instances, or *cases*: nominative, possessive, and objective.

Personal Pronouns

	Nominative	Possessive	Objective
		SINGULAR	
First Person	I	my, mine	me
Second Person	you	your, yours	you
Third Person	he, she, it	his, her, hers, its	him, her, it
		PLURAL	
First Person	we	our, ours	us
Second Person	you	your, yours	you
Third Person	they	their, theirs	them

RELATIVE OR INTERROGATIVE PRONOUN

Singular	who	whose	whom
Plural	who	whose	whom

The Nominative Case

1. Use the nominative case for the subject of a verb.

   Note: After *as* and *than*, use the nominative case if the pronoun is the subject of a verb that's understood or implied.

   Example:
   He made the decision. (Not, "Him made...")
   She's better educated than *he* (is).
   He is as informed as *they* (are).

   When you use the pronoun *who* as the subject of a verb, its nominative form isn't changed by parenthetical ideas that separate it from the verb.

   She is a person *who* I think deserves a raise.

   Use the nominative form for a pronoun that's the subject of a clause, even though you use the entire clause as an object of some verb or preposition.

   We asked only the people *who* we felt were her associates.

   We'll give a suggestion award to whoever gives us the best idea.

2. Use the nominative case after "be" verbs—is, are, were, have been etc.—especially in formal English. (However, more and more people are using the objective case in informal English.)

   It is *I* who will decide the issue. (Informal usage: It is *me* who will decide the issue.)

The Possessive Case

1. If you're speaking formal English, use the possessive case for a noun or pronoun that precedes a gerund. Otherwise, just use the objective case.

   Formal: What was the reason for *his* arriving late?
   Informal: What was the reason for *him* arriving late?

2. Use an *of-phrase* to note the possessive of inanimate objectives. Use an *'s* to note the possessive of animate objects.

   Inanimate: the top of the table
   Animate: Jim's wife

3. Use *which* or *whose*, depending upon how they sound, when you refer to impersonal antecedents.

   We saw a department whose ceiling was falling in. (Not: We saw a department the ceiling of which was falling in.)

The Objective Case

1. Use the objective case for the object of a verb, verbal, or preposition.

   (In formal English, *whom* is always used in the objective case. But you can use *who* in informal English.)

   Verb: *I saw her. Whom* did you see?
   Verbal: Seeing *them* was fun. (*Fun* is the object of the gerund *seeing*.)

   Whom does she want to choose? (*Whom* is the object of the infinitive *to choose*.)
   Preposition: Three of *us* managers were elected. To *whom* were you speaking?

Verbs

These express an action or state of being of nouns (persons, places, or things).

Example: People *sail* boats. Vegetables *grow* in the garden.

A verb is a word tool that means *to do* something or *to be*. The strongest words in your writing are active verbs that are alive with meaning.

Examples of live, active verbs in sentences:

1. Communication *opens* the door to good employee relations.
2. He *packed* his report with good ideas.

Good business writing emphasizes verbs—not nouns, adjectives, and prepositions.

HOW TO USE VERBS

What Kind of Action?

Verbs show action, or that something is happening. How you show that action depends on how you use the verb—the "voice" you choose for it. When you show the subject (noun) doing the acting, you use a verb with an *active* voice. When the subject is being acted upon, you use a verb with a *passive* voice.

Active Verbs.	These make the strongest, clearest, and usually the best language, whether written or spoken. *Examples:* Barbara *made* the decision. The chemistry technician *determined* the strength of the solution.
Passive Verbs.	When you want to put the subject in lesser light, or even want to make the identity of subject become hazy or disappear entirely from the meaning of the sentence, use a *passive* verb. By their very nature, they're weak, but they have their place in the language. Use them as seldom as you can. They strangle the meaning from more sentences than any other part of speech. *Examples:* The decision *was made* by Barbara. (Notice that the emphasis is now on the *decision*, not upon the person who made it). The strength of the solution *was determined* by the chemistry technician.

How Do You feel About What You Say?

Our verbs have three different moods or ways we use to show people how we feel about what we say. The mood we choose helps clarify our meaning and can actually emphasize our feelings more.

Indicative Mood:	This simply expresses a statement for what it is. *Examples:* This *is* the shoe department. He *walked* down the aisle.
Imperative Mood:	Use the imperative mood when you give an order, make a request, give a direction, warning or prohibition, and want to make sure people interpret it exactly. *Examples: Come* to work on time. *Do* this right. *Go* to the payroll department. *Write* the report today. *Turn* left at the third aisle. *Be* careful when you open the box.

Subjunctive Mood:	When you want to express a wish, doubt, regret, condition, or improbability—something that isn't quite as black and white as you'd show with the indicative mood—use the subjunctive mood, especially with formal English.
	Examples: I wish I *were* the one chosen. If she *could* type faster, she *would* be section head. The animal looks as if it *were* sick. If this employee *is* late, then every employee *is* late. I wish I *were* better looking.

Keep Tenses and Moods Consistent.

Don't suddenly change the verb tense or mood once you make up your mind, as it confuses the reader or listener. Pick the appropriate time and feeling, and then stick to it.

Example:	She *walked* down the aisle and *looks* for her friend. (Here, we shift from the past to the present tense. Better: She *walked* down the aisle and *looked* for her friend).
	Open the top drawer and you *should take* out the box. (Here, we shift from the imperative mood, *open,* to the indicative mood, *should take.* Better: *Open* the top drawer and *take out* the box).

When Did It Happen?

You show when things happen through the tense or time of the verb. There are six basic tenses or times you can use to show action.

Tense	How It's Used	Example
Present	Shows an action going on now, or shows something you do habitually.	They *are hiring* people now. They *hire* people weekly.
Past	Shows something you finished in the past.	They *hired* 10 people.
Future	Shows an action you'll take in the future.	They *will hire* 10 people.
Present Perfect	Shows something done in the past, and which extends to the present, but isn't necessarily finished.	They *have hired* 10 people.

Tense	How It's Used	Example
Past Perfect	Shows a past action finished before some other past action took place.	They *had hired* 10 people.
Future Perfect	Shows an action you'll finish before some future time.	They *will have hired* 10 people before next Friday.

AUXILIARY VERBS

We use auxiliary verbs to help us emphasize, clarify, or limit the meaning of some verbs. The main auxiliary verbs are *be, can, do, have, may must, shall,* and *will.* For example, we use the auxiliary verb *do* when we want to emphasize, ask, or show negation:

Present	I *do* work. She *does* work. They *do* work.
Past	I *did* work. She *did* work. They *did* work.
Subjunctive	If I do work. If she does work. If they do work

Shall and Will

Use these auxiliaries to show the future or something you expect to do. In formal English, we use the *shall* form only for the first person:

I *shall* do it; you *will* do it; he *will* do it.

In formal English, we reverse the choice of *shall/will* to show desire, determination, threat, promise, intention, willingness, or a command on the part of the speaker:

I *will* do it; you *shall* do it; he *shall* do it.

However, in everyday business English, we practially omit all reference to shall, and rely strictly on the use of the auxiliary verb, *will.*

Special Uses of Shall and Will

1. In polite commands say, "You will..."

   You *will* send me a memo on this by Friday.

2. Use *will* for everyday instructions.

   John, you *will* hire three new people.

3. When you want to convey willingness, use *will.* (Formal English replaces *will* with *shall.*)

   I *will* be happy to do it for you.

Should/Would

Use the same general rules for should and would that you do for shall and will. In most cases, business English avoids the word *should* when it shows simple future:

> I *should* like to do it.
> (Better: I *would* like to do it.)

The best guide for which word to use in questions is to substitute the same word in the answer and see how it sounds.

> *Should* you buy the stock if the price goes down?
> (Yes, I *should*).

Use *should* to show an obligation, condition, or something you expect.

> We *should* have bought the stock.
> If she *should* happen to come late today, we'll talk to her.
> They *should* have the job finished by 5 p.m.

Use *would* to show a wish or a customary action:

> Once a week, he *would* walk through the department.
> Become a top executive? *Would* that I could!

Adjectives

Adjectives modify (limit or further describe) nouns and pronouns, thus making their meaning more precise.

Defining adjectives add facts to nouns: *mental* health; *construction* worker; *intelligent* people. You need them in sentences.

Commenting adjectives give opinions about the nouns, and cause you to editorialize in your writing: a *good* report; a *late* employee; *many* reporters. They add very little to your meaning and usually clutter up good writing. Try to avoid them.

HOW TO USE ADJECTIVES

Use defining adjectives to show a quality or change the meaning of a noun or pronoun:

> to describe a quality or condition:
>   his *blue* uniform
>   the *bright* lights
>   a *clean* office
>   a *persuasive* recommendation

to limit the meaning of your nouns:
>   his *only* reason
>   the *fifth* day
>   *five* dollars

to give nouns special importance. In this case, they're called proper adjectives:
>   *Canadian* bacon
>   *English* tea

Finally, you can use adjectives with certain linking verbs to help modify the subject. Typical linking verbs are: *be, appear, seem,* and *become,* and the verbs that relate to our five senses are: *smell, look, taste, sound,* and *feel.*

>   The wine seems *sour.*
>   He became *silly.*
>   It feels *good.*

In most cases, place the adjective before the noun it modifies, unless you want to emphasize the meaning in a different way:

>   It was laziness *unparalleled.*

In a few cases, (such as *everything, anything, nothing* and *something*) we place the adjective after the noun. You have to use the sound of the word arrangement as your guide:

>   nothing *imaginable*
>   a man *eager* to learn

Adverbs

These describe or modify verbs, adjectives, or other adverbs. They tell *how, when, where,* or *why.* Examples: loudly, immediately, somewhere. Avoid "empty" adverbs like extremely, exceedingly, and very, which add little to your meaning.
Adverbs express these relationships:

Time	We met them *yesterday.*
Place	Put it *there.* Leave your dog *outside.*
Manner	He answered *slowly.* I played *well* today.
Degree	He is *very* kind. She is *too* smart.
Affirmation or *Negation*	Do *not* go in. *Certainly* she made the decision. *Yes,* they are here.
Frequency	She is *always* prompt. He called *twice.*

HOW TO USE ADVERBS

We use adverbs to help change the meaning of, or tell something additional about verbs, adjectives, or other adverbs. Often, adverbs end in *-ly*, and they're usually placed directly before the word they modify. Sometimes an adverb can modify an entire clause and act as a *sentence* adverb:

Unfortunately, he didn't pay attention to their complaints.

Use an adverb to tell how, where, why, when, or to what extent something is done. Here are some of the more common adverbs and their uses:

Degree	more, less, too, completely, much, equally
Manner	well, ill, otherwise, simply, how, softly, quickly
Number	first, second, third
Place	where, here, there, below, far, downstairs, everywhere
Purpose	why, therefore, wherefore, consequently
Time	now, when, then, finally, never, lately, soon
Interrogative	how, when

We use *yes* and *no (not)* as affirmative and negative adverbs.

Placement

You have to place the adverb as close as possible to the word it modified or risk ambiguity in the sentence.

Example: The supervisor *only* pointed out one flaw.
(Better: The supervisor pointed out *only* one flaw.)

Prepositions

These words, meaning "before-positions," show the relation of a noun or pronoun to some other word (called its "object") in the sentence. Many prepositions are short, single words: at, by, for, in, on, etc. But you'll also find them used as a group of words, a *prepositional phrase*: in front of, by means of, in place of.

Generally, too many prepositions will slow down your writing, so use them as little as possible.

HOW TO USE PREPOSITIONS

Use prepositions to relate nouns or pronouns to other words in a sentence.

He walked *down* the aisle and stopped *at* the desk.

Sometimes you can use a preposition as an adverb:

> Sometimes he talked *down* to his employees.
> The foreman entered the shop just to look *in*.
> Please stand *by* for further instructions.

We normally put the preposition just *before* its object, and it usually doesn't appear at the end of a sentence. But there's no reason you can't end a sentence with a preposition if it sounds good. Consider the response Winston Churchill was supposed to have made when an aide tried to remove a preposition he had placed at the end of one of his sentences:

> "This is nonsense, up with which I will not *put*."

Here's a list of the main prepositions you can use to show relationship, along with a few phrases used as prepositions:

aboard	by	outside
about	concerning	over
above	considering	past
according to	contrary to	per
across	down	regarding
after	due to	respecting
against	during	round
ahead of	for	since
along	from	through
amid	in	throughout
among	in back of	till
apart from	in place of	to
around	inside	toward(s)
as far as	in spite of	under
at	in view of	underneath
because of	into	until
before	like	unto
behind	near	up
below	of	upon
beneath	off	via
beside(s)	on	with
between	on account of	within
beyond	onto	without

Conjunctions

These join words, phrases, clauses, and sentences to each other. Use them as connectives to show the relationship of these elements to other elements in sentences.

HOW TO USE CONJUNCTIONS

Use *coordinating* conjunctions to connect ideas of *equal* importance.

They employed both men *and* women. (Connecting nouns)

He walked through the door *and* into the department.
(Connecting prepositional phrases)

Our board members were ready *and* they made the decision.
(Connecting two independent clauses)

I came to work early to get a head start on the day's work.
But it didn't help—I had interruptions from the start.
(Connecting one sentence with another)

These are the most common coordinating conjunctions: and, but, or, nor, for (meaning "because"), yet.

Use *subordinating* conjunctions to subordinate one idea, word, phrase, clause, or group of words to another. They help you make one word or group of words more important than the other, and explain relationships such as condition, comparison, place, purpose, reason, result, and time.

Here's a list of the most common subordinating conjunctions.

after	how	so that	whence
although	if	so...as (that)	whenever
as	in case	such...as (that)	where
as if	inasmuch as	than	wherever
as long as	in order that	that	which
as often as	in spite of	though	whichever
as soon as	in that	till	while
as though	lest	unless	whither
because	notwithstanding	until	who
before	now that	what	whoever
but that	provided that	whatever	why
even if	since	when	with a view to
for the purpose of			

Use *correlative* conjunctions to connect words or groups of words that are used in pairs. These connectives always link sentence elements of equal grammatical value. For example, if you use a noun with one conjunction, use another noun with the companion correlative; if a verb follows the first part, use a verb to follow the second:

The meeting was *neither* informative *nor* interesting.
(Adjective follows adjective.)

He could *either* work *or* talk. (Verb follows verb.)

Here's a list of the common correlatives:

> not only...but also
> though...yet
> whether...or
> either...or
> neither...nor
> both...and
> so...as
> if...then
> as...as

Sometimes you can use adverbs as conjunctions to relate one clause to another. Here's a list of the conjunctive adverbs used most often:

accordingly	nevertheless
also	notwithstanding
besides	otherwise
consequently	so
furthermore	still
hence	then
however	therefore
likewise	thus
moreover	

Like and As

Regardless of what the TV commercials have done to these two words, *like* is still a preposition to be used with nouns and pronouns, and *as* is always a conjunction. Good English usage still doesn't permit *like* to be used in place of *as*.

He worked *like* a dog. (*As* would sound foolish here, anyway).

My people worked hard, *as* I expected they would.

Interjections

Use these words to exclaim strong or sudden feelings. You don't always have to punctuate interjections with an exclamation point—sometimes a comma or period is enough. (The word interjection comes from two Latin words meaning *to throw into*. We throw interjections into sentences to make them more lively. They don't relate grammatically to other words in the sentence).

> *Examples: Ah,* look at that market plan!
> *Oh,* I really don't care.

There are three other parts of speech that work as verbs and also as other parts of speech. They're called *verbals*.

Verbals

Gerund	A *gerund* is a verbal used as a noun.
	Example: He began *running* faster. (Running is the name of a concept, running, and it also shows action. So it's part noun, part verb.)
Participle	A *participle* is a verbal used as an adjective.
	Example: The *screaming* supervisor upset the entire department. (Screaming describes the supervisor, but there's action taking place.)
Infinitive	An *infinitive* is a verbal that can be used as a noun, an adjective, or an adverb. The word *to* usually precedes it, but not always:
	Examples: Jim wanted *to train* the new employees.
	Jim helped *train* the new employees.

How to Use the Verbals

Participles

We use participles to help describe nouns, but with more action than we'd put in a simple adjective. We can use them:

As an adjective that modifies a noun	*Screaming* supervisors seldom get results. The *alarming* memo scared him.
As a verb-form that takes an object	*Telling* him the reason, she made the decision.
As a verb-form that's modified by an adverb	*Shouting* madly, the foreman left the group.

Not all the participle forms end in *-ing*. Here's how they're formed.

Stem	Present Participle	Past Participle	Past Perfect Participle
decide	deciding (add *-ing* to the stem)	decided (same form as the past tense)	having decided (add *having* to past participle)

Gerunds

We use the gerund, the verbal noun, four ways:

As the subject of a verb	*Working* helps build security.
As the object of a verb	She teaches *typing*.

| *As a predicate noun* | Giving is *sharing*. |
| *As a verb-form that takes an object* | *Making* decisions was their job. |

Note: Sometimes we give the gerund a subject:

The *supervisor's coming* into the department was a surprise.
His manager likes *his sharing* his ideas.

And we frequently use the gerund in phrases:

Before sleeping for six hours, he reads poetry.

Infinitives

Because the infinitive works both as a noun and a verb, it too is a verbal noun. Use the infinitive in these four ways:

As a subject	*To retire* is his main goal.
As an object	They decided *to wait*.
As an adjective	This is a question *to be answered*.
As an adverb	She arrived this morning *to see him*.

Irregular Verbs You'll Encounter Most Often

Present Tense	Past Tense	Participle Form*
arise	arose	arisen
bear	bore	born, borne
beat	beat	beaten
become	became	become
begin	began	begun
bend	bent	bent
bet	bet	bet
bid	bid	bid
bind	bound	bound
bite	bit	bitten
bleed	bled	bled
blow	blew	blown
break	broke	broken
breed	bred	bred
bring	brought	brought
burst	burst	burst
buy	bought	bought
catch	caught	caught
choose	chose	chosen

*(Usually used with *is, was, will, has, had, have, shall have*)

Present Tense	Past Tense	Participle Form*
cling	clung	clung
come	came	come
cost	cost	cost
creep	crept	crept
deal	dealt	dealt
dig	dug	dug
dive	dived, dove	dived
do	did	done
draw	drew	drawn
drink	drank	drunk
drive	drove	driven
eat	ate	eaten
fall	fell	fallen
feed	fed	fed
feel	felt	felt
fight	fought	fought
find	found	found
flee	fled	fled
fling	flung	flung
fly	flew	flown
forget	forgot	forgotten, forgot
forsake	forsook	forsaken
freeze	froze	frozen
get	got	got, gotten
give	gave	given
go	went	gone
grind	ground	ground
grow	grew	grown
hang (execute)	hanged	hung
hang (suspend)	hung	hung
hide	hid	hidden
hold	held	held
keep	kept	kept
know	knew	known
lay	laid	laid
lead	led	led
leave	left	left
lend	lent	lent
lie	lay	lain
light	lit	lit
lose	lost	lost
make	made	made

*(Usually used with *is, was, will, has, had, have, shall have*)

Present Tense	Past Tense	Participle Form*
mean	meant	meant
meet	met	met
pay	paid	paid
put	put	put
read	read	read
rend	rent	rent
rid	rid	rid, ridden
ride	rode	ridden
ring	rang	rung
rise	rose	risen
run	ran	run
say	said	said
see	saw	seen
seek	sought	sought
sell	sold	sold
send	sent	sent
set	set	set
shake	shook	shaken
shine	shone, shined	shone, shined
shoot	shot	shot
show	showed	shown
shrink	shrank	shrunk
sing	sang	sung
sink	sank	sunk
sit	sat	sat
slay	slew	slain
sleep	slept	slept
slide	slid	slid
sling	slung	slung
slink	slunk	slunk
speak	spoke	spoken
speed	sped	sped
spend	spent	spent
spin	spun	spun
spring	sprang	sprung
stand	stood	stood
steal	stole	stolen
stick	stuck	stuck
sting	stung	stung
stride	strode	stridden
strike	struck	stricken, struck
string	strung	strung
strive	strove	striven

*(Usually used with *is, was, will, has, had, have, shall have*)

Present Tense	Past Tense	Participle Form*
swear	swore	sworn
sweep	swept	swept
swim	swam	swum
swing	swung	swung
take	took	taken
teach	taught	taught
tear	tore	torn
tell	told	told
think	thought	thought
throw	threw	thrown
tread	trod	trodden, trod
wake	woke	waked
wear	wore	worn
weave	wove	woven
win	won	won
wind	wound	wound
wring	wrung	wrung
write	wrote	written

---

*(Usually used with *is, was, will, has, had, have, shall have*).

Comparing the Most Common Adjectives and Adverbs

We show the degree of quantity or quality of words by using adjectives and adverbs in their positive (standard) comparative and superlative forms. The positive form (fast, slowly) doesn't show any comparison. We show comparison— a greater degree—by adding -er or the word *more* to the positive form (faster, more slowly). We show the superlative, the greatest degree of a quantity or quality, by adding -est or the word *most* to the positive form (fastest, most slowly) among three or more people or things.

Whether you add *-er, -est*, more or, most to adjectives usually depends upon the number of syllables in the word. Most one-syllable adjectives form the comparative and superlative form by adding -er, -est. Two-syllable adjectives have a rather wide range of variation in their comparatives and superlatives. Three-syllable adjectives always use *more* or *most* in their comparative and superlative forms. Because words like dead, empty, entirely, perfect, and unique are absolute in their meaning, we can't really compare them.

Finally, we use the comparative form when we refer to one or two people or things. We use the superlative form only when we refer to three or more people or things.

Adverb Comparisons

When you use adverbs for comparison, simply add *more* (or less) for the comparative degree and *most* (or least) for the superlative degree (*more* quickly, *most* quickly). However, there are some adverbs that have the same spelling as adjectives, so you must add *-er* or *-est* to the positive form:

close	closer	closest
early	earlier	earliest
hard	harder	hardest
tight	tighter	tightest

Finally, there are a few adverbs compared irregularly. Here are the main ones:

Positive	Comparative	Superlative
badly	worse	worst
far	farther (further)	farthest (furthest)
late	later	latest (last)
little	less	least
much	more	most
near	nearer	nearest (next)
well	better	best

3. HOW TO USE PHRASES AND CLAUSES

Phrases

A group of words without a subject or predicate, used as a single part of speech, is called a phrase.

A prepositional phrase consists of a preposition and its object. (We walked *into the room.*) A verbal phrase consist of a verbal and its object. (We wanted *to see the machine work.*) Prepositional phrases act as adjective, adverb, and noun phrases. For example, an adjective phrase modifies a noun or pronoun. (She is a person *of substance.*) An adverb phrase modifies a verb, adjective, or adverb. (The manager arrived *on time.* We waited *in the meeting room.* He arrived late *in the afternoon.*)

Verbal phrases act as other verbals, and are called participial, gerund, or infinitive phrases. A participial phrase acts as an adjective—it modifies a noun or a pronoun. (The manager *waiting for the meeting* was impatient. The products *found in the warehouse* were old.) These participial phrases were formed using the present participle *waiting* and past participle *found.* Gerunds are used as nouns, so gerund phrases are also used as nouns. (*Deciding issues quickly* was her strength.) An infinitive phrase can be used as an adjective, adverb, or noun. (It's time *to make the decision.* He was impatient *to begin the investigation.* She wanted *to begin work soon.*)

Clauses

A clause is a group of words that has a subject and predicate. How you use the clause depends upon its position in the sentence or upon a conjunction. There are two kinds of clauses—independent or main clauses, and dependent or subordinate clauses.

An independent or main clause doesn't need a subordinating word to introduce it. It makes a statement that can stand on its own. Subordinate clauses are often introduced by a subordinating conjunction like *as, since,* and *because* or by a relative pronoun like *who, which,* and *that.* Use subordinate clauses as an adjective, adverb, or noun to show an idea that's less important than the idea expressed by the main clause in the sentence.

An adjective clause modifies a noun or pronoun. (This is the machine *that broke the part.*) (The person *who spoke may stand.* Company X is the organization that *we made the deal with.*)

An adverbial clause modifies a verb, adjective, or adverb. (The man laughed *when he thought of the idea.* I am glad *that he is the manager.* She makes decisions more quickly *than you do.*)

A noun clause acts as a noun, so it can serve as a subject, predicate nominative or the object of a preposition, (What Shirley *wants* is a new opportunity. This is *where the opening should be*. Tell them *that I will be late*. He doesn't like *what he hears*.)

4. PUNCTUATION: PUTTING FEELING INTO YOUR WORDS

You make communication clear when you punctuate properly. Good punctuation breaks up long, complex ideas into simpler ones that are easier to understand.

Today, we try to use as little punctuation as possible. But that also means you'll have to choose words carefully. Think of punctuation marks as traffic signals: stop, go, wait. For example, commas, colons, semicolons, and dashes tell your reader to pause. Periods, question marks, and exclamation points are signals to come to a complete stop.

In general, use your common sense and the sound of the words to tell you when to use a punctuation mark.

Commas

These tell your reader to pause in the sentence, but not as long as he would for a period or a semicolon. Use commas to separate words, phrases, and clauses from other parts of the sentence to make your meaning clear.

Use the Comma:	Example:
After each word or phrase in a series, when the last of the series is preceded by *and*. (You *may* leave the final comma out, if you prefer.)	Frick, Frack, Feeble, and Fine are good lawyers.
After an introductory phrase that precedes a direct quote.	The supervisor said, "Four employees made suggestions today."
To separate appositives.	Mr. Johnson, the president, entered the room.
When you want to separate parenthetic phrases, words, clauses.	Mr. Johnson, who was president at the time, entered the room.
When two or more words modify the same word, and there's no conjunction between them.	The new, untrained employee.
After a subordinate clause at the start of the sentence.	While he read the report, they listened intently.
To show you've omitted a word or phrase.	God creates, man makes.

45

Use the Comma:	Example:
Before the conjunction in a compound sentence.	He visited Rochester, and he also took a side trip.
When you separate an introductory phrase or clause from a question.	During the night, did you hear the car?
When you want to make adjoining words or figures clear.	August 15, 1978
Before the intitials that follow a person's name.	John Jones, Jr.; John Jones, Sr.; John Jones, Ph.D.; John Jones, M.D.;
After a noun or noun phrase used to address someone.	Ladies and Gentlemen, here are next year' market plans.
Inside quotation marks when the sentence continues.	He said "Yes," but he meant no.
Between the city and state in addresses.	Rochester, N.Y.

Semicolons

You signal a longer pause with a semicolon than you would with a comma, but not as long as with a period. Semicolons tell your reader that you have a string of related ideas; that you have two independent clauses linked together, but not with a conjunction (as in this sentence).

Use the semicolon:	Example:
To separate clauses or phrases that contain commas.	Michael Johnson, chairman of the board, made fast decisions; Stephen Smith, the president, was more thoughtful.
To separate contrasting statements, or statements so closely related that you need a stronger break than you'd indicate with a comma.	He said yes; she said no.
To isolate distinct thoughts in the same sentence.	She studied at Harvard; they're all college graduates.

Dashes

Dashes indicate pauses, too. They show a quick change in thought or sentence structure and help clarify your meaning. They emphasize phrases or clauses and show a hesitation in your speech. They can help separate questions and answers in a written report of a meeting. They can also show you've omitted something, such as a word root. (You indicate a dash on your typewriter with two hyphens: The Decision--an important one--was made today.)

Use the Dash	Example
To show a quick change in thought or an aside.	If he joins the company—which is qute probable—he'll do well.
In place of commas or parentheses (for greater variety).	The design had important qualities—economy and simplicity—that we needed.
To emphasize something you add to a sentence (an afterthought).	He simply walked into the room—but that was enough.
Before a final clause that explains or summarizes a string of ideas.	Promptness, dedication, honesty—what more could you want?
As a substitute for a colon, when used to introduce an idea.	Her goal—to reorganize the department.
To show a hesitation in your speech.	It's—not clear what we should do.
Before an explanatory group of words.	There's something else to be considered—for example, the cost.

Colons

These tell your reader to pause—to get ready for something that's coming: an important word that explains the previous word or phrase (called an appositive), a list, a series of items, or a long quotation.

Use the colon:	Example:
Instead of a semicolon to emphasize the last of two clauses in a compound sentence.	Because of the thin walls, the room was more than noisy: it was actually dangerous to your hearing.
When the second clause is a restatement or explanation of the first.	The trouble with him as a supervisor is that he is overemotional and quick to anger: overemotional because he reacts more strongly than he should, and angry because things upset him easily.
When you introduce a quotation directly, without using a verb such as *said, noted, remarked,* and a similar verb.	Tom paused for a moment: "What do you want me to say?"

Use the colon:	**Example:**
To separate minutes from hours in expressing: time, chapters of a book, scenes from acts of play, subtitles from titles of books, publisher and place of publication in a bibliography.	3:45 a.m. I Kings 7:2-4 *Macbeth* III:4 Englewood Cliffs, N.J.: Prentice-Hall, Inc.
To introduce a series.	Three departments were represented: Purchasing, Data Processing, and Personnel.
To punctuate memo headings and some subject lines in general business letters.	To: Through: Via: Reference: Subject:
To separate writer/typist initials in a business letter.	WR:cg
To separate carbon or blind copy abbreviations from the initials of those who receive the copies of a business letter.	cc: WR bcc: WR
To separate titles and subtitles of books.	*Job Motivation: How to Make Your Work More Fun*
To call attention to an appositive.	He had only one vice: drinking.
After the salutation in a business or formal letter.	Dear Dr. Brown: Dear Sir:
After words like *namely.*	She had two favorites among English writers, namely: Dickens and Thackeray.

Periods

These tell readers to come to a full stop. They indicate that the thought has ended.

Use the Period	**Example**
To end a declarative sentence.	Mary telephoned yesterday. Cindy went home for a week.
To end an imperative sentence.	Be sure to check with her before she leaves. Give him my best wishes.
To end sentence fragments that do the work of full sentences.	"You will remember, won't you?" "Yes." "At what time?" "Ten." "Good."

Use the Period	Example
After most abbreviations.	anon., A.B., A.W.O.L., diam.
After someone's initials.	Mr. M. Franco
To terminate a polite request.	Will you please send me the check as soon as you can.
After Roman numerals in outlines and enumerations.	I. Objectives
After Arabic numbers when they stand alone.	1. business 2. Industry 3. Education

Ellipsis Dots

Ellipsis dots tell people that you've left out something in the middle or at the end of a sentence.

Use Ellipsis Dots	Example
(Three) to show you've left something out of the middle of a sentence.	I left the room and returned to it ... some days later.
(Four) to show you've left something out at the end.	I returned some days later and....
As a stylistic device to hold the reader's attention, especially in advertising copy.	A fast way to learn to speak well ... a must for business presentations.
To show halting speech in dialogue.	"I'd like to ask you if ... that is, if you prefer ... what I mean to say is ...."
As leaders, when spaced across a page, for tables.	How to Capitalize .... page 1

Question Marks

Use the Question Mark:	Example:
After you ask a direct question. You can tell a direct question easily because it has inverted word order—the verb comes before the subject; and it often begins with an interrogative pronoun or adverb.	Did you study Latin? Who is the manager of that department? Who do you think will win the raffle?
To show ignorance or uncertainty.	

Don't Use a Question Mark:	**Example:**
After an indirect question. This is a statement that implies a question, but doesn't actually ask one.	He asked me whether I had studied Latin. We wonder who was the manager of the department.

Exclamation Points

Use the Exclamation Point:	**Example:**
To show strong feeling or emotion. Caution: Don't use it too often! It looks bad! and it really stands out as the mark of an amateur!	That's terrible! How awful!

Hyphens

Use the hyphen to help you form compound words and show that you are continuing a word from one line to the next.

Use the Hyphen:	**Example:**
To join two or more words that serve as a single adjective before a noun.	The well-known speaker A good-looking person
Don't use the hyphen if it follows the noun; if the first word ends in *ly* or if the compound is a proper name.	The speaker was well known. It was an eagerly awaited event. The Boston accent is quaint.
To avoid an ambiguous or awkward joining of letters into words.	Not: recreate But: re-create (meaning to create again) Not: catlike But: cat-like
To make compound numbers from 21 through 99, and to separate the numerator from the denominator in fractions.	sixty-nine two-thirds
With stressed prefixes like *self- ex-, all-,* and the suffix, *-elect.*	self-appointed ex-president all-important president-elect
To mark the division, at the end of a line, with a syllable of a word you carry over to the next line.	He considered the joke a milestone. But then he...
To signify "up to and including" in dates and numbers.	1970-1980; pages 2-10.

Parentheses

The parenthesis is used before and after expressions to show they're loosely related to the rest of the sentence, and to explain a word or expression more fully.

Use the Parenthesis:	Example:
For parenthetic, supplemental, or explanatory words when the interruption is stronger than you'd show by commas.	Three former managers of the company (all retired) will give their views.
To enclose numbers of letters to separate items in a series.	We need to talk about (1) goals, (2) plans to implement them, and (3) costs.
To show abbreviations you will use later in the copy.	The National Technical Institute for the Deaf (NTID) at Rochester Institute of Technology (RIT) is the world's largest technological college for deaf people.
To indicate alternate forms or omissions.	Please sign the form(s) and mail back to me, before (date).

Apostrophes

Use the Apostrophe:	Example:
To form the possessive case of singular or plural nouns. Use the form *'s* even when the noun ends in s.	Mr. Walker's store Mr. Jones's store His mother's car
To show joint possession by adding it to the last noun in a sequence.	Jones and Smith's report.
To show individual possession when added to each noun in the sequence.	Jones' and Smith's report.
To show omission of letters in contractions.	Aren't; I'm; you're; o'clock
To show omission of numbers.	The class of '80
To form plurals of letters, figures or words.	There were three b's in that sentence. His 2's and 3's look alike. He can't pronounce his the's.
With an *s* before a gerund or gerund phrase.	He didn't like his manager's changing the goals.

Brackets

Use Brackets	Example:
To set apart supplemental information (like editorial comments), especially if you include it within quotes.	She said, "I sent [sic] your letter."
As another set of parentheses within parentheses.	(I didn't like [or at least I thought I didn't like] that version of the show.)

Quotation Marks

Set off material and direct speech you quote, word for word, from someone else, or from another source, by including quotation marks.

Use Double Quotation Marks:	Example:
To enclose a direction quotation. (Don't punctuate indirect quotations.)	She said, "I need your report today." She said she needed the report today.
To enclose fragments of quoted material when you want to show it as it was originally stated.	The contract makes it obvious that he "must pay the support weekly."
To enclose words and phrases you borrow from others, to show words you use in a special way, to indicate a word you want to use informally.	He looked like just another "greaser." He called himself "supervisor" but no one reported to him. He was arrested for using "coke."
To enclose titles or reports, short poems and stories, articles, lectures, chapters of books, or songs —any work that is part of a larger work—which you would normally underline.	The report, "The Selling of the Pentagon," is... The article, "What You Should Know About Good Vision" is very well written... Robert Frost's "Mending Wall" The third chapter of *Profitable Showmanship* is called, "Think Big."

5. BETTER SPELLING MADE EASY

Frequently Misspelled Words:

abhorrence	annual	beautiful
absurd	anxiety	beggar
academy	apparatus	beginning
accede	apparent	believing
accept	appearance	beneficial
accidentally	appropriate	benefited
accommodate	apocalypse	biscuit
accompanied	apologize	bloc (political)
accumulate	archaeology	bluing
accustom	archipelago	bologna
achieved	arctic	bouillon
acknowledgment	argument	boulder
acquainted	arithmetic	boundary
acquire	arrangement	boutonniere
acquitted	article	brilliant
across	artisan	Britain
address	ascend	Britannica
advertisement	asparagus	bruised
adviser	assassin	buoy
affects	association	buoyant
aggravate	attendance	bureau
airplane	athletic	business
aisle	awkward	caddie (golf)
allotted	auditor	caddy (tea)
all right	auxiliary	cafeteria
altar	ax	calendar
alter	baccalaureate	calk
altogether	bacchanalian	cancellation
aluminum	bachelor	candidate
alumnus	balance	carriage
always	bankruptcy	career
amateur	barbarian	catalog
ambassador	barbarous	catarrh
analogous	baritone	catechism
analysis	barren	catsup
angel	baroque	ceiling
angle	bastille	cellar

cemetery
chancellor
changeable
changing
characteristic
chauffeur
chlorophyll
chrysalis
cinnamon
cigarette
clique
coarse
coconut
collar
colonel
column
commission
committed
committee
commodity
communicate
comparative
comparatively
comparison
compel
compelled
competent
competition
completely
compulsion
conceivable
conceive
conception
condemn
condescend
confident
connoisseur
conquerer
conscience
conscientious
conscious
contempt
contemptible
consumption

convenient
cooly
correspondence
councilor
counselor (legal advisor)
course
courteous
courtesy
crescendo
criticism
cruelty
cruise
cryptic
curiosity
cyanide
cyclic
cynicism
cylinder
dealt
debater
debtor
deceitful
deceive
deception
decide
decision
deference
deferred
deficient
definite
delivery
delicatessen
demigogue
derivative
descendant
descent
desiccated
describe
description
diaphragm
desirable
desperate
develop
device

devise
dialog(ue)
diarrhea
diary
dietitian
dictionary
different
dilemma
diptheria
disappear
disappoint
disastrous
disease
discipline
discuss
discussion
disk
dissatisfied
disparate
dissipate
distribute
distributor
divine
divorcee
dormitory
dormitories
doughty
drought
drudgery
duly
dumbfound
dungeon
dying
dyeing
ecclesiastical
ecstasy
edible
eerie
effects
efficiency
eighth
eligible
eliminate
embarrass

eminent
emphasize
encumbrance
endorse
enemy
envelope
environment
equaled
equipped
equivalent
Eskimo
especially
esthetic
exaggerate
exceed
excel
excellent
except
exercise
exhaust
exhibitor
exhilarate
existence
expense
explain
explanation
extraordinary
familiar
fantasy
fascinate
feasible
February
fetus
fiery
finally
financier
financially
flautist
flex
flier (or flyer)
forbade
foreign
foremost
forfeit

formally
formerly
fortuitous
forty
fourth
frantically
fraternity
friend
fulfill (or fulfil)
furniture
fungus
gage
gaily
gallant
galosh
gasoline
generally
genius
ghost
glamour (or glamor)
goddess
good-bye (or good-by)
gorilla
gourmet
government
governor
grammar
grandeur
grief
grievous
gruesome
guarantee
guerilla
guitar
guidance
gypsy
hallelujah
handkerchief
harangue
harass
height
heinous
hesitancy
hesitate

heterogenous
hiccup
hindrance
history
homogenous
hoping
horrible
hosiery
humorous
hundredths
hurriedly
hygienic
hyperbole
hypocrisy
icicle
idiosyncrasy
idyll (or idyl)
ignorant
imaginary
imitative
imitation
immediately
immigration
imminent
imperiled
impromptu
incarcerate
incidentally
incredible
incredulous
independence
indict
indigestible
indispensable
induce
inevitable
infinite
influential
innocence
instance
intellectual
intelligence
intelligible
intentionally

intercede	meanness	occasionally
interest	medicine	occur
irresistible	medieval	occurred
itself	messenger	occurrence
jeopardy	meter	o'clock
jewelry	miniature	offense
judgment	minute	omission
knowledge	miscellaneous	omit
Ku Klux Klan	mischievous	omitted
khaki	misogyny	operate
kindergarten	Mississippi	opinion
knell	misspelled	opportunity
laboratory	moccasin	organization
landlord	Mohammedan	optimistic
larynx	momentous	outrageous
legitimate	monolog	overrun
leisure	morale	pageant
lenient	mortgage	paid
liable	murmur	pajamas
library	muscle	pamphlet
licorice	mustache	pantomime
lightning	naturally	parallel
likable	necessary	parliament
likely	Negroes	particularly
literature	neither	pastime
livelihood	nestle	peculiar
llama	niche	peddler (or peddlar)
loath	nickel	periphery
loneliness	niece	perceive
loose	nil	peremptory
lose	nineteenth	permanent
lying	ninetieth	permissible
lymph	ninety	perseverance
magazine	ninth	persistent
maintain	notoriety	personnel
maintenance	noticeable	perspiration
manual	nowadays	persuade
manufacturer	obligation	phase
marital	oblige	physically
marriage	nucleus	physician
Massachusetts	nuclear	picnic
mathematics	obedience	picnicking
material	obstacle	piece
meager	occasion	piteous

pleasant
plow
politician
plebiscite
portentous
possess
possession
possibly
practically
practice
prairie
precede
precedence
preferred
prejudice
preparation
presence
prevalent
primitive
principal
principle
privilege
proceed
prodigy
professor
promissory
pronunciation
propeller
prophecy
prophesy
psyche
psychiatrist
psychology
ptomaine
pumpkin
pursue
quantity
quay
queue
quiet
quixotic
quizzes
raccoon
realize

really
recede
receipt
receive
recognize
recommend
reconnaissance
refer
referee
reference
referred
region
registrar
reign
relieve
religious
reminisce
repeat
repetition
representative
reservoir
resistance
restaurant
reticence
rhetoric
rheumatism
rhythm
ridiculous
route
sacrifice
sacrilegious
saccharin
safety
salable
salary
salmon
sarcasm
savior (or saviour)
scarcely
scenery
scepter
schedule
schism
science

screech
scythe
secession
secretary
seize
sensible
sentinel
separate
sergeant
severely
several
shepherd
shone
shown
shriek
siege
similar
simile
smolder
solemn
soliloquy
sophomore
specimen
speech
stationary
stationery
studying
strenuous
suave
suffrage
summarize
subpoena
supersede
suppress
surprise
syllable
symmetrical
symmetry
taboo
tarpaulin
temperament
temperature
tendency
theater

their
there
thorough
thousandths
tied
tying
till
tournament
trauma
tragedy
tranquility
transfer
transferred
treacherous
treasurer
tremendous
trestle
tried
tries
truly

turquoise
twelfth
typical
tyranny
unanimous
universally
until
unusual
usage
usually
vaccination
vacancy
vacuum
valuable
vengeance
victory
victual
vigilance
villian
vitiate

weather
Wednesday
weird
whether
whiskey (whisky)
wholly
who's
whose
wintry
wiry
wrestle
writing
written
yacht
yoke
yolk
your
you're
zigzag

Choosing the Right Prefixes and Suffixes

We use common root stems in English and add prefixes and suffixes to change the meaning of the word. You'll be able to determine the meaning of unfamiliar words if you can spot the prefix and suffix—along with the root.

COMMON PREFIXES:

Prefixes:	Meaning:		
ab-	away from	non	not
ad-*	to or for	ob-*	against
com-*	with	pre-	before
de-	down, away from, or undoing	pro-	for or forward
dis-*	separation or reversal	re-	back or again
ex-*	out of or former	sub-*	under
in-*	in or on	trans-	across
in-*	not	un-	not
mis-	wrong		

---

*The spelling may change, to make it easier to pronounce the word. (ad/ac/ag/at)

COMMON SUFFIXES:

These fall into three groups:

noun
verb   } suffixes
adjectival

NOUN SUFFIXES:

These show act of, state of, quality of.

Suffix:	Meaning:	Example:	Meaning:
-ance	process	continuance	continuing
-ancy	state	redundancy	being repetitious
-ation	action	flirtation	flirting
-dom	realm	freedom	being free
-ence	condition	precedence	coming before
-ency	condition	frequency	being frequent
-ery	condition	bravery	being brave
-hood	condition	manhood	being a man
-ice	quality	cowardice	being a coward
-ion	process	intercession	interceding
-ism	state	conservatism	being conservative
-ment	condition	argument	disagreement
-ness	quality	dimness	being dim
-ship	condition	friendship	having a friend
-sion	process	conversion	change
-tion	condition	corruption	being corrupt

NOUN SUFFIXES:

These show someone who does something.

Suffix:

-eer
-ess
-ist
-or
-er

These show something being made or done.

Suffix:

-ate
-en
-fy
-ize, ise

ADJECTIVAL SUFFIXES:

Suffix:	Meaning:
-ful	full of
-ish	relating to
-ate	having
-ic, -ical	consisting of
-ive	performs an action
-ous	full of
-ulent	full of

Spelling Guidelines

The English language is full of inconsistencies, and nowhere is that more evident than in the rules of spelling. The best guideline you can use is to notice how words are spelled, practice them, and ask someone who is a naturally good speller to check your work from time to time. Nevertheless, there are a few spelling rules that can be helpful.

		Examples
1. ie/ei	Write *i* before *e*	receive
	Except after *c*	
	Or when sounded as *a*	*freight*
	As in neighbor and weigh.	

2. final e   Drop the final *e* if it comes before a suffix that beings with a vowel. Don't drop the final *e* if the suffix begins with a consonant.

erase + ure = erasure
entire + ly = entirely
hide + ing = hiding
hate + ful = hateful

Exceptions:

Sometimes we keep the final *e* so we won't confuse words (like dying and dyeing).
singe + ing = singeing

We usually keep the final *e* to keep a *c* or *g* soft if it comes before an *a* or an *o*.
change + able = changeable

Some words that take the suffix -ful or -ly drop the final *e*:
judge + ment = judgment
acknowledge + ment = acknowledgment

	The ordinal numbers fifth, ninth and twelfth drop the final *e*.
3. final y	Change the final *y* to *i*, unless it comes before a suffix that begins with *i*. rely + ance = reliance thirty + eth = thirtieth cry + ing = crying
4. final consonants	Double the final consonant if it comes before a suffix that starts with a vowel, only if: (a) A single vowel comes before the consonant. (b) The consonant ends with a one-syllable word or accented vowel. hop + ing = hopping forbid + ing = fobidding roof + ing = roofing benefit + ing = benefiting
5. nouns/verbs with smooth endings	If you can add an *s* to a noun to form a plural or to a verb to form the third person singular, and the sound is smooth, simply add *s*. Otherwise, add *es*. doctor - doctors table - tables torch - torches
6. nouns ending in y	Form the plural of a noun that ends in *y* by changing *y* to *i* and adding *es*. sky - skies body - bodies But, if the noun that ends in *y* is preceded by a vowel, just add an *s*. toy - toys boy - boys
7. plurals of Latin, Greek, French words	These keep the plurals used in their own languages. analysis - analyses datum - data phenomenon - phenomena
8. able - ible	If the word ends in -ce or -ge, keep the full word and add *-able*. manage + able = manageable If the final *e* is silent, drop it and add *-able*. debate + able = debatable

If the word ends with -ation, use the ending *-able.*

demonstration - demonstrable

If the word ends with -sion or -tion, use the ending *-ible.*

collection - collectible

If the verb ends in -ate, drop it when adding *-able.*

communicate -communicable

If the verbs ends in *y*, and it's preceded by a vowel, keep the *y* before adding *-able.*

pay - payable

If the verb ends in *y*, and it's preceded by a consonant, change the *y* to *i* and take the ending *-able.*

identify - identifiable

9. ance - ence   When the root word ends with a hard *c* or *g*, use *-ance, -ancy, or -ant.*

significant - significance

When the root word ends with a soft *c* or *g*, use *-ence, -ency, or -ent.*

emerge - emergence

How to Remember Correct Spelling

Spelling rules can be helpful, but there are so many exceptions in English that it's questionable whether it's worth the time learning the rules. A better way to remember spelling is to observe correct spelling closely and practice it. Here are some suggestions.

1. If you're a poor speller, admit it and have someone check your work. Force yourself into the habit you may have neglected in grade school: write each mispelled word three, five, or ten times if necessary, until you never misspell it again. This may seem like a burden at first, but you're probably misspelling only certain words anyway. If you can learn to spell only three words correctly each day, you'll have mastered 1,000 words in one year, and your spelling problems should largely be eliminated.
2. Watch for words. Read newspapers and magazines more carefully and slowly. Watch to see how everyday words like *indispensable* are spelled. Spell out these words to yourself, either silently or out loud. As you become more conscious of words, you'll be more sensitive to spelling them correctly.

3. Admit you need help. Just like the problem drinker must admit to himself that he needs help, poor spellers must admit they need to work on their spelling. It's a poor substitute when an executive dumps his poor spelling on his secretary's desk and expects her to "clean up his act." Top executives must master the English language because 80 percent of their time is spent communicating—often in handwritten notes. An executive who tries to be direct and personal by writing his own notes (a very desirable trait and a powerful motivational tool), but who misspells the words, makes himself look foolish, to say the least.

4. Make up some trick sentences. For the -able, -ible problem, for example, you might remember the sentence, "Able managers are indispensable," or, "Be insistent on a tent."

Common Root Stems for Better Word Understanding

No one can possibly know all the words in the English language and you don't always have a dictionary near you. But one good thing about English is that a large percentage of vocabulary comes from Latin and Greek words. They form a base for many of the words we use, and we frequently combine Latin and Greek suffixes with Latin and Greek base words to form new words.

You can get a good idea of the general meaning of a word if you have a list of these frequently used bases and suffixes handy. That's why they are included in this section—so that you won't have to look up the meaning of every strange word you come upon. Just become familiar with these bases and suffixes and keep this reference handy. It'll save you a lot of time.

LATIN PREFIXES

a-, ab-, abs-	away from, off
ad-	to, toward, near
ambi-	both, around
ante-	before
bi-, bin,- bis	two
circum-	around
co-, col-, com-	together, with
contra-	opposite, against
de-	down, from
demi-	part, half
di-, dis-	separation, apart from, removal
e-, ef-, ex-	off, out of
extra-	outer, beyond
im-, in-, ir-	in, on, into, against
il-, im-, in-, ir-	not
infra-	below, lower

inter-	between
intra-	inside, within, during
intro-	within
juxta-	near, beside
non-	not
ob-, op-	against
per-	throughout, completely
post-	after, behind
poster-	behind
pre-	before, in front of
pro-	in front of, before
re-	again
retro-	behind, backward
se-	apart from
semi-	half
sub-	below, under
super-	above, over
supra-	upper, above
trans-	across, through
ultra-	excessive, beyond

LATIN SUFFIXES

-able, -ible	able to, can
-acious	tending to
-acity	inclined to
-acy	being or having
-al, -eal, -ial	relating to
-ance, -ancy	the quality of
-ence, -ency	
-an, -ane, -ian	pertaining to
-ar, -ary	pertaining to
-arium, -ary	place for
-ate	possessing, office of
-cle, -cule	little
-el	little
-esce	to begin
-(i) fic	making
-(i) fy,	to make
-ic, -tic	pertaining to
-id	tending to
-egate, -ignate	to make
-il	little
-il, -ile	pertaining to

-ile	able to be
-ine	pertaining to
-ion	act of
-itude	quality of
-itious	tending to
-ety, -ity, -ty	quality of
-ive	tending to
-(o) lence, -(u) lence	full of
-men, -ment	result of
-(i)mony	quality of
-le, -ole, -ule	little
-or	one who does something
-or, -our	state of
-ory	tending to
-orium, -ory	place for
-iose, -ose	full of
-eous, -ious, -ous	full of
-rix	woman who does something
-ulous, -uous	tending to
-ure	act of
-y	quality of

LATIN BASES

abdomen-, abdomenin-	body cavity
acid	sour
acr-, acu-	sharp
adip-	fat
adolesce-, adult-	grow up
act-, ag-, ig-	do, drive
ager-, agri-	field
agita-	shake, excite
alb-	white
aliment-	food, nourishment
alt-	high
am-	love
ambula-	walk
ampull-	bottle; flask
anim-	mind, feeling, life
anima-	breath, life
ann (u)-, enni-	year
apert	open
aqu (a)-	water
art-	art, skill

aud-, audit-	hear
aur-	ear
bell-	war
bene-	well, good
benign-	kind
bi-, bin-	two, twice
bibe-	drink
brev-	short
cad-, cas-, cid-	fall, befall
capill-	hair
calc-	limestone, pebble
cap-, capt-, cept-, cip-	take, seize
capit-, cipit-	head
carn-	flesh
cav-	hollow
ced-, cess-	to, yield
cerebr-	brain
celer-	swift
cent-	hundred
cern-, cret-	separate
cid-, cis-	kill, cut
cili-	hair
claim-, clam-	cry out
clos-, clud-, clus	shut
cord-	heart
coron-	crown
corp-, corpor-, corpus-	body
cre-, cresc-, cret-	grow
cred-, credit-	believe, trust
cruc-, crux-	a cross
culp-	blame, fault
cub-, cumb-	lie down
cours-, cur (r)-, curs-	run
cut-	skin
de-, div-	god
deci-, decim-	ten
dent-	teeth
dexter-, dextra-	right
dic-, dict-	say
digit-	finger
doc-, doct-	teach
dolo-	pain
dorm-	sleep
duo-	two

duc-, duct-	lead
dura-	hard
ede	eat
ego-	I
equ-	equal
err-	wander, deviate
exter	on the outside
fa- fat-	to speak
fac-, fact-, fect-, fic-	do, make
faci-	face, outer surface
fall-, fals-	deceive
fecund-	fruitful, fertile
fenestra-	opening, window
fer-	bear, carry
ferv-	boil, bubble
fet-	offspring; bring forth
fid-	faith
fidel-	faithful
fil-	thread
fin-	end, limit
firm-	firm, strong
flect- flex-	bend
flor-	flower
foli-	leaf
flu-, flux-	flow
fort-	strong
fract-, frang-, (fring-)	break
fruct-, frux-	fruit
(found-), fund-, fus-,	pour, melt
gen-, genit-	produce, give birth to
gen-, gener-	race, kind
genu-	knee
ger-, gest-	carry, produce
grad-, gress-	step, to
gran-	grain
grand-	great
grat-	pleasing, grateful
grav-	heavy
greg-	flock, herd
habe-, habit-	have, hold
her-, hes-	to stick
hominis-, homo-	man
hum-	earth, soil
i-, it-	go

jac-, ject-	throw
joc-	joke
judic-	judgment
join-, junct-	join
jur-	to swear
lac-, lact-	milk
lacrim-	tear
lat-	bear, carry; wide
lapid-, lapis-	stone
later-	side
lect-, leg-, lig-	choose, pick out, read
len-	soft, mild
lev-	light weight
line-	line
langu-	tongue
liter-	letter, literature
loc-	place
locut-, loqu-	speak
luc-	light, to shine
lud-, lus-	play, mock
lumin	light
lun-	moon
magn-	great
mal(e)-, malign-	bad
mamm-	breast
man(u)-	hand
matern-, matr-	mother
medi-, media,	middle
mens-	table
mel-	honey; sweet
milit-	martial
mens-, ment-	mind
mill-	thousand
miss-, mitt-	send
minor-, minus-, minut-	small, smaller
misc-	to mix
mit-	mild, soft
mis(s)-, mit(t)-	send, let go
moll-	mild, soft
mon-, monit-	warn, advise
mort-	death
mot-, mov-	to move
mult-	many
mut-	to change
nasc-, nat-	be born

neg-	to deny
noct-	night
nomen-, nomin-	name, noun
nud-	naked
nul(l)-	nothing
nunci-	to announce
oct-, octav-	eight
ocul-	eye
omn-	all
orb-	circle
ordin-	order
or-, os-	mouth
os, oss-	bone
part-	part
pass-, pati-	endure, to suffer
patern-, patr-	father
patri-	fatherland, country
pect-, pector-	chest
pecuni-	money
ped-	foot
pel(l)-, puls-	drive, push
pend-, pens-	hang, weigh, pay
pet-, petit-	seek, assail
pisc-	fish
plac-	please, appease
ple-, plet-	fill
plen-	full
plex-, plic-, plicit-, (ply-)	fold, tangle, intermingle
plur-, plus	more
pon-, posit-, (pound-)	place, put
port-	carry
pot-	have power
pota-	drink
prec-	prayer
pred-	prey
press-	press
prim-	first
prob- (prov-)	good, text
prol-	offspring
propri-	one's own, fitting
pugn-	fight
punct-, pung-	prick, point
purg-	clean
put-	reckon, think
quadr(u)-	four

quart-	fourth
quint-	fifth
quir-, quisit-, (quest-)	ask, seek
radi-	ray, spoke
radic-	root
rect-	right, straight
reg-, rect-, rig-	straighten, rule
rog-	to ask
rot-	wheel
rupt-	to break
sacr-, secr-	sacred
sal-, salt-, sil-, sult-	to leap
salut-	health
sanct-	holy
sanguin-	blood
sati(s)-	enough
sci-	know
scrib-, script-	write
sec-, sect-, seg-	cut
sed-, sess-, sid-	sit, settle
semi-	half, partly
sen-	old
sens-, sent-	feel, think
sept-, septem-	seven
secut-, sequ-	follow
serv-	serve, save
sext-	sixth, six
sicc-	dry
simil-, simul-	like
sol-	alone
sol-	sun
solut-, solv-	loosen, to free
son-	sound
sopor-	sleep
spec-, spect-, spic-	look
spri-	to breathe
st(a), stat-	stand
string-, strict-, strain-	draw tight
stru-, struct-	build
tang-, ting-, tact-	touch
tard-	slow
tempera	mix, moderate
tempor-	time

tain-, ten-, tent-, tin-	hold
tend-, tens-, tent-	stretch, strive
tenu-	thin
termin-	boundary, end
torqu-, tors-, tort-	twist
tot-	all
tract-	drag, draw
tri-	three
trud-, trus-	push, to thrust
turb-	to disturb
umbr-	shadow
un-	one
und- (ound)-	wave
vacu-	empty
val- (vail-)	be strong, be worth something
vas-	vessel
ven-, vent-	come
ver-	true
verb-	word, verb
vers-, vert-	turn
vest-	garment
vi-	way, road
vibra-	shake, vibrate
vid-, vis-	see
vinc-, vict-	conquer
vir-	man, poison, strong
viv-	to live
voc-, vok-	voice, call
vol-	wish
volut-, volv-	roll
vor-	devour
vulg-	common

GREEK PREFIXES

a-, an-	not, without
amphi-	both, around
anti-	against, opposed to
arche-, archi-	first, chief
di-	two, twice
dia-	through
dys-	bad
ek-, ex-	outside

ekto-	outside
em-, en-	inside
endo-	within
epi-	upon
exo-	outside
hemi-	half, partially
hyper-	above, over
hypo-	under, below
meta-	beyond, after
para-	near, by the side of
peri-	around
pro-	before, in front of
sym-, syn-	with

GREEK SUFFIXES AND COMBINING FORMS

-arch	one who rules
-archy	rule by
-arion, -arium	little
-ast, -st, -aste	one connected with
-cracy	rule by
-crat	an advocate or follower
-ectomy	surgical removal
-emia	condition of the blood
-gram	thing written
-graph	writing, etc.
-graphy-	writing, etc.
-hedron	solid figure
-iasis	diseased condition
-ac, -ic, -tic	relating to
-ician	specialist in, one connected with
-ics, -tics	art, science, or study of
-idum	little
-in, -ine	chemical substance
-ion, -ium	little
-iscus, -isk	little
-ism	belief in
-ist	one who believes in
-ite	one connected with
-itis	inflammation of, etc.
-ium	part, etc.
-ize	verbal ending
-logy	science of
-m, -ma, -me	result of
-mania	madness about

-maniac	a person who has a madness for
-meter	measure
-metry	art or science of measuring something
-nomy	science of
-oid	like
-oma	tumor
-osis	diseased condition of
-path	someone who suffers from a disease of
-pathy	disease of
-phobe	someone who fears or hates
-phobia	abnormal fear of
-rrhea, -rrhoea	abnormal discharge
-scope	instrument for viewing, etc.
-se, -sia, -sis, -sy	act of

GREEK BASES

acou-, acu-	hear
acr-	highest, extreme
actin-	ray, radiating structure
aden-	gland
aer-	air, gas
aesthe-, esthe-	feel, perceive
agog-, -agogue	lead
agon-	struggle, contest
alg-	pain
all-	other
andr-	man, male
angel-	messenger, message
angi-	vessel
anth-	flower
anthrop-	human being, man
archa(e)-, arche-	ancient, primitive, beginning
arthr-	joint, speech sound, or articulation
asce-	exercise
ast(e)r-	star
atm-	air, breath
aut-	self
ball-, ble-, bol-	throw, put
bar-	weight, pressure
bi-	life
bibli-	book
blast-	bud, embryonic cell, formative substance
brachy-	short
brady-	slow

bucol-	pastoral
cac-	bad
cal(l)-, kal(l)-	beauty
canon-	a rule
cardi-	heart
carp-	fruit
cau-, caus-	to burn
centr-	center
cephal-	head
cheir-, chir-	hand
chlor-	green, chlorine
chol(e)-	bile, gall
chondr-	cartilage
chore-	dance
chrom-, chromat-	color
chron-	time
cla-	break
clys-	wash
cocc(us)	berry, seed
cosm-	universe, order
cra-	to mix
cri-	to decide, to judge, to separate
cryph-, crypt-	hidden, secret
cyan-	dark blue
cycl-	circle, wheel
cyn(os)-	dog
cyst-	bladder, sac
cyt-	cell
dactyl-	digit, finger or toe
dec(a)-	ten
dem-	people
demon-	evil spirit, spirit
dendr-	tree, tree-like structure
derm-, dermat-	skin
deuter-	second
di-	double, twice
dich-	in two
didac-	teach
do-	give
dolich-	long
dog-, dox-	opinion, teaching
drom-	a course, a running
dyn-, dynam-	force, power

enter-	intestine
epi-	above
er-, erot-	love
erg-, urg-	work
eryther-	red
ethn-	cultural group, race
eury(s)-	broad, wide
gam-	marriage
gastr-	stomach
ge-	earth
gen(e)-, gon-	to originate, to be produced, to produce
gen(e)-	kind, race
ger-, geront-	old age, old people
gloss-, glot(t)-	tongue, language
glyph-	to carve
gno-	to know
gon-	generative, reproductive, sexual
gon-	angle, angled figure
gon-, (see gen (e)-)	produce
gymn-	naked
gyn(e)-, gynaec-, gynec-	female, woman
hect-	a hundred
hedon-	pleasure
hegemon-	leader
heli-	sun
hem-, hemat-	blood
hemer-	day
hemi-	half
hepat-	liver
hept(a)-	seven
heter-	different, other
hex(a)-	six
hier-	sacred
hipp-	horse
hist-, histi-	tissue
hol-	whole
hom-, home-	regular, same
hydr-	water
hygr-	moist, wet
hypno-	sleep
hyster-	hysteria, uterus
iatr-	medicine, physician
ichthy-	fish

icon-	image
ide-	idea, thought
idi-	peculiar, your own
is-	equal
kilo-	one thousand
cine-, kine-	move
lab-, (lem-), lept-	seize, take
lat(e)r-	worship fanatically
lect-, log(ue)	choose, speak
leuc-, leuk-	white
lip-	fat
lite, lith-	stone
log-, -logue	proporation, reasoning, speech, word
ly-	loosen
macr-	large, long
manc-, mant-	divine by means of
mast-, maz-	breast
mega-, megal-	large, a million
melan-	black, dark
mening-	membrane
mer-	part
mes-	middle
metr-	measure
micr-	millionth part, small
mim-	to imitate
mis-	hatred
mne-	remember
mon-	one, single
morhp-	form, shape
my-, myos-, mys-	muscle
myc-, mycet-	fungus, mold
myel-	bone, marrow, spinal cord
naut-	sailor
ne-	new, different form of
necr-	corpse, dead, dead tissue
nephr-	kidney
nes-	island
neur-	nerve
oct(a)-	eight
od-	poem, song
od-, hod-	road, way
odont-	tooth
olig-	few
onym-	name, word
oo-	egg

op-, opt-	eye, of eight
ophthalm-	eye
ora-	mouth
ornis, ornith-	bird
orth-	correct, straight
ost(e)-	bone
ot-	ear
pale-	old
pan-, pant-	all, every
pate-	walk
path-	disease, feel, suffer
patr-, patri-	father
ped-	child
pedi-	foot
pent(a)-	five
pep(t)-	digest
petr-	rock
pha(n)-	show, appear
phag-	eat
pha-, phe-	speak
phem-	voice
pher-, phor-	bear
phil-	love
phleb-	vein
phob-	fear
phon-	sound, voice
phot-	light
phra-	speak
phren-	diaphragm, mind
phy-	grow
physi-	nature
phyll-	leaf
plas(t)-	form
platy-	broad, flat
pleg-	paralysis
plex-	paralytic stroke
pod-	foot
pol-, polis	city, state
polem-	war
poly-	many, much
prot-	first, original, primitive
pragma-	deed, act
pseud-	false
psych-	mind, spirit
pter-	wing

py-	pus
pyr-	fire
rhin-	nose
schiz-, shiss-	split
scler-	hard
som-, somat-	body
soph-	wise
sperma-	seed
sta-	stand, stop
stal-, stle-, stol-	send, draw
sten-	narrow
stere-	solid, three dimensional
sthen-	strength
stom-, stomat-	mouth
stroph-	turn
tach-	speed
tachy-	swift
tact-, tax-	arrange, put in order
taph-	tomb
taut-	the same
techn-	art, craft, skill
tele-	at a distance
tetr(a)-	four
(thanas-), thanat-	death
the-	place, put
the-	god
thec(a)	ease
therm-	heat
thromb-	clot
thym-	mind, strong feeling
tom-	to cut
ton- (-tonus)	a stretching, tension
top-	place
tox-	poison
trauma-	wound, injury
tri-	three
trop-	turn
troph-	grow, nourish
typ-	model, stamp
ur-	urine, of the kidney
ur-	tail
xanth-	yellow
xen-	stranger, foreigner
xero-	dry
xyl-	wood
zo-	animal

PART *II.*

Understanding Words

6. CHOOSING SIMPLER WORDS

Business people sometimes feel that more complicated words should be used instead of everyday language. Perhaps they feel that there is a special, more precise meaning attached to a word like "minuscule," when the word "tiny" really does the job just as well. However, it could be argued that any business procedure that takes more time than it should is needless, wasteful, and cuts into profits. Thus, any business word that is harder to understand than a simpler, everyday word, is unprofitable and a needless time-waster.

The words listed in the left-hand column are those you often see in business correspondence and conversations. But they're usually harder for most people to understand. Most often, a simpler word such as those listed in the right-hand column will do the job just as well, and often better.

Synonyms for Everyday Language

Word Sometimes Used	Everyday Word
abandon	leave
abate	lessen
abbreviate	shorten
abdicate	quit
aberration	abnormal
abjure	avoid
abominate	hate
abscond	hide away
abstract (v.)	summarize
abstruse	complex
accolade	praise
accost	attack
accretion	addition
acquiesce	comply
acquit	freed of a charge
actuate	start
acumen	keenness
adamant	immovable
adjunct	helper
admixture	blend
adroit	clever
adventitious	accidental

Word Sometimes Used	Everyday Word
affray	battle
aggrandize	enlarge
aggregate	total
alacrity	haste
altercate	fight
amalgamate	blend
ameliorate	improve
amorphous	shapeless
analogous	similar
annul	repeal
anomalous	peculiar
apportion	set aside
artifice	trick
ascend	climb
ascetic	self-disciplined
asperse	malign
assuage	calm
attenuate	weaken
attrition	weakening
audacious	bold
averse	against
avouch	affrim
awry	wrong
balderdash	nonsense
banal	silly
bedeck	decorate
befit	proper
besmirch	stain
bizarre	weird
blench	flinch
boorish	crude
buffoon	clown
cabal	conspiracy
callous	thick-skinned
calumniate	slur
canny	clever
caper	frolic
captious	grouchy
cartel	agreement
censure	criticize
cessation	end
chic	style
choleric	cranky

Word Sometimes Used	Everyday Word
churl	oaf
coalesce	merge
cogent	effective
cognizant	aware
commodious	spacious
complaisant	obliging
concatenate	link
congenital	inborn
consternation	anxiety
constrain	force
construe	interpret
contentious	quarrelsome
contravene	oppose
contumely	abuse
convoke	summon
cordon	barricade
corroborate	confirm
countermand	reverse
covenant	promise
criterion	measure
debilitate	weaken
decimate	destroy
demur	disagree
demure	prim
denigrate	belittle
depose	overthrow
deprecate	insult
derogate	downgrade
desultory	haphazard
diffident	reserved
dilettante	amateur
disavow	reject
discomfit	embarrass
disinclined	opposed
distend	bloat
doddering	feeble
effete	outdated
effigy	likeness
egress	outlet
elan	enthusiasm
empiric	experience-related
enervate	drain
ennui	boredom

Word Sometimes Used	Everyday Word
ensconse	shelter
ephemereal	fleeting
epigram	witticism
epithet	characterizing word
equivocate	lie
esoteric	specialized
exacerbate	irritate
excoriate	censure
execrate	denounce
exemplary	commendable
exigency	need
exonerate	absolve
expiate	atone
expurgate	cleanse
extirpate	destroy
fabricate	make
facade	front
facilitate	help
flaccid	limp
fluctuate	change
fractious	unruly
fulsome	disgustingly excessive
gamut	scope
garrulous	talkative
germane	relevant
harbinger	omen
ideate	think
ignominy	disgrace
imbibe	drink
impalpable	vague
impetuous	impulsive
implacable	unchangeable
impromptu	spontaneous
impudent	rude
inadvertent	unintentional
inchoate	forming
incipient	beginning
inculcate	teach
indigent	poor
indubitable	certain
indurate	hardened
inestimable	valuable
infamous	disgraceful

Word Sometimes Used	Everyday Word
inimical	unfriendly
innocuous	harmless
insipid	bland
insurgent	rebel
interpolate	alter
intractable	headstrong
inveterate	habitual
invidious	hateful
involuted	intricate
judicious	careful
juxtaposition	nearness
laconic	concise
lampoon	ridicule
lascivious	sensual
lethargic	sluggish
limpid	clear
livid	angry
luxuriate	revel
macabre	grim
malevolent	evil
malleable	pliable
mendacity	lie
minuscule	tiny
mitigate	lessen
mollify	appease
morose	moody
nebulous	hazy
nullify	annul
obdurate	firm
obese	fat
obsequious	compliant
palatable	tasty
palliate	moderate
pallid	whitish
patronizing	condescending
pensive	thoughtful
peremptory	haughty
perfidy	treachery
perquisite	tip
placate	soothe
plethora	fullness
ponderous	massive
portend	foretell

Word Sometimes Used	Everyday Word
precipitate	impetuous
prevaricate	lie
pristine	unspoiled
proclivity	tendency
prognosticate	forecast
propitiate	appease
propitious	favorable
proximal	nearest
punctilious	careful
quandary	puzzle
querulous	complaining
quintessence	core
raillery	kidding
raucous	harsh
recalcitrant	unmanageable
recant	deny
recondite	hidden
rectitude	uprightness
redoubtable	fearsome
reduplicate	repeat
remunerate	pay
reparation	compensation
reprehensible	blameworthy
repudiate	deny
rescind	cancel
resplendent	glittering
restive	balky
reticent	silent
retrograde	retreat
risible	laughable
rostrum	platform
ruminate	ponder
salient	important
salutory	beneficial
saturnine	gloomy
scintilla	scrap
sedentary	settled
sententious	terse
shibboleth	slogan
sleazy	cheap
snide	false
solecism	error
sporadic	scattered

Word Sometimes Used	Everyday Word
spurious	false
staid	grave
stolid	unemotional
stringent	strict
subterfuge	deceit
surcease	end
taciturn	silent
tirade	rage
tractable	obedient
truculent	savage
umbrage	resentment
undaunted	brave
unequivocal	direct
unmitigated	unrelieved
vacuous	empty
voracious	overeager
woof	essence
zenith	peak

7. PRONUNCIATION GUIDE TO ESPECIALLY DIFFICULT WORDS ENCOUNTERED IN BUSINESS

Sample Word	Pronounce as	Sample Word	Pronounce as
ace	ays	is	iz
air	air	jay	jay
at	at	kiss	kis
alms	ahmz	lamb	lam
all	awl	my	migh
back	bak	mice	mighs
chain	chayn	nice	nighs
do	doo	sing	sing
eel	eel	told	tohld
ear	ier	oil	oil
fine	fighn	out	owt
fit	fit	race	rays
go	goh	yearn	yern
helm	helm	so	soh
hurt	hert		

Word	*Pronunciation*
aberration	ab er AY sh'n
abortive	uh BOWR tiv
absent (adj.)	AB s'nt
absent (verb)	ab SENT
absetee	ab s'n TEE
absolute	AB suh loot
absolutely	AB suh loot li
absolve	uhb SAHLV
absorb	uhb SOWRB
abstract (adj.; noun)	AB strakt
abstract (verb)	ab STRAKT
abuse (noun)	uh BYOOS
abuse (verb)	uh BYOOZ
abusive	uh BYOO siv
academe	ak uh DEEM
accelerate	ak SEL uh rayt
accelerator	ak SEL uh rayt er
accent (noun)	AK sent
accent (verb)	AK sent

Word	*Pronunciation*
accept	ak SEPT
acceptable	ak SEP tuh b'l
acceptance	ak SEP t'ns
access (noun)	AK ses
accessory	ak SES uh ri
acclamation	ak luh MAY sh'n
acclimate	uh KLIGH mit
acclimation	ak li MAY sh'n
accompaniment	uh KUHM puh ni m'nt
accomplish	un KAHM plish
accredit	uh KRED it
accuracy	AK yoo ruh si
accurate	AK yoo rit
acetate	AS uh tayt
acoustics	uh KOO stiks
acquaintance	uh KWAYN t'ns
acquiesce	ak wi ES
acquisitiveness	uh KWIZ uh tiv nis
acumen	uh KYOO m'n
acute	uh KYOOT
adamant	AD uh m'nt
addict (noun)	AD ikt
addict (verb)	uh DIKT
address (noun)	uh DRES
address (verb)	uh DRES
adept (adj.)	uh DEPT
adequate	AD uh kwit
adherence	ad HIER 'ns
ad hoc	ad HAHK
ad infinitum	ad in fi NIGH t'm
ad interim	ad IN tuh rim
adjacent	uh JAY s'nt
adjourn	uh JERN
adjudicate	uh JOO di kayt
adjunct	AJ uhngkt
adjust	uh JUHST
adjutant	AJ uh t'nt
ad libitum	ad LIB eh t'm
admirable	AD mi ruh b'l
admit	ad MIT
admittance	ad MIT 'ns
admonish	ad MAHN ish
ad nauseam	ad NAW see'm

Word	*Pronunciation*
adrenalin	uh DREN uh lin
adroit	uh DROYT
advance	ad VANTS
advantage	ed VAN tij
advantageous	ad v'n TAY juhs
advent	AD vent
adventure	uhd VEN cher
adversary	AD vuh sehr i
adverse	uhd VERS
advertise	AD ver tighz
advertisement	ad ver TIGHZ m'nt
advertiser	AD ver tigh zer
advice (noun)	uhd VIGHS
advise (verb)	uhd VIZE
advocacy	AD vo kuh si
advocate (noun)	AD vuh k't
advocate (verb)	AD vuh kayt
affair	uh FAIR
affirm	uh FERM
affirmation	af er MAY sh'n
affluence	AF loo 'ns
affluent	AF loo 'nt
affront	uh FRUHNT
agenda	uh JEN duh
aggravate	AG ruh vayt
aggregate (adj.; noun)	AG ruh git
aggregate (verb)	AG ruh gayt
aggressor	uh GRES er
agile	AJ il
agility	uh JIL i ti
alibi	AL i bigh
alien	AYL y'n
alienate	A LEE uh nayt
alienation	ay ly 'n AY sh'n
alignment	uh LIGHN m'nt
alliance	uh LIGH 'ns
allied	uh LIGHD
alloy (noun)	AL oy
alloy (verb)	uh LOY
allude	uh LOOD
allure	uh LOOR
allusion	uh LOO zh'n
alternate (adj., noun)	AWL ter nit

Word	*Pronunciation*
alternate (verb)	AWL ter nayt
alternately	AWL ter nit li
alternative	awl TER nuh tiv
altruism	AL troo iz 'm
amalgamate	uh MAL guh mayt
amass	uh MAS
amateur	am uh CHER
ambidextrous	am bi DEK struhs
ambiguity	am bi GYOO uh ti
ambiguous	am BIG yoo uhs
ambition	am BISH 'n
ambitious	am BISH uhs
ambivalence	am BIV uh l'ns
amenable	uh MEE nuh b'l
amend	uh MEND
amendment	uh MEND m'nt
amenities	uh MEN i teez
amenity	uh MEN i ti
amiable	AY mi uh b'l
amicable	AM i kuh b'l
amplify	AM pli figh
anachronism	uh NAK ruh niz 'm
analogous	uh NAL uh guhs
analogue	AN uh lawg
analogy	uh NAL uh ji
analyses	uh NAL uh seez
analysis	uh NAL uh sis
analyst	AN uh 'list
analytic	an uh LIT ik
anatomy	uh NAT uh mi
ancillary	AN si lehr i
anecdotal	AN ek doh t'l
anecdote	AN ek doht
animate (adj.)	AN uh muht
animate (verb)	AN uh mayt
annotate	AN uh tayt
annotation	an uh TAY sh'n
annuity	uh NYOO i ti
annulment	uh NUHL m'nt
anomalous	uh NAHM uh luhs
anomaly	uh NAHM uh li
anonymous	uh NAHN uh muhs
answerable	AN ser uh b'l

Word	Pronunciation
appellant	uh PEL 'nt
appellate	uh PEL it
appendage	uh PEN dij
applicant	AP li k'nt
application	ap li KAY sh'n
applicator	AP li kay ter
appointee	uh poyn TEE
apportion	uh PAWR sh'n
apportionment	uh PAWR sh'n m'nt
appraisal	uh PRAYZ 'l
appreciable	uh PREE shi uh b'l
appreciate	uh PREE shi ayt
appreciation	uh pree she AY sh'n
appreciative	uh PREE shi ay tiv
approbation	ap roh BAY sh'n
appropriate (adj.)	uh PROH pri it
appropriate (verb)	uh PROH pri ayt
approximate (adj.)	uh PRAHK suh mit
approximate (verb)	uh PRAHK suh mayt
a priori	uh pree OH ree
a propos	ap ruh POH
aptitude	AP ta tyud
arbiter	AHR bi ter
arbitrary	AHR bi trehr i
arbitrate	AHR bi trayt
arbitration	ahr bi TRAY sh'n
arbitrator	AHR bi tray ter
aseptic	uh SEP tik
askew	uh SKYOO
assert	uh SERT
assertion	uh SER sh'n
assess	uh SES
assessment	uh SES m'nt
assessor	uh SES er
assets	AS ets
assiduous	uh SIT uh wus
assign	uh SIGHN
assignable	uh SIGHN uh b'l
assignee	uh si NEE
assimilate	uh SIM i layt
assimilation	uh sim uh LAY sh'n
associate (adj., noun)	uh SOH shi uht
associate (verb)	uh SO shi ayt

Word	Pronunciation
association	uh soh shi AY sh'n
assumption	uh SUHMP sh'n
assurance	uh SHOOR 'ns
assure	uh SHOOR
astute	as TYOOT
attache	ah TASH ay
attainable	uh TAYN uh b'l
attainment	uh TAYN m'nt
attenuate	uh TEN yoo ayt
attenuation	uh ten yoo AY sh'n
attribute (noun)	A tri byoot
attribute (verb)	uh TRIB yoo t
attribution	at ri BYOO sh'n
attributive	uh TRIB yoo tiv
attrition	uh TRI sh'n
audit	AW dit
auditor	AWD i ter
authentic	aw THEN tik
authenticate	aw THEN ti kayt
authenticity	aw then TSI i ti
authoritative	uh THAW ri tay tive
authorization	aw ther i ZAY sh'n
authorized	AW ther ighzd
autonomous	aw TAHN uh muhs
autonomy	aw TAHN uh mi
averse	uh VERS
aversion	uh VER zh'n
banter	BAN ter
belligerent	buh LIJ er 'nt
beneficiary	ben i FISH i ehr i
benevolence	buh NEV uh l'ns
benevolent	buh NEV uh l'nt
biannual	by AN yoo 'l
bias	BI uhs
brevity	BREV i ti
brokerage	BROH ker ij
buttress	BUH truhs
cajole	kuh JOHL
cajolery	kuh JOHL er i
calamitous	kuh LAM i tuhs
calculable	KAL kyuh luh b'l
calculate	KAL kyuh layt
calculation	kal kyuh LAY sh'n

Word	*Pronunciation*
calendar	KAL 'n der
caliber	KAL i ber
calibrate	KAL i brayt
caliper	KAL i per
candid	KAN did
candidacy	KAN dih duh si
candidate	KAN di dayt
candor	KAN der
capital	KAP i t'l
capitalism	KAP i t'l iz 'm
capitalist	KAP i t'l ist
capitol	KAP i t'l
capitulate	kuh PIT choo layt
caricature	KAR i kuh choor
carte blanche	kahrt BLAHNSH
cashier	kash IER
castigate	KAS ti gayt
casualty	KAZH yoo 'l ti
catharsis	kuh THAHR sis
caveat emptor	KAH vi et'EMP er
censorship	SEN ser ship
censure	SEN sher
census	SES suhs
cerebral	SUH ree br'l
cessation	ses AY sh'n
chagrin	shuh GRIN
chastise	chas TIGHZ
chastisement	CHAS tiz m'nt
chattel	CHAT 'l
chronology	kroh NAHL uh ji
chronometer	kroh NAHM uh ter
cipher	SIGH fer
circuit	SER kit
circuitous	ser KYOO i tuhs
circular	SER kyoo ler
circumspect	SER k'm spekt
circumstantial	ser k'm STAN sh'l
citation	sigh TAY sh'n
clarification	klar i fi KAY sh'n
clarity	KLAR i ti
client	KLIGH 'nt
clientele	kligh 'n TEL
climactic	kligh MAK tik

Word	*Pronunciation*
closure	KLOH zher
coadjutant	koh AJ uh t'nt
coadjutor	koh AJ oo ter
coagulate	koh AG yoo layt
coalesce	koh uh LES
coauthor	koh AW ther
codicil	KAHD i sil
codify	KOD i figh
coefficient	koh i FISH 'nt
cognizance	KAHG ni z'ns
cognizant	KAHG ni z'nt
collaborator	kuh LAB uh ray ter
collate	kah LAYT
collateral	kuh LAT er 'l
colloquial	kuh LOH kwi 'l
collusion	kuh LOO zh'n
combative	KAHM bah tiv
compatibility	k'm pat i BIL i ti
compendium	k'm PEN di 'm
compensate	KAHM p'n sayt
competence	KAHM puh t'ns
competitor	k'm PET i ter
compilation	kahm pi LAY sh'n
complacence	k'm PLAY s'ns
complacent	k'm PLAY s'nt
component	k'm POH n'nt
comprehensible	kahm pri HEN si b'l
comprehensive	kahm pri HEN siv
comptroller	k'n TROHL er
compulsory	k'm PUHL suh ri
concomitant	kahn KAHM i t'nt
concurrence	k'n KER 'ns
concurrent	k'n KER 'nt
conducive	k'n DOO siv
confiscate	KAHN fis kayt
congruent	KAHNG groo 'nt
congruity	k'n GROO i ti
congruous	KAHNG groo uhs
connotation	kahn oh TAY sh'n
connotative	KAHN oh tay tiv
consensus	k'n SEN suhs
construe	k'n STROO
controller	k'n TROHL er

Word	*Pronunciation*
conversely	kahn VERS li
convocation	kahn voh KAY sh'n
coping	KOHP ing
copious	KOH pi uhs
cordial	KAWR j'l
correlative	kuh REL uh tiv
corroborate	kuh RAHB uh rayt
coupon	KOO pahn
culminate	KUHL mi nayt
cursory	KER suh ri
cybernetics	sigh ber NET iks
data	DAY tuh
datum	DAY t'm
debenture	di BEN cher
debit	DEB it
decentralization	dee sen tr'l i ZAY sh'n
decibel	DES i bel
deficit	DEF i sit
diffraction	di FRAK shuhn
diffuse (adj.)	dif YOOS
diffuse (verb)	dif YOOZ
digest (noun)	DIGH jest
digest (verb)	di JEST
diplomate	DIP loh mayt
discernible	di ZERN i b'l
discourse (noun)	DIS kawrs
discourse (verb)	dis KAWRS
discrepancy	di KREP 'n si
dynamic	digh NAM ik
dynamo	DI nuh moh
ebullient	i BUHL y'nt
eccentric	ek SEN trik
eccentricity	ek sen TRIS i ti
economic	ee kuh NAHM ik
economical	ee kuh NAHM i k'l
economics	ee kuh NAHM iks
economist	i KAHN uh mist
economy	i KAHN uh mi
efficacious	ef i KAY shuhs
efficacy	EF i kuh si
efficient	i FISH 'nt
elicit	i LIS it
eligibility	el i ji BIL i ti

Word	*Pronunciation*
elite	ay LEET
elucidate	i LOO si dayt
elude	i LOOD
elusive	i LOO siv
elusory	i LOO suh ri
emanate	EM uh nayt
amanation	em uh NAY sh'n
emulate	EM yoo layt
emulation	em yoo LAY sh'n
endemic	en DEM ik
endorse	en DAWRS
ensure	en SHOOR
envelope (verb)	en VEL uhp
envelope (noun)	EN vuh lohp
enviable	EN vi uh b'l
environment	en VIGH r'n m'nt
equalization	ee kw'l i ZAY sh'n
equate	ee KWAYT
equivocal	i KWIV uh k'l
equivocate	i KWIV uh kayt
equivocation	i kwiv uh KAY sh'n
estimate (noun)	ES ti mit
estimate (verb)	ES ti mayt
euphemism	YOO fi miz 'm
errata	i RAT uh
erratic	i RAT ik
erratum	i RAT 'm
excursion	eks KER zh'n
executor	eg ZEK yoo ter
exemplar	ek ZEM pler
exemplary	eg ZEM pluh ri
exorbitance	eg ZAWR bi t'ns
exorbitant	eg ZAWR bi t'nt
expedient	eks PEE di 'nt
expedite	EKS pi dight
fiduciary	fi DOO shi ehr i
figurative	FIG yoor uh tiv
finance (noun)	FIGH nans
finance (verb)	fi NANS
forfeit	FAWR fit
formidable	FAWR mi duh b'l
frequent (adj.)	FREE kw'nt
frequent (verb)	free KWENT

Word	Pronunciation
fruition	froo ISH 'n
futurist	FYOOCH a rist
futurity	fyoo TYOOR it i
gratuitous	gruh TOO i tuhs
guarantee	gar 'n TEE
guarantor	GAR 'n tawr
guaranty	GAR 'n ti
harass	huh RASS
hiatus	high AY tuhs
honorarium	ahn uh RAIR i 'm
illusive	i LOO siv
illusory	i LOO suh ri
illustrate	IL uhs trayt
illustrative	i LUHS truh tiv
impeccable	im PEK uh b'l
impetus	IM pi tuhs
inadvertent	in uhd VER t'nt
incisive	in SIGH siv
incisor	in SIGH zer
incline (noun)	IN klighn
incline (verb)	in KLIGHN
include	in KLOOD
inclusive	in KLOO siv
incongruous	in KAHNG groo uhs
incorporate (adj.)	in KAWR puh ruht
incorporate (verb)	in KAWR puh rayt
increment	IN kre m'nt
indicative	in DIK uh tiv
indices	IN di seez
indict	in DIGHT
indictment	in DIGHT m'nt
indigenous	in DIJ i nuhs
indigent	IN di j'nt
indiscretion	in dis KRESH 'n
inevitable	in EV i tuh b'l
inexplicable	in EKS pli kuh b'l
inextricable	in EKS tri kuh b'l
insatiable	in SAY shi uh b'l
insatiate	in SAY shi ayt
irrefutable	i REF yoo tuh b'l
irrelevant	i REL i v'nt
irrevocable	i REV uh kuh b'l
jargon	JAHR g'n

Word	Pronunciation
judicious	joo DISH uhs
kinetic	ki NET ik
kudos	KYOO dahs
logistics	loh JIS tiks
maintenance	MAYN ti n'ns
malign (adj. verb)	muh LIGHN
malingerer	muh LING ger er
mandate (noun, verb)	MAN dayt
mandatory	MAN duh taw ri
matrix	MAY triks
mediocre	MEE di oh ker
mediocrity	mee di AHK ri ti
menial	MEE ni 'l
minuscule	mi NUHS kyool
modicum	MAHD i k'm
motif	moh TEEF
naive	nah EEV
naivete	nah eev TAY
niche	NEESH
nondescript	NAHN di skript
nuance	noo AHNS
obligatory	uhb LIG uh taw ri
oblique	oh BLEEK
obsolete	AHB shu leet
ostensible	ahs TEN si b'l
ostentatious	ahs t'n TAY shuhs
panacea	pan uh SEE uh
paradox	PAR uh dahks
paradoxical	par uh KAHK si k'l
paucity	PAW si ti
penchant	PEN ch'nt
pendulum	PEN dyoo l'm
per capita	per KAP i tuh
personal	PER s'n 'l
personnel	per suh NEL
placate	PLAY kayt
precedent (adj.)	pri SEED 'nt
precedent (noun)	PRES i d'nt
precipitous	pri SIP i tuhs
precis	PRAY see
pre-empt	pri EMPT
privy	PRIV i
promissory	PRAHM i saw ri

Word	*Pronunciation*
rapport	ra PAWR
recompense	REK 'm pens
regimen	REJ i m'n
regulatory	REG yoo luh tor ee
research	ri SERCH
secretiveness	si KREE tiv nuhs
spontaneity	spahn tuh NEE i ti
spurious	SPYOOR i uhs
stamina	STAM i nuh
sauve	SWAHV
succinct	suhk SINGKT
suffuse	suh FYOOZ
superfluity	soo per FLOO i ti
superfluous	soo PER floo uhs
surfeit	SER fit
syntheses	SIN thi seez
synthesis	SIN thi sis
tenuous	TEN yoo uhs
tenure	TEN yer
transient	TRAN sh'nt
transigence	TRAN si j'ns
transition	tran ZISH 'n
tumult	TYU muhlt
tumultuous	tyu MUHLCH oo uhs
usurer	YOO zhoo rer
usurious	yoo ZHOOR i uhs
usurp	yoo SERP
usurpation	yoo ser PAY sh'n
variable	VAIR i uh b'l
versatile	VER suh til

8. WORDS AND PHRASES FREQUENTLY ENCOUNTERED

Business people often have to read literature that may be a little unfamiliar. Until now, rather than having to consult a larger dictionary all the time, you may have wished for a series of smaller dictionaries you could keep near your desk so you could look up the meaning of words peculiar to a specific profession. Following are several convenient lists for you. (If you happen to be reading about computers, for example, consult the list of computer terms and phrases first, before going to a larger dictionary. You will find that this list can save you valuable time.) The special lists include, among others:

Building and Construction Terms
The 400 Most Important Business Terms
Computer Terms
Financial, Legal, and Real Estate Terms
Foreign Words and Phrases
Clichés
Jargon and Idioms
Sales, Marketing, and Advertising Terms
Scientific Words and Expressions

Building and Construction Terms

ACCOUSTICAL TILE	Tile for walls and cellings made to control sound volume.
AIR DUCT	A pipe that carries air to rooms and back to a furnace or air conditioning system.
ANCHOR BOLT	A bolt that secures a wooden sill plate to concrete, a masonry floor, or a wall.
APRON	A paved section such as the joint of a driveway, with the street or garage entrance.
	The flat member of the inside trim of a window placed against the wall immediately beneath the sill.
BACKFILL	Gravel or earth put back in the space around a building's walls after the foundations are in place.
BALUSTERS	The upright supports of a balustrade rail.
BALUSTRADE	A row of balusters topped by a rail; the edging of a balcony or a staircase.

BASE SHOE	Molding, sometimes called a carpet strip, next to the floor on an interior baseboard.
BATT	Insulation in the form of a blanket, rather than loose filling.
BATTEN	A thin strip that covers the joints between wider boards on exterior building surfaces.
BATTER BOARD	A horizontal board nailed to posts set at the corners of an excavation to indicate the desired level. It's also used as a fastening for stretched strings to indicate the outlines of the foundation walls.
BEAM	A main horizontal wood or steel member of a building.
BEARING PARTITION	A partition that supports vertical weight besides its own.
BEARING WALL	A wall that supports any vertical weight besides its own weight.
BIB OR BIBCOCK	A water faucet to which a hose may be attached; also called a hose bib or sill cock.
BLEEDING	See page of resin or gum from lumber. Also, the process of drawing air from water pipes.
BLIND-NAILING	Nailing so that the nailheads aren't visible on the work face—usually at the tongue of matched boards.
BLIND STOP	A rectangular molding used as a stop for storm and screen or combination windows.
BRACE	A sloping piece of lumber applied to a wall or floor to stiffen the structure. Often used on walls as temporary bracing until framing has been completed.
BRACED FRAMING	A construction technique that uses posts and cross-braces for greater rigidity.
BRIDGING	Wood or metal pieces placed diagonally between floor joists.
BUILDING PAPER	Heavy paper used in walls or roofs to dampproof.
BUTT JOINT	End-to-end joint of two pieces of wood or molding.
BX CABLE	Electricity cable wrapped in rubber with a flexible steel outer covering.
CANTILEVER	A projecting beam or joist, unsupported at one end, used to support a structure's extension.

CAP	The upper part of a column, door cornice, or molding.
CARRIAGE	The support for the steps or treads of a stair.
CASEMENT WINDOW	A window sash that opens on hinges at the vertical edge.
CASING	Door and window framing.
CAVITY WALL	A hollow wall formed by firmly linked masonry walls, providing an insulating air space between them.
CHIMNEY CAP	Concrete capping surrounding the top of chimney bricks and around the floors to protect the masonry from the elements.
CHECKING	Fissures that appear with age in many exterior paint coatings.
CIRCUIT BREAKER	A safety device which opens (breaks) an electric circuit automatically when it becomes overloaded.
CISTERN	A tank to catch and store rain water.
COLLAR BEAM	A horizontal beam fastened above the lower ends of rafters for more rigidity.
COLLAR BEAM	Pieces that connect opposite roof rafters, to stiffen the roof structure.
CONCRETE PLAIN	Concrete, either without reinforcement, or reinforced only for shrinkage or temperature changes.
CONDUIT, ELECTRICAL	A pipe, usually metal, in which wire is housed.
CONSTRUCTION DRY-WALL	Construction in which the interior wall finish is applied in a dry condition, generally in the form of sheet materials or wood paneling, instead of plaster.
CONSTRUCTION, FRAME	Construction in which the structural parts are wood or depend upon a wood frame for support.
COPING	Tile or brick that caps or covers the top of a masonry wall.
CORBEL	A horizontal projection from a wall, forming a ledge or supporting a structure above it.
CORNER BEAD	A strip of wood or metal for protecting the external corners of plastered walls.
CORNER BOARDS	Used as trim for the external corners of a structure against which the ends of the siding are finished.

CORNER BRACES	Diagonal braces at the corners of a frame structure to stiffen and strengthen the wall.
CORNICE	A horizontal projection at the top of a wall or under a roof's overhang.
COUNTERFLASHING	A chimney flashing at the roofline to cover the shingle flashing and to prevent moisture entry.
COURSE	A single, horizontal row of bricks, cinder blocks, or other masonry materials.
COVE LIGHTING	Concealed light sources behind a cornice or horizontal recess that directs the light upon a reflecting ceiling.
COVE MOLDING	A molding with a concave face used for trim or interior corners.
CRIPPLES	Cut-off framing members above and below windows.
CROSS-BRIDGING	Diagonal bracing between adjacent floor joists, placed near the center of the joist span to stop the joists from twisting.
DOOR BUCK	The rough frame of a door.
DORMER	The frame of a recess that projects in a sloping roof.
DOUBLE GLAZING	An insulating window pane with two thicknesses of glass separated by a sealed air space.
DOUBLE HUNG WINDOWS	Windows with an upper and lower sash, each supported by cords and weights.
DOWNSPOUT	A spout or pipe that carries rain water down from a roof or gutters.
DOWNSPOUT LEADER	A pipe that conducts rain water from the roof to a cistern or to the ground away from the building through a downspout.
DRY WALL	A wall surface of plasterboard.
EAVES	The extension of a roof beyond the house walls.
EFFLORESCENCE	White powder that forms on a brick's surface.
EFFLUENT	Treated sewage from a septic tank or sewage treatment plant.
EXPANSION JOINT	A bituminous fiber strip that separates blocks or units of concrete to prevent cracking due to expansion as a result of temperature changes.

FACIA (FASCIA)	A flat board, band, or face, used in combination with moldings, often located at the outer face of the cornice.
FILLER (WOOD)	A heavily pigmented preparation used for filling and leveling off the pores in open-pored woods.
FILL-TYPE INSULATION	Loose insulating material.
FIRE STOP	A solid, tight closure of a concealed space, placed to prevent the spread of fire and smoke through such a space.
FISHPLATE	A wood or plywood piece used to fasten, with nails or bolts, the ends of two members together at a butt joint.
FLASHING	Material used in roof and wall construction to protect a building from water seepage.
FLOOR JOISTS	Framing pieces that rest on outer foundation walls and interior beams.
FLUE	A chimney passageway to transport smoke, gases, or fumes to the outside air.
FOOTING	The concrete base a foundation sits on.
FOUNDATION	Lower parts of walls that the structure is built on, usually of masonry or concrete below ground level.
FLUE	The space or passage in a chimney through which smoke, gas, or fumes ascend.
FLUE LINING	Fire clay or terra-cotta pipe, round or square, used for the inner lining of chimneys with the brick or masonry work around the outside.
FRAMING	A building's rough lumber-joists, studs, rafters, and beams.
FURRING	Thin wood or metal strips applied to a wall to level the surface for lathing, boarding, or plastering, to create an insulating air space, and to dampproof the wall.
GABLE	The triangular-shaped wall under the inverted "v" of the roof line.
GAMBREL ROOF	A barn-type roof with two pitches to provide more space on upper floors.
GIRDER	The key piece in a framed floor that supports the joists that carry the flooring boards. It supports the weight of a floor or partition.

GRADE LINE	The place where the ground rests against the foundation wall.
GREEN LUMBER	Lumber that hasn't adequately dried. It tends to warp or "bleed" resin.
GROUNDS	Wood inserted in wall plaster to which skirtings are attached. The wood pieces that keep the plaster from working around doors and windows.
GUSSET	A brace or bracket that strengthens a structure.
GUTTER	A channel at the eaves to carry away rain water.
HEADERS	Double pieces of wood that support floor joists; double wood pieces placed on edge over windows and doors to transfer the roof and floor weight to the studs.
HEEL	The end of a rafter; it rests on the wall plate.
HIP ROOF	A roof that slants upward on three or four sides.
JACK RAFTER	A rafter that spans the distance from the wall-plate to a hip.
JALOUSIES	Windows with movable, horizontal glass slats that admit ventilation and keep out rain.
JAMB	An upright surface that frames an opening for a door or window.
JOIST	A small rectangular piece placed parallel from wall to wall in a building, or resting on beams or girders. It supports a floor.
KILN-DRIED	Artificial drying of lumber, usually better than most air-dried lumber.
KING-POST	The center post of a truss.
LAG-SCREWS OR COACH-SCREWS	Large, heavy screws; used where much strength is needed, as in heavy framing or attaching ironwork to wood.
LATH	Thin, narrow, strips of wood nailed to rafters, ceiling joists, wall studs, etc., to make a groundwork or key for slates, tiles, or plastering.
LEACHING BED	Tiles in trenches carrying treated wastes from septic tanks.
LEDGER	A piece of wood, attached to a beam, to support joists.

LINTEL	The piece over a door or window that supports the walls.
LOAD-BEARING WALL	A strong wall that can support weight.
LOUVER	An opening with horizontal slats that permits air, but keeps out rain, sunlight and view, if desired.
LUMBER, MATCHED	Lumber that is dressed and shaped in a grooved pattern on one edge, and in a tongued pattern on the other.
MASONRY	Walls of brick, stone, tile, or similar materials.
MOISTURE BARRIER	Treated paper or metal that keeps moisture from passing into walls or floors.
MOLDING	A decorative strip with a plane or curved narrow surface prepared for ornamental application, often used to hide gaps at wall joints.
MULLION	Slender framing that separates window panes.
NEWEL	The principal upright post at the foot or the secondary post at a landing of a staircase.
NOSING	The rounded edge of a stair tread.
PARGING	A rough layer of mortar over a masonry wall as protection or finish.
PENNY	Formerly the price per hundred nails, the term now serves as a measure of nail length and is abbreviated by the letter "d."
PILASTER	A projection of the foundation wall that supports a floor girder or stiffens a wall.
PITCH	The incline slope of a roof or the ratio of the total rise to the total width of a house; i.e., a 10-foot rise and 30-foot width is a one-third pitch roof. Roof slope is expressed in the inches of rise per foot of run.
PLASTERBOARD	Gypsum board, used instead of plaster, dry wall.
PLATES	Pieces of wood placed on wall surfaces as fastening devices. The bottom member of the wall is the sole plate and the top member is the rafter plate.
PLENUM	A chamber that serves as a distribution area for heating or cooling systems, usually between a false ceiling and the actual one.

PLUMB	Exactly perpendicular; vertical.
POINTING	The treatment of masonry joints by filling them with mortar to improve their appearance or protect against weather.
POST-AND-BEAM CONSTRUCTION	Wall construction in which heavy posts, rather than many smaller studs, support the beams.
PREFABRICATION	Construction of components such as walls, trusses, or doors, before they're delivered to the building site.
RABBET	A groove cut in a board to receive another board.
RADIANT HEAT	Coils of electrical wires, or hot water or steam pipes, embedded in floors, ceilings, or walls to heat rooms.
RAFTER	A structural roof member that spans from an exterior wall to a center ridge beam or ridge board.
RAFTER, HIP	A rafter that forms the intersection of an external roof angle.
RAFTER, VALLEY	A rafter that forms the intersection of an internal roof angle.
RAKE	Trim members that run parallel to the roof slope and form the finish between the wall and a gable roof extension.
REINFORCED CONCRETE	Concrete strengthened with wire or metal bars.
RESORCINOL GLUE	A glue that is high in both wet and dry strength and resistant to high temperatures. It's used for gluing lumber or assembly joints that must withstand severe service conditions.
RIDGE POLE	A thick, longitudinal plank, to which the ridge rafters of a roof are attached.
RISE	In stairs, the vertical height of a step or flight of stairs.
RISER	The vertical boards that close the spaces between the treads of stairways.
ROLL ROOFING	Roofing material, composed of fiber and saturated with asphalt, which is supplied in 36-inch wide rolls with 108 square feet of material. Weights are generally 45 to 90 pounds per roll.

ROOF SHEATHING	Plywood sheets nailed to the top edges of trusses or rafters to tie the roof together and support the roofing material.
RUN	In stairs, the net width of a step, or the horizontal distance covered by a flight of stairs.
SADDLE	Two sloping surfaces meeting in a horizontal ridge, used between the back side of a chimney or other vertical surface, and a sloping roof.
SANDWICH PANEL	A panel with plastic, paper, or other material enclosed between two layers of a different material.
SASH	A window's movable part; the frame in which panes of glass are set in a window or door.
SCRATCH COAT	The first coat of plaster, which is scratched to form a bond for the second coat.
SCREED	A small strip of wood, usually the thickness of the plaster coat, used as a guide for plastering.
SCOTIA	A concave molding.
SCUTTLE HOLE	A small opening to the attic, crawl space or plumbing pipes.
SEEPAGE PIT	A septic tank and a connected cesspool sewage disposal system.
SEPTIC TANK	A tank that allows part of the sewage to settle and be converted into gas and sludge before the remaining waste is discharged by gravity into an underground leaching bed.
SHAKES	Handcut wood shingles.
SHEATHING *(SEE* **WALL SHEATHING)**	The first covering of boards or materials on the outside wall or roof before installing the finished siding or roof covering.
SHIM	The thin, tapered piece of wood used to level or tighten a stair or other building element.
SHINGLES	Pieces of asbestos, wood, aluminum, or other materials used as an overlapping outer covering on walls or roofs.
SHIPLAP	Boards with overlapping, rabbeted edges.

SIDING	Boards nailed horizontally to vertical studs, with or without intervening sheathing, to form the exposed surface of the outside walls of frame buildings.
SILL PLATE	The lowest member of the house framing that rests on top of the foundation wall.
SKIRTINGS	Narrow boards around the margin of a floor; baseboards.
SLAB	The concrete floor, usually about four inches thick, that is placed directly on an earth or a gravel base.
SLEEPER	A strip of wood, set on the concrete floor, to which the finished wood floor is nailed or glued.
SOFFIT	The visible underside of a roof overhang or eave and other structured members.
SOFTWOOD	Easily worked wood from a cone-bearing tree.
SOIL STACK	A vertical plumbing pipe for sewage or waste water.
SPAN	The distance between structural supports such as walls, columns, piers, beams, girders, and trusses.
SQUARE	A unit of measure—100 square feet—usually applied to roofing material.
STILE	An upright framing member in a panel door.
STRING, STRINGER	A timber or other support for cross members in floors and ceilings.
STUDS	The vertical pieces of wall frames, spaced 16 or 24 inches apart, to which horizontal pieces are nailed.
SUBFLOOR	The plywood sheets nailed to the floor joists to receive the finish flooring.
SUMP	A basement pit in which ground water collects to be pumped out with a sump pump.
SWALE	A shallow, wide excavation in the ground that forms a channel for storm water drainage.
TIE	A piece of wood that binds a pair of main rafters at the bottom.
TILE FIELD	The open-joint drain tiles laid in shallow soil to distribute septic tank effluent over an absorption area or to provide subsoil drainage in wet areas.

TOENAIL	To drive nails at an angle into corners or other joints.
TONGUE-AND-GROOVE	A carpentry joint in which the projected edge of one board fits into the grooved end of another board.
TRAP	A curve in a water pipe that holds water so gases won't move from the plumbing system into the house.
TREAD	The horizontal part of a stair step.
TRIMMER	A beam or joist to which a header is nailed into the framing for a chimney, stairway, or other opening.
TRUSS	A frame or jointed structure designed to act as a beam of long span, while each member is usually subjected only to longitudinal stress; structural members, often arranged in triangular units, forming rigid framework that spans between load-bearing walls.
VALLEY	The low point of two roof slopes.
VAPOR BARRIER	Paper, metal or paint used to prevent vapor from passing from rooms into the outside walls.
VENETIAN WINDOW	A window with a large, fixed, center pane and smaller panes on either side.
VENT PIPE	A pipe that allows gas to escape from plumbing systems.
WAINSCOTING	The lower three or four feet of an interior wall that has material that is different from the rest of the wall.
WALL SHEATHING	Material nailed to the outside face of the studs as a base for exterior siding.
WEATHER STRIPPING	Material installed around door and window openings to prevent air infiltration.
WEEP HOLE	A small hole in a wall that lets water drain away.

The 400 Most Important Business Terms

Here's a handy list of the words and phrases most often used in business literature and correspondence. Many, like "advertising mix" are seldom found in everyday dictionaries. You should find this list a valuable guide to the meaning of business terms and phrases you use daily.

ABSORPTION	One business absorbing another.
ABSTRACT OF TITLE	A property description from a government record to a deed or mortgage.
ACCELERATED DEPRECIATION	Depreciating assets as rapidly as allowed under the tax laws.
ACCORDION FOLD	Parallel folding of printed matter. Successive panels are folded in alternate directions.
ACCOUNT EXECUTIVE	An advertising agency or stock brokerage sales and service representative.
ACCRETION	Business growth caused by adding other companies.
ACCRUAL BASIS	An accounting method that shows expenses incurred and income earned during a time period, without regard to payment date.
ACCUMULATION	Things purchased in anticipation of rising prices.
ACTUALS	Commodities you have on hand, ready for shipment, manufacture, or storage.
ACTUARY	A mathematician who calculates insurance rates from available information.
ADVERTISING MIX	All the different efforts in an ad campaign.
AFFILIATE	The relationship when one company owns all or part of another company.
AGING	Any listing by age, such as accounts receivable.
ALLOWANCE	The deduction you allow as the seller, for damage or shortage, in the settlement of a debt.
ALLOWANCE FOR BAD DEBTS	An estimated amount of receivables you probably can't collect.
ALLOWANCE FOR DEPRECIATION	An amount allowed for of the gradual loss of usefulness of a fixed asset.
AMORTIZATION	Payment of a debt through scheduled installments.
ANNUAL REPORT	A printed message to stockholders signed by the chairman of the board and president. It includes the income statement and balance sheet for the company's latest fiscal year, usually with comparisons of previous periods, observations on past perform-

ance, and future prospects.

ANTICIPATION
Payment of a debt before it's due date, usually to reduce the interest.

ANTITRUST
Federal laws that limit competition through acquisitions, mergers, secret pricing, and other actions that limit public choice and bargaining power.

APPRECIATE
To grow in value.

APPURTENANCES
Expense-allowed luxuries related to someone's style of living, allowed on expense accounts.

ARBITRAGE
Buying and selling an asset in different, nearby markets, at almost the same time, to gain a profit.

ARREARS
Something due but not paid, especially dividends on cumulative preferred stock or interest on defaulted bonds.

ART DIRECTOR
A graphic arts specialist who designs advertisements and printed matter, and supervises the development of sketches and camera-ready, finished art.

ASKED
The price asked for something, often a share of stock.

ASSESSED VALUATION
Real estate value determined by assessors for taxes.

AT THE MARKET
The best price you can get at the time you execute an order to buy or sell.

BACK LABEL
A container label that states the legally required information about the product that not shown on the front label.

BACK ORDER
Accepting an order and marking it for later delivery because you can't ship from current stocks.

BALANCE OF TRADE
The value of one country's exports, less their imports.

BANKRUPTCY
The financial condition of a business or person who is legally declared unable to pay his or her debts.

BASE PERIOD
The length of time used as a reference period to present data.

BASING POINT

A geographical point from which you determine uniform prices. From it, you also add shipping costs to the destination, regardless of where the merchandise originated.

BEAR

A securities trader favored by declining prices, usually by selling borrowed securities and replacing them by purchase later, after a price decline.

BID

Your expressed willingness to buy something at a specific price.

BILL OF LADING

A list of merchandise loaded on a common carrier. When signed by the carrier, it is a receipt for the merchandise and is used for billing and collection.

BILL OF SALE

An instrument that conveys title to merchandise; an invoice.

BLISTER PACKAGING

Packaging in which you display merchandise in a transparent plastic tray attached to a card. This prevents customers from touching the merchandise.

BLURB

A short mention of a person or product in an editorial section; the baloon shape used in cartoons to surround words spoken by characters.

BOOK VALUE

The net worth of a company, as noted on its books. The value at which you carry an asset on your books, without reference to its productive or resale value.

BOND

A certificate that verifies long-term indebtedness; a guarantee of an empolyee's honesty that will insure the employer against loss.

BOTTOM OUT

The behavior of a market price to sink to a low level and establish a new base before rising.

BREAKEVEN POINT

The sales volume at which you recover your expenses, but don't show a profit or a loss.

BROADSIDE

A large, printed matter that requires two or more folds for easier mailing.

BROCHURE

A good-looking booklet or folder that reflects an institutional image in its message.

BROKER

Someone who conducts sales and purchases for others, especially in real estate, insurance, and securities.

BULL
Someone who trades in securities or commodities in order to be affected favorably by rising prices.

BUSINESS CYCLE
The economic movement through prosperity, recession, depression, and recovery.

BUYING POWER
The dollar volume of new purchases a broker will authorize in margin securities accounts without further increasing the investor's balance.

BY-PRODUCT
A valuable product of a manufacturing process in addition to the primary product.

CALL
A privilege of buying 100 shares of stock, within a limited future period such as 30, 60, 90, or 180 days, at a price based upon a current quotation.

CALLABLE
The privilege given to the bond-issuer of repayment at prices and times stated in the indenture at time of issue.

CALL MONEY
A brokers' demand loans to customers, secured by collateral.

CAMPAIGN
A marketing plan; advertisements with a planned theme appearing in series.

CAPITAL
The amount of assets over liabilities.

CAPITAL GAIN
Regarding federal income tax on individual incomes, excess proceeds over the net cost of securities, property, and other assets not normally dealt in by the taxpayer.

CARRIER
Any railroad, truck, barge line, or other facility that transports freight.

CARRY BACK
To apply a loss to decrease a previous year's profit and thus reduce taxes.

CARRY FORWARD
To apply a loss to the decrease of a subsequent year's profit and thus reduce future taxes.

CARTAGE
Transferring goods by truck from a common carrier to their destination or from their shipping point to a common carrier.

CARTE BLANCHE
Permission to spend money as necessary; to conduct organization business according to your own judgment.

CARTEL
A group of companies that agree upon the same pricing.

CASH BASIS   An accounting method in which you re-
                              cord revenues and expenses when re-
                              ceived and paid, not the period to which
                              they apply.

CASH FLOW   Your profit before you deduct deprecia-
                              tion items, adjusted to show income taxes.

CERTIFIED MAIL   First class mail, the delivery of which the
                              post office will certify.

CHANNEL   The marketing path that merchandise
                              takes from wholesale to retail channels.

CHARTIST   A person who predicts future price move-
                              ments by studying the charts of past prices.

CHATTEL MORTGAGE   A loan you make using movable goods as
                              security.

CHROMALITE   A chemical that artists use to paint por-
                              tions of commercial art, causing them not
                              to print when a dropout halftone engrav-
                              ing is made from the art.

CLEARING HOUSE   A central organization that members use
                              to clear or exchange checks, stock certifi-
                              cates, or other business instruments.

CLOSED END FUND   A mutual fund with a specified number of
                              outstanding shares.

**COLLECTIVE
  BARGAINING**   Negotiations between labor and manage-
                              ment on pay, working conditions, and
                              other matters.

COLLUSION   Agreement to conduct an unfair or illegal
                              business

**COMBINATION
  ADVERTISING RATE**   The cost for space in a combination of
                              more than one publication or station,
                              which is lower than that of the same pur-
                              chases made separately.

COMMODITIES   Contracts to buy customary, sized lots of
                              bulk goods like wheat and hogs for spot or
                              future delivery.

COMMON MARKET   Countries with the same trading agree-
                              ment.

**COMPLIMENTARY
  ADVERTISEMENT**   Space you buy in a publication instead of
                              giving a donation. It carries a complimen-
                              tary message.

COMPOUND INTEREST   Interest you receive on accumulated, un-
                              withdrawn interest.

COMPTROLLER   The senior, operating fiscal officer of a
                              business.

CONCESSIONAIRE	Someone who rents permission to conduct a business in an area occupied by other enterprises.
CONCRETE PROPOSAL	A proposal with definite provisions. If you accept them, they become a contract.
CONDEMNATION	Governemnt refusal to allow further use, such as comdemnation of an unsafe building.
CONDOMINIUM	An apartment house in which each tenant owns the quarters he occupies. He also shares some of the building and land occupied by others.
CONSIDERATION	Money or other inducement to sign a contract, as a payment for a service or merchandise.
CONSIGNMENT	Goods for which you convey title to the consignee when he resells and pays. The consignee retains the right to return any unsold goods.
CONSORTIUM	Allied companies that share in a limited business venture.
CONSTANT DOLLARS	Statistical dollars that have a fixed value as of a specific date and retain that value in statistical comparison.
CONTINGENT ASSETS AND LIABILITIES	Recorded items that haven't yet become assets or liabilities but could.
CONVEY	Transfer ownership.
COOLING-OFF PERIOD	The time in labor negotiations, during which labor is prohibited by law from striking.
COOPERATIVE	A business with special tax advantages that buys and sells for its members at better prices than those possible for individuals.
COOPERATIVE ADVERTISING	The advertising that you place as a retailer, which is partially paid for by the manufacturers whose products you advertise.
COPY	The words in an advertisement or article.
COPYWRITER	Someone skilled in marketing, selling, advertising, and writing. He or she writes ads that motivate people.
CORNER	To take ownership of all of a security or commodity that is in demand.
CORPORATE IMAGE	The total public opinion about a corporation, or what it is striving to build through public relations.

COST ACCOUNTING	Accounting procedures that show the profitability of operations in terms of the costs involved.
COST OF SALES	The cost of goods manufactured, less any excess of finished goods, divided by the inventory of finished goods at the beginning of the period.
COVER	To buy stock or commodities equal to what you previously sold short.
CUMULATIVE DIVIDEND	A fixed dividend that's payable at regular intervals. If it's not declared, it accumulates for later declarations. No dividends may be paid on junior securities until dividends in arrears on senior securities are paid.
CURRENT ASSETS	Assets you can readily convert to cash, such as accounts receivable, cash and merchandise on hand, and cash in banks.
CURRENT LIABILITIES	Accounts and loans payable within one year.
DAY ORDER	A brokerage order that expires at the close of the day's trading if it can't be executed.
DEBIT	A bookkeeping entry that's placed on the left side of a ledger account to record the increase of an asset, the decrease of a liability, or some item of revenue and net worth.
DEBTOR IN POSSESSION	A business owner appointed by a referee in bankruptcy to manage a bankrupt business and try to reestablish its solvency.
DILUTION OF OWNERSHIP	Increasing the total number of shares of a company's outstanding stock but not proportionately increasing the number of shares owned by each stockholder. This causes some stockholders to own a smaller percentage of the company than before.
DIRECT MAIL	Advertisements you send directly by mail to the customer, such as printed pieces, catalogs, and letters.
DISPLAY ADVERTISING	A window or interior display of advertising; publication advertising with larger space, type, and illustrations.
DISSIDENT STOCKHOLDER	A stockholder who doesn't support the corporation's management policy.
DIVESTITURE	The disposal of a subsidiary by spinoff or sale.

DOLLAR AVERAGING	The buying of equal dollar amounts of a security when its price falls or rises, either at set intervals or at preset prices.
DOMAIN	An owned or dominated area.
DOMICILE	A residence regarded as one's principal home.
DONOR	A giver of a charitable gift or public offering.
DOUBLE ENTRY	A bookkeeping practice in which you record each transaction with two or more balancing entries.
DOUBLE INDEMNITY	An insurance policy that provides for payment of twice the face value of the policy under certain conditions such as accidental death.
DROP SHIP	The separation of an order into small shipments to customer's branches or customers.
DUN	The attempt to collect a debt by strongly urging the debtor to pay it.
EMINENT DOMAIN	The right governments have to acquire private property needed for public use for reasonable compensation.
EMPLOYEE PROFIT SHARING	The setting aside of a specific part of the profits for a calendar period to be shared with employees, usually in proportion to their earnings for the periods.
EMPLOYEE STOCK OWNERSHIP PLAN	Any plan in which employees of a corporation can acquire stock, often at a discount or through payroll deductions.
ENTREPRENEUR	The proprietor, partner, or owner of a business.
EQUIPMENT BOND	A bond that's secured by a mortgage on rolling stock or equipment.
EQUITY	The value of property, minus any mortgages and liens against it.
EQUITY CAPITAL	The capital that's paid for, plus retained earnings.
ESCALATOR CLAUSE	A contract clause that lets the seller adjust the later delivery price to compensate for certain contingencies.
EX-DIVIDEND	The price after you deduct the dividend. It refers to the quotation on stock, on or after the record date of the dividend.

EXECUTIVE	Someone whose position calls for making decisions and exercising of power over others to conduct a business or government.
EXEMPTION	Money not taxed, such as an exemption from taxable income to support a dependant.
EXPRESS	A fast way to transport merchandise by truck, rail, or air.
EXPROPRIATION	A government acquisition of privately owned companies or properties, often for less than market values.
EX-RIGHTS	The price of stock after deducting a value of rights declared. The rights are then distributed to those who owned the stock on record date.
EXTRAPOLATE	An estimate of unknown values made by projecting known values.
FAIR TRADE AGREEMENT	An agreement between a manufacturer and all distributors or retailers that sets a minimum resale price.
FEEDBACK	The market information from the field.
FEE SIMPLE	The ownership of real property without any limitations.
FIDUCIARY	A person entrusted with securities, other valuables, or the handling of affairs, in confidence, for someone else.
FIFO	The inventory method of "first in, first out."
FIRST QUARTER	The first three months of the fiscal year of a business or government.
FISCAL YEAR	The U. S. Treasury year, usually extending from July 1 to June 30. It can also be any consistently followed, one-year period you select for accounting and tax purposes, for the convenience of your business.
FIXED ASSETS	Property, buildings, and other permanent assets.
FIXED CHARGES	Bond interest, taxes, and other charges you must meet on fixed dates.
FLOW CHART	A chart that shows steps in production, processing, order handling, or another procedures.
FOUR-COLOR PROCESS	Printing in four colors: yellow, magenta, cyan, and black, from process plates, so you can produce almost any color.

FOURTH CLASS MAIL	Merchandise or book mail, also known as parcel post.
FRACTIONAL LOT	Less than 100 shares of stock.
FRACTIONAL SHARES	Portions of shares as declared in stock dividends. They must become whole shares, either by selling, or buying a complementary fraction.
FRANCHISE	A privilege vested by government or a corporation, such as the right to operate a railroad or restaurant with a certain trademark.
FRANK	The mark on letters that indicate free postage, granted to certain government officials.
FREE ALONGSIDE	The freight is paid for transportation to the loading dock.
FREE GOODS	Adding extra merchandise with the purchase of a quantity, such as one free with a dozen, to stimulate sales.
FREE-LANCER	Someone whose services you can buy, especially an artist or writer.
FREE ON BOARD	The shipping and sometimes loading costs paid to a specific point.
FREE SURPLUS	The retained earnings that are available for common stock dividends.
FREIGHT EQUILIZATION	A partial allowance on customer-paid freight of goods from a distant location, so that the transportation costs are the same as those of goods purchased from a closer location.
FREQUENCY DISTRIBUTION	The number of statistical units in a group, such as the number of families with three or more children.
FRINGE BENEFIT	Employee compensation besides wages, such as health insurance, pension, and paid vacations.
GOLD STANDARD	The using of gold as a money standard to back currency.
GRANTEE	Someone to whom you transfer title to land.
GRAPH	A chart with rectangular coordinates that show statistics as lines or areas.
GRAPHIC ARTS	The industry that includes printing and the similar arts of making and reproducing graphics.
GRAVEYARD SHIFT	The word period from midnight to 8 a.m.

GROSS INCOME	The revenues before expenses are deducted.
GROSS NATIONAL PRODUCT	The total goods and services that industry and labor produce in one year.
GROSS PROFIT	An excess income over the cost of goods sold.
GUARANTEE	The promise to repair or replace merchandise that doesn't perform satisfactorily during the stated time-limit.
HEAD TAX	A equal tax placed on people.
HIGH FLYER	A stock issue that has extremely fluctuating prices.
HIRING HALL	An employment place, usually operated by a labor union.
HOLDING COMPANY	A company that owns equities in other companies and controls them without operating them.
HONORARIUM	An honorary payment, such as one given to a public official for a speech, when custom or propriety suggests that no price be set.
HOUSE ORGAN	A company's publication that contains articles directed to its employees and customers.
HUMAN RELATIONS	Handling the people problems you meet when you deal with employees, suppliers, customers, and others.
IMAGE	A company's public reputation, formed by your reported actions, advertising, and other impressions.
IMPARTIAL CHAIRMAN	The chairman of a panel who is agreeable to parties in negotiations and invested with power to mediate disputes and make recommendations.
IMPERIAL GALLON	The British or Canadian gallon, equivalent to 1.29 U. S. gallons.
IMPORT QUOTA	A government limit on the quantity of goods you can import within a given period.
IN ARREARS	Something that is not paid when due, such as unpaid interest due, or an account payable past due.
INCENTIVE	A reward for improved productivity, product quality, or safety.

INCOME STATEMENT	A summary of income and expenses of a business for a specific accounting period.
INCOME TAX	A tax on yearly earnings and profits.
INCREMENT	An addition.
IN DEFAULT	Owing money in the form of interest or principle beyond the due date.
INDEMNIFY	To compensate or secure against loss or damages.
INDENTURE	Your agreement with lenders, filed with a fiscal agent and printed in the prospectus under which you issue certificates of indebtedness or bonds.
INDIRECT LABOR	Work performed during processing but not directly on the product, such as supervision and maintenance.
INDUSTRIAL UNION	A union of workers in the same industry and related fields.
INJUNCTION	A court order that forbids an action under consideration.
INSIDER	Someone in a business organization who is well informed of its financial condition.
INSTALLMENT	The regular payment of part of the principal due on a loan or purchase.
INSTITUTIONAL	Something that benefits the firm itself, like advertisement that enhances the reputation of the institution.
INTANGIBLE ASSET	An asset such as goodwill, patents, trademarks.
INTEGRATE	To join together, such as business departments, or a company and its subsidary.
INTERCOMPANY TRANSACTION	A business transaction between a corporation's divisions or its wholly-owned subsidaries.
INTERPOLATE	The estimating of a value between two known values through the use of proportion or other means.
INTRASTATE	A transaction completely within a state.
INTRODUCTORY	The initial, as an introductory offer, price, coupon, etc.
INVENTORY	The merchandise you have on hand, such as raw materials, goods in process, or finished goods.
INVESTMENT	The buying of an equity or a certificate of indebtedness when you consider such factors as safety and yield.

INVESTMENT CREDIT	An income credit on a tax return in the form of total write-off of newly-purchased fixed assets, or write-down at a rate faster than normally allowed in depreciation guidelines.
INVESTMENT TRUST	A fiduciary engaged in making investments.
INVOICE	A bill of sale.
INVOLUNTARY BANKRUPTCY	A bankruptcy that occurs by a petition of creditors.
ISSUE	To sell, convey, or distribute company securities.
JOB ANALYSIS	A study of an employee's duties and responsibilities before making a job description of the position.
JOBBER	A distributor or wholesaler.
JOINT STOCK COMPANY	A company formed by many people to conduct business for profit. The stock shares may be transferred by any holder without the consent of the other stockholders.
JOINT VENTURE	A company organized for a specific temporary purpose, to be liquidated when the purpose is achieved.
JOURNAL	A record book in which you make the original entry of bookkeeping items.
JOURNEYMAN	A skilled workman.
JUDGMENT	A court award that substantiates a money claim and opens the way to its legal enforcement; a judge's ruling or opinion.
JUNIOR SECURITY	A class of bond, stock, or promissory note that is less secure than one of senior security.
JUNKET	A journey that combines pleasure with business, and the expense is borne by the employer.
KEYED ADVERTISING	Advertising designed so that you can identify the replies by the medium and issue in which the ad appears.
KEY EXECUTIVE OPTION	A privilege given to top executives to buy shares of stock in the company from a block set aside at 95 percent or 100 percent of the price specified on the day of the grant, with the privilege of deferring purchase later.

LAISSEZ FAIRE	The economic doctrine of noninterference.
LAYOFF	A temporary discharge of an employee with intent to rehire as soon as business conditions permit.
LEASE-BACK	A provision in a contract of sale. You, the seller, agree to lease back the property or facility from the buyer for a specified period.
LEDGER	A financial record book into which you make postings and from which you can compile statements.
LEGAL TENDER	The bills and coins that are legal for payment.
LESSEE	One who leases property from someone.
LESSOR	One who leases property to a tenant.
LETTERHEAD	A sheet of correspondence paper that bears your printed or engraved name and address.
LETTER OF CREDIT	A banker's letter certifying that the bearer can draw up to a specified amount.
LEVERAGE	A characteristic of common stock when it shows a wide swing in earnings per share on a relatively small difference in profit.
LIABILITIES	Amounts owed.
LIABILITY INSURANCE	Insurance you pay for to guard against accidental injuries to others or damages to the property of others.
LIBEL	Publication of an untrue, derogatory statement regarding another.
LIBERALIZATION	An increase in privileges, rights, or compensation, particularly to employees.
LIEN	A security interest a creditor holds on the real or personal property of his debtor. It secures payment of the debt and continues through any transfer of the property.
LIFO	In inventories, last in first out.
LIMITED LIABILITY	Limited responsibility for debt, such as for a corporation.
LIMITED PARTNERSHIP	A partnership in which the liability of the partners for debts is limited to a specific amount.
LINE AND STAFF	An organization of direct line authority, with staff assistants to those in the higher levels.

LIQUID ASSETS	Quick assets; see quick assets.
LIQUIDATION	Turning assets into cash.
LITIGATION	Legal action taken through the courts.
LOBBY	The attempt to influence legislation favorably or unfavorably, by personal persuasion and the dissemination of literature.
LOCKOUT	The management action of closing a plant and laying off its employees.
LONG-TERM BOND	A bond that takes 15 years or longer to mature.
LONG-TERM GAIN	Your profit on a capital asset acquired six months or longer before you sell.
LONG-TERM LIABILITY	An obligation that won't become due for one year.
LOSS LEADER	An item on which you make little or no gross profit. You offer it for sale in the hope that the customers it attracts will also buy other, more profitable items.
LUMP SUM SETTLEMENT	A single amount of money offered in payment of a claim.
LUXURY MARKET	The people who can afford to buy luxury products.
MACROCOSM	The great cosmos of the universe and, by extension, the national and international economy, rather than the individual business or person.
MAILING	Identical pieces mailed at one time.
MAIL ORDER	A type of distribution in which goods are ordered, shipped, and paid for by mail, without personal selling, as a result of advertising.
MAKE GOOD	The free republication of an advertisement to make good for an error or other dissatisfaction.
MALINGERER	One who pretends illness to avoid work or duty.
MANAGE	To organize and direct the work of others under a plan to accomplish objectives.
MAN-HOUR	The work of one person for one hour.
MANUFACTURER'S AGENT	An independent person you commission to sell the entire manufacturing output in a specified territory. He also handles non-competing lines.

MANUFACTURING EXPENSE	The cost of converting raw materials into finished goods, less the cost of raw materials and direct labor.
MARGIN	That part of the cost of a security that you put up. It immediately pledges, upon purchase, the security with the broker as collateral for the balance.
MARKETING	The total of all operations needed to move a product from the production line to the consumer.
MARKET ORDER	The order you give to a broker to buy or sell immediately at the best available price.
MARKET RESEARCH	The study of the product or service marketability, usually through store survey reports, opinion research surveys, and market testing of products.
MARKET VALUE	The price you can actually obtain in open market.
MARK-ON	The percentage of cost you add to the cost, in order to equal the selling price.
MARKUP	The percentage of the selling price you add to equal your selling price. See mark-on.
MART	The market place.
MASS PRODUCTION	Producing goods in quantity, using machinery, interchangeable parts, and automation, or short, repetitive work sequences.
MATERIAL	The physical equipment and supplies of a business, as compared to people.
MATERIALS HANDLING	The loading and unloading of materials for transportation and storage.
MEDIA	The plural of medium; vehicles for advertising, such as publications, broadcasting stations, or outdoor posters.
MEDIAN	The midpoint between maximum and minimum.
MERCHANDISING	The functions of marketing: buying, pricing, displaying, advertising, promoting, publicizing, selling, and servicing.
MERGER	A combination of two businesses, usually when one buys the other.
MISMANAGEMENT	These poor management units result from lack of knowlege, bad judgment, or serving other interests.

MONOPOLY	The exclusive ownership of all available products or services in a category, which allows you to set or control prices.
MORTGAGE	A security interest in real or personal property that you, as a debtor, convey to a creditor in order to secure a debt. The creditor usually has the right to foreclose the property, sell it at auction, and apply the proceeds of the sale to pay the debt.
MOTION STUDY	The recording of the motions of a person during a repetitive task, analyzing the findings, and recommending ways to accomplish the same task with fewer or shorter motions.
MUTUAL FUND	A company that invests in the securities of other companies.
NADIR	A low point.
NATIONALIZATION	The government acquisition of property, such as mines, and oil and gas wells.
NEGOTIABLE	The ability to transfer ownership without signature.
NET NET	The lowest amount after all discounts and deductions.
NET PROFIT	The gross profit, less operating expenses.
NET WORTH	The excess of assets over liabilities; equity; capital.
NOMINAL PRICE	The price of a commodity future during a time in which no actual trading took place.
NOMINAL VALUE	The named or face value as compared to market value.
NONNEGOTIABLE	A thing that is unable to be transferred to another.
NONOPERATING EXPENSE	A business expense not directly related to the operation, such as interest paid on loans.
NONOPERATING REVENUE	A business expense not directly related to the operation, such as rent income.
NONPROFIT ORGANIZATION	A business organized in the public interest, which enjoys tax advantages on gains, but isn't legally permitted to declare dividends.
NONRECURRING ITEM	A gain or loss not encountered in the regular business of the company; for example, the sale of capital assets.
NO PAR VALUE	A thing that is without any stated value.

NOTE PAYABLE	A written promise to pay a specific sum at a specific place and time, constituting a liability and obligation of the maker.
NOTE RECEIVABLE	A note issued to or endorsed to you that is in your possession.
OCCUPATIONAL HAZARD	The danger of incurring certain diseases and having types of accidents as a result of employment, such as silicosis in mineworkers.
ODD LOT	The shares of stock in a trade on an exchange, less than the 100 shares.
OFFER	A stated willingness to sell at a stated price.
OF RECORD	Stock ownership as of the date on which holders become entitled to a dividend that was declared earlier and is payable later.
OLIGOPOLY	The leadership or rule by a small group of companies or suppliers.
ONE-PRICE STORE	A store that charges all customers the same price for each item, where no bargaining is permitted.
OPEN END FUND	A mutual fund that seeks expansion through sales of additional, authorized shares at prices equal to the asset value per share, plus a loading charge.
OPENING PRICE	The price of a security on a day's first transaction.
OPEN ORDER	A commercial customer's order on a supplier's books for merchandise not available now, but that is expected.
OPEN RATE	The base rate for the minimum number sold. From it you can sometimes get a reduction for larger purchases.
OPERATING INCOME	The excess revenue over expenses for an enterprise's usual operations. It includes other income, such as interest and dividends.
OPERATING STATEMENT	An income statement.
OPTION	The right to buy or sell at a future time and at a specific price.
OVERHEAD	All costs, other than direct labor and raw materials.
OVERSOLD	The market condition in which prices, lowered by persistent sellers and reluctant buyers, are now ready to rise as the low prices attract new buying and discourage more selling.

OVER-THE-COUNTER	Those stocks not listed on major exchanges.
PARITY	A contrived statistical price applied to a quantity of wheat, or other farm commodity, to compare the farmer's purchasing power with the August 1909-July 1914 base period, and to serve as a base for a government crop loan.
PARTICIPATION	The right to share in the earnings of preferred stock above preferred requirements.
PARTNERSHIP	A contract between two or more persons, based on their agreement to combine in a business enterprise their resources, talents, or both.
PAR VALUE	The value stated on the face of a security.
PASS THE DIVIDEND	The refusal to declare a dividend at a meeting of the Board of Directors that was called to declare dividends.
PAY-AS-YOU-GO	The running of a business without borrowing.
PENSION PLANS	An employer plan that covers a specified class or all employees, providing for a fund to pay benefits to employees after their retirement.
PERCENTAGE	A ratio between any real number and 100, used to express interest rates and statistical comparisons.
PERPETUAL INVENTORY	A way to keep stock records in which daily entires provided up-to-date information on inventories.
PERQUISITES	The special favors, luxuries, or other advantages given as a right to the holder of an office, such as the use of an automobile for business.
PETTY CASH	A small amount of cash kept on hand for minor expenses.
PIECEWORK	Any work paid for on the basis of units completed.
PIE CHART	A circular chart divided into sectors. Each represents a share of the whole.
PILOT PLANT	A manufacturing plant in which you make production runs for a new product in order to learn about it, to eliminate problems, and to decide whether you should

construct more extensive production facilities.

POINT OF PURCHASE ADVERTISING
The counter displays and literature found in retail outlets.

PORTFOLIO
A person's total security holdings.

PREEMPTIVE RIGHTS
The rights of current stockholders to be the first to buy shares offered for sale.

PREFERRED STOCK
The stock that is redeemable, up to the stated redemption value, before repayment of any common stock liquidating dividends. Holders are also entitled to dividends from earnings that may be declared on the common stock.

PRESENTATION
A sales solicitation with aids.

PRICE-EARNINGS RATIO
The ratio between the current market price of a share of stock and the earnings per share.

PRIME RATE
The interest rate commercial banks charge on 60- to 90-day loans made to their large customers who enjoy the best credit rating.

PRODUCTION PROCESS
All the functions involved in producing goods.

PRODUCTIVITY
The ratio of finished work to the man-hours needed to produce it.

PROFIT
Excess income over expenses.

PROFITABILITY
The ability of a business to earn a profit.

PROFIT AND LOSS STATEMENT
A financial statement for a specific period showing sales, cost of sales, other expenses, and gross and net profits.

PROMISSORY NOTE
An unconditional, written promise to pay a certain sum of money, with or without interest, at a fixed place, at a fixed or determinable future date.

PRORATE
To assign proportionately, such as shares of stock.

PROXY
A stockholder's written authorization, to nominees of management or their opponents, to vote his shares at a stockholders' meeting.

PROXY FIGHT
A contest between two opposing groups of stockholders to control a corporation's management.

PUBLIC DOMAIN
The creative works like poems, songs, and speeches, that are not protected by copyright, which may be freely quoted or adapted, parodied, or plagiarized.

PUBLICITY	The communication of favorable information about a company or its products, through, and at the discretion of, a medium without charge to the company.
PUBLIC RELATIONS	The good performance of an organization communicated to its public such as customers, employees, and stockholders, in order to enhance its reputation.
PUT	A privilege to sell within a limited period, such as 30 or 60 days, 100 shares of stock, at a price based upon a current quotation.
QUALITY CONTROL	A production control system in which you maintain quality by inspection, machine improvement, and adjustment of conditions.
QUICK ASSETS	Assets easily converted into cash.
QUITCLAIM	A deed that releases a right or interest in land, but does not include any covenants of warranty.
RECEIVABLES	Accounts, notes, and accrued income receivable.
RECESSION	The business cycle characterized by decline of employment, inventories, capital investment, savings, and prices.
RECIPROCITY	The purchasing from your customers, the materials and services they sell, which are required in your business.
RECORD DATE	The date for determining stock ownership.
REGRESSIVE TAX	A tax that requires the payment of larger percentages of lower incomes than higher incomes, such as sales and excise taxes.
REPLACEMENT COST	The cost to replace existing equipment, regardless of its age.
RESTRAINT OF TRADE	An action that interferes with or restricts the business rights of others.
RESUME	A summary of your goals, job history, education, skills, and qualifications used to help you seek employment.
RETAINED EARNINGS	Those earnings not distributed as dividends but kept in the business.
RETURN ON INVESTMENT	The returns accrued on a yearly basis.
REVOLVING FUND	A fund from which you continuously take and refund money.

RISK CAPITAL	Equity capital.
ROUND LOT	A lot of 100 shares of stock.
SALES PROMOTION	Display, sales ideas, publicity, and advertising to help sell a product or service.
SECONDARY OFFERING	Off-the-floor selling of a large block of stock shares owned not by the company, but by the selling stockholders, as is the case in original stock offering.
SECOND MORTGAGE	A mortgage that must be paid only after payment in full of a first mortgage and other liens, such as back tax claims.
SELF-LIQUIDATING	A debt that's paid off in stated installments.
SHOP STEWARD	An employee who is also a union official elected by members of his own company. He negotiates with the company on minor matters, such as employee grievances.
SHORT SALE	The selling of borrowed stock to be returned at a later date when the stock is bought back. You make a profit in a short sale if there is a decline in price; you lose money if there is an increase in price.
SHORT TON	2000 lbs., the long ton is 2240 lbs., and the metric ton is 2204.6 lbs.
SILENT PARTNER	A person with an investment in a partnership, who takes no active part in day-to-day operations.
SLIDING SCALE	A scale of fees, prices, or wages, in which the unit amount changes with other factors, such as the total volume.
SPECIALIST	A stock exchange member who specializes in the shares of a limited number of companies, quoting prices and making sales and purchases of those issues for himself and others.
SPECULATION	The buying and selling of securities and commodities to gain on the transactions instead of on the dividends and interest.
SPINOFF	Divesting a subsidiary to stockholders of a parent company by issuing stock shares in the subsidiary proportional to their holdings in the parent company.
STOCKBROKER	A company or person who buys and sells securities for others.
STOCK DIVIDEND	A dividend payable in shares of the company's stock.

STOCK EXCHANGE	A federally regulated exchange for trading stocks.
STOCKHOLDER	Someone who owns shares in a corporation.
STOCK MARKET	A stock exchange.
STOCK SPLIT	The issuing of new shares of stock for old, such as a ratio of two to one.
STOP LOSS ORDER	An order to a stockbroker to sell on the next sale after the price drops to a specified level.
STRAIGHT LINE DEPRECIATION	Depreciation at a constant rate, through the calculated life of the asset.
SUBCONTRACT	The contracting to others of a part or all of a contract.
SUBSIDIARY	A self-contained business acquired and managed by another company.
SUCCESSOR	One who follows in office.
SUPERIOR	Someone of higher rank or office than another. Someone or something of higher standing, better quality.
SUPERMARKET	A very large retail store selling food and associated products principally by display and checkout.
SUPERSONICS	The realm of materials' performance, machine operation, and human behavior at speeds greater than Mach 1. Also, the study and use of sound waves at frequencies beyond the range of the human ear, or more than 20,000 cycles per second.
SUPERVISION	The close observation of the work of others having the authority and responsibility to manage.
TACIT AGREEMENT	The unspoken agreement, sometimes from failure to disagree with an overall situation.
TIE-IN SALE	Merchandise sold, as tied-in with other merchandise the seller wants to sell.
TRADEMARK	A special mark or symbol, identified and associated with a product or company.
TRIAL BALANCE	Adding the debit and credit balances of the open accounts to show that the debits equal the credits.

UNION SHOP	A company in which the employees are represented by a union. New non-union employees must join the union within a specified time.
VERTICAL ORGANIZATION	A company organized for the complete handling of a product, such as an oil company that explores, drills, refines, stores, and retails its products.
VESTING	Giving title to another, such as an employer giving an employee title to part or all of the company contributions to a pension fund.
VOUCHER	A document that supports the payment of cash.
WARRANT	A privilege to buy a future share of stock at a price currently determined.
WARRANTY	A seller's declaration that merchandise is as represented.
WHITE-COLLAR WORKER	A salaried worker whose job requires a well-groomed appearance.
WORKING CAPITAL	The excess of current assets over current liabilities.
WRITE-OFF	An accounting function to reduce to zero the undepreciated value of an asset.
WRITE-UP	An increase in net worth achieved through accounting methods.
YIELD	A stock's annual dividends in dollars, divided by its current price.

9. COMPUTER TERMS USED IN BUSINESS

ABSOLUTE ADDRESS   An address permanently assigned to a storage location.

ACCESS, DIRECT   The getting of information from storage when the access doesn't depend on the location recently accessed.

ACCESS TIME   The time it takes a computer to transfer data to or from storage.

ACRONYM   A word formed from the first letters of the words in a name or phrase (ALGOL from *ALGOR*rithmic *L*anguage).

ADDRESS   A name, number, or other reference that names a data storage location.

ADDRESS MODIFICATION   The change of address in a prescribed way by a stored program computer.

ADP   (Automatic Data Processing). Data processing performed automatically by a system of electronic machines.

ALGOL   (*ALGO*rithmic *L*anguage). A procedure-oriented language used to express computational algorithms developed by international cooperation.

ALGORITHM   A set of rules to solve a problem in a specific number of steps.

ALPHANUMERIC   A character set that includes both alphabetic characters (letters) and numeric characters (digits).

ANALOG   Representing numbers by physical variables such as voltage, resistance, or rotation.

ANALOG COMPUTER   A computer that works on data presented in the form of constantly changing physical quantities.

APPLICATION PACKAGE   A computer routine for a specific application.

ARITHMETIC UNIT   The section of hardware in which you perform arithmetical and logical operations.

ASCII   (American Standard Code for Information Interchange). A seven-bit (or compatible) standard code that facilitates the interchange of data.

ASSEMBLE	To prepare a machine language from a program written in symbolic coding.
ASSEMBLER	A computer program that assembles programs.
ASYNCHRONOUS	Not synchronized; operating independently.
ASYNCHRONOUS COMPUTER	A computer in which each operation begins at a signal generated by the completion of the previous operation.
AUDIT TRAIL	A way (such as the order of documents) to identify the actions taken in processing data.
AUXILIARY STORAGE	A storage to supplement a computer's primary internal storage.
BACKUP	The equipment or procedures available in the event of the failure or overloading of the regular equipment or procedures.
BASE	A number base that identifies a system of representing numbers by noting their position; a radix.
BATCH PROCESSING	The term used to describe when items to be processed are collected into groups (batched) for convenient and efficient processing.
BATCH TOTAL	The sum of the items in a batch used to check the accuracy of operations.
BAUD	A signaling speed of 1 bit per second.
BCD	(Binary Coded Decimal). A way to represent the decimal digits zero through nine by a distinct group of binary digits.
BINARY	The number system with a root of 2. The binary numeral 1101 means: $(1 \times 2^3) + (1 \times 2^2) + (0 \times 2^1) + (1 \times 2^0)$ which is equivalent to decimal 13.
BIT	A binary digit (o or 1).
BLOCK	The words, characters, or digits held in one section of an input/output medium and treated as one unit.
BLOCK DIAGRAM	A graphic illustration that shows the logical sequence in which you process data.
BLOCKING	The combining of two or more records into one block.
BRANCH	An instruction to transfer control. It causes a unit to select one of two or more program paths.

BREAKPOINT	The point in a program at which you can stop the program manually or by a monitor routine.
BUFFER	A storage device you use to compensate for differences in the rates of data flow.
BUG	A mistake in the design of a program or system.
BYTE	A group of adjacent bits that are considered a unit (usually shorter than a word).
CAI (COMPUTER-ASSISTED INSTRUCTION)	A way to use a computer to present individualized material to many students simultaneously.
CALL	To transfer control to a subroutine.
CALLING SEQUENCE	The instructions and data needed to call a subroutine.
CATHODE RAY TUBE	(CRT) An electronic vacuum tube that contains a screen on which information is displayed.
CENTRAL PROCESSOR	A computer system unit that includes the circuits that control the interpretation and execution of instructions. Also called the central processing unit (CPU) or main frame.
CHANNEL	The path used to carry signals between a source and a destination.
CHECK BIT	A binary check digit.
CHECK DIGIT	A digit used to check accuracy
CLOCK	A clock which records the actual passage of time.
COBOL	(*CO*mmon *B*usiness *O*riented *L*anguage). A procedure-oriented language that makes it easier to prepare and change programs that form business data processing functions.
CODING	The instructions that make a computer perform a process.
COLLATE	(Merge). To form a single file by combining two or more similar files.
COMPILE	To prepare a machine language program from a program written in another programing language.
COMPILER	A computer program that compiles. It permits the use of procedure-oriented languages that can greatly reduce the work needed to prepare computer programs.

COMPUTER, ANALOG	A computer that operates by using an electrical representation of the variables in the problem.
CONSOLE	That part of a computer which operators or maintenance engineers use to communicate with the computer, usually by visual displays and manual controls.
CONSOLE OPERATOR	A computer operator.
CONTROL CARD	A punched card that has input data needed for the specific application of a general routine.
CONTROL CLERK	A person who controls data processing operations.
CONTROL PROGRAM	A routine that helps control the operations of a computer system.
CONVERSATIONAL MODE	A mode of operation that simulates a "dialog" between a computer and its user. The computer examines the input supplied by the user and prepares the questions or comments directed to the user.
CRT	A cathode ray tube display device.
CRYOGENICS	The study and use of devices that use the properties of materials at temperatures near absolute zero.
CYBERNETICS	The study of the control and communication of information-handling machines to understand and improve communication.
CYCLE TIME	The least amount of time between the starts of successive accesses to a storage location.
DATA BASE	The data items stored to meet information processing and retrieval needs.
DEBUG	The process of detecting and stopping mistakes in a program, the repairing of defects in equipment.
DENSITY, CHARACTER	The number of characters you can store per unit, such as per inch of magnetic tape.
DESK CHECKING	A manual checking process in which selected data items, used to detect errors in program logic, are traced through the program before it's checked on the computer.
DETAIL FILE	A file that contains relative information that changes, such as transactions.

DIAGNOSTIC ROUTINE	A routine that performs diagnostic functions.
DIAGRAM, BLOCK	A system flowchart.
DIGITAL COMPUTER	A computer that operates on digital data. It performs arithmetic and logical operations on the data.
DIGIT CHECK	An extra digit you add to a group of digits to find errors.
DIRECT ADDRESS	An address that specifies a storage location.
DISC, MAGNETIC	A rotating metal disc that has a magnetized surface on which you store information.
DOCUMENTATION	The preparation of a document that describes the program and its preparation, its approval, and its later changes.
DRUM, MAGNETIC	A fast-revolving cylinder that stores information in the form of small, polarized dots on its surface.
DUMP	To transfer data from one storage location to another.
DUPLEX	(1) A channel that lets you transmit simultaneously in two directions. (2) A standby unit you use when equipment fails.
EAM	(Electrical Accounting Machine). Data processing equipment that is mostly electromechanical, like keypunches, collators, mechanical sorters, and tabulators.
EDIT	A change in the data format.
EDP	(Electronic Data Processing). Data processing on electronic equipment.
EFFECTIVE ADDRESS	An address developed by changing another address.
EXECUTIVE ROUTINE	A routine that controls the flow of work in a computer.
FACILITIES MANAGEMENT	The use of an independent service organization to operate and manage a data processing installation.
FEEDBACK	Presentation of information to someone, based upon his responses.
FIELD	In a punched card, the columns that represent one item. A subdivision of a computer work instruction or record.
FILE	Related records, often arranged in sequence.

FILE MAINTENANCE	The updating of a file to show changes by adding, altering, or deleting data.
FILE PROCESSING	The periodic updating of master files to reflect current data.
FIXED-LENGTH RECORD	A record that always has the same number of characters.
FIXED-WORD LENGTH	A machine word that always has the same number of bits or characters.
FLOWCHART	A diagram of symbols and interconnecting lines that illustrates the structure and general sequence of the operations of a program or system.
FORTRAN	(*FOR*mula *TRAN*slator). A procedure-oriented language that makes it easier to prepare programs that perform mathematical computations.
GAP	A space of time interval that separates words, records, or files on magnetic tape.
GATE	A circuit that provides an output signal that depends on past or present input signals.
GENERATOR	A computer program that constructs other programs which perform certain types of operations.
HEADER LABEL	A machine-readable record at the start of a file which contains data that identifies the file.
HEURISTIC	The exploratory methods of problem solving; a careful trial-and-error system.
HOUSEKEEPING	Those program operations that do not help solve problems, but which are necessary to maintain processing control.
INDIRECT ADDRESS	An address that notes a storage location of either a direct address or another indirect address.
INITIALIZE	To set the changeable items of a process at initial values before you start the process.
INPUT/OUTPUT	The techniques, devices, and media used to communicate with data processing equipment.
INPUT/OUTPUT CHANNEL	A channel that transmits data to or from a computer.
INSTRUCTION	The characters that specify an operation.
INSTRUCTION, ONE ADDRESS	An instruction with a code and address for one data unit.

INSTRUCTION, PSEUDO	An instruction that can be executed without interpretation.
INTEGRATED CIRCUIT	A complete electronic circuit that performs all the functions of a conventional circuit made in a single, integrated process.
INTERBLOCK GAP	The space on a magnetic tape between the end of one block and the start of the next.
INTERFACE	A connection or relationship between systems.
INTERLOCK	A device or procedure that prevents one device or operation from interfering with another.
INTERPRETIVE ROUTINE	A routine that translates instructions into machine instructions and executes them before translating the next instructions.
INTERRUPT	A signal that causes an operation to stop.
INTERRUPTION	A temporary halt in a set of instructions.
ITEM	Any data treated as a unit.
KEY	Those characters linked with an item that identifies it.
LANGUAGE, ALGORITHMIC	A language used to state numerical procedures.
LANGUAGE, BUSINESS-ORIENTED	The language used for business file processing procedures (COBOL).
LANGUAGE, OBJECT	The language you develop by translating procedure-oriented language statements, usually machine language instructions.
LANGUAGE, PROBLEM-ORIENTED	A language that doesn't depend upon machines, and requires only that you state the problem, not the procedures.
LANGUAGE, PROCEDURE-ORIENTED	A language that doesn't depend on machines, and which you use to solve a problem (COBOL, FORTRAN).
LIBRARY ROUTINE	A treated routine kept in a program library.
LINKAGE	The coding that links two separately coded routines.
LOADER	A service routine that reads programs into internal storage to prepare for their execution.
LOG	A record of the EDP operations.
LOOP	A sequence of instructions you can execute repeatedly.

MACHINE INSTRUCTION	An instruction that a computer recognizes and executes.
MACHINE LANGUAGE	The language used by a computer.
MACRO INSTRUCTION	An instruction written in a machine-oriented language that doesn't have an equivalent operation in the computer.
MAIN FRAME	A central processor.
MANAGEMENT INFOR-MATION SYSTEM	A system that gives the managers of a business information to keep informed about the business, and helps them make operative decisions.
MAP	A list that indicates areas of data storage.
MARK	A symbol that shows the end of a word, group, or message record.
MARK SENSING	A technique to detect pencil marks on punched cards or other documents.
MASK	The extracting of characters from a computer word.
MASTER FILE	A file that contains relatively permanent information for future reference.
MERGE	The forming of a single, sequenced file, by joining two or more similar files.
MESSAGE SWITCHING	A technique to control the traffic within a data communications network.
MICR	(*Magnetic Ink Character Recognition*). Machine-reading of graphic characters printed with magnetic ink.
MICROLOGIC	A permanent, stored program that interprets instructions in a microprogram.
MICROPROGRAM	The pseudo instructions translated by micrologic hardware.
MICROSECOND	One-millionth of second, abbreviated μsec or μs.
MILLISECOND	One-thousandth of second, abbreviated msec or ms.
MIS (MANAGEMENT INFORMATION SYSTEM)	A system designed to give information to management.
MNEMONIC	A technique you use to assist your memory.
MONITOR ROUTINE	A routine that shows the progress of work in a computer system.
MULTIPLEX	To transmit two or more messages simultaneously over the same channel.
MULTIPROCESSING	Simultaneous execution of two or more sequences of instructions in the same computer system.

MULTIPROGRAMMING	A technique to handle two or more independent programs simultaneously.
NANOSECOND	One-billionth of a second (i.e., 10^{-9} second), abbreviated nsec or ns.
OCR	(*Optical Character Recognition*). Machine-reading of graphic characters using light-sensitive devices.
OFFLINE	(Off-line). Equipment not in direct communication with the central processor.
ONLINE	(Online). Equipment in direct communication with the central processor.
OPERAND	A unit of data upon which you perform an operation.
OPERATION CODE	A code that represents the operations of a computer.
OPERATING SYSTEM	The routines and procedures used to operate a computer.
OVERFLOW	The generation of a quantity beyond the capacity of the register or storage location.
OVERHEAD	The nonproductive operations of a computer system.
PACK	A group of several data units in a single storage cell for later recovery.
PADDING	The dummy characters, items, or records that fill out a fixed-length information block.
PAGE	A section of a program.
PARALLEL	The handling of all the bits or characters simultaneously.
PASS	A complete cycle of input, processing, and output in a computer program.
PATCH	To change a program in a somewhat rough way.
PERIPHERAL EQUIPMENT	The input/output units and backup storage units of a computer system.
PICOSECOND	One-thousandth of a nanosecond.
PLUGBOARD	A perforated board that normally controls the operation of some automatic data processing equipment.
PL/1 (PROGRAMMING LANGUAGE, VERSION 1)	An IBM combination algebraic and business language for a System 360.
POSTMORTEM ROUTINE	A diagnostic routine that is used after a program fails.
PRECISION, DOUBLE	The use of twice as many digits as a computer normally uses to represent a number.

PROCESSING, PARALLEL	The running of two or more programs in a computer simultaneously.
PROCESSING, REALTIME	The processing of information as it's received to further influence the process.
PROCESSOR	A device or system that performs operations on data.
PROGRAM	A plan advice or routine used to solve a problem; the writing of a computer routine.
PROGRAM FLOWCHART	A flowchart that shows the processing steps of a computer program.
PROGRAMMING LANGUAGE	A language that expresses computer programs.
PROGRAMMING, SYMBOLIC	Any programming that uses addresses and memory-related operation codes.
PSEUDO INSTRUCTION	An instruction in the same format as a machine instruction but which a computer can't execute; used for a machine control.
RADIX	The basis for a number system.
RANDOM ACCESS	A storage device whose access time isn't seriously affected by the location of the data.
RATE, CLOCK	The speed pulses are emitted from a timing circuit. The speed regulates all operations in a synchronous computer.
REALTIME	(or REAL-TIME). The actual time during which a process takes place.
RECORD	A collection of related-data items.
RECORDING DENSITY	The number of useful storage cells in a specified area.
REDUNDANCY	The extra characters, bits, or operations not needed for the operation, which are used to check the process.
REGISTER	A device that can store data, such as one word, intended for a special purpose.
ROUTINE	The instructions arranged in correct sequence so that a computer will perform a process.
ROUTINE, EXECUTIVE	A routine that controls the loading of programs, their relocation in memory, the scheduling of runs, and other functions that would require manual intervention otherwise.
RUN	A specific process by a computer on certain data.

RUN MANUAL	A manual that documents the processing system, procedures, and instruction in a computer run.
SECONDARY STORAGE	The storage that backs up a computer's primary storage.
SELECTOR CHANNEL	A device that can transfer data to or from just one peripheral device at a time.
SENSING, MARK	The marking of a box on a punched card, for sensing on special equipment. The pencil markings are translated and punched as regular punches.
SERIAL	The handling of the parts of a word one after another.
SETUP TIME	The time it takes to get equipment ready between runs.
SIMPLEX	A communications link that transmits data in only one direction.
SIMSCRIPT	A procedure-oriented language used to write simulations.
SOFTWARE	Those computer programs and routines that facilitate the operation of the computer. Contrast with HARDWARE.
SOLID STATE	The electronic components that depend on the electric or magnetic phenomena in solids, such as transistors.
SPECIAL CHARACTER	A character that is neither a letter nor a digit.
STORAGE, ALLOCATION	The assignment of programs or data blocks to specific areas of a computer's storage.
STORAGE, ASSOCIATIVE	A content-addressable storage in which you identify storage locations by contents instead of by name of position.
STORAGE PROTECTION	The protection against unauthorized writing in, or reading from, any part of a storage device.
STORAGE, SECONDARY	A storage device that's usually less expensive and has slower access than the main memory. Magnetic tapes and disc files are examples.
SUBPROGRAM	A part of a larger program.
SUBROUTINE	A routine that's part of another routine.
SYNCHRONIZATION CHECK	A check that shows whether an event occurs at the right moment.

SYNCHRONOUS COMPUTER	A computer that starts from a signal generated by a clock.
SYSTEM FLOWCHART	A chart that shows the flow of work, in a data-processing application.
SYSTEM, OPERATING	The routines used to supervise the operations of a computer system, such as program loading, program location, and assembly.
TABLE LOOK-UP	The using a known value (the argument) to locate an unknown value in a table.
TABULATING EQUIPMENT	The predominantly electromechanical machines that use punched cards.
TELECOMMUNICATIONS	The transmitting of signals over long distances, e.g., by radio or telegraph.
THROUGHPUT	The useful work data processing system performs during a given period of time.
TIME, ACCESS	The time you need to locate data in storage and transfer it to a unit for processing.
TIME SHARING	The use of a given device by a number of other devices, programs, or human users, one at a time and in rapid succession.
TRACE ROUTINE	A diagnostic routine that checks a program's operation.
TRACK	The recording paths.
TRANSLATOR	A device program that translates from one language or code to another.
UNCONDITIONAL TRANSFER	An instruction that always triggers a new departure from the normal sequence of instructions.
UNIT RECORD	A record that is physically separate, like a record on a punched card.
UNPACK	The separating of parts of a tape record or computer work and storing of them in separate locations.
UPDATE	To put changes into a master file.
UTILITY ROUTINE	A routine used to help the operation by performing a frequently required process, such as sorting or merging.
VARIABLE-LENGTH RECORD	A record with a variable number of characters.
VARIABLE WORD LENGTH	A machine word with a variable number of bits or characters.
VERIFY	The checking of accuracy by comparing two operations performed on the same record.

WORD	The bits or characters that are treated as a unit, which can be stored in one location.
WORD LENGTH	A symbol you use to mark the beginning or end of a word.
X PUNCH	A punch in the X row (or 11 row) of an 80-column punched card, usually used to note a negative number.
Y PUNCH	A punch in the Y row (or 12 row) of an 80-column punched card, usually used to note a positive number.
ZERO SUPPRESSION	The elimination of meaningless zeros in a number.

10. GUIDE TO SCIENTIFIC WORDS AND EXPRESSIONS

ABSCISSA	The perpendicular direction from a given point on a graph.
ABSOLUTE	Pure, exact, unmixed.
ABSOLUTE ZERO	The temperature at which a system undergoes a reversible thermal process.
ABSORBENT	The capacity to take up another substance.
ABSORPTION	The penetration of a liquid or solid into another liquid or solid.
ABSTRACT	A summary of a publication or article that summarizes all relevant data, arguments, and conclusions.
ACID	A compound that contains hydrogen, which can replaced by metallic elements, and which produces hydrogen in solution.
ACOUSTICS	The science of sound and hearing.
ADSORPTION	An action in which one substance is taken at the solid surface of another, resulting in a change of concentration at the interface.
AERODYNAMICS	The study of the relationship between air and the objects moving through it.
AERONAUTICS	The art and science of flight.
AEROSOL	A dispersion of particles of a solid or solids in a gas.
AGGREGATE	The sum of particles.
ALDEHYDE	The intermediate stage of oxidation of an alcohol to a volatile fluid characterized by the CHO radical.
ALDEHYDE	A generic term for a class of compounds derived from a hyd-carbon by oxidation, i.e., by the substitution of an oxygen for two hydrogen atoms; they contain the -CHO group.
ALGEBRA	That part of mathematical science in which letters, characters, or symbols are used for the calculations instead of, or in addition to, numbers. The numerical value of the letter characters or symbols may be different for different calculations.
ALGEBRAIC	Relating to algebra.

ALGEBRAIC EXPRESSION	Any quantity expressed by literal and arithmetical numbers combined by means of the fundamental operations defining algebra.
ALGEBRAIC SUM	The sum of two numbers in algebra. To be distinguished from arithmetical sum," in which the sum of the two numbers is always greater than either of them. In algebra, the sum of two numbers can be smaller than one of them if one is negative. Example: $5 + (-2)$ equals 3.
ALIDADE	An instrument used to measure vertical elevations and distances.
ALKALI	The oxides or hydroxides of the alkali metals.
ALLOY	A substance that has the properties of two or more substances.
ALTERNATING CURRENT	The current in which the flow charge regularly reverses, as compared to direct current.
AMALGAMATION	In a strict sense, an alloy of mercury, mixed with some other metals. Sometimes, although improperly used, in the sense of an alloy in general.
AMBIENT	Local or environmental.
AMPERE	A unit of the flow of electric current. One ampere equals the current that will flow with a potential of one volt through a conductor with a resistance of one ohm.
ANALYSIS	The breaking down of a substance systematically into its parts in order to examine it.
ANION	A negative ion in an electrolytic solution is then attacted to the positive pole or anode.
ANODE	An electrode through current enters an electrode.
ANTISEPTIC	The absence of infection-producing bacteria.
APOGEE	The point of an orbit or trajectory that is farthest from the earth.
ASTRONAUTICS	The science of space flight.
ATOM	The smallest building block of chemical elements; it cannot be divided or broken up by chemical means.

AUTOCLAVE	A vessel, usually constructed of thick steel plates, used to carry out chemical reactions under high pressure and at high temperature.
AVERAGE	The sum of a number of quantities divided by the number.
AXIOM	A self-evident and generally accepted principle.
AXIS	Any real or imaginary straight line that divides a plane into two equal or symmetrical parts.
AZIMUTH	In a system of coordinates by which a point is located by its distance from another fixed point, the angle that the line from the point to the given point makes with a fixed line called the polar axis.
BOND	A linkage between atoms.
BUFFER	The addition of a substance to a solution, compound, or system that enables the latter to resist changes in hydrogen concentration when an acid or alkali is added.
BURETTE	A graduated, cylindrical glass tube fitted with a ground glass stopcock, used to measure and deliver a small volume of liquid.
CALIBRATION	The comparison of an unknown reading to a known reading on an instrument.
CAPACITANCE	A material that changes a device to maintain a current in the same direction.
CATALYST	A substance that changes the rate of a chemical reaction, without being consumed by the reaction, which is also recoverable unchanged chemically at the conclusion.
CATHODE	An electrode from which electrons leave a unit.
CENTRIFUGAL FORCE	The force which a mass, forced to move in a circular path, exerts outward/
CENTRIFUGE GRAVITIES	An instrument to separate liquids of different specific weights by the use of centrifugal force.
CENTRIPETAL FORCE	The force that restrains a body in rotation from going in straight line, directed toward the center of rotation.
CLOSED LOOP	A continuous chain formed by automatic control units that are connected together.

COEFFICIENT	A number, letter, or symbol that has a fixed value.
COLLIMATE	To make something parallel to a line or direction.
COMMUTATOR	A motor or generator device used to maintain current in the same direction.
COORDINATE	A number that locates a point in space.
DECIBEL	A unit used to express the intensity of sound.
DEDUCE	To infer something from information obtained to draw a conclusion by reasoning from given principles.
DEDUCTIVE REASONING	The reasoning technique that starts out from an assumption or premise, which proceeds by logical steps to a solution to the problem.
DESICCATION	Drying.
DIFFERENTIAL RELAY	A relay that works because of the difference between two alike quantities, such as current or voltage.
DOPPLER RADAR	The radar that detects the movement of a distant object by measuring the change in radio frequency of the echo signal caused by its motion.
EDDY	Any current of fluid that flows differently from the main stream.
EDDY CURRENT	The electrical currents affected by the application of a magnetic field.
ELECTROLYTIC RECTIFIER	An electrolytic system that changes alternating current to direct current.
ELECTROMOTIVE FORCE	The potential difference between the terminals of a unit used to as a source for electrical energy.
ELECTRON	The smallest known particle having a negative charge.
ELECTRON MICROSCOPE	A microscope that uses electrons instead of light rays, and electrical magnetic fields instead of glass lenses. It sends a beam of electrons through a thin sample of the material and magnifies the shadow it causes.
ELLIPTIC POLARIZATION	The polarization that produces an elliptically polarized wave.

ELLIPTICALLY AT POLARIZED WAVE	A polarized wave in which the direction of the displacement point rotates about a point in a plane and the magnitude displacement varies as the radius of an ellipse.
ELLIPTICITY	In an ellipse, the ratio of the difference between the two diameters to the major semidiameter; it is a measure of the oblateness of the ellipse.
ELUTION	The extraction of a solid from a mixture of solids with the aid of a liquid.
E.M.F.	The abbreviation for electromotive force.
EMISSION	The radiation of energy, or the liberation or sending out of particles.
EMISSION SPECTRUM	The spectrum showing the radiations emitted by a substance.
EMISSIVE POWER	The time rate, at a given temperature, of the total emission of radiant energy per unit area of the radiating surface. (called intrinsic radiance.)
EMISSIVITY	The ratio of the emissive power of a radiating surface to the emissive power of a black body at the same temperature.
EMPIRICAL CURVE	A curve determined and drawn to conform fully or nearly with certain empirical or statistical data.
EMPIRICAL EQUATION	The equation of an empirical curve.
EMULSION	A dispersion of one liquid in another. both do not mix, such as oil-in-water.
ENERGY	The capacity to do work.
FARAD	A unit of capactance.
GALVANIC CELL	Two plates of dissimilar metals immersed in an electrolyte, more frequently called a voltaic cell.
GALVANIC SERIES	A synonym for an electrochemical series.
GALVANISM	An obsolete term for the science of electrical currents.
GALVANIZE	To coat a metal with a think layer of zinc by dripping it into a bath of molten zinc.
GALVANOMETER	An instrument used for detecting or measuring a small electrical current.
GALVANOSCOPE	An instrument capable of detecting, but not measuring, electric currents.

GAMMA RAY	The electromagnetic radiation of nuclear origin, of short wave-length, emitted by the nuclei of certain atoms as they decay radioactively.
GROUND RESISTANCE	The earth's opposition to the current flowing through it.
HEAT COIL	A protective device that opens or grounds a circuit, by a mechanical element that moves when a fusible substance which holds it in place is heated to a certain temperature.
HELIX	A curve that resembles a corkscrew.
HYDRODYNAMICS	The study of fluid motion dynamics.
HYDROSTATICS	The study of fluids in a state of equilibrium.
HYGROMETER	The instrument that measures humidity in the air.
ION	An electrically charged atom or group of atoms, formed when an ordinarily neutral atom gains or loses an electron.
MACH	A unit of the velocity of sound.
MASS	A measure of the inertia of a body.
MEDIAN	The value of the middle term of a series.
MENISCUS	The curved surface of a liquid in a vessel.
OSMOSIS	The movement of a fluid through a porous membrane into another fluid of a different density.
OXIDATION	In the original and litcral sense, the chemical combination of an element with oxygen.
PARALLAX	The apparent displacement of the location of an object caused by a shift in the observation point.
POLYHEDRAL ANGLE	An angle formed by three or more planes (the faces of the polyhedral angle) that meet at a point (the vertex). Each two successive faces form a dihedral angle of the polyhedral angle, and the edges of these dihedral angles are the edges of the polyhedral angle; the angles formed by any two consecutive edges are referred to as the face angles of the polyhedral angle.
POLYHEDRON	A solid that is bounded by planes.

POLYMER

Any of two or more polymeric compounds, especially one of higher molecular weight; in particular, one produced from another by polymerization.

POLYMERIC

Consist of the same chemical elements in the same proportion by weight, but differing in molecular weight.

POLYMERIZATION

A chemical reaction in which two or more molecules of the same substance combine to form a new compound.

RADIOLOGY

The science that deals with x-rays, radioactivity and other radiation.

THERMOCOUPLE

A device used to measure temperature in which a pair of electrical effect conductors are joined as they produce thermoelectricity.

TITRATION

The determing of the strength of a solution of an acid, base, oxidizing, or reducing agent by adding an appropriate reagent of known strength.

VISCOSITY

The internal friction of a fluid.

YAW

The angular displacement about an axis that is parallel to the normal axis of a vehicle.

11. FINANCIAL, LEGAL, AND REAL ESTATE TERMS

Contracts, correspondence, and literature related to the more complicated aspects of law, real estate, and business finance often contain words having unclear meaning. Here's a quick guide to words you're likely to come across most often. This list should save you valuable time that would be wasted by looking for definitions in a larger dictionary.

ABANDONMENT	The giving up of any right or claim to ownership or property
ABEYANCE	A temporary suspension of title to property until the proper owner is determined.
ABROGATION	The cancellation of a contract or law.
ABSTRACT (OF TITLE)	A written history of the title to property, which lists former owners, liens, or changes in the property.
ACCELERATION CLAUSE	A clause in an installment contract stating that the entire amount must be paid if an installment is not paid when due.
ACCEPTANCE	The acceptance of an offer that ends in a valid agreement.
ACCOMMODATION PAPER	An agreement to allow someone to get credit or to raise money without collateral. If you make the agreement, you guarantee the credit of the borrower.
ACCORD AND SATISFACTION	An agreement by both parties to change a contract to their mutual satisfaction.
ACCOUNT STATED	An agreement between parties who have previous transactions that fixes the amount one owes the other.
ACKNOWLEDGMENT	A formal declaration made before an authorized person (such as a NOTARY PUBLIC, by someone who has signed a document, that he actually signed it.
ACT OF GOD	An event caused exclusively by the force of nature.
ACTUARY	A statistics expert who calculates rates and risks.

ADMINISTRATOR	Someone named to manage an estate of another person.
ADVERSE POSSESSION	The acquiring of property by someone who doesn't actually have title to it.
AFFIDAVIT	A written statement of facts declared under oath before an authorized person.
AGENCY	A relationship in which one party contracts to represent another party.
AGENT	A person authorized to transact business for another.
AGENCY SHOP	A workplace in which all employees contribute to a union, whether or not they belong to it.
AIR BILL	Evidence that goods have been received and shipped by air.
AIR RIGHTS	The right to use or not to use the open space above a property.
ALL-TIME BOTTOM	The lowest period of business activity.
ALL-TIME HIGH	The highest period of business activity.
AMORTIZATION	The paying off of a debt by installments.
ANNUAL REPORT	A yearly financial statement to the stockholders of a corporation, audited by independent accountants.
ANNUITY	A sum of money received yearly.
ANTITRUST LEGISLATION	Those laws prohibiting trade practices that monopolize, inhibit, or restrain interstate commerce.
APPRAISAL	An expert's opinion of the worth of a business, home, or property.
ARBITRAGE	The buying of securities on one market in order to sell them immediately on another market to make a profit.
ATTACHMENT	The legal seizure of a person or property.
ATTENTION LINE	The naming of a specific department or person in a business letter.
AUTHORIZED CAPITAL STOCK	The amount of stock a corporation can issue, according to the incorporation certificate.
BAIL	The money or security given to a court guaranteeing that someone will appear as scheduled. The money is returned when the person appears.
BAILMENT	The process of providing bail.

BANKRUPTCY	A legal proceeding whereby a debtor's property is turned over to a receiver and distributed equally among those he owes money to.
BALANCE OF PAYMENTS	A record of a country's payments to other countries, including capital and gold, and the total receipts from those countries.
BALANCE SHEET	A concise summary of the financial condition of a company that shows assets, liabilities, and capital.
BALLOON PAYMENT	The remaining amount of principal due on a loan after all the monthly amortization payments have been made.
BEAR MARKET	The stock market when prices are going down.
BIG BOARD	The New York Stock Exchange.
BILL OF EXCHANGE	A written order (the draft) by one person (the drawer) to another (the drawee) to pay a sum of money to a third person (the payee).
BALANCE OF POWER	The arrangement of power between nations, often by agreements and alliances, so that no nation can dominate the others.
BALANCE OF TRADE	The value difference in the imports and exports of a country.
BILL OF LADING	The contract between someone who ships goods and a carrier who describes the goods received and the terms of shipment.
BINDER	A written agreement, usually confirmed with money, which makes a contract legally binding until the full contract is completed.
BILL OF SALE	A written statement from the seller to the buyer showing transfer of title to the property described.
BIRD DOG	A slang expression for a real estate salesperson who "flushes out" prospects or leads, then turns them over to another salesperson or broker who is better at closing sales.
BLACKLIST	A list of people under suspicion or censure.
BLANKET INSURANCE	The insurance which covers more than one kind of risk.

BLANKET MORTGAGE	A mortgage that covers more than one piece of property.
BLUE CHIP	A stock that sells at a high price because of public confidence in its steady record of performance.
BLUE LAWS	Those laws developed in colonial times which restricted business on Sundays and other days for religious reasons.
BLUE SKY LAW	Any law designed to protect people against fraud, especially with regard to securities.
BOARD OF DIRECTORS	A group elected by the stockholders of a corporation to set policy and manage the business of the corporation.
BOND	A written agreement, especially by a corporation or a government body, to pay a stated amount of money at a specific time in the future (the maturity date).
BOND ISSUE	A way to raise money by issuing a large number of similar bonds.
BOND AND MORTGAGE	A legal instrument that combines a bond (written evidence of a debt) and a mortgage (pledge of some security for the debt).
BOOK COST	An asset's value as noted on the company ledger.
BOOK DEPRECIATION	The amount you can deduct for depreciation from the cost of a business asset as noted on your accounting books.
BOOK VALUE	The value of an asset you carry on your accounting books.
BREACH OF CONTRACT	The failure of one party in a contract to perform an act the contract calls for.
BREACH OF WARRANTY	Any warranty of a seller that is proven to be false.
BULK SALES LAW	The laws used to protect a seller's creditors from his selling all his assets to only one buyer in a single transaction.
BULL MARKET	The stock market when prices are rising.
BUSINESS CERTIFICATE	A certification of registration required by some states if you conduct business under an assumed name.
BUYER'S MARKET	A time when property for sale is so plentiful that sellers have to lower their prices to make a sale.

BY-BIDDING

The fake bidding at an auction that is used to stimulate the bidding. The fraudulent by-bidder (also called a "shill," "decoy," "puffer," or "sham") rarely buys the items he bids on.

BYLAWS

The rules adopted by a corporation for its own management, as well as requirements for stockholders, directors, and officers.

CALL

Loaned money payable on demand.

CALL LOAN

A loan repayable on demand.

CALL MARKET

The current market for call money.

CALL MONEY

The money that banks lend which is repayable on demand, and usually lent to stockbrokers.

CANCELLATION CLAUSE

A clause in some contracts and leases that gives either party the right to cancel the agreement in the event of a specific occurrence.

CAPITAL

The net worth of a business—money, accumulated assets such as materials, stocks and bonds, and equipment used in business; the actual wealth of a business.

CAPITAL ASSETS

Any property a taxpayer holds under the capital gain and loss provision of the federal income tax law. It doesn't include property held for ordinary sale, stock in trade, real or depreciable property, copyrights, accounts receivable, or government obligations.

CAPITAL GAINS

The profits from the sale of a capital asset after you deduct its cost or appraised value. The price at which you sell something, less the price you paid for it. The appreciation in value of an asset over a period of time.

CAPITAL STOCK

The total amount of stock in a corporation that is authorized for issue.

CAPITALIZATION RATE

The percentage rate of return you consider reasonable for your investment. Often used by appraisers and investors to set commercial real estate values.

CAPITALIZE

To provide capital or cash, or the establishment of an asset's value.

CARNET	A permit that allows you to take a car into a foreign country for a short time without paying an import duty.
CARRIER	Someone who agrees to transport merchandise for a shipper or consigner to a specific designation or consignee.
CARRY-BACK, CARRY-OVER	A provision in the tax law that lets you use an operating or capital loss in one year to reduce taxes in a preceding or succeeding year.
CARTEL	A group of independent businesses that agrees to regulate producing, pricing, and marketing, thus eliminating competition.
CASH	Ready currency; liquid funds, negotiable instruments you can easily convert into usable money.
CASH FLOW	Net income; your usable cash after you meet your expenses.
CASH ON DELIVERY	A contract in which you agree to pay the price when you receive the product, but you're not allowed to inspect the goods before payment. The contract usually specifies the time in which you have to inspect the goods and return them for a refund if they don't conform to the contract.
CASH ON THE BARRELHEAD, CASH ON THE LINE	A slang expression that means you pay a deposit or a complete cash payment immediately.
CASH VALUE	The amount of money an asset will bring you on the open market, with little delay. A better term is "market value."
CATS AND DOGS	Those low-priced stocks that involve a fair amount of risk, but which have the opportunity to produce a substantial profit.
CAVEAT EMPTOR	A Latin phrase that means, "Let the buyer beware." You're expected to inspect the property carefully before you buy it, usually at your own risk, as long as the property has been represented accurately.
CAVEAT VENDOR	A Latin phrase that means, "Let the seller beware."

CERTIFICATE OF DEPOSIT	A bank's acknowledgement that it has received your money along with an agreement to repay it.
CERTIFICATE OF DOING BUSINESS	A permit issued by a state or local government that allows you to do business under an assumed name.
CERTIFICATE OF INCORPORATION	A document granted by a state that allows persons to form a corporation.
CERTIFICATE OF STOCK	The written evidence that you own a specified number of shares in a corporation.
CERTIFICATE OF TITLE	A written document showing that you have good title to property you want to convey to another person.
CERTIFIED CHECK	A check that a bank guarantees is covered by enough funds on deposit.
CHATTEL MORTGAGE	A mortgage in which you ensure payment by giving security of your personal property.
CLEAR MARKET PRICE	The fair market price.
CLEAR TITLE	A good, marketable title to property that is free from encumbrances.
CLOSED CORPORATION	A corporation in which the directors and officers own most of the voting stock, and thus control all policies and actions of the corporation.
CLOSED SHOP	A place of work in which the employer agrees that all employees must belong to the union as a condition of hiring.
CLOSER	A person who is responsible for getting the contract signed, closing the deal, or making the sale.
CODICIL	A written addition or change in a will.
COLLATERAL	The cash or valuables deposited as pledge to a lender that you will repay a loan. The value of the collateral is often much higher than the value of the loan. If you don't pay the loan, you lose the entire collateral.
COLLECTIVE BARGAINING	The negotiation of wages, terms of employment, benefits, and work hours between labor and management.
COLLECTION AGENCY	A company that specializes in collecting overdue accounts receivable. They charge the creditor a fee for their service and are often more successful because they don't

care about the good will of the debtor, often threatening to damage the creditor's credit rating if the bill isn't paid.

COMMERCIAL BANKS Banks that get most of their money from depositors' checking accounts. They specialize in short-term loans.

COMMERCIAL PAPER A banking term that means a written agreement to pay a specific amount of money at a specific future date. Commercial paper includes mortgage and collateral promissory notes, drafts, checks, bank drafts and checks, cashier's checks, certificates of deposits, and trade acceptances.

COMMINGLE FUNDS The combination of personal money with escrow funds in a common account.

COMMON CARRIER A person who is in business to transport public goods for a fee.

COMMON MARKET The European Economic Community, or any customs union.

CONCEALMENT The withholding of facts in contracts, insurance, and sales when you have an obligation to reveal them.

CONGLOMERATE A large corporation made up of smaller ones, often in totally unrelated kinds of businesses.

COMMON STOCK Corporate stock that is secondary to preferred stock. Common stockholders receive dividends shared among them only if there is enough profit left after the preferred stockholders receive their share.

CONSIDERATION The necessary part of a contract that shows the price, motive, or cause that made a party agree to the contract.

COMMUNITY PROPERTY In certain states, the property a husband and wife acquire during their marriage. Each owns one-half of it.

CONSPIRACY Any agreement between two people to commit a crime.

CONSIGNEE A person you ship goods to on consignment so that he can sell them.

CONSUMMATE To bring an agreement to a successful end.

CONTRACT A written or oral binding agreement between people to do or not to do something.

COPY Any writing a printer will set in type.

COPYRIGHT A government protection for a writer, which covers the production, sale, or publication of artistic or literary works.

CORPORATION A group of people who form a legal association to act as a single person, for a specific purpose.

CORNER The holding of a monopoly by buying all or most of the available supply, in order to raise the price.

COST AND FREIGHT The sales price that includes the cost of goods and the freight to a specific destination.

COST, INSURANCE AND FREIGHT The sales price that includes the cost of goods, any insurance to cover possible loss, and freight to a specific destination.

COST PLUS A construction contract term in which you agree to reimburse a builder for the cost of labor and materials, plus a fee for his services.

COUNTERSIGN The use of a second signature on a document to back up the authenticity of the first signature.

CREDIT The money due a person. In bookkeeping, what's owed to you.

DAMAGES Money you recover in court when you suffer injury or loss because of negligence or an unlawful act of another person.

DEAL An agreement to do business.

DEBENTURE A corporate bond not backed up by any security of corporate property—the company simply promises to pay a debt out of its assets.

DEBIT A charge or debt. In bookkeeping, what you owe.

DEBT INSTRUMENT The note, bond, or document you sign to create a debt.

DEBT SERVICE The money you need to pay your debt, including principal and interest payments.

DECLARATION OF TRUST A statement that you, as someone who holds property, make that you're keeping it in trust for someone else.

DECREMENT A decrease in value because of economic and social changes; the opposite of increment.

DEDUCTIBLE	The amount you can take away from a larger amount of money.
DE FACTO	Really; in actual fact (Latin).
DEFAULT	The failure to meet an obligation of a contract.
DEFICIENCY	A shortage in money or standards; a shortage.
DEFICIENCY JUDGMENT	A legal judgment that is issued when the security for a loan is not enough to pay a debt.
DELINQUENT DEBT	An overdue loan or debt; the failure to make a loan payment.
DEPLETION	The reduction or loss of an asset that decreases its value.
DEPRECIATION	A reduction in the value of property.
DIRECTOR'S MEETINGS	The meetings at which a corporation's directors formally take action on the corporation's business.
DISBURSEMENTS	The money you pay out. In a real estate closing, these are the funds that buyer and seller spend to transfer ownership.
DISCHARGE	The cancellation of a contract obligation.
DISCOUNT	A sum of money taken away from the original amount.
DISCOUNT FEE	In real estate, the points or charges made by a lender to gain more money than the usual mortgage interest rate allows.
DIVEST	To give up or relinquish personal or real property.
DRAFT	The same as a bill of exchange: an order you (the drawer) write to someone who owes you money (the drawee) telling him to pay money to a third person (the payee).
EASEMENT	Any right you have, as the owner of real property, to use another person's property as a right of way.
ECONOMIC LIFE	The estimated time in which you can use a property profitably.
EMBEZZLEMENT	The theft of someone's property, money, or benefits.
EMINENT DOMAIN	The power governments have to take private property for public use.

EMPLOYMENT CONTRACT	A written agreement between an employer and employee. The employer agrees to hire the employee for a specified amount of money, for a specific period of time, and under certain specific conditions and terms.
ENJOIN	To impose or prohibit by legal authority.
ESCROW	Any money or personal property held by a third person until a specific condition of the contract is met.
EXCISE TAX	A tax imposed on an act or practice, such as the sale of tobacco, the issue of licenses, or sales taxes.
EQUITY	The current market value of a certain property, less any liens against it.
FACE VALUE	The value shown on the outside of an instrument such as a stock certificate or bond.
FACT FINDING	The process of getting all the facts in a labor negotiation. The results of the process are presented to all parties to either be accepted or rejected.
FAIR TRADE	An agreement in which distributors sell products of a specified class at no less than the minimum price determined by the manufacturer.
FAMILY CAR DOCTRINE	In some states, the law that makes a car owner responsible for any damage that results when any member of the family operates it.
FANNIE MAE	The nickname of the Federal National Mortgage Association.
FEATHERBEDDING	The practice of forcing an employer to pay for services that were not performed.
FEDERAL ESTIMATED TAX	The estimate of tax you expect to pay over $100 if you earn over $500 from sources other than your wages or if your income will exceed a certain amount.
FIDELITY	The obligation you have to your employer to carry out your responsibilities faithfully.
FIDUCIARY	A person or organization who holds an official position of trust and confidence so that he places the interests of those he represents ahead of his own interests.

FISCAL YEAR	The business year, rather than the calendar year. The most common is July 1 to June 30.
FIXED ASSETS	Those permanent assets with a long economic life, such as office equipment and machines and the land they're located in.
FLOAT	In banking, a check that has not been cleared for collection.
FLOATER POLICY	An "allrisk" insurance policy that covers your home's personal property.
FLOATING INTEREST RATE	An interest rate that changes as the mortgage market changes.
FLUID ASSETS	Those assets you can readily change into cash.
FOREIGN CORPORATION	A corporation that does business in a different state than the one it is incorporated in.
FRANCHISE TAX	A tax states levy on corporations for the privilege of operating as a corporation. It's also called a corporate fee, license fee, or qualification tax.
FRANK	An official mail mark used by certain government employees so that their mail can be sent free of postage.
FREE ALONGSIDE SHIP (F.A.S.)	A contract term that shows the delivery point of goods sold. It is the seller's responsibility to deliver the goods to that point.
FREE ENTERPRISE	Your personal right to run a business freely and openly for a profit, as long as you don't break the law.
FREE ON BOARD	A contract term that specifies the place of delivery of goods sold. The seller has to deliver the goods to that place at his own expense.
FUNGIBLE GOODS	The units of merchandise that are blended together uniformly, such as grains, oils, wines, and gasolines.
FUTURE DEPRECIATION	The asset depreciation you anticipate.
GAIN	Any increase in profit or value/
GARNISHMENT	A legal procedure in which a court orders a person's earnings withheld to repay a debt.
GENTLEMAN'S AGREEMENT	A verbal agreement, usually in secret, often to monopolize prices or to exclude a minority group.

GIVE NOTICE	To let someone know, legally, of some impending action.
GOOD TITLE	The title to property showing that it is marketable and free of defects or liens, so that its owner can enjoy it without major problems.
GOOD WILL	The estimated value of a business in addition to its assets, because of its good reputation with the public.
GOODS	Stock, inventory, and merchandise.
GILT-EDGED SECURITIES	Those securities with high quality value.
GRACE PERIOD	The time during which a debt is past due, but which is allowed before the debt goes into default.
GROSS	The opposite of net: the entire amount, with nothing subtracted.
GROSS INCOME	Money before taxes, operating expenses, depreciation, salaries, fees, and other items are deducted.
GROWTH COMPANY	A firm that is growing faster than others in its field or faster than the normal economic growth.
GROWTH STOCK	The stock of a company with earnings that are continually increasing.
GUARANTY	A direct agreement to perform some action; an agreement to the honest and faithful performance of a sales contract.
HANDSHAKE DEAL	A deal that's bound or closed with a handshake, and with nothing in writing to verify the transaction.
HARD MONEY	A down payment; good faith money, a deposit. (The opposite is **SOFT DOLLAR,** which means notes, mortgages, deferred payments, and the like.)
HARD SELL	A high-pressure, very persuasive method of selling something, as opposed to **SOFT SELL.**
HOLDER IN DUE COURSE	A person who has a negotiable instrument, acquired in good faith, without knowing any defect in it, before the instrument matures. The holder in due course is assured payment by the debtors or indorsers.
HOLDING COMPANY	A company that owns or controls some or all of the interest in other companies.

HONORARIUM	A payment you give to a professional person for services when fees aren't legal or traditional.
HOT CARGO AGREEMENT	An agreement between an employer and a labor organization in which the employer agrees not to handle, use, sell, or transport products of a certain company. (It's usually unlawful and unenforceable.)
HOUSE ORGAN	A publication issued by a business for its employees, customers, or clients.
HYPOTHECATE	To pledge property as security for a debt, without giving up its possession.
IN-AND-OUT	The buying and selling a security within a short time period.
INCOME	Your return in property, money, or services from a business; return on capital you've invested.
INCOME STOCK	A security that regularly pays high dividends, although its price stays relatively stable.
INCOME TAX	Federal, state, and local taxes that may be levied against the yearly income of a person or a corporation.
INCORPORATION	The process of forming a corporation, or of joining or merging a document or property with another document or property.
INCREMENT	An increase in value.
INDEMNITY	An agreement in which you are compensated for loss or damages in a specific transaction.
INDENTURE	A deed or contract between two parties that involves the rights and duties of each party; an official list or inventory; a contract that binds you to the service of another person for a specific time period.
INDORSEMENT	The notation you make and sign on the back of commercial paper to transfer title to another person.
INDUCEMENT	Something of value you offer to a person in order to influence him to do something or refrain from doing something.
INJUNCTION	A court order that prohibits you from a specific course of action.

INNOCENT PURCHASER FOR VALUE	Someone who enters a contract and pays money without knowing a defect in the seller's title.
INSOLVENCY	A debtor's financial condition in which he cannot pay what he owes because he has more liabilities than assets.
INSTALLMENT CONTRACT	An agreement to buy merchandise and pay for it later, in installments. In the Uniform Commercial Code, the installment contract of sale requires that goods be delivered in separate lots and be accepted separately.
INSTRUMENT	Any legal, written document like a bill of sale, deed, contract, option, bond, will, or mortgage that you use to transact legal business.
INSURANCE	A method to guarantee or indemnify yourself or your company against loss from a specific hazard.
INTANGIBLE ASSET	Something you cannot see, or a quality that adds to the value of your business.
INTEREST	A fee or charge for the use of money.
INTESTATE	A person who dies without a will, or who leaves an invalid will. Administrators receive the estate to settle it.
INVALID	Not binding; unfounded in law; unenforceable.
INVENTORY	A list of real or personal property to help determine its value.
INVESTMENT	The money or property you use to make a profit at a later time.
INVESTOR	A person who puts money into a business or venture with the idea of making a good profit on his capital at a later time.
INVOICE	A written, itemized list of services or products sold for a specific amount of money; a bill.
IRONCLAD AGREEMENT	A specific, written agreement so clear and binding that there is no way to escape its provisions. An agreement that cannot be broken by the parties who made it.
IRREVOCABLE	Unchangeable, unalterable; can't be recalled.
ISSUE	To publish, circulate, or distribute securities of a company by an official group.

JOINT VENTURE An association of two or more people for a limited, specific purpose, but without the normal duties, powers, and responsibilities that go along with partnership.

JOINT STOCK COMPANY A business association formed by a contract so that all the members take personal responsibility for the organization's debts.

KITE A check used to sustain credit temporarily when there is no money in the account to back up the check. The usual intention is to deposit money in the account before the check is presented for payment. The practice is unethical and sometimes illegal. A bank can close your account if you're found doing this deliberately.

LARCENY The taking and carrying away of the personal property of another person; theft.

LATE CHARGE A charge you pay on installment loans and mortgage payments when you don't pay them on time.

LEAD A prospective buyer; a prospect.

LEASE A written agreement in which a property owner (lessor) and a tenant (lessee) agree on the possession and use of the property for a specific period of time, and for a specific amount of money or services.

LEASEBACK A seller who keeps possession of property as a tenant after completing the sale and delivering the deed.

LEGAL INSTRUMENT A written, formal document such as a bill of sale, deed, lease, or will. The formal expression of a legal act or agreement.

LETTERS OF ADMINISTRATION A legal document that entrusts a person with the administration of the estate of someone who has died.

LETTER OF ADVICE A letter in which you include specific information about a commercial transaction, from consignor to consignee.

LETTER OF CREDIT A letter a bank issues that authorizes a person to draw a specific amount of money from it, its branches, or associated banks.

LETTERS OF CREDENCE A document that officially conveys the credentials of a diplomatic envoy to a foreign government.

LETTERS, PATENT	A document the government issues that grants a patent to an inventor.
LIABILITY	A debt or obligation; something that acts to your disadvantage. The opposite of an asset.
LIEN	Any claim against the property of a debtor as security or payment for a debt.
LIMITED ORDER	An order to buy stock at or below a certain price, or above a certain price, and within a certain period of time.
LIMITED PARTNERSHIP	An agreement that limits the partner's liability to the amount invested, and also limits the amount of profit he can make. A limited partner does not usually have a voice in managing the company.
LIQUID ASSETS	The assets you can easily turn into cash, or cash on hand; also called **CURRENT ASSETS** or **QUICK ASSETS.**
LIQUIDATION VALUE	The amount of cash you could raise if you were forced to sell an asset.
LIQUIDATE	To pay off or settle an obligation; to turn assets into ready cash.
LIQUIDITY	The amount of cash you can raise quickly; your cash position.
LISTED STOCK	The stock that is traded on the securities exchange.
LISTING	A written or verbal agreement with a broker to sell or lease real estate that you own.
LOAN COMMITMENT	An approved loan application in which the lender states the loan amount, the interest rate, the years on the loan, and the amount of monthly payment.
LOAN COSTS	The actual cost for services you pay to obtain a loan. It includes survey and attorney fees, along with loan commissions.
LOCK, STOCK, AND BARREL	A real estate expression that means everything on the premises is included in the sale.
LONG	The possession of a large holding of a security or commodity because you expect a rise in price.
LOW-PRESSURE SELLING	The use of logic and reasoning instead of agressive, high-pressure tactics. Also called **SOFT SELL.**

MAKER	Someone who issues a promissory note and is primarily responsible for its payment.
MANIFEST	A list of passengers or cargo; a list of railroad cars by owner and location.
MARKET ORDER	An order that lets you buy or sell stocks, bonds, or other securities at the prevailing market price.
MARKET VALUE	The going price at which merchandise, commodities, or securities are sold. What you, as a seller, can expect for merchandise, securities, or services in the open market.
MERGER	The transfer of the assets of one corporation to another, so that the first corporation ceases to exist. This includes changing one agreement in a contract into another agreement that you can enforce more easily.
MONEY MARKET	The availability of bank money and the interest rate charged to borrow it, which fluctuates with supply and demand.
MONOPOLY	The exclusive ownership or control of one industry, field, or product, to the extent that you are in a position to limit, exclude, or stifle competition.
MORTGAGE	A written agreement to provide property as security until full payment is made for it. The written agreement promises payment of the loan, the amount and number of payments, the interest rate, and the first and last payment dates.
NEGOTIABLE INSTRUMENT	A written agreement by a maker or drawer that contains an unconditional promise or order to pay money. You can pass the instrument, such as a check, from one person to another.
NEGLIGENCE	The failure to use reasonable care required by the circumstances, especially in corporations and partnerships.
NAKED CONTRACT	An agreement in which there is no consideration given. This makes the contract unenforceable.
NET INCOME	The money you have left after you subtract the expenses from the income.

NET WORTH	The current market value, after you total the assets and subtract the liabilities.
NONPROFIT CORPORATION	A corporation specifically formed to advance charitable, benevolent, fraternal, scientific, political, or educational purposes instead of a profit motive.
NONRECURRING EXPENSE	An expense that does not occur regularly or periodically, such as repairs you have to make for vandalism.
NOTARY PUBLIC	Someone authorized to take acknowledgments, administer oaths, and certify the accuracy of business and legal documents.
NOVATION	The substitution of a new contract or party in a contract for an older contract or party.
OATH	A declaration in which you show you must act or speak truthfully.
ODD LOT	A stock market term that means the sale of less than 100 shares.
OFFER TO BUY	An agreement between buyer and owner, which names the price, terms, conditions, and date of occupancy of real estate.
OFFICER OF A CORPORATION	Someone who has the power and duty to manage and carry out the business of the corporation.
OPEN MORTGAGE	A mortgage you can pay off at any time before it matures, without payment of a penalty.
OPERATING EXPENSES	The expenses you incur to keep a property or business in usable or rentable condition, for example, management, maintenance, taxes, furniture replacement, and insurance.
OPERATING INCOME	The income you receive directly from a property or business before you deduct the expenses.
OPERATING PROFIT	Your financial gain from a business after you pay the operating expenses. The return you receive on your investment after you deduct all the operational charges.
OPERATING RATIO	The ratio of business expneses to gross income.
OPTION	The exclusive right to buy or sell property, within a specific time and at a specific price.

OUTAGE	The amount lacking after the delivery or storage of an item.
OVERAGE	The money or goods you keep on hand exceeding the amount you list on your records. Rent payments, usually a percentage of a retail tenant's sales over a fixed-base rental.
OVERBUY	To buy stock on margin, in excess of your ability to provide further security if prices drop.
OVERRIDE	A percentage of sales commission paid to an executive or sales manager in addition to the salesperson's commission.
OVERSELL	An agreement to sell more of a stock or commodity than you can deliver within the terms of the contract.
OVER-THE-COUNTER	Stock not listed or available on an officially recognized stock exchange, but which is traded in direct negotiation. Something you can buy legally without a prescription.
PAPER PROFIT	An increase in the value of your securities.
PAR VALUE	The value noted on a stock certificate or bond, on which you base the interest or dividend; its face value.
PARTNERSHIP	A contract in which two or more people agree to do business for a profit.
PASSPORT	An official government document that certifies your identity and citizenship, and lets you travel abroad.
PAYEE	The person who receives a payment.
PAYER	The person who makes a payment.
PERFORMANCE BOND	A bond that guarantees a builder will complete a construction contract satisfactorily, and that it will be free of liens.
PERSONAL PROPERTY	Merchandise and tangible items you can move, along with intangibles such as bonds, stocks, mortgages, and leases.
PETTY CASH FUND	The cash you keep on hand to pay bills that are too small to justify payment by check.
PLAT	A survey or map that shows how land has been subdivided into blocks and lots.
POINT	A unit that is equal to one dollar, used to quote the current stock or commodity

prices. In real estate, a unit of one percentage point.

PORTFOLIO An itemized list of investments, securities, or commercial paper owned by a person, bank, or another investment organization.

POWER OF APPOINTMENT The authority you grant to another person to succeed to property upon your death.

POWER OF ATTORNEY A legal instrument that authorizes someone to act as another person's attorney or agent.

PREEMPTIVE RIGHT The right of a corporate shareholder of common stock to buy as much as needed from a new issue to keep the same level of ownership.

PREFERRED STOCK A corporation's stock that has priority over the common stock in the distribution of dividends and assets.

PREPAYMENT PRIVILEGE The amount you, as a lender, will let the borrower pay on the principal in addition to the monthly payments.

PREPAYMENT PENALTY The percentage you, as a lender, may require to be paid in addition to the loan if the loan is paid ahead of schedule.

PRICE INDEX A number that relates the price of a commodity to its price during a chosen base period.

PROFIT SHARING A system in which employees share in the profits of a business.

PROSPECTUS A formal summary of a proposed commercial venture. A printed notice that describes securities offered for sale.

PROXY Someone authorized to act for another.

PROFIT Income or earnings. What you have left of a business or other venture after you've paid the expenses.

PROFIT AND LOSS STATEMENT The exact amount of profit or loss of a business, itemized on a statement according to income and expenses.

PRIME RATE The interest rate banks reserve for prime or preferred customers such as the highest credit-rated, public corporations.

PRINCIPAL The person who authorizes an agent to act in his behalf.

PRODUCT LIABILITY Your responsibility, as the maker and seller of a product, for any defect in parts, construction, or operation that harms a person or his property.

PROFESSIONAL CORPORATION
An agreement among members of a profession, such as law or medicine, to conduct the practice of their profession as a corporate entity.

PROMISSORY NOTE
A written promise you, as a debtor (maker), make to a creditor (payee) to pay a specific amount of money within a specific period of time.

PROMOTER
An independent contractor who develops and organizes the financing and creation of a corporation with the understanding that he will be paid after the corporation is formed.

QUORUM
The number of people who must be present at a meeting so that the organization can legally transact business.

QUALIFIED ENDORSEMENT
Any endorsement that limits the endorser's liability.

RECEIVER
A neutral party appointed by the court who takes possession and manages the property of a person or firm undergoing bankruptcy or some other litigation.

REAL PROPERTY
The buildings, and land permanently attached to the land, along with any rights or easements in the adjoining land.

REDLINING
A practice of certain banks and private lenders in which they put certain neighborhoods off limits for mortgages, usually where there exists an estimated high risk.

RESTRAINT OF TRADE
Any agreement or contract designed to stop competition or create a monopoly, regulate prices or stop the natural development of trade.

RETAINER
A fee paid for the services of a consultant, lawyer, or other professional.

RIDER
A change or addition made to an existing document.

ROYALTIES
Those payments made to a patent or copyright owner for the privilege of making or using the patented device or document.

SAVINGS AND LOAN ASSOCIATION	A financial institution that is state or federally chartered, or privately owned by the stockholders or depositors.
SALE AND RETURN	A sales agreement in which you and the other party both agree that ownership is transferred when the goods are delivered, but the buyer can return them within a specified time.
SATISFACTION PIECE	A document that acknowledges the payment of a debt.
SELLER'S MARKET	A market in which the commodity is in short supply and the seller is in the better position to set prices.
SHORT COVERING	The buying of stock, securities, or commodites to close out a short sale.
SHORT SALE	The sale of securities or commodities not in your immediate possession, but whose delivery you can anticipate before you close the contract.
SILENT PARTNER	A partner who doesn't have a voice in the management of the business.
SIMPLE INTEREST	The interest you pay only on the original principal, not on the accumulating interest.
SINKING FUND	A fund you accumulate to pay off a public or corporate debt.
SHOP RIGHT	Your right, as an employer, to use an invention in your business for free, if it came from an employee during working hours, using your tools and equipment. However, the employee still owns the invention.
SOFTWARE	The printed material such as programs, instructions, routines, and symbolic language used to operate computers.
SOLE OWNERSHIP	The ownership of a business in which you are responsible for its debt and obligations. Your personal property may also be used to pay your business debts.
SOFT DOLLARS	A jargon term that means any payments you defer such as notes and mortgages. They are the opposite of **HARD MONEY,** which means cash or its equivalent.
SOFT SELL	A sales technique in which you sell by the use of logic and reasoning, rather than

loud, overly aggressive tactics. Low-pressure selling.

SPINOFF
An object, product, or enterprise that is generated from a larger and often unrelated enterprise.

STOCKBROKER
Someone who acts as an agent in buying and selling stocks and other securities.

STOCK CERTIFICATE
A certificate that indicates ownership of a specific number of shares in a corporation's stock.

STOCK COMPANY
A company or corporation whose capital is divided into shares.

STOCK DIVIDEND
A dividend paid in securities instead of cash.

STOCK EXCHANGE
A place where securities such as stocks and bonds are bought and sold.

STOCK SPLIT
A division of the shares of a company's stock, which gives its holders two or more shares for each share they hold.

STOP ORDER
An order you give to a broker to buy or sell a stock when it reaches a specified level of gain or decline.

STOP PAYMENT
An order you give to your bank not to honor a check.

STANDBY COMMITMENT
A financing term that means you receive a pledge for a loan to be used some time in the future, usually for a construction project.

STATUTE OF LIMITATIONS
A state law that limits the time in which you can take legal action.

STRAW MAN
Someone who buys property for another person to hide his identity, also called a dummy purchaser.

SUBCONTRACT
A contract you give out, when you hold the original or general contract, to perform any or all of the work.

SURETY
A personal guarantee you give to fulfill an obligation.

SURETY BOND
A bond you use when you trust employees with money or hold them responsible for sizeable assets. Bonding and insurance companies guarantee that the employees will carry out their responsibilities honestly.

SURVEY	Locating the boundaries, areas, or elevations of land.
SYNDICATE	An association of people who gather together for a specific business transaction; similar to a joint venture.
TANGIBLE PROPERTY	A property you can touch, such as a building, its furnishings, or the land the building is located on.
TAXABLE INCOME	Income that is subject to government taxation. In a real estate investment, taxable income is your net return from a property, after you deduct the depreciation and interest you pay on the mortgage.
TAXABLE VALUE	Your property's assessed value, often only a percentage of the actual market value, placed on an asset for tax purposes.
TAX BASE	a property's assigned value for tax purposes. With an income tax, the base is the net taxable income. With a property tax, it is the assessment.
TAX CERTIFICATE	A certificate given to the buyer of tax-delinquent land before a **TAX DEED** is delivered. If the back taxes are not paid within the time allowed by law, the person who holds the tax certificate becomes the owner.
TAX DEED	A deed used for land that is sold for nonpayment of taxes.
TAX EXEMPTION	The elimination of taxes for certain kinds of ownership, such as church property, schools, and nonprofit organizations. In some states, tax exemptions are allowed on homes owned by widows.
TAX LEASE	A lease you receive when you buy tax-delinquent land and the law forbids its outright sale.
TAX LIEN	A legal encumbrance put on real estate or chattel because the taxes are not paid; an unpaid tax.
TAX RECEIVER	A person or organization appointed by the court or provided by law to receive property when there is a tax default.
TAX ROLL	The official record of the property owners of an area, which gives their addresses, the

assessed valuation of the property, and the amount of taxes to be paid.

TAX SALE
A sale of property that is in default because of nonpayment of taxes.

TAX SEARCH
A records search to see if there are unpaid taxes on a property.

TAX SHELTER
A tax protection provided by the tax law.

TAX TITLE
The title to property you obtain when you buy land that is up for sale because of unpaid taxes.

TENANCY
The occupying of property that belongs to someone else.

TENANCY AT WILL
A tenancy based upon the persmission of the owner, but without any fixed term or lease.

TENANCY IN COMMON
The ownership of property by two or more people, each of whom has a separate, undivided interest without any right of survivorship.

TENANCY IN PARTNERSHIP
A tenancy that occurs when property is bought with money from a business partnership.

TENANT
Someone who owns and uses a property legally, although the property belongs to someone else; the lessee to whom you make a lease.

TERM MORTGAGE
A mortgage that has a specified duration, usually less than five years, during which you pay only the interest. At the end of the term, you have to pay the entire amount of the principal.

THIRD PARTY
Someone besides the principals in a contract, such as an escrow agent or real estate broker.

TICKER
Any device that receives and records stock market quotations.

TITLE
In real estate, the lawful ownership and right to property.

TITLE COMPANY
A company that specializes in examining records to see if a property title is clear and free of liens and encumbrances.

TITLE INSURANCE
A special insurance to assure that you have clear title to property.

TOPPING-OFF	The highest point of a building's construction. Workers often mark it by attaching a tree or branch to the highest point.
TORT	An act in which one person causes damage to another person or his property.
TRADE ACCEPTANCE	A written agreement, signed by a buyer, to pay the purchase price of goods to the seller at a specified future date.
TRADE BOOK	A book for the general public, rather than a textbook or limited edition, which is distributed through booksellers.
TRADE DISCOUNT	A manufacturer's or wholesaler's discount given to buyers in the same trade.
TRADE MAGAZINE	A magazine published for a specific business or industry to provide news and development within that industry.
TRADEMARK	A symbol that a person or an organization uses to identify a product or service.
TRADE NAME	The name a business uses to identify itself. The public name of the company.
TRADER	A person on a stock exchange who trades for himself, not as a broker for other people.
TRADE SECRETS	The ideas, formulas, or manufacturing processes a company uses to give it an advantage over its competitors.
TRANSFER OF TITLE	A change in the title to property from one person to another.
TRANSFER TAX	A tax some states levy when real estate title is transferred.
TRUST	A responsible position in which one person (the trustee) acts in the best interests of another person.
TRUSTEE	Someone who legally holds property in trust for someone else. A person placed in a responsible position of trust.
TRUST ESTATE	An estate held in trust for someone's benefit.
TRUST FUND	A fund you set up to benefit another person.
TRUST RECEIPT	A written statement that you, as a lender, receive as security for the payment of a debt.

TRUST RECEIPT	A written statement that you, as a creditor or lender, can receive as security for payment of a debt. The debtor gives you a receipt for merchandise, which makes him a trustee of the goods.
TRUTH IN LENDING ACT	A federal law (Consumer Protection Act) that requires lenders to provide full, accurate information on the interest charges made to people who borrow money.
TURNKEY JOB	A complete construction job, from groundbreaking to turning the key in the door when everything is finished.
UNIFORM COMMERCIAL CODE	A federal act designed to simplify and clarify the laws governing commercial transactions, especially among the state and local jurisdictions.
UNION	An employee or labor organization designed to deal with employers regarding work conditions, pay, labor disputes, and similar work issues.
USURY	The charging of excessivly high or unlawful interest rates for the use of money.
UNION SHOP	A place of employment in which a new employee doesn't have to belong to a union in order to be hired, but which must be joined within a specific period of time in order to keep the job.
UTILITY	A privately owned, government-franchised company that serves the general public, usually to provide service such as electricity, water, gas or telephone service.
VARIABLE INTEREST RATE	An interest rate that fluctuates with the mortgage market.
VARIANCE	Any cost that changes because of outside factors.
VENDEE	A purchaser or buyer.
VENDIBLE	Salable; capable of being sold.
VENDOR'S LIEN	The amount of money due a seller at a real estate closing, when any portion of the purchase price is not yet paid.
VESTED	In possession or in control. Something authorized, committed, or given to another person.

VESTED RIGHT	A legal right of a person that is immediate and fixed, and cannot be taken away without his consent.
WAGE EARNER'S PLAN	A plan provided in the National Bankruptcy Act through which a wage-earner can submit a plan to pay for his debts over an extended period of time.
WAIVER	The deliberate giving up of a right, privilege, or claim, or the document that indicates this.
WARRANTY	An affirmation of a promise or specific, material fact by a seller, in order to persuade a buyer to make a purchase.
WARRANT	To promise, affirm, or guarantee a fact.
WASH SALE	The buying of a stock illegally by a seller's agents to create the impression of an active market.
WAYBILL	A document that contains a list of goods and shipping instructions regarding a shipment that is prepared and transported by a common carrier.
WILL	A legal declaration of how you want your estate to be disposed of after your death.
WINDFALL	Something fortunate that happens through no special wisdom, foresight, or effort on your part.
WORKING CAPITAL	The assets of a business that you can apply to its operation. Your current assets as compared with your current liabilities.
WORKING PAPERS	Those documents that certify a person's right to employment.
WRITTEN INSTRUMENT	A document in writing that serves as proof or evidence of agreement.
WITHOUT RECOURSE	An agreement that an endorser of commercial paper secures so that there is no recourse against him if the instrument is not paid.
YIELD	That which a property or investment will return in profit or income from a business venture. It is usually determined by dividing the annual net income, interest, and dividends by the market value or cost.

12. COMMON FOREIGN WORDS AND PHRASES

Latin

bona fide	good faith
carpe diem	enjoy the present
casus belli	a cause justifying war
causa sine qua non	an indispensable condition
cui bono	for whose advantage, to what end
degustibus non est disputandum	there is no disputing about tastes
dei gratia	by the grace of god
deo volente	god willing
ecce homo	behold the man
ex cathedra	unofficially, with authority
ex more	according to custom
gaudeamus igitur	let us be joyful
hoc anno	in this year
in extremis	at the point of death
in hoc signo vinces	by this sign you will conquer
in loco parentis	in the place of a parent
in medias res	into the midst of things; into the heart of the matter
in omnia paratus	prepared for all things
in perpetuum	forever
in situ	in its place; in proper position
in statu quo	in the state in which it was before
in toto	altogether; entirely
in transitu	in transit
ipso jure	by the law itself
labor omnia vincit	labor conquers all things
laborare est orare	to work is to pray
loco citato	in the place cited
loquitur	he (or she) speaks
mens sana in corpore sano	a sound mind in a healthy body
mirabile dictu	wonderful to say
modus operandi	a mode of operating
morituri te salutamus	we who are about to die salute you

nemo me impune lacessit	no one attacks me with impunity
nihil	nothing
non possumus	we are not able
nunc	now
obiit	he died; she died
O tempora! O mores!	O times! O customs!
omnia vincit amor	love conquers all
opere citato	in the volume cited
pater patriae	father of his country
paucis verbis	in few words
pax vobiscum	peace be with you
persona non grata	an unacceptable person
pleno jure	with full authority
primus inter pares	first among equals
pro bono publico	for the public good or welfare
pro deo et ecclesia	for god and the church
pro forma	as a matter of form
pro tempore	temporarily; for the time being
quantum sufficit	as much as suffices
quo jure?	by what right?
quo modo?	in what way?
quod erat demonstrandum	which was to be shown
requiescat in pace	may he (or she) rest in peace
scripsit	he or she wrote (it)
secundum	according to
semper paratus	always ready
sic passim	so throughout
sic semper tyrannis	thus always to tyrants
sic transit gloria mundi	thus passes away the glory of the world
sine die	without fixing a day for future action or meeting
sine qua non	something essential
summum bonum	the highest or chief good
sui cuique	to each his own
tempus fugit	time flies
ubique	everywhere
ut dicta	as directed
vade mecum	go with me; companion
vale	farewell

French

affaire de coeur	a love affair
au revoir	till we see each other again
avec plaisir	with pleasure
bête noire	something that one especially dislikes or dreads
bon jour	good day; hello
bon soir	good evening; good night
c'est la vie	such is life
chef de cuisine	head cook
cherchez la femme	look for the woman
en rapport	in sympathy or accord
fait accompli	an accomplished fact
grand monde	the world at large; refined society
lettre de cachet	a sealed letter; usually containing orders for imprisonment
mal de mer	seasickness
mal du pays	homesickness
mon ami	my friend
monde	world; society
object d'art	a work of art
pièce de résistance	the principal meal or event
raison d'être	reason for being
sans doute	without doubt
sans gene	without embarrassment
sans pareil	without equal
sans souci	carefree
voilà	see! look!

13. SALES, MARKETING, AND ADVERTISING TERMS

ADVERTISING
A communication that informs mass or selective audiences about a product or service. The purpose is to encourage sale, inform markets, and impress the trademark upon the customer.

AUTOMATIC SELLING
The retail sale of goods or services through money-operated machines activated by the consumer.

BRAND
A name, term, sign, symbol, or design used to identify the goods or services of a seller.

BRAND NAME
A brand or part of a brand consisting of a word, letter, group of words, or letters in a name to identify a seller's goods or services.

COMPETITIVE ADVERTISING
Advertising in direct competition with other advertisements. Once the public accepts a new product, it is in direct competition with similar articles.

CONSUMERS' COOPERATIVE
A retail business owned and operated by consumers to buy and distribute goods and services primarily to the membership.

CONSUMERS' GOODS
Those good destined for use by consumers or households, which can be used without commercial processing.

CONVENIENCE GOODS
Those consumer goods which the customer purchases regularly and with a minimum of effort in comparison buying.

COOPERATIVE ADVERTISING
A sharing of advertising expenses by manufacturer and dealer. A manufacturer supplies a dealer with mats or tapes and the dealer places the ad in his local media. Both parties agree in advance what percentage each will pay.

CUSTOMER RELATIONS
The offering of services that attract customers to a store; working in the interest of customers.

DIRECT ADVERTISING
Advertising literature that appears in folders, leaflets, throwaways, letters, and is

	delivered to prospective customers by mail, salesmen, or dealers.
DIRECT SELLING	The process in which the firm responsible for production sells to the user, without middlemen intervening.
DISCRETIONARY INCOME	An individual's personal income, in excess of the amount needed to maintain a standard of living.
DISPOSABLE INCOME	An individual's personal income after deducting the taxes on personal income and compulsory payments.
FLYER (ADVERTISEMENT)	A handbill or circular, distributed by hand.
INDIRECT ADVERTISING	That advertising which builds up the good points of a product with the hope of getting sales in the future.
INDUSTRIAL GOODS	Those goods destined to be sold primarily for use in producing other goods or services.
MAIL-ORDER HOUSE	A retailing business that receives its orders primarily by mail or telephone and offers its goods and services for sale from a catalogue or other printed material.
MARKET	All the factors buyers and sellers consider in making decisions that result in the transfer of goods and services.
MARKET ANALYSIS	That marketing research which involves measuring the extent of a market and the determination of its characteristics.
MARKETING	All the activities that go into buying and selling.
MARKETING BUDGET	The planned dollar sales and marketing costs for a specified future period.
MARKETING POTENTIAL	The maximum possible sales opportunities for all sellers of a product or service during a stated period.
MARKETING RESEARCH	A systematic gathering, recording, and analyzing of data about problems relating to the marketing of goods and services.
MARKET SHARE	The ratio of a company's sales to the total industry sales, either actually or potentially.
MERCHANDISING	The planning and supervision that involves marketing the merchandise or service.

MOTIVATION RESEARCH	The techniques developed by behavioral scientists and used by marketing researchers to discover factors that influence marketing behavior.
NATIONAL BRAND	A manufacturer's brand that has wide territorial distribution.
PERSONAL SELLING	The oral presentation of a product or service in a conversation with one or more prospective buyers.
POINT-OF-PURCHASE ADVERTISING	The displays used to inform customers about various products. They may be photographs, oversized package reproductions, streamers, cutaways, floor stands, or wall signs. The displays are usually next to the merchandise they are advertising.
PRIVATE BRANDS	The brands sponsored by merchants or agents, as compared to those sponsored by manufacturers or producers.
PRODUCT LINE	A group of closely-related products.
PRODUCT MANAGEMENT	The planning, direction, and control of all phases of a product's life cycle.
PRODUCT MIX	All the products offered for sale by a firm.
PROMOTION, BUSINESS	The building of good-will in other ways than direct selling, such as community affairs participation, exhibitions and demonstrations at schools and clubs, and the mailing of greeting cards on special occasions. The object is not to sell products, but to create a wholesome atmosphere about the company, which in turn, makes selling easier.
PUBLICITY	The stimulation of demand for a product, service, or business by placing commercially significant news about it in a published or broadcast medium.
PUBLIC RELATIONS	The creation of a pleasant atmosphere with a targeted public to whom to sell a product or an idea. Some techniques: (a) publicity (announcing the results of a board of directors' meeting); (b) direct mail (seeking support from the public for the sale of Christmas seals); (c) public speaking (supporting a political candidate for office); (d) open house in a factory

(showing the operations of a plant to the public); (e) films used as an educational vehicle (an insurance company explains the benefits of a policy when an emergency arises); (f) personal follow-up calls (either by telephone or in person, to check on a purchase); (g) company relations with the public (the proper way to answer the telephone, write a letter, or to greet a customer).

RETAILER
A merchant whose main business is to sell directly to the consumer.

SALES BUDGET
The part of the marketing budget concerned with planned dollar sales and costs of personal selling.

SALES FORECAST
A sales estimate, in dollars or physical units, for a specified period within a marketing plan.

SALES LETTER
A sales message sent through the mail to promote the completion of a sale.

SALES MANAGEMENT
The planning, direction, and control of the personal selling activities of a business.

SALES MANAGER
The executive who directs, plans, and controls the activities of salesmen.

SALES PROMOTION
Those marketing activities which stimulate consumer purchasing and dealer effectiveness, such as display, shows and exhibitions, and demonstrations.

SPECIALTY GOODS
Those consumer goods with unique characteristics or brand identification, such as hi-fi products, men's clothing, and photo equipment.

TRADEMARK
A brand given legal protection because of its exclusive qualities.

TRADE NAME
The name by which an article is known among buyers and sellers.

ULTIMATE CONSUMER
A person who buys or uses goods or services to satisfy personal or household desires rather than to resell or use further in business.

VALUE ADDED BY MARKETING
The value of a product or a service that results from marketing activities.

WHOLESALER
A business that buys and resells merchandise to retailers and other merchants.

14. WORDS NOT TO USE: CLICHÉS, OUT-OF-DATE WORDS, AND SLANG

Clichés

Cliches are phrases used so much that they've become tired and worn out. They lack any real meaning, so that when you use them, you simply fill up valuable space ... and waste time. It's better to choose a specific phrase that describes what you really mean, as exactly and as simply as possible.

Here are some cliches we see often ... too often.

A

able to make head or tails of, not
accidents will happen
Achilles' heel, the
acid test, the
act in cold blood
ad nauseam
add insult to injury
again and again
alive and kicking
all in a day's work
all things considered
all things to all men, be
almighty dollar, the

ample opportunity
any port in a storm
apple of one's eye
armed to the teeth
as a matter of fact
as far as that goes
as well as can be expected
at death's door
at long last
at your earliest convenience
at his wit's end
axe to grind, an

B

back to the wall
balmy breezes
baptism of fire
be in good hands, to
be that as it may
beat about the bush
beaten track, off the
bed of roses
bee in one's bonnet, have a
beginning of the end
behind the scenes
beneath contempt
best is yet to be
best of all possible worlds

better half, one's
better left unsaid
between a rock and a hard place
birds of a feather (flock together)
bite off more than you can chew
blaze a trail
blessing in disguise
blind leading the blind
blissful ignorance
blood-curdling yell
blow off steam
blow your own trumpet
blown to smithereens
blue blood

bolt from the blue
bone of contention
bored to death (or tears)
born and bred
born under a lucky star
born with a silver spoon in
  his (her) mouth
bottomless pit, the
break the ice
breath of spring
breathe freely
bright and early
bring to his knees
brute force

build upon sand
bundle of nerves
burden of proof
burn your fingers
burn the candle at both ends
burning question
bury the hatchet
buy a pig in a poke
buy for a song
by hook or by crook
by the same token
by the sweat of your brow
by word of mouth

C

call a spade a spade
call in question
calm before the storm
can say safely that ...
cart before the horse
casual encounter
casual remark
charmed life
chip off the old block
circumstances beyond one's control
clear the decks
coast is clear, the
come home to roost

come on the scene
come to light
come to the end of one's rope
considered opinion, my
constant communication, be in
controversial question
cook someone's goose
crocodile tears
cry over spilt milk
cry wolf once too often
crystal-clear
cut off your nose to spite your face

D

dark horse
days are numbered
dead and gone
deliver the goods, to
devoted soley to
dictates of your conscience
dim and distant path
do a good turn, to
do or die, to

dog's life, a
don't you know?
down and out
down to the last detail
drag into the mire
drenched to the skin
drift apart, to
drown your sorrows in drink
dyed in the wool

E

each and every
eat out of someone's hand
eat humble pie
eat one's heart out
eat out of house and home
eleventh hour, the
ends of the earth, the
entertain high hopes

escape by the skin of your teeth
escape unscathed
even if the worst happens
every last one
every man has his price
explore every avenue
express concern, to
express appreciation

F

fair and square
fall on deaf ears
far and away
far and wide
far cry from
far from accurate
far-reaching effects
far-reaching policy
fast and furious
feel in your bones
feet of clay
festive occasion
few and far between
fight tooth and nail
filled to capacity
find it in your heart, to
fingers are itching
firm footing
first and foremost
fish out of water
fit for a king
fit to hold a candle to, not
flashed through my mind
flesh and blood

fly in the ointment
foam at the mouth
follow in the footsteps of
for all I know
for better or worse
for love or money
for the life of me
for what it's worth
fobidden fruit
force to be reckoned with
foregone conclusion
formulate a plan
four corners of the earth
fraught with danger
free and easy
friend in need
frightened out of one's wit
from A to Z
from bad to worse
from head to heels
from pillar to post
from the bottom of your heart
from the cradle to the grave
further the interest

G

gala occasion
generous to a fault
get down to brass tacks
get more than you bargained for
get a second wind

get your teeth into
get up on the wrong side of the bed
gift of tongues
five and take
give the Devil his due

go at it hammer and tong
go by the board
go hat in hand
go in one ear and out the other
go off with your tail between
  your legs
go on the warpath
go the whole hog
go through fire and water for
go to the dogs

go to the other extreme
goes without saying
gone but not forgotten
good, bad or indifferent
good clean fun
good for nothing
good Samaritan
grand finale, the
grievous error
grin and bear it

H

handle with kid gloves
hang by a thread
happy ending, a
hard and fast
hard facts
hat in hand
have a bone to pick with
have a shot at something
have at your fingertips
have your cake and eat it too
have too many irons in the fire
have too much of a good thing
head and shoulders above
hear a pin drop

heart bleeds for
heart of gold
heavy responsibilties
helping hand
here today and gone tomorrow
hide your light under a bushel
high and dry
hit below the belt
hit or miss
hit the nail on the head
hold forth
hold your own
horse of another color

I

I could hardly believe my eyes
if the truth were known
in a nutshell
in a word
in one ear and out the other
in hot water
in my opinion

in no uncertain terms
in the nick of time
in the same book
ins and outs
it goes without saying
it may interest you to know that
it stands to reason that

K

keep a stiff upper lip
keep body and soul together
keep the ball rolling
kill the goose that lays the
  golden eggs
kill two birds with one stone

kindred spirit
know full well
know which side your bread is
  buttered on
know where you stand

L

labor of love
last but not least
last legs to be on
last straw, the
late in the day
lay down the law
lead a dog's life
leave much to be desired
left out in the cold

left to his own devices
let the cat out of the bag
let slip through your fingers
little bird told me, a
live from hand to mouth
live in the past
lock, stock and barrel
long and short of it

M

make a clean breast of it
make ends meet
make your hair stand on end
make your mouth water
man to man
milk of kindness

monumental effort
more or less
move heaven and earth
much as I hate to do it
must, if necessary
my opinion, in

N

neck and neck
needle in a haystack
needs no introduction
neither fish nor fowl
nip it in the bud
no expense has been spared

no mistakes of any kind
no uncertain terms (words)
nodding acquaintance
nose to the grindstone
not one iota
not worth the paper it's written on

O

of no avail
off and on
official capacity
once and for all
one in a thousand

only too glad
out of the blue
outstanding features
overcome by emotion
own worst enemy

P

paramount importance
parting shot
personal attack
pick and choose
picture of health
play with fire

pool our resources
powers that be
pay on your mind
proud parents
pull some strings
put all your eggs in one basket

R

rain cats and dogs	risk life and limb
rank and file	root of the matter
rap on the knuckles	rough and tumble
really and truly	rough diamond
reply in the affirmative	rub the wrong way
return to the fold	rule the roost

S

salt of the earth	so far as that goes
say the least	social whirl
scathing criticism	sound policy
second to none	sour grapes
see eye to eye	spare no pains
see it through	spend money like water
sell like hot cakes	spick and span
set your house in order	square deal
shake in your shoes	stab in the back
short and sweet	steer clear of
sight for sore eyes	step by step
sit on the fence	stick to your guns
skate on thin ice	strike while the iron is hot
smell a rat	sum and substance
sneaking doubt	supply and demand

T

take immediate steps	through thick and thin
take the bull by the horns	time and time again
take the rough with the smooth	time immemorial
taken aback	to a fault
task confronts us	to say the least
team spirit	too numerous to mention
tear your hair out	touch and go
thing of the past	trials and tribulations
thorn in your flesh	turn the tables on

U

under the sun	up in arms
untold advantages	ups and downs

V

venture a guess	visible to the naked eye

W

wash your hands of	win hands down
ways and means	with a vengeance
weather the storm	with bated breath

Y

your earliest convenience	your guess is as good as mine

Tired Expressions

Words to Avoid	Better
above (mentioned)	this
accede to	grant
accordingly	so
according to our record	we find
activate	start
acquaint (with)	tell
acquire	get
active consideration, under	under consideration
ad hoc	this, temporary, specific
adjunct	tool; assistant
agreement, be in	agree
amount	number, quantity
ancillary	secondary
and/or	both; either
appear	seem
appreciates, (it will be appreciated)	I appreciate
approximately	about
as per your request	as you requested
assist	help
attached hereto;	here is
at the due date	when due
at this time	now
bilateral	two-sided
by reason of	because of
causal factors	causes; reasons
cognizance of, take	notice
communicate	write, tell
comprehensive	complete
conflagration	fire
consequently	so
consider	think

Words to Avoid	Better
consume	eat
create	establish
decided, (it has been decided)	we decided; it is decided
demonstrate	show
determine	decide
disparity	difference
domicile	home
due to the fact that	because
effect (a change)	make
effectuate	do
employ of, be in the	work for
enclosed you will find	I've enclosed
encounter	meet
entail	mean; require; impose
entertainment-value	fun
entity	thing
erratum	mistake; error
expedite	speed up
facilitate	make it easy
feasible, it is	we can do it
following, the	these
for the purpose of	to, for
for your information	(not needed at all)
future, in the near	soon
gear	modify
give particular attention to	read carefully
have the effect of	result in
have the need for	need
in all cases	always
increment	increase
indicated	told
in due course	soon
initial	first
initiate	start
in my opinion	I think
innumerable	many
in order to	to
inquire	ask
in the interim	meanwhile
it has come to my attention	I've learned
modification	change
multiplicity of	many
on the basis of	by

Words to Avoid	Better
opinion, I am of the	I think
optimum	best
partake of	eat
per capita	each
per se	itself
personnel	people
peruse	read
please don't hesitate to …	please …
prior	before
proceed	go
procure	get
productivity	output
render inoperable	disable
require	need; order
signature, under one's	signed by
subsequent to	after
take into account	consider
tangential	incidental
tantamount to	the same as
terminate	end
the undersigned	me, I
transpire	happen
viable alternative	choice

Business "In" Words: Jargon

There are other words chosen to confuse a reader. Here are 30 words, often used at random and in combination, to make a business letter, memo, or report seem more impressive than it really is. (A good business writer will generally try to avoid using them unless there is a specific, clear meaning intended.)

capability	integrated	policy
compatible	logistical	programming
concept	management	projection
contingency	mobility	reciprocal
digital	monitored	responsive
enhanced	optimal	synchronized
flexibility	options	systematized
functional	organizational	third-generation
hardware	parallel	time-phase
incremental	parameter	transitional

Bureaucratic Doublespeak

Doublespeak Words	What They Mean
above, the	this, that
adjust	help, tune
administrative democracy	equal authority
amount	quantity, number
appear to be	seem
approximately	about
bureaucracy	structure
category	class
comprised of	composed of
concerning	about
conflagration	fire
conservative	moderate
considerate	thoughtful
correspondence	letters
create	make, establish
data	facts
demise	death
due to	because of
duplex	double
education	learning
effect	do
effected	caused
elemental	basic
entity	thing
explore	investigate
finances	money
function	duty
hiatus	gap
however	but
impact	influence
incident to	related to
indicate	seem necessary
initiate	start
integrate	combine, unite
involuntary separation	firing
liquidate	destroy
objective	goal, purpose
obtain	get
overall	general
partially	partly
pending	awaited, not decided
picture	situation
planned parenthood	birth control

Doublespeak Words	What They Mean
portion	part
prior to	before
probative	probable
psychological	mental
purchase	buy
pursuant to	after
rehabilitate	repair, restore
relating to, regarding	about
state	condition
status	condition, state
subsequent to	after
tangential	borderline, irrelevant
through channels	red tape
undersigned, the	I, we
unique	unusual
utilize	use

15. WORDS FREQUENTLY CONFUSED

The English language is one of the most difficult for foreigners to learn because there are so many exceptions to the rules. Furthermore, many of our words sound alike but have quite different meanings—such as allusion, elusion, and illusion.

Here's a list of words often confused with each other.

ABJURE	renounce or reject
ADJURE	command or entreat
ABSORPTION	taking up or drinking in;
ADSORPTION	adhesion of gas or liquid to a solid's surface
ACCEDE	adhere to an agreement
EXCEED	surpass
ACCEPT	receive
EXCEPT	exclude
ADAPT	adjust to a new use
ADEPT	skilled
ADOPT	choose your own
ADHERENTS	followers
ADHERENCE	steady attachment
ADHESION	sticking together
ADMISSION	the right to enter
ADMITTANCE	permission to enter
ADVERSE	opposing
ADVERSE TO	not inclined to
ADVICE	(noun) recommendation, counsel, notice given
ADVISE	(verb) counsel, notify.
AFFECT	influence, change
EFFECT	accomplish (verb); result (noun)
AGENDA	list of things to be done at a meeting
ADDENDA	(plural) things to be added, as in a supplement or an appendix
AID	help; helper
AIDE	confidential assistant
ALL READY	entirely ready
ALREADY	action has occured

ALL TOGETHER	in a body
ALTOGETHER	entirely
ALLUSION, ALLUDE	reference by suggestion
DELUSION, DELUDE	a false idea
ELUSION, ELLUDE	avoidance
ILLUSION, ILLUDE	visual deception
ALTAR	place of worship
ALTER	change
ALTERNATE	substitute
ALTERNATIVE	choice between two things
ALTOGETHER	entirely
ALL TOGETHER	in one group
AMNESIA	loss of memory
APHASIA	loss of speech
ASPHYXIA	suffocation
ASTASIA	inability to stand
AMONG	reference to more than two
BETWEEN	reference to only two persons
AMOUNT	bulk; the sum total
NUMBER	something counted
QUANTITY	something measured
ANALYST	someone who analyzes
ANNALIST	writer of annals (records)
ANTE-	prefix meaning "before"
ANTI-	prefix meaning "against"
ANTEDATE	date back
POSTDATE	date forward
ANTIDOTE	remedy
ANECDOTE	interesting story
ANTISEPTIC	something that destroys bacteria
ANESTHETIC	something that desensitizes
ASEPTIC	free from germs
ANY WAY	in any single way
ANYWAY	in any event
A PIECE	by the piece
APIECE	each
APPRAISE	put a value on
APPRISE	inform
APPRIZE	put a value on
APPRIZE	inform

APPERTAIN	belong
PERTAIN	belong
APPURTENANCE	an accessory
PERTINENT	applicable
APT	suitable
LIABLE	legally bound
LIKELY	possible
ARC	curved line
ARK	place of refuge
ARRAIGN	call into court
ARRANGE	put in order
ASCETIC	austere
ACETIC	sour
ASSAY	analyse or test
ESSAY	short composition
ASSEMBLAGE	unorganized gathering
ASSEMBLY	organized gathering
ASSENT	consent
ACCENT	stress
ASCENT	rise
ASTRAY	off the right path
ESTRAY	thing out of place
STRAY	wanderer
ASTROLOGY	study of the influence of the stars on people
ASTRONOMY	science of the heavenly bodies
AUGER	tool
AUGUR	foretoken, foreshadowing
AUGHT	anything
OUGHT	should
AVIARY	place for birds
APIARY	place for bees
AWAY	away from
AWEIGH	lift anchor
A WHILE	short period
AWHILE	for a while
BAD	defective
BADE	told or commanded
BAIL	dip up; parachute from, release security; pail handle
BALE	large, compacted bundle

BAIT	lure
BATE	moderate, lessen
BARBARIAN	uncivilized
BARBARIC	primitive, crude
BARBAROUS	cruel, primitive, crude
BARK	outer part of a tree
BARQUE	three-masted sailing ship
BARON	nobleman
BARREN	unfruitful
BASE	material foundation
BASIS	fundamental theory
BATHOS	move from the sublime to the ridiculous
PATHOS	sadness
BAZAAR	fair
BIZARRE	fantastic
BELLOW	loud noise
BILLOW	high wave or mass
BESIDE	at the side of
BESIDES	in addition to
BIANNUAL	twice a year
BIENNIAL	every two years
BLOC	combination for political strength
BLOCK	quantity or unit
BOAR	swine
BOOR	rude person
BORE	drill; carried
BORN	brought into life
BORN	held, carried
BOURNE	brook; a goal
BOUILLON	clear soup
BULLION	uncoined gold or silver bars or ingots
BOW	tie, weapon, violin bow, bend
BOW	foward part of a ship;
BOUGH	branch of a tree
BRAISE	brown and then cook slowly
BRAZE	solder or join
BREACH	break or gap
BREECH	rear or lower part
BRIDAL	related to a wedding
BRIDLE	horse's headgear; something restraining

BRITAIN	Great Britain: England, Wales, and Scotland
BRITON	native British subject
BRETON	native of Bretagne (Brittany, in France)
BRITISHER	British subject
BROACH	open, introduce
BROOCH	ornamental pin
BULLION	gold or silve metal
BOUILLON	broth
CAGEY	sly; shrewd
CADGING	begging or sponging
CALENDAR	time schedule
CALENDER	press for cloth, paper rubber, rubber
COLANDER	strainer
CALLOUS	(adj.) hardened
CALLUS	(noun) a hardened surface
CANE	walking stick
CAIN	the brother of Abel
CANNON	huge gun
CANON	law or rule
CANVAS	strong tent cloth
CANVASS	to solicit
CAPITAL	chief, weath
CAPITOL	the official building of Congress in Washington, D.C.
CAROUSAL	boisterous drinking
CARROUSEL	military horseback tournament; a merry-go-round
CASH	money
CACHE	hiding place
CACHET	seal or stamp
CASTER	small wheel or roller
CASTOR	beaver or its fur; dull color
CASUAL	incidental; unimportant
CAUSAL	related to a cause
CENSOR	critic
CENSURE	condemn
CENSER	vessel for burning incense
CITE	quote an authority or proof
SIGHT	view, see
SITE	place, spot

CHAFE	anger, irritate
CHAFF	worthless; teasing
CHAMPAGNE	sparkling white wine
CHAMPAIGN	flat expanse or open country
CHASED	pursued; ornamented, as "chased gold"
CHASTE	virtuous; pure in design or style, not ornate
CHILDISH	petty; small
CHILDLIKE	innocent
CLAMBER	climb
CLAMOR	noise
CLAQUE	paid applauders; admirers
CLICK	light, sharp sound
CLICHÉ	stereotyped or trite phrase
CLIQUE	small social set
CLIENT	person who uses the services of a professional person
CUSTOMER	person who buys a commodity or service
CLIMATIC	related to climate
CLIMACTIC	related to a climax
CLIMACTERIC	crisis; crucial period of time; a period of physiological change
CLINCH	grab or clamp
CLENCH	grip tensely
COARSE	rough
COURSE	direction; action; part of a meal
COLLEAGUE	associate in a profession
PARTNER	member of a business partnership
COLLISION	clash
COLLUSION	secret agreement to defraud
COMPARE	examine for similarities
CONTRAST	show differences
CONTINUAL	frequently recurring
CONTINUOUS	uninterrupted
CRUMBLE	break into fragments
CRUMPLE	crush and wrinkle
CUE	signal
QUEUE	line of people
CURRANT	berry
CURRENT	flowing, general course; present
DAM	barrier
DAMN	curse

DECENT	respectable
DESCENT	downward
DISSENT	disagreement
DECRY	censure
DESCRY	spot something distant; detect
DISCREDIT	destroy confidence in
DISPARAGE	show disrespect for
DEMEAN	degrade
DEMESNE	lands or estate
DEPOSITORY	place where something is deposited
DEPOSITARY	person or trustee with whom you deposit something
DEPRECATE	disapprove
DEPRECIATE	decrease in value
DESECRATE	profane
DESCENDANT	an offspring
DESCENEDENT	descending
DESERT	abandon
DESERT	barren land
DESSERT	last course of a meal
DESERVE	be worthy of
DISSERVE	treat badly
DESIRABLE	worth desiring
DESIROUS	entertaining desire
DETRACT	take away from
DISTRACT	divert attention
DICTOGRAPH	interoffice telephone
DICTAPHONE	dictation device
DISINTERESTED	lack of self-interest
UNINTERESTED	not interested, indifferent
DISCOMFIT	baffle
DISCOMFORT	pain
DISCREET	prudent
DISCRETE	distinct or separate
DISINTERESTED	impartial
UNINTERESTED	not interested
DISPENSE	distribute
DISPENSE WITH	do without
DISPERSE	scatter
DISBURSE	pay out

DISSEMINATE	spread widely or broadcast
DISSIMULATE	conceal by pretending
DISTINCT	individual; separate
DISTINCTIVE	characteristic
DISTRAIT	absent-minded
DISTRAUGHT	distracted
DRAFT	an air current, an order
DRAUGHT	damper; drawn drink
DROUGHT	dryness from lack of rain
DYING	about to die
DYEING	coloring
DIEING	stamping with a die
EGOISM	excessive thought of self
EGOTISM	excessive talk of self
ELDEST	relate to the age of people in one family
OLDEST	relates to the age of other people and things
ELEMENTAL	primal, natural
ELEMENTARY	basic; rudimentary
ELIGIBLE	qualified
ILLEGIBLE	hard to read
LEGIBLE	easy to read
EMERGE	rise from
IMMERGE	plunge into water
EMIGRATE	leave a country
IMMIGRATE	come into a country
EMOLLIENT	soothing application
EMOLUMENT	remuneration
EMPIRE	imperial organization
REFEREE	one who decides issues in a game
UMPIRE	a judge
ENERVATE	weaken
INNERVATE	stimulate
ENERGIZE	give energy to
ENORMOUSNESS	vastness of size
ENORMITY	greatness of horror
ENTOMOLOGY	insect zoology
ETYMOLOGY	the history of words
ENVELOP	to wrap around
ENVELOPE	cover or wrapper
EPIC	action poem in heroic style
EPOCH	memorable period of time

EPITAPH	inscription for the dead
EQUITABLE	fair; just
ERASABLE	can be erased
IRASCIBLE	quick-tempred
ERR	to make a mistake
ERE	before
E'ER	a contracton of "ever"
AIR	expose
ERRANT	notoriously bad
ARRANT	wandering
ERUPTION	bursting out
IRRUPTION	bursting in
EUPHEMISM	a softened statement
EUPHUISM	high-flown language style
EXALT	glorify
EXULT	rejoice
EXCEED	surpass
ACCEDE	yield
EXCEPT	leave out
ACCEPT	receive
EXCEPTIONABLE	open to exception
EXCEPTIONAL	uncommon
EXCESS	beyond the usual
EXCESSIVE	beyond what is reasonable
EXCITE	stir up emotionally
INCITE	stir into action
EXERCISE	put into practice; to train
EXORCISE	drive out an evil spirit
EXHIBIT	to display; something displayed
EXHIBITION	a public display, such as artwork or skill
EXPOSITION	explanation; show
EXIT	go out
EXODUS	going away
ESOTERIC	private; understood by only a few
EXOTIC	of foreign origin
EXOTERIC	popular
EXPATIATE	enlarge
EXPIATE	atone for
EXPEDIENT	personally advantageous
EXPEDITIOUS	speedy

EXTANT	still existing
EXTENT	measure; degree
EXTRACT	large, selected literary passage
EXCERPT	small, carefully selected literary passage
FACET	one of many small flat surfaces
FAUCET	tap
FACETIOUS	causing laughter
FACTIOUS	caused by a faction
FACTITIOUS	artificial
FICTITIOUS	not real
FAIN	gladly
FEIGN	to pretend
FAINT	weak
FEINT	trick
FAKER	one who fakes
FAKIR	wandering religious wonder-worker
FAMOUS	celebrated
NOTED	well-known
NOTORIOUS	unfavorably noted
FARTHER	relates to actual distance
FURTHER	additional
FATAL	causing death or destruction
FATEFUL	full of dangerous possibilities
FATE	destiny
FETE	festival; to honor
FINELY	in a fine manner;
FINALLY	at last
FLARE	spreading out
FLAIR	aptitude
FLAUNT	to display or show off
FLOUT	to insult
FLEW	did fly
FLU	influenza
FLUE	a chimney
FLOUNDER	struggle clumsily
FOUNDER	fill with water and sink
FLOW	move smoothly
FLOE	flat mass of floating ice
FOGGY	clouded
FOGY	someone behind the times

FOLLOW	to come after
FALLOW	to plow land but leave it unseeded
FONT	receptacle for holy water
FOUNT	spring; source
FOR	in place of, in the interest of
FORE	first; preceding
FOUR	numeral
FORBEAR	refrain from
FOREBEAR	ancestor
FORCEFUL	effective
FORCIBLE	powerful
FORGO	go without
FOREGO	go before
FORMALLY	in a formal manner
FORMERLY	previously
FORT	fortified place
FORTE	special talent
FORWARD	eager
FORWARD	obstinate
FREEZE	to become ice
FRIEZE	an ornamental strip
FULL	abundant
FULSOME	coarse; offensive
FUNERAL	burial
FUNEREAL	sad or solemn
GAMBLE	wager
GAMBOL	frolic about
GAMUT	scale or range
GANTLET	punishment
GAUNTLET	glove
GAP	opening
GAPE	yawn
GENTEEL	well-bred
GENTILE	someone not a Jew
GENTLE	mild
GOURMAND	someone overly fond of good food
GOURMET	connoisseur of fine food
GRILL	gridiron
GRILLE	wrought-iron framework

GRISLY	ghastly
GRIZZLY	somewhat gray
GUARANTEE	to warrant performance
GUARANTY	financial security
HAIL	frozen rain; to call
HARDY	able to withstand hardship
HEARTY	vigorous
HART	stag
HEART	part of the body
HEALTHFUL	producing good health
HEALTHY	enjoying good health
HEARSAY	rumor
HERESY	an opinion that is opposite the accepted belief
HEW	cut or chop
HUE	color; tint
HIE	hurry
HIGH	lofty
HISTORIC	history-making
HISTORICAL	relating to history
HISTRIONIC	relating or pertaining to theatrics
HOARD	hidden supply
HORDE	roaming pack or tribe
HOLEY	full of holes
HOLY	sacred
WHOLLY	entirely
HOLLY	a shrub
HOMELY	plain
HOMEY	homelike
HOMOGENEOUS	having like parts
HOMOGENOUS	similar because of origin in structure
HYPERCRITICAL	overcritical
HYPOCRITICAL	deceitful
IDLE	inactive
IDOL	object of worship
IDYL	rustic scene
ILLICIT	unlawful
ELICIT	draw out
IMAGINARY	existing only in the imagination

IMAGINATIVE	actually existing, but created by imagination
IMBRUE	stain (with blood)
IMBUE	saturate
ENDUE	clothe
IMMERGE	plunge under
EMERGE	rise out of
IMMANENT	inherent
IMMINENT	impending
EMANATE	originate
EMINENT	distinguished
IMMORAL	sinful
AMORAL	neither moral nor immoral
UNMORAL	without morals
IMPASSABLE	not passable
IMPASSIBLE	not feeling pain
IMPASSIVE	unemotional
IMPERIAL	relating to an empire
EMPIRICAL	based on experience
EMPYREAL	celestial
IMPOSSIBLE	not possible
IMPRACTICABLE	not possible under current conditions
IMPLY	suggest indirectly
INFER	deduce from
IMPOSTER	pretender
IMPOSTURE	the act of a pretender
INCARCERATION	imprisonment
INCARNATION	embodiment in a living form
INCIDENTS	occurences
INCIDENCE	range of occurence
INCREDIBLE	unbelievable
INCREDULOUS	skeptical
INDITE	put into words
INDICT	charge with an offense
INDIGENOUS	originating from a certain region
INDIGENT	poor
INDISCREET	imprudent
INDISCRETE	compact, having similar elements
INEPT	awkward

INAPT	unsuited
INFECT	have germs
INFEST	overrun with
INGENIOUS	clever
INGENUOUS	artlessly frank
INSENSATE	incapable of sensation
INSENSIBLE	unable to feel
INSENSITIVE	not sensitive
INSENTIENT	inanimate
INSIGHT	mental vision
INCITE	spur to action
INSIPIENT	unwise
INCIPIENT	beginning
INSOLUBLE	incapable of being dissolved
INSOLVABLE	not solvable
INSOLVENT	someone who can't pay his debts
INSTANCE	example
INSTANT	a moment
INSULATE	to protect from
INSOLATE	to expose to the sun
INSURE	to guarantee against
ENSURE	to make sure
ASSURE	to make confident
INTERPELLATE	to ask for an explanation
INTERPOLATE	to insert computed values
EXTRAPOLATE	to deduce unknown values from known values
INTERSTATE	between two or more states
INTRASTATE	within one state
INURE	to toughen
IMMURE	confine
JIBE	to agree; to shift a sail
GIBE	to taunt
JUDICIAL	A relating to a judge
JUDICIOUS	wise
JUNCTION	joining things
JUNCTURE	joining times or events
KARAT	a measure for gold
CARAT	a measure for precious stones
CARET	a correction mark

LATER	at a subsequent time; more recent
LATTER	second of two; near the end
LATH	a strip of wood (lath)
LATHE	a machine for turning materials
LEACH	filter through something
LEASH	strap for a dog
LEECH	blood-sucking worm; the edge of a sail
LEAD	heavy metal
LED	guided
LEGIBLE	easy to read
ELIGIBLE	qualified to be chosen
LESSEE	tenant
LESSOR	one who give a lease
LEVEE	embsnkment; warf
LEVY	assess or collect
LIABLE	responsible
LIBEL	written, published defamation
LIFELONG	lasting through life
LIVELONG	long in passing
LIGHTENING	making lighter
LIGHTNING	sudden electrical charge in the sky
LINEAMENTS	outline or contour
LINIMENT	ointment
LINEAL	relates to ancestral lines
LINEAR	relates to lines or measurement
LIQUEUR	an alcoholic cordial
LIQUOR	liquid, alcoholic
LITERAL	exact facts
LITTORAL	relating to a shore;
LIVID	discolored, black and blue
LURID	ghastly
LOATH	reluctant; unwilling
LOATHE	to detest
LOCAL	pertaining to a limited space
LOCALE	locality
LUXURIANT	abundant
LUXURIOUS	promoting luxury
MADDENING	enraging
MADDING	raging
MAGNATE	influential, rich person

MAGNET	something with magnetic attraction
MAGNIFICENT	having spelndor
MUNIFICENT	unusually generous
MAJORITY	more than half
PLURALITY	the largest number of votes cast
MANTEL	structure around a fireplace
MANTLE	cloak
MARINE	relating to the ocean
MARITIME	bordering on the ocean
MARITAL	pertaining to marriage
MARTIAL (MARSHAL)	pertaining to war, military
MARSHAL	arrange; an official
MASTERFUL	filled with power
MASTERLY	having superior skill
MATERIAL	substance
MATERIEL	equipment
MEAN	intend
MESNE	middle
MIEN	appearance
MEAT	food; the flesh of animals
MEET	join (Law) just,
METE	measure out
MERITORIOUS	deserving of praise
MERETRICIOUS	tawdry
METICULOUS	careful
METAL	hard substance
METTLE	spirit, courage
METER	measure
METIER	profession
MILLENARY	thousandth
MILLINERY	pertaining to hats
MINER	someone who mines
MINOR	someone under age; smaller
MISSIVE	letter or written message
MISSILE	something thrown or shot
MITIGATE	make less severe
MILITATE	operate against
MODAL	relating to a mode (modal)
MODEL	pattern or example
MODE	method
MOOD	disposition or feeling

MORAL	right conduct
MORALE	state of mind
NAUGHT	zero
NOUGHT	nothing
NAVAL	relating to the navy
NAVEL	central part
NAVE	center of a church
KNAVE	rogue
NAY	no
NEE	born (woman's maiden name)
NEIGH	sound a horse makes
NECESSITIES	things urgently needed
NECESSARIES	things usually needed
NEEDED	wanted
NEEDFUL	necessary
NEEDY	in need
NEGLECT	act of neglecting
NEGLIGENCE	habit of neglecting
OBSERVANCE	complying with
OBSERVATION	seeing, watching
OCCULTIST	believer in supernatural powers
OCULIST	physician who treats diseases of the eyes; an ophthalmologist
OPTICIAN	person who makes optical glasses according to prescriptions
OPTOMETRIST	person who measures the range or powers of vision and prescribes corrective glasses or contact lenses
OFFICIAL	a person with executive powers
OFFICIOUS	unauthorized; meddlesome
ONE	single thing
WON	past tense of win
ORAL	something spoken
VERBAL	by word of mouth; word for word
ORDINANCE	law
ORDNANCE	military ammunition and supplies
ORDONNANCE	an arrangement in order
OSCILLATE	swing back and forth
OSCULATE	kiss
VACILLATE	waver
OVERDO	do to excess
OVERDUE	past due

PACKED	crowded
PACT	an agreement
PALATE	part of the mouth
PALETTE	an artist's color board
PALLET	shabby bed
PARTAKE	take some of
PARTICIPATE	take part in
PARTLY	in part
PARTIALLY	to some degree
PAST	time gone by
PASSED	gone beyond
PIQUE	provoke
PIQUÉ	a ribbed cotton fabric
PEARL	gem
PURL	to flow in swirls; a knitting stitch
PEDAL	a foot lever
PEDDLE	sell from house to house
PEER	equal
PIER	support pillar
PENDANT	something that hangs
PENDENT	suspended
PERCENT	number of parts to 100
PERCENTAGE	relationship of a part to the whole of 100 parts
PEREMPTORY	decisive; dictatorial
PREEMPTIVE	right of preference
PERQUISITE	an extra privilege
PREREQUISITE	something required
PERSECUTE	torment; oppress
PROSECUTE	pursue in order to accomplish; (Law) to sue
PERSONALITY	personal qualities
PERSONALTY	personal property
PERSONAL	individual
PERSONNEL	staff
PERSPECTIVE	mental view
PROSPECTIVE	expected
PESPICACIOUS	mentally sharp
PERSPICUOUS	clear
PHYSIC	medicine
PHYSIQUE	the body's structure
PSYCHIC	relating to the soul, mind, or spirit

PICARESQUE	relating to rogues
PICTURESQUE	charming qualities of a picture
PIDGIN	Chinese corruption of "business,"
PIGEON	dove
PLAINTIFF	someone who brings suit
PLAINTIVE	mournful
PLAT	piece of land
PLAIT	braid
PLATE	flat piece
PLEAT	fold cloth
PLUM	fruit
PLUMB	weight
POLE	long wooden rod
POLL	voting place
POLITICALLY	relating to politics
POLITICLY	discreetly
POPLAR	tree
POPULAR	relating to people
POPULACE	common people
POPULOUS	thickly populated
POST CARD	a private mailing card
POSTAL CARD	a card printed by the government with the stamp already on it
POWER	strength
PROWESS	combined strength and courage
PRACTICABLE	can be efficiently accomplished
PRACTICAL	efficient
PRECEDE	go before
PROCEED	advance
PRECEDENCE	priority
PRECEDENTS	established rules
PRECIPITOUS	steep as a precipice
PRECIPITATE	sudden; hasten; to condense and fall, as rain or snow
PRECIPITANT	rash; cause of condensation
PREDICATE	assert
PREDICT	foretell
PREMIER	chief
PREMIERE	the opening performance
PRESCRIBE	designate
PROSCRIBE	outlaw

PRESENTIMENT	foreboding
PRESENTMENT	presentation or report
PRESENTATION	showing
PRESENTS	gifts; present writings
PRESENCE	attendance
PREVIEW	an advance view
PURVIEW	the range or scope
PRINCIPAL	chief; main
PRINCIPLE	rule
PROCEEDING	moving forward; a course of action
PRECEDING	going before
PRODIGY	marvel
PROGENY	offspring
PROTÉGÉ	someone cared for by another
PROPORTIONAL	determined by proportion
PROPORTIONATE	in proportion to
PROPOSAL	offer for consideration
PROPOSITION	project for adoption, with terms and good points outlined
PROTAGONIST	chief advocate
ANTAGONIST	an opponent; foe
PURPOSE	have as a purpose; intend
PROPOSE	offer for consideration
RACK	frame; torment
WRACK	debris thrown ashore by the sea
RAIL	bar; scold
RAILING	bar, composed of several rails
RAIN	falling drops of water
REIGN	rule
REIN	curb; restraint
RAISE	lift or produce something
RAYS	beams
RAZE	destroy
RISE	lift itself or oneself
RAPPED	struck with quick blows
RAPT	engrossed
REAL	true
REEL	winding device
REALITY	something that is real
REALTY	real estate

REBOUND	bounce back
REDOUND	return, react
RECOGNIZANCE	legally, a recorded promise
RECONNAISSANCE	survey tour
RECOURSE	resorting to for assistance
RESOURCE	something or someone you turn to for support
REFECTORY	dining hall
REFRACTORY	unmanageable
REFERENCE	directing attention toward
REFERRAL	act of referring something
REGIMEN	regulated procedure
REGIME	term of government
REGISTER	record; list
REGISTRAR	keeper of records
REGISTRY	place where you keep a register
REPULSIVE	driving back or repelling
REVULSIVE	causes a desire to turn away from
RESPECTFULLY	with respect
RESPECTIVELY	in the order designated
RESTIVE	balky; fretting
RESTLESS	fidgety; constantly moving
RESTFUL	giving rest
RESTRAIN	hold back
RESTRICT	confine
RESUME	begin again
RÉSUMÉ	summing up
SAMPLE	part of anything inspected
SPECIMEN	part intended to show the quality of the whole
REVERENCE	profound respect
REVEREND	worthy of reverence
REVERENT	expressing reverence
SAC	pouch containing fluid
SACK	bag; dismiss; ("sack coat," a man's coat)
SALARY	fixed compensation for office work
WAGES	daily or weekly pay for manual labor
SANGUINARY	attended with bloodshed
SANGUINE	hopeful

SCRIP	certificate
SCRIPT	style of handwriting
SEASONABLE	timely; in keeping with the season
SEASONAL	periodical; affected by the seasons
SELL	transfer for a price
CELL	small place of confinement
SELLER	one who sells
CELLAR	underground storeroom (saltcellar)
SENSES	faculties
SENSITIVE	easily offended or affected
SENSUAL	relating the baser senses
SENSUOUS	appealing to the finer senses
SESSION	assembly
CESSION	giving over
SECESSION	withdrawal
CESSATION	stopping or ceasing
SLEW	killed
SLUE	twist
SLOUGH	mudhole
SLOUGH	slowly flowing water in a marsh
SLOUGH	cast off
SLICK	slippery
SLEEK	glossy
SLIGHT	small
SLEIGHT	skill
SLOW	not rapid
SLOE	plumlike fruit
SEW	stich
SOUGH	the sighing or murmuring of the wind (sou, or suf)
SOW	scatter
SOME TIME	period of time
SOMETIME	an indefinite time
SOMETIMES	now and then
SPACIOUS	large
SPECIOUS	something that only appears to be right
SPECIAL	specific
ESPECIAL	extraordinary
SPATIAL	pertaining to space
SPECIALLY	in a special manner
ESPECIALLY	particularly

SPECIE	coin
SPECIES	kind
SPY	discover
ESPY	catch sight of
STABLE	steady, firm
STAPLE	chief, regular
STATIONARY	fixed, not moving
STATIONERY	writing materials
STATUE	carved likeness
STATURE	height of a person
STATUTE	enacted law
STAUNCH	firm; steadfast
STANCH	stop the flow of blood
STIMULANT	excitant
STIMULATION	effect produced
STIMULUS	incentive
STRAIGHT	not curved
STRAIT	narrow; tight
SUBJECTION	exposing to some force
SUBJUGATION	conquering and controlling
SUBTITLE	secondary title
SUBHEAD	subdivision heading
SIDEHEAD	subdivision heading at the side
SURGE	rising and falling
SERGE	fabric
SUSPECT	imagine
EXPECT	count on
SUPPOSE	think
SUSTENANCE	something which sustains life
SUBSISTENCE	maintenance
SWATH	sweep of the blade in mowing
SWATHE	wrap
SYMBOL	emblem
CYMBAL	platelike musical instrument
TALISMAN	charm
TALESMAN	persons added to a jury
TANTAMOUNT	equivalent
PARAMOUNT	highest
TEMBLOR	earthquake
TREMBLER	vibrating hammer
TREMOR	vibration

TEMERITY	rashness
TIMIDITY	shyness
TENANT	someone paying rent
TENET	shyness
TENOR	trend; intent; vocal range
TENURE	holding, length of term
TERMINAL	end
TERMINUS	boundary or goal
THEIR	pronoun
THERE	in that place
THEY'RE	they are
TIMBER	building wood
TIMBRE	tonal quality
WAIVER	giving up of a claim
WAVER	hesitate
WEIGHING	measuring the heaviness
WEIGHTED	made heavy
WEIGHTING	adding weight to

16. CAPITALIZATION MAKES A WORD SPECIAL

We use capital letters for two basic reasons; to show a beginning of something (such as a sentence), or to show that a proper noun or adjective is more important than a common noun. Here are the basic rules and examples of capitalization.

When to Capitalize:	Examples:
Abbreviations, if they represent proper nouns and adjectives	Jan. (for January), ABC (for American Broadcasting Company
Most acronyms (unless they've become a common word in everyday speech)	NATO, OPEC (but not radar, laser)
The first word of a sentence	We postponed the meeting.
The first word of a direct quote	"No, you can't go," he said.
The first word of a direct question	The question is this: Is it true?
The pronoun I	He and I both like it.
All proper nouns of specific persons, races, nationalities	William, Caucasian, American
Specific places and organizations	New York City, NAACP, AFL/CIO
Days of the week, months, holidays	Monday, June, Labor Day
Religious terms that are special	God, Christ, the Savior, the Virgin
Titles of books, plays, magazines, newspapers, articles, poems	*A Bell for Adonis, South Pacific, Apartment Life, The Times* "The Healing Touch," "Mending Wall."
Titles, when they precede a proper noun	Reverend Jones, President Robert Jones
(Unless the titles show especially high distinction, do not capitalize them after the nouns)	Robert Jones, president, said he …
Common nouns essential to a proper noun	Sterling Square; Jefferson Road

227

When to Capitalize:	Examples:
Compass directions, when they come at the start of a sentence or refer to specific geographical locations	North, south, east, and southeast appeared on the map. It's charming in the Old South
The names of seasons	Spring, Fall, Summer, Winter
Family relationships, unless they're preceded by a possessive (mother and father are exceptions)	My aunt has 10 children. My Uncle Charlie is fun. I wrote Mother. I wrote to my mother. I went to high school.
Nouns and adjectives used in place of proper nouns, nouns and adjectives	I went to Monroe High School. I took a psychology course. I took Psychology 201 last year.

Capitals and Abbreviations for Special People and Organizations

MILITARY TITLES

AIR FORCE

Titles for commissioned officers are the same as those in the Army. Capitalization is used when the rank precedes the name.

Enlisted Personnel

Chief Master Sgt.	Staff Sgt.
Senior Master Sgt.	Airman 1st Class
Master Sgt.	Airman
Tech. Sgt.	

ARMY

Commissioned Officers

Gen.	Ft. Col.
Lt. Gen.	Maj.
Maj. Gen.	Capt.
Brig. Gen.	1st Lt.
Col.	2nd Lt.

Warrant Officers

Chief Warrant Officer	Warrant Officer

Enlisted Personnel

Army Sgt. Maj.	Spec. 6
Command Sgt. Maj.	Sgt.
Staff Sgt. Maj.	Spec. 5
1st Sgt.	Cpl.
Master Sgt.	Spec. 4
Platoon Sgt.	Pfc.
Sgt. 1st Class	Pvt. 2
Spec. 7	Pvt.
Staff Sgt.	

MARINE CORPS

Ranks and abbreviations for commissioned officers are the same as those in the Army. Warrant officer ratings use the same system as the Navy. The Marines have no specialist ratings.

Sgt. Maj.	Sgt.
Master Gunnary Sgt.	Cpl.
Master Sgt.	Lance Cpl.
1st Sgt.	Pfc.
Gunnary Sgt.	Pvt.
Staff Sgt.	

NAVY, COAST GUARD

Commissioned Officers

Adm.	Cmdr.
Vice Adm.	Lt. Cmdr.
Rear Adm.	Lt.
Commodore	Lt. j.g.
Cpt.	Ensign

Warrant Officers

Commissoned Warrant Officer Warrant Officer

Enlisted Personnel

Master Chief Petty Officer	Petty Officer 3rd Class
Senior Chief Petty Officer	Seaman
Chief Petty Officer	Seaman Apprentice
Petty Officer 1st Class	Seaman Recruit
Petty Officer 2nd Class	

ACADEMIC DEGREES

Bachelor of Aeronautical Engineering
Bachelor of Agricultural Science
Bachelor of Agriculture
Bachelor of Applied Science
Bachelor of Architectural Science
Bachelor of Architecture
Bachelor of Arts
Bachelor of Arts in Education
Bachelor of Business Administration
Bachelor of Chemical Engineering
Bachelor of Chemical Science
Bachelor of Chemistry
Bachelor of Christian Science
Bachelor of Civil Engineering
Bachelor of Civil Law
Bachelor of Dental Surgery
Bachelor of Divinity
Bachelor of Education
Bachelor of Electrical Engineering
Bachelor of Engineering
Bachelor of Finance
Bachelor of Fine Arts
Bachelor of Forestry
Bachelor of Journalism
Bachelor of Laws
Bachelor of Letters
Bachelor of Liberal Arts
Bachelor of Library Science
Bachelor of Literature
Bachelor of Mechanical Engineering
Bachelor of Medicine
Bachelor of Mining Engineering
Bachelor of Music
Bachelor of Pedagogy
Bachelor of Pharmacy
Bachelor of Philosophy
Bachelor of Physical Education
Bachelor of Public Health
Bachelor of Sacred Theology
Bachelor of Science
Bachelor of Science in Education
Bachelor of Scientific Agriculture

ACADEMIC DEGREES, cont'd

Bachelor of (Science in) Social Sciences
Bachelor of Surgery
Bachelor of Theology

Master of Agriculture
Master of Arts
Master of (or in) Business Administration
Master of Civil Law
Master of Dental Surgery
Master of Education
Master of Laws
Master of Liberal Arts
Master of Library Science
Master of Music
Master of Pedagogy
Master of Pharmacy
Master of Physical Education
Master of Sacred Theology
Master of Science
Master of Surgery

Doctor of Canon Law
Doctor of Chemistry
Doctor of Chiropractic
Doctor of Christian Science
Doctor of Civil Law
Doctor of Commercial Science
Doctor of Divinity
Doctor of Dental Medicine
Doctor of Dental Science
Doctor of Dental Surgery
Doctor of Education
Doctor of Engineering
Doctor of Humanities
Doctor of Juridical Science
Doctor of Laws
Doctor of Letters (or Literature)
Doctor of Library Science
Doctor of Medicine
Doctor of Music
Doctor of Osteopathy
Doctor of Pedagogy

Academic Degrees

    Doctor of Pharmacy
    Doctor of Philosophy
    Doctor of Podiatry
    Doctor of Public Health
    Doctor of Public Hygiene
    Doctor of Sacred Theology
    Doctor of Science
    Doctor of Theology
    Doctor of Veterinary Medicine
    Doctor of Veterinary Medicine and Surgery

    Licentiate in Dental Surgery
    Licentiate in Medicine (or Midwifery)
    Licentiate in Surgery

DIPLOMATIC TITLES

    The American Consulate
    The Consulate of the United States of America
    The American Counsul
    The Counsul of the United States of America
    The Honorable John Doe, Consul
    The Ambassador of the United States of America
    Her Excellency, Jane Doe, Ambassador of...
    American Charge d'Affaires
    Minister of the United States of America

EDUCATIONAL TITLES

    Chancellor
    Chaplain
    Dean
    Instructor
    President
    Principal
    Assistant/Associate Professor
    Professor

FOREIGN GOVERNMENT OFFICIAL TITLES

    Premier of ...
    President of ...
    Prime Minister

Government Official, Federal

The Attorney General
The Secretary of ...
Chairman, Committee on ...
Commissioner
Director ... Agency
District Attorney
Judge of the United States District Court for the District of ...
The Postmaster General
President of the United States
Press Secretary to the President
The Honorable ... United States House of Representatives
The Honorable ... United States Senate
Senator-Elect
Speaker of the House of Representatives
Mr. Justice Doe, The Supreme Court of the United States
The Chief Justice of the United States
Delegate of ... House of Representatives
Undersecretary of ...
The Vice President of the United States

Government Official, Local

Alderman
Clerk of ...
Judge of ...
Court of ...
Mayor of ...
Attorney General of the State of ...
Clerk of the Court of ...
Governor of
Lieutenant Governor
The State Assembly
President of the Senate of the State
The Senate of ...
Speaker of ...
Associate Justice of the Supreme Court of ...
Presiding Justice ... Division

Religious/Clerical

The Right Reverend ... Abbot of ...
The Most Reverend ... Archbishop of ...
The Apostotic Delegate
The Venerable ...

Religious/Clerical

The Archdeacon of ...
The Lord Bishop of ...
Bishop of ...
Presiding Bishop of ...
Brother John Doe O.F.M.
Superior
Canon of ... Cathedral
His Eminence John Cardinal Doe Archbishop of ...
The Reverend John Doe
The Reverend Dr. Joyce Brown
Dean John Doe
The Moderator of ...
The Right Reverend Monsignor John Doe
The Very Reverend Monsignor John Doe
His Beatitude the Patriarch of ...
His Holiness the Pope
His Holiness Pope John XXIII
Rabbi John Doe
Sister Mary Joan
The Reverand Mother Superior
The Reverend Sister Superior

17. ABBREVIATIONS AND ACRONYMS

Common Abbreviations

A

a;A;@	at (refers to price; altitude; atomic weight; area; absolute (temperature); ampere
aa.	author's alteration (in printing)
AA	Alcoholics Anonymous; antiaircraft
A-1	first class
AAA	American Automobile Association; Amateur Athletic Association
a.a.r	against all risks
AASE	Association for Applied Solar Energy
A.B.A.	American Bankers Association; American Booksellers Association
abbr.; abbrev.	abbreviation
ABC	American Broadcasting Company; Atomic, Biological and Chemical (weapons)
abr.	abridged; abridgment
abs.	absolute; abstract
a.c.; A.C.	alternating current; Athletic Club
a/c; ac.;acct.	account; accountant; acre; account current
A/C	account current
A/cs Pay; A/P	accounts payable
A/cs Rec; A/R/	accounts receivable
ack.	acknowledge; acknowledgment
A.C.P.	American College of Physicians
acpt.	acceptance (in banking)
ACS	American Chemical Society
actg.	acting
a/d	after date
ad lib.	freely; not in the script
ad	advertisement
ad.	adapted; adaptor
a.d.;a/d	after date
A.D.	in the year of our Lord (anno Domini)
A.D.A.	American Dental Association; American for Democratic Action; American Dairy Association
add.	addendum; addenda; addition; address; add to, append

ad hoc	for this purpose
adj.	adjacent; adjective; adjourned; adjunct; adjustment
ad-lib.	not in the script
ad loc.	at or to the place
adm.; admin.; admr.; adms.; admstr.	administrator; administrative
admrs.; admx.	administratrix (female)
afore	combining form; before
Afro.	combining form that means Africa (Afro-American)
ADP	automatic data processing
adv.	advance, adverb; advertisement; advise; advocate
ad. val.	according to the value (ad valorem)
advt.	advertisement
AEC	Atomic Energy Commission
aeron.	aeronautic; aeronautics
AF; a.f.	audio frequency
affd.	affirmed
AFL-CIO	American Federation of Labor, Congress of Industrial Organization
afft.	affidavit
a.g.b.	a good brand
agcy.	agency
agr.; agric.	agriculture; agricultural; agriculturist
agt.	agent; agreement
A.I.B.	American Institute of Banking
AIDA	steps that stimulate a sale: attention; interest; desire; action
AKC	American Kennel Club
A.L.A.	American Library Association
ald.; aldm.	alderman
A.L.R.	American Law Reports
Als.; A.L.S.	autograph letter signed
alt.	alternate; alternating; alternative; altitude; alto
a.m.; A.M.	before noon (ante meridian); amplitude modulation; in the year of the world (anno mundi)
AMA	American Management Association; American Marketing Association; American Medical Association
Amb.	ambassador
amd.	amended
AMEX	American Stock Exchange; American Express

AMG.	Allied Military Government
amp.	ampere(s); amperage
Am. Rept.	American Reports
amt.	amount
angl.	anglicized
ann.	annual; annuity; annals
anon	anonymous
ans.	answer; answered
ant.	antenna; antiquarian, antiquity; antonym
ANTA	American National Theatre and Academy
Anzac	Australian and New Zealand Army Corps
Anzus	Australia; New Zealand; U.S. Alliance
a/o	account of
AP	Associated Press; American Plan (all meals included with the price of the room); Air Police
A/P	additional premium
apd	assessment paid
API	American Petroleum Institute
apmt.	appointment
APO	Army Post Office
app.	appended; appendix; appointed; apprentice; apparent
appd.	approved
approx.	approximate(ly)
apt(s).	apartment(s)
ar.	arrive; arrival; aromatic
A/R	all risks
ARC	American Red Cross
arch.	archaic; architect
arith.	arithmetic(al)
arr.	arrange(d); arrangement(s); arrive(d); arrival
art.	article; artificial; artist
a.s.	at sight
ASA	American Standards Association
ASCAP	American Society of Composers, Authors and Publishers
assigt.	assignment
assmt.	assessment
assn.	association
asst.	assistant; assorted
A.S.T.	Atlantic Standard Time
ASTA	American Society of Travel Agents; American Spice Trade Association
A.t.	Atlantic time
A.T.	American Terms

ATA	Air Transport Association
ATC	Air Traffic Control; American Transport Conference; Air Traffic Conference of America
A. to O.C.	attached to other correspondence
att.; attn.; atten.	attention
atty.	attorney
aud.	auditor
Aus.	Australia
AUS	Army of the United States
auth.	author; authentic; authority; authorized
aux.; auxil.	auxiliary
av.; ave.	average
av., avdp.	avoirdupois
A/V	according to value (ad valorem)
A.V.	Authorized Version
Ave.	avenue
avn.	aviation
A/W	Actual Weight
A.W.G.	American Wire Gauge
a.w.o.l.	away without official leave
AYH	American Youth Hostels

B

b.	boils at; breadth (width)
B.	brightness; Baume (Hydrometer scale)
b7d; b10d; b15d	buyer 7, 10, 15 days to take up
bal.	balance; balancing
bar.	barometer; barometric; barrel; barrister
b-b.	bial bond; bill book
B/B	bank balance
BBC	British Broadcasting Corporation
bbl.; bbls.	barrel; barrels
B.C.	Before Christ
B/C	bill of collection
bd.	bond; board; bound
B/D; b.d.	bank draft; bar draft; bills discounted; brought down
bd. ft.	board feet
bdl.; bdle.	bundle
B/E; B.E.; b.e.	bill of exchange; bill of entry
Bev.	billion electron volts (measure for atom-smashing machines)
bf; b.f.; bld.	boldface (heavy type in printing)
B/F; bf; b.f.	brought forward
bg.; bgs.	bag; bags

B/G	bonded goods
B/H	bill of health
b. hp.	brake horsepower
bibl.	bibliographical
bibliog.	bibliographer; bibliography
biog.	biography
biol.	biology
Birdie	battery integration and radar display equipment (a system for missles)
bk.	bank; block; book
bkpt.	bankrupt
bkt. bsk.	basket
bl.	bale; barrel; black; blue
B.L; b.l.; Bs?l	bill(s) of lading
Bldg.	building
BLS.	Bureau of Labor Statistics
Blvd.	boulevard
b.m.	board measure
BMEWS	Ballistic Missle Early Warning System
BMT	Brooklyn Manhattan Transit (a N.Y.C. subway system)
B.N.	bank note
b.o.	back order; bad order; box office; branch office; broker's order; buyer's option
B/O	brought over
B.O.	branch office
B.O.T.	Board of Trade
B.P; b.p.; B. Pay.	bills payable; bill of parcels
b.p.b.	bank post bill
B/R; b.r.; B. Rec.; b. rec.	builders' risks; bills receivable
B/R; B.R.	Bill of Rights
br.	branch; brown; bronze; brother
Brit.	British; Britain
Bro(s).	brother(s)
B/s; bs.	balance sheet; bill of sale
B.S.A.	Boy Scouts of America; Bibliographical Society of America; British South Africa
B/St.	bill of sight
BTS; B.T.U.; B.Th.U.	British Thermal Unit(s)
bu.	bushel
bul.; bull.	bulletin
bus.	business; bushels
Bus. Mgr.	business manager
B/v	book value
Bvt.	brevet

B.W.G.	Birmingham wire gauge
bx.	box

C

c.	centi = one-hundredth (0.01); cycle (kc only); curie; cent; circa
C.	Catholic, Celsius, Cellic
Ca.	Centore(s) (a metric unit); circa
c.a.; C.A.	chartered accountant; chartered agents; chief accountant; claim agent; commercial agent; consular agent, controller of accounts
C/A	capital account; credit account; current account
C. and s.c.	caps and small caps
CAB, C.A.B.	Civil Aeronautics Board; Consumers Advisory Board
C a/c	current account
C.A.F., c.a.f.	cost, assurance, and freight; cost and freight
Calif.	California
canc.	cancel; canceled; cancellation
cap, caps	capital(s); capitalize; capacity; capital letter(s)
CAP; C.A.P.	Civil Air Patrol
CAPIS	Customs Accelerated Passenger Inspection System
Capt.	Captain
CARE	Cooperative for American Remittance to Everywhere
Cart.	cartage
cat.	catalog
CB	citizens band (radio)
C/B	cash book
CBC	Canadian Broadcasting Corporation
CBD; C.B.D.;; c.b.d.	cash before delivery
CBI	China, Burma, India
CBS	Columbia Broadcasting System
cc.; c.c.; CC; cc	carbon copy; cashier's check; chief clerk; circuit court; city council; city councilor; common councilman; consular clerk; contra credit; county clerk; county commissioner; county council; county court; current account (French: comple courant)
C.C.A	Circuit Court of Appeals
CCC	Civilian Conservation Corps; Commodity Credit Corporation
C.C.F.	Cooperative Commonwealth Federation of Canada

CCM	Centimerer(s)
cd	cord
c.d.	cash discount
C.D.	Civilian Defense
CD(s)	Certification(s) of Deposit Commercial Dock
c/d	carried down
cd-ft.	cord-foot
C & D; c & d	collection and delivery
C.E.	Common Era
CEA	Council of Economic Advisers
Cent.	centered; central; century; centigrade; centimeter
cert.; certif.	certificate; certify; certificated
cf.; Cf	compare; confer
C/F; c/f	carried forward
C.F.; c.f.; c. & f.	cost and freight
CFA	Colonies Francais d'Afrique
C.F.I.; c.f.i.	cost, freight, and insurance
c.f.m.	cubic feet per minute
c.f.s.	cubic feet per second
c.f.m.; cfm	cubis feet per minute
c.f.o.	cost for orders
cg.; cgr.	centigram(s)
cge. pd.	carriage paid
Ch.; ch.	chain; champion; chancery; chaplain; chapter; chief; child
c.-h.	candle-hour
C.I.	consular invoice
Cia, cia	company (compania-Spanish)
CIA	Central Intelligence Agency
c.i.f.	cost, insurance, and freight
c.i.f. & c.	cost, insurance freight, and commission
civ.	civil
ck(s)	check; cask; cook
cl.	claim, class; classification; clause; clearance; clerk; centiliter
C.L.; c.l.	carload; carload lots; center line; civil law
c/l	craft loss
C/L	cash letter
clk	clerk; clock
CM.; cm	centimeter(s)
CM^2	square centimeter
CM^3	cubic centimeter (cc preferred)
c.m.	circular mil (wire measure)
cml	commercial

cm. pf.	comulative preferred
cn.	consolidated
C/N; c.n.	circular note; consignment note; credit note
Co.	Company; county
C/O, c.o.	care of; carried over
C/O	cash order; certificate of origin
COBOL	Common Business Oriented Language (a computer program language used in business data processing)
C.O.D.; c.o.d.	cash on delivery; collect on delivery; certificates of deposit
col.	collected; collector; college; colonial; colony; color; column
Col.	Colonel
Collat.	collateral
coll. tr; cit.	collateral trust
Colo.	Colorado
Comdr.	Commander
Comm.	Committee; Commission
Comp. Dec.	Comptroller's Decisions and Treasury
Comp. Gen.	Comptroller General General Decisions
Com'r.	Commissioner
CONARC	Continental Army Command
conf.	confer; conference
consgt.	consignment
cont.	continued
co-op	cooperative
CORE	Congress of Racial Equality
Corp.	Corporation
cos.	cosine
C.O.S.; c.o.s.	cash on shipment
cosh.	hyperbolic cosine
cp.	compare; candlepower; chemically pure
c-p.	candle-power
CP	Continental Plan (only continental breakfast included in hotel room rate)
CPA; C.P.A.	Certified Public Accountant
CPI	Consumer Price Index
Cpl.	corporal
c.p.m.	cycles per minute
c.p.s.	cycles per second
CPS	Certified Professional Secretary
cr.	credit; creditor
Cr.	Cranch (U.S. Supreme Court Reports)

C.R.	class rate; current rate; company's risk; carrier's risk
CRP	C-reactive protein
C.S.; c.s.	capital stock; civil service
c/s	cases
csc.	cosecant
CSC	Civil Service Commission
csch.	hyperbolic cosecant
CSS	Commodity Stabilization Service
C.S.T.	Central Standard Time
ct.; Ct	cent; county; court; one hundred
C.T.; c.t.	Central Time
ctge.	cartage
cu. cm.	cubic centimeter
cu.	cubic
cu. ft.	cubic feet
cu. in.	cubic inch
cum.	with; cumulative
cu. mi.	cubic mile
cum. pref.; cu. pf.	cumulative preferred
cur.	current
C.W.	Commercial weight
CWO	chief warrant officer
C.W.O.	cash with order
cwt.	hundredweight(s)
C.Z.	Canal Zone

D

d.	pence, dyne; deci
d/a	days after acceptance
D/A	deposit account; documents against acceptance
DALPO	do all possible
DAR	Daughters of the American Revolution
DATA	Defense Air Transportation Administration
db.	decibel
d.b.a.	doing business as
dbk	drawback
db. rts	debenture rights
d.c.	direct current
D.C.	District of Columbia
D/C	deviation clause
dd.; d/d; D/D; D/d	delivered; demand draft; delivered at docks; delivered at destination; days after date
D.D.	Doctor of Divinity

D.D; D/D	demand draft
D-Day	Date of Normandy landings (June 6, 1944)
D.D.S.	Doctor of Dental Surgery
DDT.	dichlorodiphenyl trichloroethane, an insecticide
deb.; deben.	debenture
dec.	decision
decim.	decimeter(s)
def.	deferred
dep.	deposit; department; departure; deponent; depot; deputy
dep. ctfs.	deposit certificates
depr.	depreciation
dept.; dpt.	department
DEW	Distant Early Warning (line)
d.f.	dead freight
D.F.A.	division freight agent
dft.	draft
dg.	decigram
dict.	dictator; dictation; dictionary
dir.	director
Dist. Ct.	District Court
dist.	district
dk.	deka (10)
DL	day letter
d.l.c.	dispatch loading only
dld.	delivered
D. Lit.	Doctor of Literature
DM, dm	Deutschemark
DME	Distance Measuring Equipment
D/N	debit note
do.	ditto (the same)
D/O	delivery order
doc.	document
dom.	dominion
do. P.	did; done
doz.	dozen
d.p.	direct port
DP	demi-pension; displace person
D/P	documents against payment
dr.	debit; debtor; drachma; dram; dram (p); drawer
D/R	deposit receipt
Dr.	Doctor

D.R.; d.r.; D/R	deposit receipt; dead reckoning
dr. ap.	apothecary's dram(s)
dr. av.	dram(s) avoirdupois
D/S	days after sight
d.w.	dead weight
D/W	dock warrant
d.w.c.	dead weight capacity
dwt.	pennyweight(s)
d.w.t.	deadweight tons
DDT	dichlorodiphenyltrichloroethane, an insecticide

E

e.	erg (unit of energy)
E.	east
ea.	ea
EAM	electronic accounting machine
E.A.O.N.	except as otherwise noted
E. & O.E., e. & o.e.	errors and omissions excepted
ed., edit.	edited; edition; editor(s)
Ed. Note	editorial note
EDP	electronic data processing
E.D.T.	Eastern Daylight Saving Time
e.e.	errors excepted
E.E.C.; EEC	European Economic Community
EEE	eastern equine encephalitis
EER	energy efficiency rating
eff.	effective
e.g.	for example (Latin: exempli gratia)
EHF	extremely high frequency
elec.	electric
e.m.f.	electromotive force
enc.	enclose; enclosed; enclosure
Encyc.	Encyclopedia
end.	endorse; endorsement
eng.	engineer; engine; engraved
e.o.h.p.	except as otherwise herein provided
e.o.	ex officio
e.o.m.; EOM	end of month
EP	European Plan (no meals included in charge for hotel room)
eq.	equal; equation; equator; equivalent
equip.	equipment
ERDA	Energy Research and Development Administration

ERISA	Employee Retirement Income Security Act (1974)
ERP	European recovery program
erron.	erroneous; erroneously
est.	estate; estimated
E.S.T.	Eastern Standard Time
e.s.u.	electrostatic unit
e.t.	eastern time
ETA; e.t.a.	estimated time of arrival
et al.	and others (Latin: et alia)
	and elsewhere (Latin: et alibi)
etc.	and so forth (Latin: et cetera)
ETD; e.t.d.	estimated time of departure
et seq.	and the following (Latin: et sequens)
Ex. B.L.	exchange bill of lading
ex cp.; ex/cp	ex coupon
exd.	examined
ex.d.; ex div.	ex dividend
Ex. Doc.	executive document
exec.	executive
ex int.	ex interest
ex n.	ex new
exp.	express; expenses; export
exr.	executor
ex r.	ex rights
exrx.	executrix
ex ship	delivered out of ship
ext.	extension; external; extinct; extra; extract
extra sess.	extraordinary session

F

f.	following; feminine; farad; and following pages(s)
F.	Fahrenheit
F.A.; f.a.	free alongside; freight agent
FAA	Federal Aviation Agency
fac.	facsimile
f.a.c.	fast as can
Fahr.	Fahrenheit
FAO	Food and Agriculture Organization
f.a.q.	fair average quality; free at quay
f.a.q.s.	fair average quality of season
F.A.S.; f.a.s.	free alongside ship
FAS	Foreign Agricultural Service

f.b.	freight bill
FBI;F.B.I.	Federal Bureau of Investigation
FBLA	Future Business Leaders of America
fmb	feet board measure
f.c.	follow copy (in printing)
FCA	Farm Credit Administration
FCC; F.C.C.	Federal Communications Commission
FDA; F.D.A.	Food and Drug Administration
f.d.	free delivery; free dispatch
f. & d.	freight and demurrage
FDIC; F.D.I.C.	Federal Deposit Insurance Corporation
F.D.R.	Franklin Delano Roosevelt
FEA	Federal Energy Administration
Feb.	February
Fed.	Federal Reporter
ff.	following (pages); folios
f.f.a.;	free from alongside;
F.F.A.	free foreign agency
F.F.A.	Future Farmers of America
F.H.A.	Federal Housing Administration; Farmers Home Administration
FHLBB	Federal Home Loan Bank Board
f.i.a.	full interest admitted
FICA	Federal Insurance Contributions Act
fid.	fiduciary
fig.(s)	figure(s)
f.i.o.	free in and out
f.i.t.	free of income tax; free in truck
f.i.w.	free in wagon
Fla.	Florida
flex.	flexible
F.L.N.	following landing numbers
fl. oz.	fluid ounce(s)
fm	fathom(s); from
F.M.	frequency modulation
FMB	Federal Marine Board
FMCS	Federal Mediation and Conciliation Service
fn.	footnote
FNMA	Federal National Mortgage Association
f.o.	for orders; firm offer
F.O.	firm offer; free overside; Foreign Office
f.o.b.;	free on board;
F.O.B.	freight on board

f.o.c.	free on car; free of charge
f.o.d.	free of damage
f.o.f.	free on field
fo	sheet folded once (in printing)
fol.	folio; following
f.o.q.	free on quay
f.o.r.	free on rail
f.o.s.	free on steamer
f.o.t.	free on truck
F.P.	floating policy; fully paid
FPA; F.P.A.	Foreign Press Association
FPC; F.P.C.	Federal Power Commission
f.p.m.	feet per minute
FPO	fleet post office
f.p.s.	feet per second
FPV	free piston vessel
fr.	fragment; Franc; from
FR	full rate
F.R.	Federal Register
F/R	freight release
FRELP	Flexible Real Estate Loan Plans
F.R.G.	Federal Republic of Germany (West Germany)
Fri.	Friday
f.r.o.f.	fire risk on freight
FRS	Federal Reserve System
F.R.S.	Fellow of the Royal Society
frt.	freight
F. Supp.	Federal Supplement
FSLIC	Federal Savings and Loan Insurance Corporation
ft.	foot
f.t.	full terms
ft. b.m.	feet board measure
ft.-c.	foot-candle
FTC	Federal Trade Commission
FTD	Florists Transworld Delivery
Ft.-1.	foot-lambert
ft.-lb	foot-pound
f.v.	on the back of page
fwd.	forward
f.w.d.	fresh water damage
F.X.	foreign exchange
F.Y.I.	for your information

G

g.	gram; gravity
Ga.	Georgia
G.A.; g.a.; G/A	general average
gal.	gallon(s)
GAO	General Accounting Office
G.A.R.	Grand Army of the Republic
CARP	Global Atmospheric Research Program
GATE	*GARP Atlantic Tropical Experiment*
GATT	General Agreement of Tariffs and Trade
G.A.W.	guaranteed annual wage
GCA: G.C.A.	ground control approach
g.c.d.; gcd; G.C.D.	greatest common divisor
gcf; g.c.f.; G.C.F.	greatest common factor
gcm; g.c.m. G.C.M.	greatest common measure
G.c.t.	Greenwich civil time
g.f.a.	good fair average
G.F.A.	general freight agent
g.gr.	great gross
gi.	gill(s)
GI; G.I.	general issue; government issue; (by extension a U.S. soldier)
gm.	gram(s)
G.m.a.t.	Greenwich mean astronomical time
GMT; G.M.T.; G.m.t.	Greenwich mean time
GNP; G.N.P.	gross national product
govt.	government
G.P.A.	General Passenger Agent
gpm; g.p.m.; G.P.M.	gallons per minute
GPO; G.P.O.	General Post Office; Government Printing Office
g.p.s.	gallons per second
gr.	grade; grain; gram; grammar; great; gross; group
gro	gross
gr. wt.	gross weight
G.S.	General Secretary; Girl Scouts
GSA;G.S.A.	General Services Administration
g.t.c.; G.T.C.	good till cancelled (or countermanded)
G.T.M.	good this month
GTS	gas turbine ship
G.T.W.	good this week
guar.; gtd.	guaranteed

H

h.	hecto (metric system = 100)
ha.	hectare
H.B.	House Bill
H.C.	held covered; House of Commons
hcf; h.c.f.; H.C.F.	highest common factor
H. Con. Res. (with number)	House concurrent resolution
hd.	head; hand
H. Doc. (with number)	House document
hdkq.	handkerchief(s)
hdwr.	hardware
HE	high explosive
HEW	Department of Health, Education and Welfare
hf.; h.f.; HF; H.F.	high frequency
H.F.M.	hold for money
hg.	hectogram
hhd.; Hhd.	hogshead(s)
H.J. Res. (with number)	House joint resolution
hl.	hectoliter
H.L.	House of Lords
hm.	hectometer
hm²	square hectometer
HOLC; H.O.L.C.	Home Owner's Loan Corporation
hon.	honorably; honorary
Hon.	Honorable
How.	Howard (U.S. Supreme Court Reports)
hp; H.P.	horsepower; high pressure
hp.-hr.	horsepower-hour
hq.; h,q.; HQ; H.Q.	headquarters
hr.	hour(s)
H. Rept. (with number)	House Report (With number)
H. Res. (with number)	House Resolution
H.W.	high water
H.W.M.	high-water mark
H.W.O.S.T.	high water ordinary spring tide
hyp.	hypothesis

I

IADB	Inter-American Defense Board
IAEA	International Atomic Energy Agency
IANF	Interallied Nuclear Force
IATA	International Air Transportation Association
I.B.	invoice book; in bond
ib.; ibid.	in the same place (Latin: ibidem)
I.B.A.	Investment Bankers Association
IBI	invoice book; inwards

I.B.O.	invoice book; outwards
IBRN	International Bank for Reconstruction and Development
ICA	International Cooperation Administration
ICAO	International Civil Aviation Organization
ICBM	intercontinental ballistic missle
ICC	Interstate Commerce Commission
I.C.'C.	Invoice cost and charges
id.	the same (Latin: idem)
IDA; I.D.A.	International Development Association (of the World Bank)
IDP	integrated data processing
i.e.	that is (Latin: id est)
if.; i.f.; IF; I.F.	intermediate frequency
IFC	International Finance Corporation
IFF	Identification, friend or foe
I.H.P.	indicated horsepower
I.L.A.	International Longshoreman's Association
I.L.G.W.U.	International Ladies' Garment Workers Union
Ill.	Illinois
ILO	International Labor Organization
ILS	instrument landing system
IMCO	International Maritime Consultative Organization
imit.	imitation; imitative
imp.	imperative; imperfect; imperial; impersonal; import (ed, er); important; imprimatur; improper
impf.	imperfect
imp. gal.	imperial gallon(s)
in.	inch(es)
inc.	inclosure; including; inclusive; income; incorporated; increase
Inc.	incorporated
incl.	inclosure; including
incor; incorp.	incorporated
incr.	increased; increasing
ind.	independent; index; indicated; indicative; indigo; indirect; industrial
Ind.	Indiana
IND	Independent Subway System (N.Y.C.)
indef.	indefinite
indic.	indicating; indicative; indicator
individ.	individual
inf.	inferior; infinitive; information

init.	initial; in the beginning (latin: initio)
in.-lb.	inch-pound
ins.	inches; inspector; insular; insulated; insulation; insurance
Insp. Gen.	Inspector General
inst.	instant; instantaneous; instrument(al)
Inst.	Institute; Institution
int.	intelligence; interest; interior; interjection; internal; international; interval; intransitive
inter.	intermediate
internat.	international
interrog.	interrogative
introd.	introduction; introductory
inv.	invoice; invented; invention; inventor
invt.	inventory
IOU; I.O.U.	I owe you
IPA; I.P.A.	International Phonetic Alphabet (or Association)
i.q.	the same as (Latin: idem quod)
I.Q.	intelligence quotient
IRE	Institute of Radio Engineers
IRO	International Refugee Organization
I.R.S.	Internal Revenue Service
IRT	Interborough Rapid Transit (N.Y.C.)
is.	island
ISES	International Solar Energy Society
ital.	italics
ITO	International Trade Organization
ITU	International Telecommunications Union; International Typographical Union
i.v.	invoice value; increased value

J

j.	joule
J.	Judge; Justice; journal
J.A.	Judge Advocate
J/A	joint account
Jan.	January
JATO	jet-assisted takeoff
jct.; jctn	junction
jg.	junior grade
J.J.; JJ	Justices
jnt. stk.	joint stock
jour.	journal
J.P.	Justice of the Peace
Jr.	Junior

Judge Adv. Gen.	Judge Advocate General
jus.; just.	justice

K

k.	carat; knot; kilo
K.	Kelvin
kc.	kilocycle(s)
K.D.	knocked down
Kev.	kilo-electron volts
kg.; kgr.	kilogram(s)
kilo.	kilometer(s)
km.	kilometer(s)
km²	square kilometer
km³	cubic kilometer
kt.	carat; kiloton
kv.	kilovolts
kv.-a.	kilovolt-ampere
kw.	kilowatt(s)
kw.-hr.	kilowatt-hour(s)
Ky.	Kentucky

L

L.	lake; latitude; law(s); leaf; left; length; line; link; lira; lire; low; book (Latin: liber)
L	Latin; length; listed; longitude.
l.; l	line; liter(s)
La.	Louisiana
L/A	letter of authority; landing account
lat.	latitude
lb(s).	pound(s)
lb. ap.	pound, apothecary's
lb. av.	pound, avoirdupois
lc; l.c.	lower case (in printing); in the place cited (Latin: loco citato)
LC	Deferreds (cables)
L.C.	Library of Congress
L/C	letter of credit
lcd; l.c.d.; L.C.D.	least (or lowest) common denominator
l.c.l.	less-than-carload lot
lcm; l.c.m.; L.C.M.	least (or lowest) common multiple
ld.	lead (in printing)
Ld.	limited; Lord
ldg.	loading
ldg. & dely.	landing and delivery
lds.	loads
lect.	lecture; lecturer
L. Ed.	Lawyers Edition

leg.	legal; legate; legislation; legislature
legis.	legislation; legislature
lf; l.f.	lightface (in printing)
l-f; l.f.; LF; L.F.	low frequency
lg; lge.	large
lg. tn.	long ton(s)
L.I.P.	life insurance policy
Litt. D or D. Litt.	Doctor of Literature
lin.	lineal; linear
lkg. & bkg.	leakage and breakage
L.L.B.	bachelor of laws
L.L.D.	Doctor of Laws
L.M.S.C.	let me see correspondence
LMT	local mean time
loc. cit.;	in the place cited (latin: loco citato)
log.	logarithm
L.O.G.	left own goods
long.	longitude
LORAN	long-range navigation
lox.	liquid oxygen
LPN; L.P.N.	Licensed Practical Nurse
lr.	lire
L.S.	the place of the seal (Latin: locus sigilli)
LSD	lysergic acid diethylamide (hallucinogen)
l.s.t.	local standard time
l.t.(n)	long ton; local time
Lt.	leiutenant
LT	letter message
Lt. Col.	lieutenant colonel
Lt. Comdr.	lieutenant commander
Lt. Gen.	lieutenant general
Lt. Gov.	lieutenant governor
Lt. (jg)	lieutenant (Junior Grade)
ltd.; Ltd.	limited (limited liability company; a corporation)
Lt.V.	light vessel
lv.	leave
LVN	Licensed Vocational Nurse
L.W.	low water

M

M.	Noon (meridian); monsieur
m; M	meridian; noon
m.	male; married; meter(s); mile; milli (one-thousandth)

M	thousand (Latin: mille); master, Majesty (in titles); mark; mill (in currency); medieval; Monday; monsieur; month
m.^{2}	square meter
m.^{3}	cubic meter
ma.	millampere
m/a	my account
MA	machine account/ Maritime Administration
mach.	machine; machinery; machinist
MAG.	Military Advisory Group
Maj.	major
Maj. Gen.	major general
MAP	Modified American Plan—hotel rate that includes breakfast and one other meal
mar.	maritime; married
Mar.	March
marg.	margin; marginal
Mass.	Massachusetts
math.	mathematics; mathematical
MATS	Military Air Transport Service
max.	maximum
max. cap.	maximum capacity
mb.	millibar
Mb.m.	thousand (feet) board measure
mc.	marked capacity; megacycle
M.C.	Master of Ceremonies
M/C	marginal credit
Mcf.	thousand cubic feet
m/d	months after date
M/D; m/d	memorandum of deposit; months/after date
Md.	Maryland
M.D.	doctor of medicine
MDAP	Mutual Defense Assistance Program
Mdse.	merchandise
Me.	Maine
M.E.	Methodist Episcopal
mech.	mechanical; mechanics; mechanism
med.	medical; medicine; medium
memo.	memorandum(s)
m.e.p.	mean effective pressure
meq.	milliequivalent
Messrs.	Misters (plural of mister)
Mev.	million electron volts

mf.	millifarad
M.F.	medium frenquency
mfg.	manufacturing
mfr.; mfg.	manufacturer; manufacturing; manufacture
mG	milligauss
mg.; mgm	milligram(s)
Mgr.	manager; Monsignor; Monseigneur
M.H.	main hatch
μa	microampere
μg	microgram
$\mu\mu$	micromicron (one millionth of a micron)
$\mu\mu$f	micromicroforad (one millionth of a millionth part)
μ^2	square micron
μ^3	cubic micron
μsec.	microsecond
μv.	microvolt
μw	microwatt
mμ	millimicrom
mil.	military
mi.	mile(s); mill (in currency)
min; min.	minute(s); mineralogical; mineralogy; minimum; mining
min. B/L	minimum bill of lading
M.I.P.	Marine Insurance Policy
MIRV	Multiple Intercontinental Re-Entry Vehicle
misc.	miscellaneous
mk.	mark
mkt.	market
ml	milliliter
MLD	minimum lethal dose
Mlle(s).	Mademoiselle(s)
mm.	millimeter(s)
mm.^{2}	square millimeter
mm.^{3}	cubic millimeter
MM.	Messieurs
m.m.	with the necessary changes made (Latin: mutatis mutandis)
Mme.	Madam
Mmes.	Mesdames
mmf; m.m.f.	magnetomotive force
mmfd.	microminiforad
mo.	month(s)
M.O.	money order; mail order; medical officer
Mo.	Missouri

Mol	Manned Orbital Laboratory
mol.	molecular; molecule
M.O.M.	middle of the month (discount)
Mon.	monetary; monastery
Mon.	Monday
MOS	military occupational specialty
m.p.	melting point
M.P.	Member of Parliament
MP, M.P.	military police
mpg; m.p.g.	miles per gallon
mph; m.p.h.	miles per hour
Mr.	Mister
MRBM	Medium-Range Ballistic Missile
Mrs.	Missus (married woman)
Ms.; MS.;	Miz (married or unmarried woman)
ms.; ms.	manuscript (plural: MSS)
MS.	motorship
M.S.	Master of Science
M/s	months after sight
msec.	millisecond
msg.	message
msgr.	Monsignor
M.Sgt.	master sergeant
m.s.l.	mean seal level
mst.	measurement
M.S.T.; m.s.t.	Mountain Standard Time
MSTS	Military Sea Transportation Service
mt.	empty; megaton; mountain
Mt.; mt.	mountain
m.t.	mountain time
mt. ct. cp.	mortgage certificate coupon
mtg.	mortgage; meeting
MTST	Magnetic Tape "Selectric" Typewriter
mus.	music
m.v.; M/V	marked value
mV	millivolt
MV	megavolt; motor vessel (also M/V)
MVD	the uniformed police of the Ministry of Public Law and Order of the U.S.S.R.
mW	milliwatt
MW	megawatt
mya.	myriare
	N
N.	normal; north; noun
n/a	no account; not applicable

N/A	no advice
N. A.	Narcotics Anonymous; National Academician; National Academy; North America
N.A.A.	National Aeronautic Association; National Automobile Association
NAACP; N.A.A.C.P.	National Association for the Advancement of Colored People
NAC	National Agency Check
N.A.M.	National Association of Manufacturers
N.A.S.	National Academy of Science
NASA	National Aeronautics and Space Administration
nat.	national; native; natural
natl.	national
NATO	North Atlantic Treaty Organization; National Association of Travel Organizations
NATS	Naval Air Transport Service
naut.	nautical
n.b.; N.B.	note well (latin: note bene)
NBC; N.B.C.	National Broadcasting Company
N,B.	New Brunswick, Canada
NBS	National Bureau of Standards
N/C	new charter; no charge
N.C.	North Carolina
NCAR	National Center of Atmospheric Research
NCR	no carbon required
n.c.u.p.	no commission until paid
N.C.V.	no commercial value
n.d.; N.D.	no date
N. Dak.	North Dakota
n.e.	not exceeding
N.E.	New England; Northeast
NE.	Northeast
N/E	no effects
NEA; N.E.A.	National Education Association; National Editorial Association
n.e.c.	not elsewhere classified
n.e.s.	not elsewhere specified
n/f; N.F.	no funds
ng.; N.G.	no good
N.H.	New Hampshire
N.H.P.	nominal horsepower
N.J.	New Jersey
N.L.; NL	night letter

N.L.T.	night letter cable
nm; n.m.	nautical mile
n/m	no mark
N.M.	night message
N. Mex.	New Mexico
No.; no.; nos.	number(s)
N/O	No orders
N.O.E.	not otherwise enumerated
N.O.H.P.	not otherwise herein provided
noibn	not otherwise indexed by name (used in freight)
nol. pros.	unwilling to prosecute
nom.	nominative
NOMA	National Office Management Association
nom. std.	nominal standard
non. pros.	he does not prosecute
non. seq.	does not follow (Latin: non sequitur)
n.o.p.	not otherwise provided (for)
N.O.S.	not otherwise specified
Nov.	November
n/p	net proceeds
N.P.	no protest; notary public
N.P.L.	nonpersonal liability
np. ord.	no place or date
nr.	near
n.r.	no risk; net register
n.r.a.d.	no risk after discharge
NS	nuclear ship
N.S.	National Society; New Series; New Style; Nova Scotia
N/S; N.S.F.	not sufficient funds
n.s.; N.S.	not specified
NSA	National Shipping Authority; National Student Association; National Secretaries Association
NSC	National Security Council
NSEP	National Solar Energy Program
NSF	National Science Foundation
N.S.P.C.A.	National Society for the Prevention of Cruelty to Animals
n.s.p.f.	not specifically provided for
n.t.	net tons; new terms
n.t. wt.	net weight
nv.	nonvoting

N.W.; NW.	Northwest
N.Y.	York York
NYSE	New York Stock Exchange

O

o/a	on account of
OAG	Official Airline Guide
OAPC; O.A.P.C.	Office of Alien Property Custodian
OAS	Organization of American States
ob.	he or she died (Latin: obit)
O.B./L; ob/l	order bill of lading
obs.	obsolete
o/c	old charter; open charter; overcharge
OCAS	Organization of Central American States
Oct.	October
o/d	on demand
o.d.	olive drab
O.D.	overdraft; overdrawn; officer of the day
o.e.	omissions excepted
OE	Old English
OEEC	Organization for European Economic Co-operations
OEO	Office of Economic Opportunity
OEP	Office of Emergency Planning
off.	office, officer; official
Off. Interp.	Official Interpretation
OIT	Office of International Trade
O/o	Order of
o.p.; O.P.; op; OP	out of print
O.P.	open (floating) policy
op.	opinion; operation; opposite; opus
Op.	operation; opus
op. cit.	in the work cited (Latin: opere citato)
OPEC	Organization of Petroleum Exporting Countries
o.&r.; O.&.R.	ocean and rain
o.r.; O/R; O.R.	owner's risk
Orderly Sgt.	orderly sergeant
o/s	out of stock
O/S	on sale; on sample
O.S.	old series
o.s.&d.	over, short, and damaged
o/t	old terms; on truck
oz.	ounce(s)

P

p.	page (pp. pages); past tense; pence; penny
pa.	paper
p.a.; per an.; per ann.	by the year (Latin: per annum)
PA.	Pennsylvania
PA	public address system; press agent
P/A	power of attorney; purchasing agent; passenger agent; private account
Pac.	Pacific Reporter; P. (2d): Pacific Reporter, second series
P.A.C.	put and call
P. and L.	profit and loss
pam.	pamphlet
par.	paragraph; parallel; parenthesis; parish
part.	participating
pat.	patent (ed); patrol; pattern
pat. pen.	patent pending
P/Av.	particular average
P.A.Y.E.	pay as you earn; pay as you enter
P.B.X.; PBX	private branch exchange (telephone)
pc.; pcs.	piece(s); price(s)
p.c.	per cent; post card; petty cash; price(s) current
P/C	price current; petty cash; per cent
pct.	percent
p.d.	per diem; potential difference
pd.	passed; paid
P.D.	port dues; pupilary distance
P/E	price-earnings ratio
per.	period, person; by; by means of; on account of
pert.	pertaining
pF.	water energy (p = logarithm; F = frequency)
Pfc.	private, first class
pfd.	preferred
ph.	phase
pH.	Hydrogen-ion concentration
Ph.	phenyl
PHA	Public Housing Administration
p.&i.	protection and indemnity
Phar. D.	doctor of pharmacy
pk(s).	peck; pack; park; peak
pkg.	package
pl.	place; plate, plural

p.l.	partial loss
P.&.L.	profit and loss
p.m.	afternoon (Latin: post meridian)
P.M.	postmaster; Provost Marshall
pm.	premium
pmk.; pmkd.	postmark(ed)
P/N; p.m.	promissory note
P.O.	petty officer
P.O.D.; p.o.d.	pay on delivery
p.o.r.	pay on return
P.O.R.	payable on receipt
P.P.	parcel post
pp.	pages; past participle; privately printed
P.P.	parcel post; parish priest; postpaid
ppd.	prepaid; postpaid
pph.	pamphlet
p.p.i.	policy proof of interest
p.p.m.; ppm	parts per million
P.P.S.; p.p.s.	additional postscript
ppt.	prompt loading
p.q.	previous question
pr.	pair; price; power; present; priest; prince; printing; pronoun; preferred
PR	public relations; proportional representation
P.R.	Puerto Rico
prec.	preceding
pref.	preface; prefatory; preference; prefix
Pres.	President
prin.	principal
proc.	proceedings; procedure; process
prod.	produce(d); product
Prof.	Professor
pron.	pronoun
prop.	properly; property; proposition; proprietor; proprietary
pro tem.	for the time being
prox.	proximate
ps.	pieces
P.S.; p.s.	postscript (P.P.S.; p.p.s. additional postscript) passenger steamer; privy seal; public sale; public school
p.s.f.	pounds per square foot
p.s.i.	pounds per square inch
P.S.T.	Pacific Standard Time

P/S	Public Sales
pt.	pint(s); part; payment; point(s); port
p.t.	for the time being (Latin: pro tempore)
P.T.	Pacific time
ptg.	printing
P.T.O.: p.t.o.	please turn over (page)
pub.	public; publisher
Public Res.	public resolution
PUC	Public Utilities Commission
Pvt.	private
p.w.	packaged weight
pwt.	pennyweight
P.X.	please exchange
PX	post exchange

Q

Q.	question; query
q.d.a.	quantity discount agreement
Q.E.D.	which was to be proven (Latin: quod erat demonstrandum)
Q.E.F.	which was to be done (Latin: quod erat faciendum)
ql.	quintal
qlty.	quality
Q.M. Gen.	Quartermaster General
Q.M. Sgt.	Quartermaster Sergeant
qn.	quotation
q. pl.; Q.P.	as much as you please (Latin: quantum placet)
QQ.	questions; queries
qr.	quarter
qt.	quart(s)
q.v.	which see (Latin: quod vide)

R

R.	Riaumur (thermometric scale on which 0° is freezing and 80° is boiling point of water)
R/A	refer to the acceptor
radar	radio detection and ranging; radarman; radarscope
R.A.F.	Royal Air Force
R.B.	Renegotiation Board
R/C	reconsigned
rcd.	received
Rd.	road

R/D	refer to drawer
R. & D.	research and development
r.d.	running days
R.D.B.	Research and Development Board
re	in regard to
R.E.	real estate
REA	Rural Electrification Administration
Rear Adm.	Rear Admiral
recd.	received
ref.	referee; reference
reg.	registered; regulation
reg. sess.	regular session
rep.	report
res.	residue
retd.	returned
Rev.	Reverend
rev. A/C	revenue account
revd.; rev'd.	reversed
revg.; rev'g.	reversing
rf.; rfg.	refunding
r.f.	radio frequency
R.F.D.	Rural Free Delivery
rfg.	refunding
R.I.	reinsurance
r. & l.	rail and lake
r.l. & r.	rural, lake, and rail
rm.	ream; room(s)
r.m.s.	root mean square
r. & o.	rail and ocean
R.O.G.	receipt of goods
ROK	Soldier of the Republic of South Korea
ROTC	Reserve Officers' Training Corps
rotn. no.	rotation number
R.P.	return premium
R/p	return to post for orders
r.p.m.	revolutions per minute
r.p.s.	revolutions per second
R.R.	railroad
RRB; R.R.B.	Railroad Retirement Board
R.S.V.P.	please reply
Rt. Rev.	Right Reverend
R.S.V.P.	please reply at once
r. & w.	rail and water
Ry.	Railway

S

s.	shilling
S.	south; Senate bill (with number)
s3d; s7d; s10d	seller 3, 7, 10 days to deliver
s/a	subject to approval; safe arrival
SAC	Strategic Air Command
SAE	Society of Automotive Engineers
SAM	surface-to-air missile
s. and s.c.	sized and super charged
s.a.n.r.	subject to approval no risk
SAR; S.A.R.	Sons of the American Revolution
S.B.	short bill
S/B	statement of billing
SBA; S.B.A.	Small Business Administration
s.c.	small capitals; same case
S.C.	South Carolina
sc.; scil.	namely (Latin: scilicet)
S.C.	salvage charges
s. & c.	shipper and carrier
s.d.	without a day being named (Latin: sine die)
S. Dak.	South Dakota
S.D.B.L.	sight draft, bill of lading attached
S. Doc.	with number, Senate Document
S.E.; SE	southeast
SEATO	Southeast Asia Treaty Organization
sec.; secy.; sec'y	secretary
sec.	section(s); sector; secondary; second(s); secant; according to (Latin: secundum)
sec.-ft.	second-foot
2d. Lt.	second lieutenant
SEC; S.E.C.	Securities and Exchange Commission
Sept.	September
seq.; et seq.	subsequent lines (Latin: et sequentes)
ser.	series; serial; sermon
SERI	Solar Energy Research Institute
Sf.	Svedberg flotation
S.F.	sinking fund
S. & F.A.	shipping and forwarding
Sfc.	sergeant first class
sgd.	signed
Sgt.	sergeant
sh.	shore(s); sheet; shilling(s); sheep; share agent
S.H.F.	superhigh frequency
s.hp.	shaft horsepower
shpt.	shipment

sh. tn.	short ton
sic.	so; thus (used to confirm a questioned word)
Sig.; sig.	signature; signor; signore; signori
sin.	sine
sink.	hyperbolic sine
s.i.t.	stopping in transit
sk	sock(s)
s.l.	salvage loss
S/N	shipping note
SNAFU	situation normal, all fouled up
s.o.; S.O.	seller's option; shipping order
soc.	society
sol.	solicitor(s)
Sol. Op.	Solicitor's Opinion
S.O.L.	shipowner's liability
SONAR	sound navigation and ranging
SOP; S.O.P.	standard operating procedure
sp.	special; species; specific; specimen; spelling; spirit(s)
s.p.	without issue (Latin: sine prole)
S.P.	supra protest; shore patrol
S.P.C.A.	Society for the Prevention of Cruelty to Animals
S.P.C.C.	Society for the Prevention of Cruelty to Children
s.p.d.	steamer pays dues
spec.	specification; speculation; special
specif.	specifically
Sp. 3 c.	specialist, third class
sp. gr.	specific gravity
SPIRIT	Solar Powered Isolated Radio Transceiver
Sp. Op.	special opinion
sp. term	special term
sq. ft.	square feet
sq. in.	square inch(es)
sq. mi.	square mile(s)
sq. rd.	square rod(s)
sq. yd.	square yard(s)
Sr.	Senior; Senor
S. Rept.	with number, Senate report
S. Res.	with number, Senate resolution
SRO; S.R.O.	standing room only
S.S.	steamship
SSA: S.S.A.	Social Security Act (or Administration)

S. Sgt.	staff sergeant
SSM	surface to surface missile
SST	Supersonic transport plane
S.S.U.	standard saybolt universal
st.	statute(s); stationary; statistics; statute(s) (miles); immediately (Latin: statim)
St.	street
St.; Ste.; SS	Saint, Sainte, Saints
St.	Saint
sta.	station; stamped
stat.	statute(s)
std.	standard
std. c. f.	standard cubic foot
stg.	sterling
stk.	stock
STOL	short takeoff and landing
str.	streamer
S. to S.	station to station
SSE	south-southeast
SSW	south-southwest
subj.	subject; subjective(ly); subjunctive
subpar.	subparagraph
sup.	supplement; supplementary; supply; superior; superlative; supreme; supine; above (Latin: supra)
Sup. Ct.	Supreme Court Reporter
supp.	supplement
supt.	superintendent
sur.	surcharged; surplus
Surg.	surgeon
Surg. Gen.	Surgeon General (Army, Navy, and Public Health)
s.v.	sailing vessel; under the word or heading (Latin: sub verbo, sub voce)
S.W.	southwest; shipper's weights
S.W.	southwest
S.W.G.	standard wire guage
syn.	synonym(ous)
	T
t.	metric ton(s)
T.	township
T.A.	Traffic Agent
TAA	Technical Assistance Administration

TAB	Technical Assistance Board
tan.	tangent
tanh.	hyperbolic tangent
t.b.; T/B	trial balance
TB.	tuberculosis
tbs.	tablespoonful
T/C	until countermanded
T/D	time deposits
T/D.	Treasury Decisions
TDN	total digestible nutrients
T.E.	trade expenses
TECS	Treasury Enforcement Communications System
tel.	telegram; telegraph; telephone
Telesat	telecommunication satellite
TELEX	automatic teletypewriter exchange service
Ter(r).	terrace
tf.; t.f.; T.F.	till forbidden (advertising: run the copy until further notice)
tfr.	transfer
T.H.I.: H.-H.I.	temperature-humidity index
T/L	time loan
t.l.o.	total loss only
t.m.	true mean
TM(s)	trademark(s)
tn.	ton
TNT.	trinitrotouol; trinitroluene
t.o.	turnover
T/O	transfer order
tp(s).	township
t.p.	title page
tr.	trace; train; translated; translation; translator; transpose; treasurer; trust; transitive
T/R	trust receipt
T.R.	tons registered
trans.	translated; translation; transportation; transaction; transferred; transpose; transverse; transitive
transp.	transportation; transparent
trav.	traveler; travel(s)
treas.	treasurer; treasury
trfd	transferred
T. Sgt.	technician sergeant
tsp.	teaspoonful(s)
T.T.	telegraphic transfer

T 2g.	technical, second grade
TVA.	Tennessee Valley Authority
twp.; TWP	township
TWS	timed wire service
TWX	teletypewriter exchange service
ty.; ter.	territory

U

U.	University
U/A	underwriting account
U.A.W.	United Auto Workers
uc; u.c.	upper case (printing)
UDC	Universal Decimal Classification (Dewey decimal system of library items)
UGT	urgent
UHF; U.H.F.; uhf.	ultra-high frequency
ult.	of the last month
UMTS	Universal Military Training Service (System)
U.N.	United Nations
UNCCP	United Nations Conciliation Commission for Palestine
UNEF	United Nations Emergency Force
UNESCO	United Nations Educational, Scientific, and Cultural Organization
UNICEF	United Nations Children's Fund ("International" and "Emergency" have been dropped from the name)
Univ.	Universal; University
UNRRA	United National Relief and Rehabilitation Administration
UNRWA	United Nations Relief and Works Agency
u.p.	under proof
UPI; U.P.I.	United Press International
UPU	Universal Postal Union
URA	Urban Renewal Administration
U.S.	U.S. Supreme Court Reports
USA	U.S. Army
U.S.A.	United States of America
USAF.	U.S. Air Force
USAREUR	U.S. Army, Europe
U.S.C.	United States Code
U.S.C. Supp.	United States Code Supplement
U.S.C.A.	United States Code Annotated
USCG.	U.S. Coast Guard
USDA; U.S.D.A.	United States Department of Agriculture
USES; U.S.E.S.	United States Employment Service

USIA	United States Information Agency
USMC; U.S.M.C.	U.S. Marine Corps
USN; U.S.N.	U.S. Navy
USNR; U.S.N.R.	U.S. Naval Reserve
U.S.P.	United States Pharmacopoeia
U.S.P.O.	United States Post Office
U.S.S.	United States Senate; United States Ship underwriter; U.S. Ship
U.S.S.R.;	Union of Soviet Socialist Republics
UW	underwriter
u.t.	universal time

V

v.	verb; verse; version; verso; versus; vide; violin; volt; village
V.	venerable (in titles); viscount; viscountess; volt; village
VA; V.A.	Veterans Administration
Va.	Virginia
val.	valuation; value
var.	variable; variant; variation; variety; various
V.C.	valuation clause; vice chairman; vice chancellor; vice consul; Victoria Cross; Vietcong
v.d.	various dates; vapor density
VD	veneral disease
ver.	version; verse
vet.	veteran; veterinarian; veterinary
V.F.	video frequency; visual field
vhf; VHF	very high frequency
V.I.	Virgin Islands
vic.	vicinity; vicar
vid.; v.	see (to direct reader's attention)
VIP	very important person
VIR	variable interest rate
vis.	visibility; visual
VISTA	Volunteers in Service to America
viz.	namely (to introduce examples or items)
vlf; VLF	very low frequency
vol.	volume; volcano; volunteer
v.o.p.	value as in original policy
vou.	voucher
VRM	variable rate mortgage
vs.	verse; versus
vt.	voting
Vt.	Vermont

VTOL	vertical takeoff and landing
vv.	verses
v.v.	vice versa

W

w.	week; width; with
w; W.	watt
W.	West
WAAF	Woman's Auxiliary Air Force (British)
WAC	Woman's Army Corps
w.a.e.	when actually employed
WAF	women in the Air Force
war.	warrant
WATS	wide area telephone service
wb.	waybill; westbound; water ballast; warehouse bill
w.c.	without charge; water closet (British bathroom)
W.C.T.U.	Women's Christian Temperance Union
wd.	wood; word
w/d	warranted
W.D.	Western District
w.f.; wf.	wrong font (printing)
WFTU	World Federation of Trade Unions
w.g.	weight guaranteed; wire guage
whf.	wharf
WHO	World Health Organization
W-hr	watt-hour
whs.	warehouse
whsle.	wholesale
w.i.	when issued
wk.	week
wkly.	weekly
WL; w.l.	water line; wave length
W/M	weight and/or measurement
wmk.	watermark
WNW	west-northwest
WO; W.O.	wait order; warrant officer
w.o.c.	without compensation
w.p.	without prejudice
w.p.m.	words per minute
w.p.p.	waterproof paper packing
wrnt.	warrant
W.R.	warehouse receipt
w. & r.	water and rail

wt.	weight
W. Va.	West Virginia
w.w.; W.W.	with warrants
W/W	warehouse warrant

X

x-c; x-cp.	ex coupon
x-d; x-div.	ex dividend
x-i; x-in; x-int.	ex interest
x-n.	ex-new
x-pr.	privileges
x-rts.	ex rights

Y

yb.	yearbook
yd.	yard
yr(s)	year(s); your(s); younger

Z

z.	zone; zero
ZIP	Zone Improvement Plan
zool.	zoology; zoological

Abbreviations of Popular Acronyms and Familiar Organizations

A

AA	Aircraft (Air Force); aircraft carrier; air-launched (Department of Defense missile designation)
AA	Administrative assistant
A-A	Air-to-air
AAA	Antiaircraft artillery
AAAA	American Association of Advertising Agencies
AAAS	American Academy of Arts and Sciences
AABM	American Association of Battery Manufacturers
AAC	Aeronautical Advisory Council; Aeronautical approach chart. Alaskan Air Command; Antiaircraft common (U.S. Navy)
AACB	Aeronautics and Astronautics Coordinating Board
AACC	American Automatic Control Council
AACE	American Association of Cost Engineers
AACP	Air carrier contract personnel
AACS	Airways and Air Communications Service
AACSM	Airways and Air Communications Service Manual
AADCP	Army air defense command post
AAE	American Association of Engineers; Army Aviation Engineers

AAFB	Andrews Air Force Base
AAFES	Army and Air Force Exchange Service
AAFPS	Army and Air Force Postal Service
AAI	Air-to-air identification
AAIC	Allied Air Intelligence Center
AAJCS	Anglo-American Joint Chiefs of Staff
AAM	Air-to-air missile
AAMI	American Association of Machinery Importers
AAOC	Antiaircraft Operations Center
AAP	Aerodynamics Advisory Panel (Atomic Energy Commission)
AAPD	American Academy of Professional Draftsmen
AAPMA	Automotive and Aviation Parts Manufacturing Association
AAR	Association of American Railroads
AAS	American Astronautical Society
AASE	Association for Applied Solar Energy
AAUP	American Association of University Professors
ABA	American Bankers' Association
ABB	Automatic back bias
ABC	American-British-Canadian; Atomic, biological, chemical
ABM	Automated batch mixing
ABMA	Army Ballistic Missile Agency
ABMEWS	Anti-ballistic-missile early warning system
ABN	Airborne
ABS	Acrylonitrile-butadiene-styrene (insulation material)
ABT	About
AC	American Communications Association
ACCCE	Association of Consulting Chemists and Chemical Engineers
ACEC	Association of Consulting Engineers of Canada
ACEW	Association of Communications Workers
ACIL	American Council of Independent Laboratories, Inc.
ACK	Acknowledge
ACL	Automatic carrier landing system; Armored cable, lead sheath
ACLD	Above clouds (CAA term)
ACM	Active countermeasures, Association of Canadian Manufacturers; Association for Computing Machinery
ACMA	Alumina Ceramics Manufacturers' Association
ACME	Association of Consulting Management Engineers
ACSM	American Congress on Surveying and Mapping

ACSR	Aluminum conductor, steel-reinforced (cable)
ACSS	Analog computer subsystem
ACT	Acetate cloth tape
ADAPSO	Association of Data Processing Service Organizations
ADAT	Automatic data accumulator and transfer
ADCI	American Die Casting Institute
ADF	Air Defense Force, Automatic direction finder
ADFAP	Automatic direction finder approach
ADI	American Documentation Institute
ADMA	Aviation Distributors and Manufacturers' Association
ADPC	Automatic data processing center
ADPS	Automatic data processing system
ADPT	Adapter
ADR	Adder. Analog-to-digital recorder
ADRAC	Automatic digital recording and control
ADRS	Address
A-E	Architect-Engineer
AEA	Atomic energy act
AEBA	Automatic emergency broadcast alerting
AEC	Atomic Energy Commission
AED	Association of Electronic Distributors
AEP	American Electric Power (integrated, electrical power network)
AEPM	Association of Electronic Parts and Equipment Manufacturers
AEPS	American Electroplaters' Society
AES	Aerospace Electrical Society; Aircraft Electrical Society; American Electroplaters' Society; Audio Engineering Society
AF	Admiral of the Fleet; Air Force; Alternating flow
AFA	Air Force Association
AFC	Asbestos-covered, heat-resistant cord; Automatic flight control; Automatic frequency control
AFCAL	Association Francaise De Calcul (French Computing Association)
AFCCE	Association of Federal Communications Consulting Engineers
AFCEA	Armed Forces Communications and Electronics Association
AFG	Analog function generator
AFI	Air Filter Institute
AFIPS	American Federation of Information-Processing Societies
AFROTC	Air Force Reserve Officers Training Corps

AFRS	Armed Forces Radio Service
AFS	American Field Service; American Foundrymen's Society
AFSC	Armed Forces Staff College
AFT	Acetate, film tape; Automatic fine tuning
AFTRA	American Federation of TV and Radio Artists
A/G	Air-to-ground
AGA	American Gas Association; As good as
AGA-CS	Automatic ground-to-air communications system
AGB	Accessory gear box
AGET	Advisory Group on Electron Tubes
AGF	Army ground force
AGR	Advanced gas-cooled reactor
AGREE	Advisory group on reliability of electronic equipment
AGU	American Geophysical Union
AHP	Air horsepower
AHR	Aqueous homogeneous reactor
AHS	American Helicopter Society
AIAA	American Institute of Aeronautics and Astronautics
AIBS	American Institute of Biological Sciences
AICA	International Association for Analog Computation
AICBM	Anti-intercontinental ballistic missile
AICE	American Institute of Consulting Engineers
AICHE	American Institute of Chemical Engineers
AIIE	American Institute of Electrical Engineers
AIEC	All-Industry Electronics Conference
AIF	Atomic Industrial Forum
AIHA	American Industrial Hygiene Association
AIIE	American Institute of Industrial Engineers
AIMC	American Institute of Medical Climatology
AIME	American Institute of Mining, Metallurgical, and Petroleum Engineers
AIP	American Institute of Physics
AIPA	American Ionospheric Propagation Association
AIPE	American Institute of Plant Engineers
AIRA	Air Force Attache
AIRBM	U. S. Air Force communications complex
AIRCOM	U.S. Air Force communications complex
AIRCOMNET	U. S. Air Force Operational Network
AISE	Association of Iron and Steel Engineers
AITA	Air Industries and Transports Association
AIUS	Man-in-Space International Association
AIWI	American Industrial Writing Institute
ALCEA	Airline Communication Employees' Association

ALDA	Airline Dispatchers' Association
ALM	Air-launched missile
ALMAJCO	All major command letters
ALO	Air liaison officer
ALU	Arithmetic and logic unit
AM	Air ministry (British); Auxiliary memory; Minesweeper (U.S. Navy)
A/M	Auto-manual
AMA	Academy of Model Aeronautics; American Management Association; American Medical Association; American Municipal Association; Automatic message accounting
AMCA	Air Moving and Conditioning Association
AME	Angle-measuring equipment
AMERSTD	American Standard
AMH	Alaska Military Highway
AMIS	Air movements information service
AMM	Antimissile missile
AMOS	Automatic Meterological Observation Station (U.S. Weather Bureau)
AMPAS	Academy of Motion Picture Arts and Sciences
AMPH	Amphibian
AMP-HR	Ampere-hour
AMPL	Amplifier
AMPS	Auotmatic message-processing system
AMRI	Association of Missile and Rocket Industries
AMS	Army Map Service; Army Medical Staff
AMSA	American Metal Stamping Association
AMSL	Above mean seal level
AMSOC	American Miscellaneous Society (National Academy of Sciences)
AMST	Association of Maximum Service Telecasters, Inc.
AMTDA	American Machine Tool Distributors' Association
AMVER	Atlantic Merchant Vessel Report
ANACOM	Analog computer
ANATRON	Analog translator
ANC	Air Navigation Conference; All-number calling
ANCOR	Angle extrusion and corner casting
ANI	Automatic number identification (telephone term)
ANIP	Army-Navy Instrumentation Program
ANMB	Army and Navy Munitions Board
ANOVA	Analysis of variance
ANP	Aircraft nuclear propulsion

ANS	American Nuclear Society; Automatic navigation system
ANSAM	Antimissile surface-to-air missile
ANT	Antenna
AOA	American Ordnance Association
A-O-AMPL	And-or-amplifier
AOPA	Aircraft Owners' and Pilots' Association
AOS	Add-or-subtract
APCO	Associated Police Communications Officers, Inc.
APD	Association of Professional Draftsmen
APDA	American Power Dispatchers' Association, Inc.
APEP	Association of Professional Engineering Personnel (engineers union)
API	American Petroleum Institute
APICS	American Production and Inventory Control Society
APJA	Appliance Parts Jobbers' Association
APM	Antipersonnel missile
APMI	American Powder Metallurgy Institute
APN	Nonmechanized artillery transport
APO	Army Post Office
APPA	American Public Power Association
APRT	Airport
APRXLY	Approximately
APS	American Physical Society; Assimilations per second (term used in illumination); Automatic pilot systems; Auxiliary power system
APT	Automatic picture transmission
APTS	Automatic picture transmission system
AQ	Any quantity
AQL	Acceptable quality level
AR	Acoustic reflex
ARA	Agricultural Research Administration
ARBA	American Road Builders Association
ARC	American Red Cross
AREA	Amateur Radio Emergency Association; American Railway Engineering Association
AREC	Advanced Rocket Engineering Club
ARENTS	Advanced research environmental test satellite
ARF	Aeronautical Research Foundation; Armour Research Foundation
ARI	Air Conditioning and Refrigeration Institute
ARL	Association of Research Libraries
ARMA	American Records Management Association

ARRL	American Radio Relay League (Association of U.S. radio amateurs)
ARTC	Air route traffic control
ARTCC	Air route traffic control center
ARTS	Associated Radio and TV Servicemen
AS	Add-subtract
ASA	Acoustical Society of America; American Standards Association; American Statistical Association; Army Security Agency
ASB	Air Safety Board
ASCE	American Society of Civil Engineers
ASEE	American Society for Engineering Education
ASHAE	American Society of Heating and Air Conditioning Engineers
ASII	American Science Information Institute
ASL	Association of Standards Laboratories
ASLE	American Society of Lubrication Engineers
ASLO	American Society of Limnology and Oceanography
ASM	Air-to-surface missile; American Society for Metal
ASME	American Society of Mechanical Engineers
ASNE	American Society of Naval Engineers
ASP	American Society of Photogrammetry
ASQC	American Society for Quality Control
ASSE	American Society for Safety Engineers
ASTIA	Armed Service Technical Information Agency
ASTM	American Society for Testing Materials
ASTME	American Society of Tool and Manufacturing Engineers
ASW	Antisubmarine warfare
A/T	Action time
ATA	Air Transport Association
ATAE	Association of Telephone Answering Exchanges
ATAS	Academy of TV Arts and Sciences
ATC	Air traffic Control
ATCA	Air Traffic Control Association
ATS	American Television Society
AU	Air University (U.S. Air Force)
AUS	Army of the United States
AUSA	Association of the United States Army
AVS	American Vacuum Society
AWA	Aviation Writers' Association
AWG	American wire gauge
AWRTV	American Women in Radio and TV
AWS	Air Weather Service (U.S. Air Force); American Welding Society

B

BA	Binary add
BBC	British Broadcasting Corp.
BC	Binary code; Binary counter
BCB	Broadcast band
BCD	Binary coded decimal
BCF	Bureau of Commercial Fisheries (U.S. Department of the Interior)
BDC	Binary decimal counter
BDD	Binary-to-decimal decoder
BDSA	Business and Defense Services Administration (U.S. Department of Commerce)
BPR	Bureau of Public Roads
BRAMATEC	Brain-mapping techniques
BRANE	Bombing radar and navigation equipment (IBM system)
BRI	Building Research Institute
BRS	Business Radio Service
BSDC	Binary symmetric dependent channel
BSF	Bulk shielding facility
BSI	British Standards Institution
BSIC	Binary symmetric independent channel
BSR	Bulk shielding reactor (Oak Ridge, Tenn.)
BSSRS	Bureau of Safety and Supply Radio Service (FCC bureau)
BTC	Basic Training Center
BuAer	Bureau of Aeronautics (U.S. Navy)
BuOrd	Bureau of Ordnance (U.S. Navy)
BUR	Bureau
BuSandA	Bureau of Supplies and Accounts (U.S. Navy)
BUSARB	British-United States Amateur Rocket Bureau
BuShips	Bureau of Ships (U.S. Navy)
BuWeps	Bureau of Naval Weapons
BuWepsRep	Bureau of Naval Weapons Representative (U.S. Navy)

C

CAA	Civil Aeronautics Administration
CAB	Cellulose acetate butyrate; Civil Aeronautics Board
CABRA	Copper and Brass Research Association
CACOM	Chief Aircraft Communicator
CAC&W	Continental air control and warning
CADSS	Combined analog-digital systems simulator
CADW	Civil air defense warning
CAI	Canadian Aeronautical Institute; Computer analog input

CAI/OP	Computer analog input/output
CAirC	Caribbean Air Command
CanUKUS	Canada-United Kingdom-United States
CANUSE	Canadian-United States Eastern Interconnection
CAR	Center for Aging Research (National Institutes of Health)
CARTB	Canadian Association of Radio and TV Broadcasters
CATV	Community antenna TV system
CCBA	Central Canada Broadcasters' Association
CCBS	Clear Channel Broadcasting Service
CCC	Commodity Credit Corporation (Department of Agriculture)
CCPE	Canadian Council of Professional Engineers
CDCE	Central data-conversion equipment
CDPC	Central data processing computer
CDSE	Computer-driven simulation environment
CDU	Coast defense unit
CEC	Consulting Engineers' Council
CEMA	Canadian Electrical Manufacturers' Association; Communications Equipment Manufacturers' Association
CEMS	Central electronic management system
CEWA	Canadian Electronic Wholesalers' Association
CGAS	Coast Guard Air Station
CHINFO	Chief of Naval Information
CIA	Central Intelligence Agency
CIB	Central Intelligence Board; Concrete Industry Board
CITE	Council of the Institute of Telecommunication Engineers
CMA	Canadian Manufacturers' Association
CMRU	Committee on Manufacturers' Radio Use (National Association of Manufacturers)
CMSCI	Council of Mechanical Specialties Contractors Institute
CNO	Chief of Naval Operations
COFI	Confidential
CofS	Chief-of-Staff
COGB	Certified Official Government Business
COGO	Coordinate geometry (MIT-developed programming system)
COMINT	Communications intelligence
COMM	Communication
COMMCEN	Communications center
COMPAC	Computer program for automatic control
COMPOOL	Communications pool
Com Sat	Communications satellite
COMSEC	Communications security

COMSND	Commissioned
COMSOC	Communications Spacecraft Operations Center
CRPL	Central Radio Propagation Laboratory (National Bureau of Standards)
CRS	Citizens Radio Service
CRTA	Chicago Radio Traffic Association
CRTOG	Cartography
CSAR	Communication satellite advanced research
CSC	Civil Service Commission
CSI	Construction Specifications Institute
CTCA	Channel and Traffic Control Agency
CTCU	Channel and traffic control unit
CTMA	Cutting Tool Manufacturers' Association
CTUNA	Commercial Telegraphers' Union of North America
CWA	Communications Workers of America

D

DAC	Digital-to-analog converter
DBA	Daytime Broadcasters' Association
DCA	Defense Communications Agency (U.S. Dept. of Defense)
DCMA	Defense Contract Management Association
DDD	Direct distance dialing
DESK FAX	Desk-top facsimile (Western Union)
DFL	Development Loan Fund
DHE	Data-handling equipment
DIA	Defense Intelligence Agency
DIGICOM	Digital communication system
DIY	Do-it-yourself
DNA	Deoxyribonucleic acid (genetics)
DNCC	Defense National Communications Control Center
DOD	Department of Defense
DOF	Degree of freedom
DO/IT	Digital output-input translator
DPE	Data-processing equipment
DPG	Data processing group (Division of the Office Equipment Manufacturers' Institute)
DPMA	Data Processing Management Association
DPS	Data processing subsystem
DRV	Data recovery vehicle
DSE	Data-storage equipment
DTG	Data-time group
DTP	Directory tape processor
DTS	Data-transmission system
DUO	Datatron Users' Organization

E

EA	Electroacoustic Engineers' Association
EAA	Engineer and Architects Association; Experimental Aircraft Association
EAS	Extended area service (telephone term)
EASA	Electrical Apparatus Service Association
EASTAF	Eastern Transport Air Force
EBU	European Broadcasting Union
ECA	Economic Cooperation Administration
ECAP	Electric companies' advertising program
ECC	European Coordinating Committee
ECCANE	East Coast Conference on Aerospace and Navigational Electronics
ECChart	Electrocardiocharter
ECG	Electrocardiogram. Electrocardiograph
ECLA	Economic Commission for Latin America
EIB	Export-Import Bank of the U.S. ("Eximbank")
EJC	Engineers' Joint Council
EKG	Electrocardiogram
EKW	Electrical kilowatts
ELPG	Electric Light and Power Group
ELSEC	Electronic security
ELSIE	Electronic letter sorting and indicator equipment
EM	Electromagnetic. Electromechanical
EMA	Electronic Manufacturers' Association
EMC	Engineering Manpower Commission
EMCON	Emission Control
EMEA	Electronic Maintenance Engineering Association
EMI	Electromagnetic interference
EMIS	Electromagnetic Intelligence System
EMMA	Eye-movement measuring apparatus
EMP	Electromechanical power
EMR	Executive management responsibility
EMSA	Electron Microscope Society of America
EOM	End of message
EOT	End of tape. End of transmission
EP & EM	Association of Electronic Parts and Equipment Manufacturers, Inc.
EPMA	Electronic Parts Manufacturers' Association
EQ	Equalizer
EQL	Expected Quality Level
EQP	Equipment
ERNIE	Electronic random numbering and inciating equipment

ERR	Error
ESA	Engineers and Scientists of America
ESBC	Electronics Small Business Council
ESMA	Electronic Sales and Marketing Managers' Association
ESPS	Engineering Societies Personnel Service
ETA	Estimated time of arrival
ETD	Estimated time of departure
ETG	Electronics Technician Guild
ETI	Engine test information
ETIM	Elapsed time
ETV	Educational Television
EURATOM	European Atomic Energy Community
EW	Early warning. Electronic warfare.
EWP	Emergency war plan
EWR	Early Warning radar
EWS	Early warning system
EX	Execute; Experimental; Extract
EXCH	Exchange
EXCLU	Exclusive
EXCP	Except

F

FAA	Federal Aviation Administration
FCA	Farm Credit Administration
FCBA	Federal Communications Bar Association
FCC	Federal Communications Commission
FCCA	Forestry, Conservation Communications Association
FCCN	Federal Communications Commission Network
FCDA	Federal Civil Defense Administration
FCDR	Failure cause data report
FCI	Fluid Controls Institute
FDA	Food and Drug Administration
FDIC	Federal Deposit Insurance Corporation
FET	Field-effect transistor
F-F	Flip-flop
FHA	Federal Housing Administration
FIANI	International Federation of National Associations of Engineers
FIER	Foundation for Instrumentation Education and Research
FLF	Flip-flop
FM	Feedback mechanism. Frequency modulation
FMA	Ferrite Manufacturers' Association
FMC	Federal Maritime Commission

FNMA	Federal National Mortgage Association ("Fannie Mae")
FPC	Federal Power Commission
FPE	Fixed price with escalation
FRED	Fiendishly rapid electronic device; Figure-reading
FRS	Federal Reserve System
F-to-F	Face to face
FTC	Federal Trade Commission
FTR	Film tracing reproduction
FTS	Federal Telecommunications System
FYI	For your information

G

GAES	Gas Appliance Engineers' Society
GAIT	Government and industry team
GAMA	Gas Appliance Manufacturers' Association
GAO	General Accounting Office
GBL	Government bill of lading
GCMA	Government Contract Management Association of America
GIFS	Gray Iron Founders' Society
GPO	Government Printing Office
GSA	General Services Administration
GWT	Gross weight
GZ	Ground Zero

H

HEI	Human Engineering Institute
HEPC	Hydroelectric Power Commission
HES	Home Entertainment Service (pay TV)
HEW	Department of Health, Education and Welfare
HSP	High-speed printer
HSS	High speed steel
HTA	Heavier-than-air
H-T-H-W	High-temperature, hot-water
HTO	Horizontal takeoff
HTOHL	Horizontal takeoff, horizontal landing
HUD	Department of Housing and Urban Development
HV	High voltage
HVDC	High-voltage direct current
HVPS	High-voltage power supply
HY-COM	Highway communications system
HYD	Hydraulic
Hz	Hertz

I

IAA	International Academy of Astronautics
IAAC	International Association for Analog Computation
IAARC	International Administrative Aeronautical Radio Conference
IACC	Industrial Analysis and Control Council
IACOMS	International Advisory Committee on Marine Sciences
IACS	International Arms-Control Symposium
IAD	Initiation area discriminator; International Astrophysical Decade
IAEA	International Atomic Energy Agency
IAEI	International Association of Electrical Inspectors
IAEL	International Association of Electrical Leagues
IAESTE	International Association for the Exchange of Students for Technical Experience
IAF	International Astronautical Federation
IAGS	Inter-American Geodetic Survey
IAL	International Algebraic Language
IAM	Institute of Appliance Manufacturers
IAMS	Instantaneous audience measurement system
IAO	Internal automation operation
IAPO	International Association of Physical Oceanography
IAS	Institute of the Aeronautical Sciences
IASA	Insurance Accounting and Statistical Association
IATA	International Air Transport Association
IATCS	International Air Traffic Communication Station
IATSE	International Alliance of Theatrical Stage Employees
IAU	International Astronomical Union
IAW	In accordance with
I & C	Installation and checkout
IBEW	International Brotherhood of Electrical Workers
IBO	International Broadcasting Organization
IBRD	International Bank for Reconstruction and Development
ICA	Industrial Communications Association
ICAO	International Civil Aviation Organization
ICBM	Intercontinental ballistic missile
ICC	Interstate Commerce Commission
ICDO	International Civil Defense Organization
ICE	Input-checking equipment. Institution of Civil Engineers (British organization)
ICECAN	Iceland-Canada telephone cable
ICES	International Council for the Exploration of the Sea
ICET	Institute for the Certification of Engineering Technicians

ICI	Investment Casting Institute
ICIP	International Conference on Information Processing
ICL	Incoming line
ICME	International Conference on Medical Electronics
ICO	Interagency Committee on Oceanography
ICR	International Congress of Radiology
ICRP	International Commission on Radiological Protection
ICRU	International Commission on Radiological Units and Measurements
ICSU	International Council of Scientific Unions
IDA	Institute for Defense Analysis; International Development Association
IDHA	Intelligence data handling system
IDI	Industrial Designers' Institute
IEC	International Electrotechnical Commission
IECEJ	Institute of Electrical Communications Engineers of Japan
IEE	Institute of Environmental Engineers
IES	Illuminating Engineering Society; Institute of Environmental Sciences
IFAC	International Federation on Automatic Control
IFALPA	International Federation of Airline Pilots' Associations
IFATCA	International Federation of Air Traffic Controllers' Associations
IFC	International Finance Corp.
IFEMS	International Congress of the Federation of Electron Microscope Societies
IFF	Identification, friend, or foe
IFI	Industrial Fasteners Institute
IFIPS	International Federation of Information Processing Societies
IFME	International Federation for Medical Electronics
IFN	Information
IGY	International Geophysical Year
IHE	Industrial Heating Equipment Association
IHFM	Institute of High Fidelity Manufacturers
IHP	Indicated horsepower
IISL	International Institute of Space Law
ILG	Instrument-landing guidance
ILS	Instrument landing system
ILSAP	Instrument landing system approach
IMS	Image-motion simulator; Industrial Management Society. Institute of Management Sciences
IMSA	International Municipal Signal Association
IMST	Institute of Marine Sciences and Technology

IN	Input
INACS	Interstate Airways Communications Station
INCR	Increase, Increment
IND	Indicator
INTEL	Intelligence
INTL	International
I/O	Input/Output
IOCS	Input-Output Control System
ION	Institute of Navigation
IOP	Input/output processor
IOPS	Input-output programming system
IOR	Input-output register
IORU	International Commission on Radiological Units and Measurements
IOS	International Organization for Standardization
IOU	Immediate operational use
IOVST	International Organization for Vacuum Science and Technology
IPBM	Interplanetary ballistic missile
IPC	Institute of Paper Chemistry; Institute of Printed Circuits
IPCEA	Insulated Power Cable Engineer's Association
IPM	Impulses per minute
IPPMA	In-plant Powder Metallurgy Association
IPRO	International Patent Research Office
IPY	International Polar Year
IR	Information retireval
IRE	Institute of Radio Engineers
ISO	International Organization for Standardization; International Science Organization
ISR	Information storage and retrieval
ITE	Institute of Telecommunications Engineers
ITU	International Telecommunications Union
ITV	Industral television
IUB	International Union of Biochemistry
IUE	International Union of Electrical, Radio, and Machine Workers (AFL-CIO)
IUPAP	International Union of Pure and Applied Physics
IUTAM	International Union of Theoretical and Applied Mechanics

J

JAAF	Joint Army-Air Force
JAN	Joint Army-Navy

JANAF	Joint Army-Navy-Air Force
JCC	Joint Communications Center
JCET	Joint Council on Educational Television
JCS	Joint Chiefs of Staff

L

LASER	Light amplification by stimulated emission of radiation
LASL	Los Alamos Scientific Laboratory
LAT	Latitude
LIM	Limit
LIQ	Liquid
L-I-W	Loss-in-weight
LL	Loudness level. Lower limit
LOG	Logarithm
LOGANDS	Logical commands
LOGIPAC	Logical processor and computer
LOGLAN	Logical language
LOGRAM	Logical program
LPG	Liquid petroleum gas. Liquid propane gas
LRD	Long-range data
LRG	Long range
LRP	Long-range plans
LS	Laser system, Light source
LSP	Low-speed printer
LV	Low-voltage

M

MANOP	Manual of operation
MAPI	Machinery and Allied Products Institute
MAR	Memory address register
MATS	Military Air Transport Service
M-B	Make-break
MCP	Master control program
MDT	Mean down time
MEC	Manufacturing Engineering Council
MEDLARS	Medical literature analysis and retrieval system
MET	Meteorological
MF	Medium frequency. Microcard Foundation
MICR	Magnetic ink character recognition
MIL	One thousandth of an inch
MIR	Memory-information register
MISA	Military Industrial Supply Agency

MLC	Motor load control
MP	Maintenance point. Melting point
MPA	Metal Powder Association
MPCA	Metal Powder Core Association
MPIF	Metal Powder Industries Federation
MPPA	Metal Powder Producers' Association
MPTA	Mechanical Power Transmission Association
MRIA	Magnetic Recording Industry Association
MS	Memory system; Military secret
MSL	Mean sea level
MSS	Manufacturers' Standardization Society

N

NAB	National Association of Broadcasters
NABET	National Association of Broadcast and Engineering Technicians
NABUG	National Association of Broadcast Unions and Guilds
NACE	National Association of Corrosion Engineers
NACOR	National Advisory Committee on Radiation (U.S. Public Health Service)
NACR	National Advisory Committee on Radiation
NAEB	National Association of Educational Broadcasters
NAEC	National Aviation Education Council
NAED	National Association of Electrical Distributors
NAIP	National Association of Industrial Plants
NAM	National Association of Manufacturers
NAMF	National Association of Metal Finishers
NAMM	National Association of Music Merchants
NANAC	National Aircraft Noise Abatement Council
NAPA	National Association of Purchasing Agents; National Automotive Parts Association
NAPE	National Association of Power Engineers
NAPM	National Association of Photographic Manufacturers
NAR	National Association of Rocketry
NARAS	National Academy of Recording Arts and Sciences
NARDA	National Appliance and Radio-TV Dealers' Association
NARM	National Association of Relay Manufacturers
NARTB	National Association of Radio and TV Broadcasters
NAS	National Academy of Sciences
NASA	National Aeronautics and Space Administration
NATO	North Atlantic Treaty Organization
NAW	National Association of Wholesalers
NBAA	National Business Aircraft Association
NBFAA	National Burglar and Fire Alarm Association

NBFU	National Board of Fire Underwriters
NBS	National Bureau of Standards
NCAR	National Center for Atmospheric Research
NCI	National Cancer Institute
NCRL	National Citizens Radio League
NCSBEE	National Council of State Boards of Engineering Examiners
NCSL	National Conference of Standards Laboratories
NCTA	National Community Television Association, Inc.
NDEA	National Defense Education Act
NDT	Nondestructive testing
NDTA	National Defense Transportation Association
NEDA	National Electronic Distributors' Association
NELA	National Electric Light Association
NEMA	National Electrical Manufacturers' Association
NESC	National Electrical Safety Code
NET	National Educational Television
NETRC	National Educational Television and Radio Center
NFFS	Nonferrous Founders' Society
NFPA	National Fire Protection Association; National Fluid Power Association
NFTW	National Federation of Telephone Workers
NHI	National Heart Institute
NI	Noise index
NIC	National Inventors' Council
NICB	National Industrial Conference Board
NIH	National Institutes of Health
NIL	Nothing
NIMA	National Insulation Manufacturers' Association
NIMH	National Institute of Mental Health
NIRNS	National Institute for Research in Nuclear Science
NLRB	National Labor Relations Board
NMA	National Management Association; National Microfilm Association
NMTBA	National Machine Tool Builders' Association
NOHP	Not otherwise herein provided
NOIBN	Not otherwise indexed by name
NORAD	North American Air Defense Command
NOS	Not otherwise specified
NRC	National Research Council; National Rocket Club
NRECA	National Rural Electric Cooperative Association
NRL	Naval Research Lab
NRMA	National Retail Merchants' Association
NSC	National Safety Council; National Security Council National Space Council

NSEC	Nanosecond
NSF	National Science Fair; National Science Foundation
NSIA	National Security Industrial Association
NSMPA	National Screw Machine Products Association
NSMR	National Society for Medical Research
NSPE	National Society of Professional Engineers
NSRB	National Security Resources Board
NSSCC	National Space Surveillance Control Center
NTDMA	National Tool and Die Manufacturers' Association
NTDPMA	National Tool, Die, and Precision Machining Association
NTID	National Technical Institute for the Deaf
NVPA	National Visual Presentation Association
NWAHACA	National Warm-Air Heating and Air-Conditioning Association
NYSF	National Youth Science Foundation

O

OABETA	Office Appliance and Business Equipment Trades Association
OAO	Orbiting Astronomical Observatory
OAS	Organization of American States
OASR	Office of Aeronautical and Space Research (NASA)
OCCA	Overseas Communications Cooperation Association
ODM	Office of Defense Mobilization
OECD	Organization for Economic Cooperation and Development
OEMI	Office Equipment Manufacturers' Institute
OEP	Office of Emergency Planning
OMGUS	Office of Military Government, United States
ONI	Office of Naval Intelligence
ORSA	Operations Research Society of America
OSA	Optical Society of America
OSD	Office of the Secretary of Defense
OSIS	Office of Scientific Information Service
OSRD	Office of Scientific Research and Development
OT	Overtime
OTUS	Office of the Treasurer of the United States
OUT	Output

P

PATCO	Professional Air Traffic Controllers' Organization
PBX	Private branch exchange
PC	Petty cash

PD	Paid; Per diem
PEC	Photoelectric cell
PEI	Porcelain Enamel Institute
PERT	Program evaluation review technique
PHS	Public Health Service
PLATO	Programmed logic for automatic teaching operations
PMA	Phonograph Manufacturers' Association
PMEA	Powder Metallurgy Equipment Association
PMI	Pressed Metal Institute
PMPMA	Powder Metallurgy Parts Manufacturers' Association
PPM	Parts per million
PPMA	Precision Potentiometer Manufacturer's Association
P-S	Pressure-sensitive
P/S	Point of Shipment
PSE	Please

Q

QF	Quality Factor

R

RADAR	Radio detection and ranging
RARAD	Radar advisory
RAREP	Radar weather report
RCOA	Radio Club of America
RCPA	Rural Cooperative Power Association
R & D	Research and development
RDBL	Readable
RDO	Readout
RDT & E	Research, development, test, and evaluation
REA	Rural Electrification Administration (Department of Agriculture)
REM	Rapid eye movement
REP	Request for proposal
RFQ	Request for quote
RIAA	Recording Industry Association of America
RPRT	Report
RPT	Repeat
RRB	Railroad Retirement Board
RTDA	Radio and Television Dealers' Association
RTDG	Radio and TV Directors Guild
RTES	Radio-TV Executives' Society
RTF	Radiotelephone
R/W	Rights-of-way
RWG	Radio Writers' Guild

S

SAC	Strategic Air Command
SAMA	Scientific Apparatus Makers' Association
SAP	Society for Applied Spectroscopy
SBA	Small Business Administration
SBIC	Small Business Investment Company
S/C	Short circuit
SEC	Securities and Exchange Commission
SFP	Straight fixed price
SHAPE	Supreme Headquarters, Allied Powers in Europe
SIT-REP	Situation report
S & L	Systems and logistics
SLA	Special Libraries Association
SMPTE	Society of Motion Picture and TV Engineers
SORD	Society of Record Dealers of America
SPAA	Systems and Procedures Association of America
SPE	Society of Plastics Engineers
SPIE	Society of Photographic Instrumentation Engineers
SPSE	Society of Photographic Scientists and Engineers
SSA	Social Security Administration
SSS	Selective Service System
STOL	Short takeoff and landing
SUB	Subtract

T

TAGA	Technical Association of the Graphic Arts
TAPPI	Technical Association of the Pulp and Paper Industry
TBO	Time between overhauls
TCMA	Tabulating Card Manufacturers' Association
TCPC	Tab card punch control
T/D	Tons per day
TESA	Television and Electronics Service Association
T-M	Time and materials
TVA	Tennessee Valley Authority
TWX	Telegraph; Teletype. (Teletypewriter exchange service)

U

UCC	Uniform commercial code
UERMWA	United Electrical-Radio Machine Workers of America
UEW	United Electrical Workers
UFN	Until further notice
UFO	Unidentified flying objects

UGGI	International Union of Geodesy and Geophysics
UHF	Ultra-high frequency
UMA	Ultrasonic Manufacturers' Association
UMT	Universal military training
UMW	Ultra-microwaves
UNAECC	United Nations Atomic Energy Control Commission
USES	United States Employment Service
UNESCO	United Nations Educational, Scientific, and Cultural Organization
UNSC	United Nations Security Council
USAFI	United State Armed Forces Institute
USCC	United States Chamber of Commerce
USCSC	United States Civil Service Commission
USDC	United States Department of Commerce
USIA	United States Information Agency
USITA	United States Independent Telephone Association

V

VA	Veterans Administration
VHF	Very high frequency
VLF	Very low frequency

W

WC	Write and compute
WO	Write out
WOC	Without compensation

Z

ZD	Zero defects
ZIP CODE	Zoning improvement plan code

Abbreviations of Academic Degrees

A.B.	Bachelor of Arts (Latin: Artium Baccalaureus)
A.M.	Master of Arts (Latin: Artium Magister)
Ar.M.	Master of Architecture (Latin: Architecturae Magister)
B.A.	Bachelor of Arts (Latin: Baccalaureus Artium)
B.A.E.	Bachelor of Aeronautical Engineering; Bachelor of Arts in Education
B.Agr.; B.Ag.	Bachelor of Agriculture (Latin: Baccalaureus Agriculturae)
B.Ag.Sc.	Bachelor of Agricultural Science

B.Ar.; B. Arch.	Bachelor of Architecture
B.A.S.; B.A.Sc.	Bachelor of Architectural Science; Bachelor of Applied Science
B.B.A.; B.Bus.Ad.	Bachelor of Business Administration
B.C.	Bachelor of Chemistry
B.C.E.	Bachelor of Chemical Engineering; Bachelor of Civil Engineering
B.Ch.E.	Bachelor of Chemical Engineering
B.C.L.	Bachelor of Civil Law
B.C.S.	Bachelor of Chemcial Science
B.D.	Bachelor of Divinity
B.D.S.	Bachelor of Dental Surgery
B.E.	Bachelor of Education; Bachelor of Engineering
B.E.E.	Bachelor of Electrical Engineering
B. ès L.	Bachelor of Letters (French: Bachelier ès Lettres)
B.F.	Bachelor of Finance; Bachelor of Forestry
B.F.A.	Bachelor of Fine Arts
B.J.	Bachelor of Journalism
B.L.	Bachelor of Laws
B.L.A.	Bachelor of Liberal Arts
B.Lit; B. Litt.	Bachelor of Letters; Bachelor of Literature (Latin: Baccalaureus Litterarum)
B.L.L.	Bachelor of Laws (Latin: Baccalaureus Legum)
B.L.S.	Bachelor of Library Science
B.M.	Bachelor of Medicine (Latin: Baccalaureus Medicinae)
B.M.E.	Bachelor of Mechanical Engineering; Bachelor of Mining Engineering
B.Mech.E.	Bachelor of Mechanical Engineering
B.Mus.	Bachelor of Music
B.P.	Bachelor of Pharmacy (Latin: Baccalaureus Philosophiae)
B.Pd.; B.Pe.	Bachelor of Pedagogy
B.P.E.	Bachelor of Physical Education
B.P.H.	Bachelor of Public Health
B.S.; B.Sc.	Bachelor of Science (Latin: Baccalaureus Scientiae)
B.S.A.	Bachelor of Scientific Agriculture
B.S.Ed.	Bachelor of Science in Education
B.S.S., B.S.Sc., B.S. in S.S.	Bachelor of (Science in) Social Sciences
B.T.; B.Th.	Bachelor of Theology (Latin: Baccalaureus Theologiae)

C.B., Ch.B.	Bachelor of Surgery (Latin: Chirurgiae Bacalaureus)
Ch.D.	Doctor of Chemistry
Ch.E.	Chemical Engineer
Ch.M., C.M.	Master of Surgery (Latin: Chriurgiae Magister)
C.S.B.	Bachelor of Christian Science
D.C.	Doctor of Chiropractic
D.C.L.	Doctor of Canon Law; Doctor of Civil Law
D.C.S.	Doctor of Christian Science; Doctor of Commercial Science
D.D.	Doctor of Divinity (Latin: Divinitatis Doctor)
D.D.S.	Doctor of Dental Surgery
D.D.Sc.	Doctor of Dental Science
De.ès.L.	Doctor of Letters (French: Docteur ès Lettres)
De.ès S.	Doctor of Sciences (French: Docteur ès Sciences)
D.Lit.;D.Litt.	Doctor of Letters (or Literature) (Latin: Doctor Lit(t)erarum)
D.L.S.	Doctor of Library Science
D.M.D.	Doctor of Dental Medicine (Latin: Dentariae Medici nae Doctor)
D.Mus.	Doctor of Music
D.O.	Doctor of Osteopathy
D.Ph.;D.Phil.	Doctor of Philosophy
D.P.H.	Doctor of Public Health
D.P.Hy.	Doctor of Public Hygiene
D.S.;D.Sc.	Doctor of Science (Latin: Doctor Scientiae)
D-S.T.	Doctor of Sacred Theology
D.Th.;D.Theol.	Doctor of Theology
D.V.M.	Doctor of Veterinary Medicine
D.V.M.S.	Doctor of Veterinary Medicine and Surgery
Ed.B.	Bachelor of Education
Ed.D.	Doctor of Education
Ed.M.	Master of Education
E.E.	Electrical Engineer
Eng.D.	Doctor of Engineering
J.C.D.	Doctor of Canon Law (Latin: Juris Canonici Doctor); Doctor of Civil Law (Latin: Juris Civilis Doctor)
J.D.;Jur.D.	Doctor of Laws (Latin: Juris Doctor)
L.A.M.	Master of Liberal Arts (Latin: Liberalium Artium Magister)
L.B.	Bachelor of Letters (Latin: Litterarum Baccalaureus)
L.D.S.	Licentiate in Dental Surgery
L.H.D.	Doctor of Humanities (Latin: Letterarum Human iorum Doctor)
Lit.B.;Litt.B.	Bachelor of Letters (or Literature) (Latin, Lit(t)erarum Baccalaureus)

Lit.D.;Litt.D.	Doctor of Letters (or Literature) (Latin: Lit(t)erarum Doctor)
LL.B.	Bachelor of Laws (Latin: Legum Baccalaureus)
LL.D.	Doctor of Laws (Latin: Legum Doctor)
LL.M.	Master of Laws (Latin: Legum Magister)
L.M.	Licentiate in Medicine (Or Midwifery)
L.S.	Licentiate in Surgery
M.A.	Master of Arts (Latin: Magister Artium)
M.Agr.	Master of Agriculture
M.B.	Bachelor of Medicine (Latin: Magister Chirurgiae)
M.B.A.	Master in (or of) Business Administration
M.Ch.	Master of Surgery (Latin: Magister Chirurgiae)
M.C.L.	Master of Civil Law
M.D.	Doctor of Medicine (Latin: Medicinae Doctor)
M.D.S.	Master of Dental Surgery
M.Ed.	Master of Education
M.L.S.	Master of Library Science
M.Pd.	Master of Pedagogy
M.P.E.	Master of Physical Education
M.S.	Master of Science (also M.Sc); Master in Surgery
Mus.B.; Mus.Bac.	Bachelor of Music (Latin: Musicae Baccalaureus)
Mus.D.; Mus.Doc. **Mus.DR.**	Doctor of Music (Latin: Musicae Doctor)
Mus.M.	Master of Music (Latin: Musicae Magister)
Pd.B.	Bachelor of Pedagogy (Latin: Pedagogiae Baccalaureus)
Pd.D.	Doctor of Pedagogy (Latin: Pedagogiae Doctor)
Pd.M.	Master of Pedagogy (Latin: Pedagogiae Magister)
Phar.B.	Bachelor of Pharmacy (Latin: Pharmaciae Baccalaureus)
Phar.D.; Pharm. D.	Doctor of Pharmacy (Latin: Pharmaciae Doctor)
Pharm. M.	Master of Pharmacy (Latin: Pharmaciae Magister)
Ph.B.	Bachelor of Philosophy (Latin: Philosophiae Baccalaureus)
Ph.D.	Doctor of Philosophy (Latin: Philosophiae Doctor)
Pod.D.	Doctor of Podiatry
S.B.	Bachelor of Science (Latin: Scientiae Baccalaureus)
Sc.B.	Bachelor of Science (Latin: Scientiae Magister)
Sc.D.;S.D.	Doctor of Science (Latin: Scientiae Doctor)
Sc.M.	Master of Science (Latin: Scientiae Magister)
S.J.D.	Doctor of Juridical Science (Latin: Scientiae Juridicae Doctor)
S.M.	Master of Science (Latin: Scientiae Magister)
S.T.B.	Bachelor of Sacred Theology (Latin: Sacrae Theologiae Baccalaureus)

S.T.D.	Doctor of Sacred Theology (Latin: Sacrae Theologiae Doctor)
S.T.M.	Master of Sacred Theology (Latin: Sacrae Theologiae Magister)
Th.B.	Bachelor of Theology (Latin: Theologiae Baccalaureus)
Th.D.	Doctor of Theology (Latin: Theologiae Doctor)
U.J.D.	Doctor of Civil and Canon Law (Latin: Utriusque Juris Doctor)
V.M.D.	Doctor of Veterinary Medicine

Abbreviations of Military Titles

AIR FORCE

Ranks/abbreviatons for commissioned officers are identical to those in the Army.

Enlisted Personnel

Rank	**When Used Before a Name**
chief master sergeant	Chief Master Sgt.
senior master sergeant	Senior Master Sgt.
master sergeant	Master Sgt.
technical sergeant	Tech. Sgt.
staff sergeant	Staff Sgt.
sergeant	Sgt.
airman first class	Airman 1st Class
airman	Airman
airman basic	Airman

ARMY

Commissioned Officers

general	Gen.
lieutenant general	Lt. Gen.
major general	Maj. Gen.
brigadier general	Brig. Gen.
colonel	Col.
lieutenant colonel	Lt. Col.
major	Maj.
captain	Capt.

| first lieutenant | 1st Lt. |
| second lieutenant | 2nd Lt. |

Warrant Officers

Rank	**When Used Before a Name**
chief warrant officer	Chief Warrant Officer
warrant officer	Warrant Officer

Enlisted Personnel

sergeant major of the Army	Army Sgt. Maj.
command sergeant major	Command Sgt. Maj.
staff sergeant major	Staff Sgt. Maj.
first sergeant	1st Sgt.
master sergeant	Master Sgt.
platoon sergeant	Platoon Sgt.
sergeant first class	Sgt. 1st Class
specialist seven	Spec. 7
staff sergeant	Staff. Sgt.
specialist six	Spec. 6
sergeant	Sgt.
specialist five	Spec. 5
corporal	Cpl.
specialist four	Spec. 4
private first class	Pfc.
private 2	Pvt. 2
private 1	Pvt. 1

MARINE CORPS

The abbreviations of rank for commissioned officers are the same as those in the Army. Warrant officer ratings use the same system as the Navy. The Marines have no specialist ratings.

Other

Rank	**When Used Before a Name**
sergeant major	Sgt. Maj.
master gunnery sergeant	Master Gunnery Sgt.
master sergeant	Master Sgt.
first sergeant	1st Sgt.
gunnery sergeant	Gunnery Sgt.
staff sergeant	Staff Sgt.
sergeant	Sgt.

Rank	When Used Before a Name
corporal	Cpl.
lance corporal	Lance Cpl.
private first class	Pfc.
private	Pvt.

NAVY, COAST GUARD

Commissioned Officers

admiral	Adm.
vice admiral	Vice Adm.
rear admiral	Rear Adm.
commodore	Commodore
captain	Cpt.
commander	Cmdr.
lieutenant commander	Lt. Cmdr.
lieutenant	Lt.
lieutenant junior grade	Lt. j.g.
ensign	Ensign

Warrant Officers

Rank	When Used Before a Name
commissioned warrant officer	Commissioned Warrant Officer
warrant officer	Warrant Officer

Enlisted Personnel

master chief petty officer	Master Chief Petty Officer
senior chief petty officer	Senior Chief Petty Officer
chief petty officer	Chief Petty Officer
petty officer first class	Petty Officer 1st Class
petty officer second class	Petty Officer 2nd Class
petty officer third class	Petty Officer 3rd Class
seaman	Seaman
seaman apprentice	Seaman Apprentice
seaman recruit	Seaman Recruit

Abbreviations and Acronyms of Government and Military Terms

GOVERNMENT

AEC	Atomic Energy Commission
A.F.T.R.	American Federal Tax Reports
ARPA	Advanced Research Projects Agency
Bd. of Rev.	Board of Review
BLS	Bureau of Labor Statistics
BTA	Board of Tax Appeals
CAA	Civil Aeronautics Administration
CAB	Civil Aeronautics Board
C.I.D.	Criminal Investigation Department
CIR	Commissioner of Internal Revenue
Coll.	Collector (internal revenue)
Comp. Gen. Op.	United States Comptroller General's Opinion
CSC	Civil Service Commission
CSS	Commodity Stabilization Service
Dem.	Democrat
DLF	Development Loan Fund
D.L.O.	Dead Letter Office
ERP	European Recovery Program
FCA	Farm Credit Administration
FCC	Federal Communications Commission
FDA	Food and Drug Administration
Fed. Reg.	Federal Register
F.H.A., FHA	Federal Housing Administration
FMCS	Federal Mediation and Conciliation Service
FPC	Federal Power Commission
F.R.B.	Federal Reserve Board (Bank)
F.R.S.	Federal Reserve System
FSA	Federal Security Agency
FTC	Federal Trade Commission
G.A.	General Assembly
GAO	General Accounting Office
GNP	Gross National Product
G.S.	General Statutes
H.B.	House Bill (state)
H.C.	House of Commons
HEW	Department of Health, Education, and Welfare
HHFA	Housing and Home Finance Agency
H.L.	House of Lords

H.R.	House Resolution (federal); House of Repre sentatives
H. Rep. (with number)	House Report
H. Res. (with number)	House Resolution
ICC	Interstate Commerce Commission
I.L.P.	Independent Labour Party (Britain)
IRC	Internal Revenue Code
IRO	International Refugee Organization
IRS	Internal Revenue Service
Judge Adv. Gen., J.A.G.	Judge Advocate General
M.C.	Member of Congress
M.P.	Member of Parliament
NA	Nonacquiescence (by CIR)
N.A.T.O., NATO	North Atlantic Treaty Organization
NBS	National Bureau of Standards
NLRB	National Labor Relations Board
NMB	National Mediation Board
NOVS	National Office of Vital Statistics
Pat. Off.	Patent Office
PHA	Public Housing Administration
PHS	Public Health Service
REA	Rural Electrification Administration
SBA	Small Business Administration
S.E.A.T.O.	Southeast Asia Treaty Organization
SEC	Securities and Exchange Commission
Sen.	Senate; Senator
S.F.	State Senate Bill
S. Rept. (with number)	Senate Report
S. Res. (with number)	Senate Resolution
SSA	Social Security Administration
TC	Tax Court of the United States
TVA	Tennessee Valley Authority
U.N. or UN	United Nations
UNESCO	United Nations Educational, Social, and Cultural Organization
UNICEF	United Nations Children's Fund
U.N.R.R.A.	United Nations Relief and Rehabilitation Administration
VA	Veterans Administration

WHO	World Health Organization

MILITARY

Adj.	Adjutant
A.G.	Adjutant General
Brig. Gen.	Brigadier General
Capt.	Captain
Col.	Colonel
D.S.C.	Distinguished Service Cross
D.S.M.	Distinguished Service Medal
GI	General issue; government issue
ICBM	Intercontinental ballistic missile
Lt.	Lieutenant
Lt. Col.	Lieutenant Colonel
Lt. Comdr.	Lieutenant Commander
Lt. Gen.	Lieutenant General
M.H.	Medal of Honor
MP	Military Police
M. Sgt.	Master Sergeant
N.C.O.	Noncommissioned Officer
OSD	Office of the Secretary of Defense
POW	Prisoner of war
Pvt.	Private
PX	Post exchange
Q.M. Gen.	Quartermaster General
Q.M. Sgt.	Quartermaster Sergeant
ROTC	Reserve Officers' Training Corps
Sgt.	Sergeant
USA	U.S. Army
USAF	U.S. Air Force
USCG	U.S. Coast Guard
USMC	U.S. Marine Corps
USN	U.S. Navy
USNR	U.S. Naval Reserve
WAC	Women's Army Corps
WAF	Women in the Air Force
WAVES	Women Appointed for Volunteer Emergency Service
WO	Warrant officer

Postal Abbreviations for the States

Here's a listing of the traditional abbreviations for the states, along with the newer, two-letter abbreviations recommended by the Post Office. Leave two spaces between the state abbreviation and the ZIP code.

	Traditional	**Two-Letter**		**Traditional**	**Two-Letter**
Alabama	Ala.	AL	Montana	Mont.	MT
Alaska	Alas.	AK	Nebraska	Nebr.	NB
Arizona	Ariz.	AZ	Nevada	Nev.	NV
Arkansas	Ark.	AR	New Hampshire	N.H.	NH
California	Cal.	CA	New Jersey	N.J.	NJ
Canal Zone	C.Z.	CZ	New Mexico	N.M.; N. Mex	NM
Colorado	Colo.	CO	New York	N.Y.	NY
Connecticut	Conn.	CT	North Carolina	N.C.	NC
Delaware	Del.	DE	North Dakota	N.D.; N. Dak.	ND
District of	Dist. Col.	DC	Ohio	Ohio	OH
Columbia			Oklahoma	Okla.	OK
Florida	Fla.	FL	Oregon	Oreg.	OR
Georgia	Ga.	GA	Pennsylvania	Pa.	PA
Hawaii	Hawaii	HI	Puerto Rico	P.R.	PR
Idaho	Idaho	ID	Rhode Island	R.I.	RI
Indiana	Ind.	IN	South Carolina	S.C.	SC
Iowa	Iowa	IA	South Dakota	S.D.; S. Dak.	SD
Kansas	Kans.	KS	Tennessee	Tenn.	TN
Kentucky	Ky.	KY	Texas	Tex.	TX
Louisiana	La.	LA	Utah	Utah	UT
Maine	Maine	ME	Vermont	Vt.	VT
Maryland	Md.	MD	Virginia	Va.	VA
Massachusetts	Mass.	MA	Virgin Islands	V.I.	VI
Michigan	Mich.	MI	Washington	Wash.	WA
Minnesota	Minn.	MN	West Virginia	W. Va.	WV
Mississippi	Miss.	MS	Wisconsin	Wisc.	WI
Missouri	Mo.	MO	Wyoming	Wyo.	WY

18. PROOFREADER'S MARKS

∧ Make the correction shown in the margin.

Stet Keep the crossed-out word or letter. (Latin: let it stand.)

· · · · Keep the words underlined by the dots. (Write "Stet" in margin.)

✗ Appears broken; examine.

≡ Straighten the lines.

✓✓✓ Unevenly spaced; correct the spacing.

⎸⎹ Line up. (Make lines even with other copy.)

run in No break in the reading; no paragraph.

no ¶ No paragraph. (Sometimes written "run in.")

out see copy Omit; see copy.

¶ Make a new paragraph here.

tr Transpose words or letters as shown.

ℐ Take out the matter shown; delete.

ℐ̃ Take out the character shown and close up.

¢ Lower case if a line is drawn through a cap.

⑨ Upside down; reverse.

⌒ Close up; leave no space.

Insert more space here.

⊥ Lower this space.

⎕ Indent line the space of one letter "M."

⊏ Move this to the left.

⊐ Move this to the right.

⌐⌐ Raise to correct position.

∟⊿ Lower to correct position.

//// Hair space letters.

w.f. Wrong font; change to correct font.

Qu? Is this right?

l.c. Put in small letters (lower case).

s.c. Put in small capitals.

Caps Put in capitals.

C ∤s.c. Put in caps and small caps.

rom Change to Roman letters.

ital Change to Italic letters.

≡ Use caps, if under letter or word.

⹀ Use small caps, if under letter or word.

⌐ Italic, if under letter or word.

∿ Bold face, if under letter or word.

⸓/ Insert comma.

;/ Insert semicolon.

:/ Insert colon.

⊙ Insert period.

/?/ Insert question mark.

/!/ Insert exclamation mark.

/=/ Insert hyphen.

⸌ Insert apostrophe.

⸜⸝ Insert quotation marks.

ᵃ⌄ Insert hyperscript or figure.

₂⌃ Insert subscript or figure.

⌐/⌐ Insert brackets.

(/) Insert parenthesis.

1/M One-em dash.

2/M Two-em parallel dash.

PART III.

Executive's Guide to Effective Letters, Reports, and Memos

19. HOW TO GET YOUR READER'S ATTENTION

It's not always easy to get the attention of a busy person, especially when you're asking for an order or trying to persuade him or her to accept your point of view. But there are a few tricks you can use to make your reader take notice of your ideas faster—and remember them.

Pay a compliment.	Mr. Jones, ever since you presented your ideas on cost control at the product manager's meeting, we've wanted to hear more from you. We think you can have an important impact on the profitability of this department.
Ask a question.	Mrs. Benson, have you ever had the excitement of participating in a product promotion—one you've helped design personally?
State something the reader can agree with.	If there's one subject we both agree on, it's the need for more and better research. We've both talked about it often, haven't we? Here's an idea about how we can get more research data on product X—with some guidance from you and your staff.
State a basic problem the reader can relate to.	Ideas for the RX-15 project have stopped coming into the research lab and we're not happy about it. Unless you can help us think of something to stimulate interest in this project, there's a good chance the entire effort will be scrapped. Here's what happened so far.
State a noteworthy accomplishment.	Last year, nearly a thousand people like you made an important decision that paid off in higher earnings, saved time and had the chance to grow into an important leadership position.
Ask a favor.	Will you help us save the RX-15 project? It's in trouble, and we think you're one of the few people who can revive it.

Say something important.	Give your family a head start toward financial security!
Use a simulating newspaper headline.	NEW SAVINGS POSSIBLE WITH FULL-CASE PURCHASES—SAVE $.44 PER ITEM!
Use a hypothetical statement.	If three of your top employees walked into your office tomorrow morning and quit, what would you do?
Use a comparison or short story.	Bob Jones and Helen Brown both started working at Ace Packing just six months ago. They both have the same education, skills, and training to do their jobs—package design experts. Yesterday afternoon, Jack Whittaker, President of Ace Packing, called Helen to his office and told her, "Helen, you and Bob have been co-workers, and we want to promote a talented woman to a position in another department. The trouble is, Bob has the same qualifications, and may quit if we give you the job. What do you think we should do?
Refer to something personal or important in the reader's life.	Congratulations on moving into your new home. With care, it'll give you years of pleasure and security. That's why it's important to consider extra insurance protection now—rather than waiting a year or two, when you'll probably be thinking about other things.
Use a famous quotation.	"If you can keep your head, when all about you are losing theirs and blaming it on you...."
Scare the reader.	This Friday, 400 people in New York State will be planning their vacation. By Sunday evening, their families will be planning their funerals.
Highlight a major product benefit.	The ACME 314 widget has the best laser production capability of any product on the market today. Who says? The National Laser Certification Agency ... for starters.
Offer something special.	For just one week, you can take 10 percent off our price tag—on any item we sell. We have an absolutely free gift waiting for you—just for coming to our store to see

	our new display of widgets. You don't even have to try out the widget—just come to the store to pick it up.
Solve a problem.	Here's a great solution to your Father's Day gift problem. It's a pipe made from crackers that Dad can smoke ... or eat ... or both.
Challenge the reader.	Try to think of five reasons why you wouldn't want to do business with us. We don't think you can. Heres' why: We'll bet you can't make this piece of new plastic break without bending it less than 50 times. Go ahead. Try it.
Use a testimonial.	"This Model 103 is the best copier we've ever used," says Tom McCaffery, office supervisor for Perry Paper Forms. "We found that all of our 47 employees could handle the instructions easily...."

Sample Outlines for Letters and Memos

I. *Good News*

    A. State the good news right away.

    B. Add more information.

        1. Include more facts, details, figures, statistics, terms, reasons.

        2. Show how to use the idea, product, or service.

        3. Re-sell your idea, product, or service.

        4. Promote an additional idea, product, or service, if it is appropriate.

    C. End on a friendly note.

        1. Say how pleased you are.

        2. Recommend some action the person might take.

        3. Say you are willing to provide further help.

II. *Bad News*

    A. Cushion the jolt to make your reader more receptive.

        1. Say thank you for something (even if it's just cooperation).

        2. Say something complimentary (carefulness, past record, etc.)

        3. Say you understand the position the person is in.

        4. Share any good news, but don't make it too positive (so you won't mislead).

5. Offer to help any way you can.
6. Say you have considered all the facts.
7. Show how you agree with the reader.

B. Explain your position.

1. Don't quote company policy—tell the reasons behind the policy.
2. Show how the decision is really in the reader's best interest.
3. Tell how you arrived at the decision—give whatever facts you can.
4. Be indirect when you can, letting the reader understand the unpleasant news by implication or suggestion. (However, if there is any possibility that you might be misinterpreted, use a more direct approach.)

C. Offer some positive suggestions.

1. Offer to help in some other way.
2. Say something constructive.
3. Re-direct the person's attention to another service or product you can provide (or show where the person can get it outside your firm).

D. Close on a friendly note.

1. Tell the reader what can be done easily, or what action can be taken.
2. Ask for future help, suggestions, support. Let the reader know you value his opinion.
3. Let the person know he or she is a valuable client, customer, or prospect.
4. Describe any further benefits.

III. *Requests*

A. State your key idea.

1. Introduce the request gently, but get to the point soon.
2. Give the reasons for your request.

B. Explain why you are asking for something.

1. Add details, facts, figures, statistics, reasons.
2. Organize your facts from most to least important, in terms of the reader's benefit.

C. Close with a message that will motivate.

1. Say what you want done—and when you want it done.

   2. Make it easy for the person to act. Include your phone number, a postage-paid reply envelope and any other information the reader will need to dispel any concern that action on his part may be difficult.
   3. Describe your appreciation and, if possible, restate how this will benefit the reader.

IV. *Motivational Letters and Memos*

   A. Grab his or her attention.

      1. Use a startling statement that will interest the reader.
      2. Ask a question the reader will want to answer.
      3. Make sure your opening sentence has the "You Attitude" and stresses reader benefits. (Check the list of benefits that motivate people, included in this chapter).

   B. Stimulate his interest.

      1. Describe the features, functions or attractiveness of your idea, product, or service.
      2. Describe the benefits (less work, more money, respect of other people, greater profits, friendship, customer satisfaction, greater comfort).

   C. Make the reader really *want* what you have to offer.

      1. Prove your statements with facts, figures, guarantees, samples.
      2. Stress the positive benefits.

   D. Tell the reader what to do.

      1. Ask for the order—tell the reader what you want.
      2. Make it easy (provide a postage-paid envelope, a phone number, a dime for the pay phone).

20. HOW TO ORGANIZE FORMAL REPORTS AND MEMOS

You may not want to use all thses headings, but they'll help you organize your thoughts more clearly and present your ideals logically.

Title Page	Include the title, usually near the center of the page. Near the bottom put your name, the date, and your division or department.
Contents	This listing of the major and minor headings in your report gives the reader a fast overview of what's in it and on what pages you've located the topics.
Authorization	This tells the reader who authorized you to write the report and why. It can be as short as a paragraph or a few sentences, or you may want to include the actual letter or memo from the person who told you to prepare the report. It also defines the project clearly and precisely.
Transmittal	This is an introduction you write to the person who requested or authorized the report.
Subject	This is a concise statement of the purpose of the report. Ideally, you should be able to state the purpose, or summarize the topic, in one sentence. When you can't do this (it isn't easy) without a lot of modifiers and restrictions, you may not have clarified the topic enough in your own mind.
Summary	This gives the highlights of the report so the reader understands the key points easily. It should be thorough enough so the reader doesn't have to read the entire report if he doesn't want to.
Introduction	This section states the purpose of the report, gives background information that can help the reader better understand the data in the report, and defines its scope. You should tell the reader how you've handled your research, and explain any unfamiliar terms or techniques.

Problem	You may wish to include this in the introduction, but many people prefer to put it in a separate section to emphasize it even more. For example, if the problem you're dealing with is absenteeism, you might say that the company is experiencing an absentee rate of 10 percent each Monday morning. The purpose of the report, then, is to find out why people are absent on Monday and to develop ways to correct the problem.
Purpose	This section tells what you hope to accomplish with your report. You should state it this clearly: "The purpose of this report is to..." or, "This report will explain why 10 percent of our people are late on Monday,s and suggest corrective action."
Scope	Here you explain how much or how little information you've included. You define the limits of your investigation. For example, in the absenteeism report, you might say you interviewed only the supervisors in the production area, as a pilot project, but did not interview supervisors of the clerical areas. You might also add that you conducted your survey by asking only one out of 10 employees, by random sampling, rather than asking each one.
Limitations	If there were factors that stopped you from doing a more complete job, such as time, money, clerical help, or availability of research data, you can mention that here. Don't mention it negatively, as if you were trying to cover yourself or complain, but simply to state the facts clearly.
Methods	Now you can say where you got your information, how you collected it, and how you analyzed it. You may want to concentrate on one or all of these ways to collect material:

Observation	Count the number of employees absent each Monday morning.
Experiment	Compare two groups, using the same factors for each, except for one experimental action. For example, take two production departments, and offer only

one of them a free, departmental beer party for 98 percent attendance over an eight-week period, and watch the results.

Library Find out what the experts say, through books, pamphlets, articles in trade journals and consumer magazines, newspapers, and government publications.

Survey Interview people directly, by mail, or by telephone. For example, talk personally with 10 department heads and 10 employees to find out what they think is the reason for absenteeism.

Discussion This contains the background of the problem, the facts from which you make your analyses and draw your conclusions. It should include all the statistics and data, illustrations, charts, and necessary information. It's the body of your report, so it should be organized logically, in a pattern that's appropriate for the material and easy to understand. Here are some options:

Causes/Effects Show how each of the items was a cause for something, or what effect it had on something else.

Chronology Discuss items in terms of the time in which they took place—hour by hour, day by day, month by month.

Compare Show the *similarities* among all the facts.

Contrast Show the *differences* among all the facts.

Criteria Organize the information according to the standards by which you measured it, accepted it, or rejected it.

Definition Simply define your terms, one after the other, either in the order in which they appear in the discussion, or in alphabetical order.

Details List all the facts, examples, and illustrations that help explain your topic. Describe all the details specifically.

Elimination One by one, eliminate the alternatives. Show why each idea or option won't work, until you reach the final idea or option that *will* work. Then show why it works.

Problem/Solution	Show how each item is a problem, and indicate the possible solutions.
Familiarity	Move from what the reader already knows and is familiar with, to what he doesn't know and isn't familiar with, but needs to know. You build new facts and ideas on ones already established.
Importance	Proceed from the least important item to the most important, or from the most important to the least important, depending upon the topic.
Repetition	Repeat and restate your point(s) in a variety of ways to explain your position and help the reader to see exactly what you mean.
Spatial	Organize according to the space relationships—east to west, outside to inside, lower to higher, big to little.
Results/Conclusions	This amplifies what you summarized at the beginning, but gives the information in greater detail. It follows logically from all that's gone before, and is a reasonable ending to the facts and statistics you presented in the previous section.
Recommendations	Here's where you say exactly what action you think should be taken, or what policies should be changed. If you've put this in the conclusion, there's no need to repeat it again. But when you locate this information under a separate heading, it sets it off more clearly for all to see.
Attachments	If you'd like to include more background material that's too cumbersome to include in the body of the report, attach it at the end and refer to it in the report. Certain kinds of background material will be more interesting to some people than to others, so whoever is interested can study the data in greater detail, if necessary.

21. BUILDING BETTER PUBLIC RELATIONS THROUGH LETTERS AND MEMOS

Each letter or memo you write can be another way to improve the image of yourself and your company. Here are 12 ways to build respect and good will.

1. Say words like "Thank you" and "We appreciate" often.
2. Do more than the minimum required. Offer a suggestion or extra service whenever you can show you want to cooperate.
3. Answer inquiries promptly—it builds good will.
4. Put enthusiasm and friendliness into your letter. You *can* influence the reader's attitude. Your letters reflect the image of your organization.
5. Let the reader know immediately that you welcome the request for information that you can't supply now. Say when you expect to write again.
6. Say what you *can* do and don't emphasize what you *can't* do.
7. Write so the reader feels your letter is only for him or her—even though you're sending the message to many other people.
8. Recognize another viewpoint even if you can't share it. Try to present your message in terms of reader benefits.
9. Admit a mistake, as long as you're not making the company legally liable.
10. Compliment the reader whenever you can.
11. Say what the reader wants to know in the first paragraph.
12. Tell your reader in your last paragraph what action you'd like him to take. This helps make your message clear.

Fifty Benefits that Motivate People

When you want to motivate a person in a letter, promise something that will meet a human need. We all have one or more needs we would like to fill if we see it's possible to attain them. *Benefit* is the key. When you present something that will clearly benefit a person, you've got an excellent chance of convincing him or her to accept your proposal. That's the basis of selling: probe for the benefit, then present your idea or product in terms of that benefit.

Here's a list of the most common benefits people want. Try to put them into your introduction when you're asking for a favor or trying to secure approval of an idea. You may want to restate it in the conclusion, too.

Appreciation of other people	Beauty
Agreement	Cleanliness
Approval of other people	Cleaner environment
Attractiveness	Compatibility

Comfort	Money
Convenience	Peacefulness
Customer satisfaction	Pleasure
Economy	Personal satisfaction
Efficiency	Popularity
Ease of operation	Prestige
Enjoyment	Pride
Entertainment	Profit
Extra money	Protection for yourself, family,
Fairness	business, or future
Freedom from worry	Provision for your future
Freedom to act	Recognition
Friendship	Safety
Fun	Savings
Good reputation	Security
Happiness	Self-fulfillment
Health	Solution to a tough problem
Improvement	Success
Independence	Thrift
Less work	Trouble-free operation
Love (of other people, spouse,	Uniqueness
home, family, or children)	Usefulness

How to Write Bad-News Letters and Memos

Handling bad-news messages is probably one of the toughest tasks you'll face as a writer of business letters or memos. But, with a little forethought and sensitivity on your part, you can make the best of something that in fact is quite negative. Here are some suggestions.

START WITH A POSITIVE ATTITUDE

You'll win half the battle if you begin your letter only when you have the right attitude toward the person you're writing to. Look for the best things you can find in the other person, and keep him or her in mind as you write the letter. Assume that the person really *wants* to do the right thing, that he isn't a vicious, conniving, lazy thief who wants to do you in. For example, once you develop the right attitude toward the person, the tone of your letter will improve and you'll have a better chance of keeping the reader *on your side,* instead of against you.

DON'T SINGLE HIM OUT

If you have to criticize something, don't single the person out for your wrath; put him or her in a group. (Of course, if you're praising the person, then it's not only desirable, but advantageous, to single him out.) Here's an example:

| *Criticism:* | Sometimes employees forget that we need to rely on them to come to work on time. (Put the employee in the group.) |
| *Praise:* | Barbara, we're really pleased that your reports are always done well and are presented on time. (Single out the employee.) |

FORGET COMPANY POLICY

Who cares about company policy? Certainly not the customer, and certainly not the employee or person who is acting against it. You weaken your argument in a bad-news letter when you cite company policy. (The rule was established for a reason, but that reason won't stimulate a person to act differently or change his ways.) Figure out another angle that will motivate the person to change his or her actions. Try to *sell* your position in terms of what will benefit the person or meet his or her needs.

DON'T LET THE PERSON LOSE FACE

We all need to keep our heads up, to feel proud about ourselves. Any bad-news message you send has to let the receiver keep that sense of pride. So, try to be as tactful as possible. Here are two different ways to do the same thing:

| *Tactless:* | If you had studied the policy manual as you were supposed to, you would have realized that you have to give us 30 days advance notice about taking vacation time. |
| *Tactful:* | To meet our production quotas, we have to ask for 30 days' advance notice about taking vacation time. Perhaps you missed that when you read our employee handbook. However, it does say how important we think it is to let us know... |

SEE IT FROM THE OTHER SIDE

Try to look at the problem from the other person's viewpoint. Then, put your ideas in terms of what will benefit him or her. Show why your plan or policy will actually benefit the person, perhaps in the long run, if not immediately.

START WITH A BUFFER

Never hit the other person with the bad news right away, whether you're talking face-to-face, or in a letter or memo. Relate your opening buffer to the topic so it helps you prepare your reader psychologically for what is to follow. It helps the reader put up necessary, ego-protecting, face-saving mechanisms to take your bad news in the best way possible. There are many ways you can do this.

Say thank you. There's almost always a reason to say thank you, even if it's only for the person's giving attention to the problem you're dealing with. But maybe you can thank the receiver of bad news for his request, for his attentiveness, for the information he gave you, for his check, his cooperation—whatever you can think of that's reasonable.

Say you agree. Find at least something you can agree with.

Say something nice. Compliment the person. Say something good about his sincerity, his concern for solving the problem, his previous record of success or dependability, or his conscientious listing of the facts related to the problem.

Provide assurance. Tell him you've carefully considered the situation and will explain all the facts related to the issue.

Tell him the good news. If there's *anything* good you can say about the issue, start with that. If you can grant part of the request, say so, and move on from there.

Offer to help. If there's any way you can provide support or help to the other person, say so right at the start. At least show your intention of wanting to be helpful.

Express sympathy. If you have to give really bad news, it may be best if you begin by saying how sorry you are to be the one to carry this news, since you know how disappointing the news is likely to be.

Say you understand. If you think you really understand the situation from the other person's viewpoint, show it. Explain how you've considered the person's needs and problems, his desire to pay part of the bill, his wish to have a product he can depend on.

Be neutral. You may have to rely on something very neutral or noncommittal. If you're changing a product that many people have liked, you may start out with something like this: "Change is something we all live with daily, and we've made some needed changes recently that will interest you."

EXPLAIN THE PROBLEM

Give your reader all the facts that led you to your decision. Provide the favorable facts first, then those less favorable. Let the reader know you're trying to act in his or her best interest, especially during the long term, and be as sincere as possible.

GIVE YOUR DECISION

Make certain that the reader clearly understands the decision. This is the time when the reader has to be absolutely clear what you're *saying. There can be no room for doubt.*

You may want to share bad news directly. But you can also imply it. Instead of saying, "We have decided not to hire you for this position," you might say, "We're sorry we can't offer you any further encouragement in seeking this position."

You might also indicate what you *can't* do for the reader by stressing what you *can* do ... and you don't have to say "no" so directly. Finally, if there's any way you can offer a compromise, do so.

MAKE CONSTRUCTIVE SUGGESTIONS

Offer your reader something to replace the bad news you've given, such as an alternative way to get the loan, another company that might be more responsive, or a different product or program. Try to help wherever you can. If appropriate, resell your company's programs, products, or services.

MAKE YOUR GOOD-BYE FRIENDLY

Your last paragraph is important, because that's the last thing your reader will remember. Assure the person that he or she is valued and appreciated as a present or future customer or client. Say you continue to be interested in his or her idea, product, or program. If you want the reader to take some action, make it clear what he or she has to do, along with how and when it should be done. Finally, invite your reader's support and cooperation in the future. Let him know you want his or her suggestions for the future.

Above all, be sincere and honest. Deep down, people know they have to receive bad news from time to time. But how you do it, and how you help people save face, makes all the difference in the world as to whether or not you'll make a friend or an enemy as a result of the bad news you give.

Choosing the Right Words

There's an old song that says, "Accent the positive and eliminate the negative." It's the same with the words we use. Try to use positive words and eliminate those that are negative.

POSITIVE WORDS

ability	active	advantage
abundant	admirable	ambition
achieve	advance	appreciate

approval
aspire
attainment
authoritative

benefit

capable
cheer
comfort
commendable
comprehensive
concentration
confidence
conscientious
cooperation
courtesy

definite
dependable
desirable
determined
distinction
diversity

ease
economy
effective
efficient
energy
enhance
enthusiasm
equality
excellence
exceptional
exclusive
expedite

faith
fidelity
fitting

genuine
good
grateful
guarantee

handsome
harmonious
helpful
honesty
honor
humor
imagination
improvement
ingenuity
initiative
integrity
intelligence

judgment

kind

lasting
liberal
life
loyalty

majority
merit
meritorious

notable

opportunity

perfection
permanent
perseverance
pleasant
please
popularity

practical
praiseworthy
prestige
proficient
progress
prominent
priority
punctual

reasonable
recognition
recommend
reliable
reputation
responsible

satisfactory
service
simplicity
stability
substantial
success
superior

thorough
thought
thoughtful
thrift
truth

useful
utility

valuable
vigor
vital
vivid

wisdom

you
yours

NEGATIVE WORDS

abandoned
abuse

affected
alibi

alleged
apology

bankrupt
beware
biased
blame

calamity
careless
cheap
collapse
collusion
commonplace
compliant
crisis
crocked
cut-and-dry

deadlock
decline
desert
disaster
discredit
dispute

evict
exaggerate
extravagant

fail
failure
fault
fear
fiasco
flagrant
flat
flimsy

gloss over

gratuitous

hardship
hazy

idiot
ignorant
illiterate
imitation
immature
implicate
impossible
improvident
insolvent
in vain

liable
long-winded

meager
mediocre
misfortune
muddle

neglect
negligence

obstinate
odds and ends
opinionated
oversight

plausible
precipitate
prejudiced
premature
pretentious

rude
ruin

shirk
shrink
sketchy
slack
smattering
split hairs
squander
stagnant
standstill
straggling
stubborn
stunted
stupid
superficial

tamper
tardy
timid
tolerable

unfair
unfortunate
unsuccessful
untimely

verbiage

wanton
waste
weak
worry
wrong

22. SAMPLE COLLECTION LETTERS

One good reason you're a successful manager is probably because you manage your money well. And you probably pay your bills on time. But not everyone is that organized, and some people just forget sometimes. Of course, there are always a few people who try to get away with as much as they can. If you find you're on the receiving end of their dishonesty, then you have every right to come down on them hard, with all the legal ammunition you have, to get the money that's owed you.

But before you write a collection letter to someone who owes you money, make sure you have a good attitude. Start with the idea that the person who owes you money is simply a little forgetful and will appreciate your reminding him or her that your bill is due. And remember, too, that this person is likely to continue to be a valued customer. Why would you want to alienate a good customer? It's a good idea to remember this when you feel the anger mounting in you because you're short on cash and people owe you money. So don't hit the person with a shotgun blast right at the start.

Begin with a gentle nudge. Then fire a BB gun, next a rifle, and finally, if you must, a shotgun. Only at the last step should you threaten to turn the account over to a collection agency, garnish wages, or file a lawsuit.

Here are a series of collection letters that start with a gentle reminder and get more serious. Once you've developed your own letters, it won't cost you much more than typing and postage to send out the series.

Letter #1

Dear Mr. Jones:

We're all apt to overlook things now and then, and perhaps that's the case with your installment loan payment of $156.75, which was due May 1.

If you've overlooked this, we'd appreciate your sending the payment to us by return mail.

If you've already sent us payment, please accept our thanks, and disregard this notice.

Sincerely,

Letter #2

Dear Mr. Jones:

Just a reminder.

Perhaps you overlooked your payment to us, but your account is now overdue. Would you please send us the amount shown on the enclosed bill by return mail? Just use the convenient postage-paid envelope we've included with this letter.

Thank you for your prompt attention to this matter.

Sincerely,

Letter #3

Dear Mr. Jones:

You've been a valued customer of ours for a long time and, frankly, we hate to nag our good customers.

Unfortunately you're damaging your good credit rating with us, and this third reminder is costing both of us time and money, since service charges are mounting on your bill.

Please take some time right now to send us your check for the $175.89 due on your account. We've enclosed a convenient envelope to help you bring your account up to date.

If there's some reason you can't pay us now, please phone us at 123-4567 and let us know what the problem is. It's entirely possible that we can help you make arrangements to pay the bill and delay reclassifying your account with us.

Yours truly,

Letter #4

Dear Mr. Jones:

We have considered you a valued customer for a long time, and have tried to work with you in settling your past due account. As you can expect, every company has to collect its bills to stay in business.

We're sorry to inform you that we've had to set a time limit for final action on this account in the amount of $193.74, which includes service charges to date.

If you make payment before July 1, you can avoid our having to turn your account over to a collection agency. Won't you please act now to prevent us from taking this action?

Your truly,

23. MODEL BUSINESS LETTERS AND MEMOS

Correct Forms for Business Letters

FULL-BLOCKED STYLE

January 1, 19_____

} Space six blank lines

Mr. John Jones
District Manager
Acme Sales Division
Topmost, Inc.
236 Field Street
Buffalo, NY 12345

Dear Mr. Jones

The Full-Blocked style is popular in business today, and it's modern. It looks efficient, and it's the easiest one to type. However, it's not always best for longer letters.

When you use the Full-Blocked style, you begin every line at the left margin. In this letter, I've used open punctuation; no punctuation appears at the end of any of the lines of the standard parts of a letter. However, you may wish to use mixed punctuation with the Full-Blocked style, as we do in the Modified Block and Simplified Block styles.

If you'd like to include your company name, even though this style doesn't require it, you can do it under the complimentary close. Place the letter reference initials under the close, along with any other notation, such as "Enclosure" or "cc" under them, as we've done here.

Some sources recommend wider margins, such as 2¼" at the left, with a 4" line length. However, that often requires you to use a second page for a longer letter, and that can cause more work with the possibility of it being lost.

Yours truly

} Space three lines for a signature

Robert Powers, Director
Customer Relations Department

RP/ar
Enclosure

HALF-BLOCK STYLE

January 1, 198_____

} Space four lines

Sales Department
Acme Sales Division
236 Field Street
Buffalo, NY 12345

<u>Attention Mr. Jones</u>

Gentlemen:

The Half-Block style business letter is like the Block style, except that you indent the paragraphs at least five spaces. Place the date to the right of center, but don't let it extend into the right margin. It's easiest if you simply type the date at the center of the page.

One advantage of the style is that you use an attention line, underlined, two lines below the inside address. This is a good way to get your reader's attention. As an alternative style, you could also center the attention line in capital letters, without underlining. Of course, if you prefer not to use the attention line, you can leave it out. In that case, include the individual's name in the inside address, as in the example of the Modified-Block letter style.

Finally, place the complimentary close in the center of the page, as you do with the date. You can put your name below the close if you like or, as I've done in this letter, place it flush left.

Yours truly,

} Space four lines for signature

Robert Powers:AR   Director
Encl.—Check

MODIFIED-BLOCK

January 1, 19_____

}Space three
lines after date

Mr. John Jones, District Manager
Acme Sales Division, Topmost, Inc.
236 Field Street
Buffalo, NY 12345

Dear Mr. Jones:

This letter illustrates the Modified-Block style of letter writing. It's probably the most popular used in businesses today, because it looks businesslike and it's easier to type than the more traditional styles. With the exception of the date, the closing, and the signature, you begin everything at the left margin.

You can center the date or begin it anywhere to the right of center, but it shouldn't extend into the right margin. In this letter, I've put the manager's title right after his name, on the same line. However, you may want to write to people who have longer names and titles than you can accommodate easily. If that happens, you can continue the title on a second line—simply indent two spaces. Of course, if you know the addressee personally, you're free to address him, "Dear John": and you can sign your letter, "John."

Place the complimentary close at the center of the page, or just to the right of center—as long as the longest line of the signature doesn't extend in the margin. You can leave out the company name in the signature, but it's a good idea to include the department or division and your business title four lines below the complimentary closing. Then, type your title below your name.

Your secretary's initials are placed on the next line, flush left, and in capital letters. If you're enclosing something with the letter, indicate that on the line below the secretary's initials. Say, "Enclosure" if there's only one piece; say "Enclosures/2" if you're including two pieces. Finally, type "cc" on the next line, flush left, if you're sending a carbon to one or more people. Side margins are 1¼″, and the line length is 6″.

Sincerely,

}Allow three lines
for signature

Robert Powers, Director
Customer Relations Department

RP:AR
Enclosure 1
cc: Mr. Robert Johnson

SIMPLIFIED-BLOCK STYLE

January 1, 19_____

} Three blank lines

Mr. John Jones, District Manager
Acme Sales Division, Topmost, Inc.
236 Field Street
Buffalo, NY 12345

STYLE OF THE SIMPLIFIED-BLOCK LETTER

This style of letter, Mr. Jones, is recommended by many management associations as an effective time-saver in preparing business letters. It has the advantage of being easily typed, yet has some attractive features business people seem to like. Consider its good points:

1. You can leave out the word "subject" and type the subject line in full capitals. This makes it easier to read and helps you grab the reader's attention fast.
2. You can leave out the salutation and complimentary close. However, so your reader won't think you're sending a form letter, you include his or her name on the first line.
3. Use open punctuation, and the Full-Block form.
4. Sign your name and title in capitals.
5. Place the typist's initials at the left margin, two lines below your name. After that, include the indication of enclosures and the names of people receiving carbon copies.

Mr. Jones, why not try this style in your next business letter? You'll find it a refreshing change!

} Leave four blank lines for signature)

ROBERT POWERS—CUSTOMER RELATIONS DIRECTOR

ar
Enc 3
Messrs. Thomas Spalding, William Brown, Mike Smith

HANGING PARAGRAPH STYLE

January 1, 19_____

{ Space five
blank lines

For Sales People Who Want to
Show a Product or Service in
the Best Light Possible ... and Make People Act!

Dear Sales Manager:

Look at the terrific advantages you have when you use the hanging
paragraph letter style with open punctuation. With it, you can
highlight many different ideas about your product or service. Also
using the call-out technique of beginning only the first line at the
margin, you draw attention to each idea ... fast!

We call this style "hanging" because the first line hangs out, and all
other lines are indented. That means you write your sentences in
such a way that the first few words are action-oriented. And, for
even greater emphasis, you could type the first word or two in
capitals.

Sales promotion ... merchandising ... motivational appeals ... these
are just some of the reasons you'd use this style. (It has too much
zing and assertiveness for everyday writing, and you'd probably
drive your typist mad.)

The main advantage of this style is the paragraph starters. They grab
your reader and yank him or her into the message. Simply ask your
typist to set the stop five or seven spaces to the right of the margin.
Then he or she indents all lines after the first one. If he or she finds
it easier, the margins could also be set for the bulk of the copy and
the margin release used to hang the openers closer to the page
edge.

Your company's name is typed in capitals, if you like, and you include
your name and title four lines below that, located to the right of the
center of page. Place the reference information at the left margin.

Try it today, won't you, and let me know how it worked? You can call
me direct at (123) 456-7890.

Cordially yours,
ACME SALES DIVISION, Topmost, Inc.

Space three }
blank lines

Robert Powers, Director

rp/ar

331

PERSONAL BUSINESS LETTER STYLE

123 Oak Street
Chicago, IL 98102
January 1, 19_____

Mr. John Jones
District Manager,
Acme Sales Division
236 Field Street
Buffalo, NY 23456

Dear Mr. Jones:

Subject: Personal Business Letters—Quotations

When you need to supply quotations and specific data, and you don't want to use a company letterhead, use this format. It features a subject line, tabulation of listed items and plenty of white space to make sure your quotations aren't lost.

Place the subject line two lines below the salutation, and use capitals if you like. Some people prefer to start the subject line at the left margin, but it gets more attention if you center it.

Now, about quoted matter, or other data you'd like to emphasize. Include a double space before you begin the material and one immediately after it. Indent the quote seven or eight lines. Look at this example:

> When you quote something, such as information from a technical manual, you need to set it apart from the rest of your letter. You can do that with spacing and strong indentation. In fact, it's probably a good idea to center the information, as in this case.

If you want to list several items, or provide figures, use the same technique. Center the material, use single spacing, and separate the information from the rest of the letter. See the example below:

	1979	*1980*
Estimated newspapers	456	512
Number accepting copy	23	27
Number yet to be reached	433	485

Page 2
January 1, 19_____

Another technique you can use is to number the items in your letter. Again, it's appropriate to center this information. Some writers prefer to use bullets, instead of numbers, to set off the material. (You make bullets by using the small letter "o" and filling it in with black ink.)

1. Numbers help your reader to refer to each item specifically.
2. They help you keep track of facts.
3. They help you emphasize the order of your ideas.

- Bullets have impact too.
- They tend to draw attention to the idea, not the number.
- Your items seem to stand out more dramatically.

If you need to go on to a second or third page using this letter style or any other, place the name of the person you're addressing the letter to at the top, about 1″ from the top, and below it, the number of the page and the date.

Sincerely,

Robert Powers

RP:AR
Enclosure: Brochure No. 4

24. TEN STEPS TO MORE POWERFUL LETTERS

You can put your business letters to work for you by following a few simple steps. Some of these are discussed in further detail in the twenty-two item checklist for better writing. But here's a ten-step system you can use to put more punch into your business letters and memos, and get people to respond quickly to your ideas:

1. *Answer every question.* Review the letter or issue you're responding to and make sure you're answering all the points raised. Don't leave any questions unanswered and don't be evasive. (If you try to fudge an answer, you'll probably just invite more correspondence, anyway).

2. *Pick the right words.* Choose the exact word that makes your meaning clear. If you think there's the least possibility that you may be misunderstood, confirm the meaning with your secretary or an associate. It's a good idea to rely on secretaries for letters and memo-writing advice. They can save you a lot of grief.

3. *Make an outline.* When you're writing a really important memo or letter, a short outline can help you give it more impact. The outline needn't be more than a few words:

Absenteeism on Mondays

1. State the problem (facts)
2. Why the company is concerned
   Downtime
   High labor cost
   Morale
3. Possible results if continued
   Lost orders
   Layoffs
4. Possible solutions
   Charge against sick days
   Note on permanent records
   Award work credits for coming in
   Hold contests for full employment

4. *Use active verbs.* These help you get to the point quickly. Say, "We sampled batches every fifteen minutes," not, "Batches were sampled by us every fifteen minutes."

5. *Use variety.* Put both long and short sentences in your letter. Long sentences come easy, because we often find it so difficult to stop writing a

334

sentence once we get started. So, work on including some short ones: "Here's another point." "But, look." "Isn't that true?" "Don't you agree?"

6. *Don't beat around the bush.* Get to the point quickly, and make your statements clear and definite. Don't use any words you don't really need.

7. *Put your important ideas first.* State your key ideas right at the start, when you've got your reader's attention. Then offer supporting details.

8. *Stay positive.* Make it easy for the reader to agree with you by being positive, not negative, and writing for the reader's benefit. Just before you start to write the second draft, check to see if you've included any negative words.

9. *Make it personal.* Use the person's name whenever you can, just as you would in conversation, and add personal pronouns. For example: "I think you'll like this new binding machine, Mary, because it'll help you manage your department." Asking your reader questions will help make it personal, too. Questions naturally stimulate reader interest, and require a response, at least internally. Even a question like, "That makes good sense, doesn't it?" will help you involve your reader.

10. *Use graphics.* Make your letter or memo look good by <u>underlining</u> beginning words or key words, by using CAPITAL letters for emphasis, or by placing items in a list instead of running one after the other. Group similar ideas in a single paragraph, and use each paragraph as a single unit of thought. Use white space and subheads to draw reader attention to what you're saying.

25. TWENTY-TWO WAYS TO WRITE BETTER REPORTS AND MEMOS

Here's a checklist of things you can do to put more punch into your writing, and make your words *work* for you. Take each point, one at a time, and apply it once a day to the first draft of each letter or memo you write. In a short time, you'll see dramatic improvement in your writing. But be patient with yourself. It probably took you years to get into the writing habits you have now, and they won't change easily. So take your time, but start working on just one memo or letter each day ... every day.

• Keep your average sentence length to no more than 17 words. Of course, you may want to use some longer sentences to describe the fullness of your ideas, and some short ones to put sparkle into your writing. You don't want all long sentences (they'll put your reader to sleep) or all short ones either (they'll make your writing sound like baby talk). So, mix them up for variety; but if you count 100 words, the average sentence should not be any longer than 17 words.

• Put variety into your sentences by beginning them in different ways. Of course, the beginning you choose will depend upon the context, and the degree of comfort you feel with each technique. Try some different beginnings. Here are six different ways to begin a sentence:

Subject/Verb:	Our *director said,* during an informal meeting, that product A will sell better.
Prepositional Phrase:	*During an informal meeting,* the director said that product A will sell better.
Verbal Phrase:	*Speaking informally,* the director said that product A will sell better.
Expletive: (There, It)	*It* was during an informal meeting that the director said product A will sell better.
Subordinate Clause:	*As he spoke* during the informal meeting, the director said that product A will sell better.
Coordinating Conjunction:	The director, *during an informal meeting,* said product A will sell better.

• Get rid of words you don't need. Make your writing as concise as possible, so you don't waste your time or the reader's. One way to do this is "hunt the which'es" and "kill the be's." Wherever you see a which, which introduces a subordinate clause like this one, strike it out, and begin a new sentence. That'll make your sentences clearer and easier to read. And when you see the verb "be" in any of its forms—is, are, was, were, am, been, being—try to get rid of that, too, and use a stronger, active verb.

• Put just one idea into each sentence. A sentence is a group of words that express a complete thought—*one* complete thought. If you have to qualify something you've said, do it in the next sentence. The longer the sentence, the harder it is to grasp as a thought unit. The best sentences are simple, declarative ones, containing a subject, a verb, and an object.

• Put just one main idea into each paragraph. After you've arranged your one-idea sentences around a common subject, put them all into a single paragraph. For example, you could use the first sentence of the paragraph as the topic sentence, with the rest of the sentences arranged to support that topic idea.

• Use simple words. Try to use everyday words people understand easily, and keep them to one or two syllables. (Think about this: the most important words in our lives are one-syllable words—peace, joy, health, love, sex, birth, death, God, warmth). To do this, try to use verbs, then nouns, then adjectives. Don't use words formed by prefixes and suffixes tacked on to nouns. For example, instead of using the word, "*preparation,*" say, "*prepare*"—the verb form. Instead of *growth,* say *grow;* instead of *development,* say *develop.*

• Use the active voice instead of the passive. That way, you make it a point to say *who* did *what.* The passive voice is wordy and evasive. It's much better to say, "The production manager made the decision," rather than "The decision was made." In the first sentence, you immediately identify who's doing the action.

• Use transition words to make sentences flow easily. Some of these tell your reader to "go-ahead," to keep on reading:

> more than that, also, in addition, similarly, more,
> furthermore, besides, further, likewise, moreover.

Others tell your reader that you're coming to a more important idea, or that you're summarizing what you've already said:

> thus, so, therefore, it's clear, then, accordingly, consequently,
> it follows that, so it's inevitable that.

Still others say to keep on reading, but indicate you'll soon come to a stop:

> as a result, concluding, finally, in conclusion

Other transition words tell your reader that you're changing the direction of your thought:

> but, nevertheless, in spite of, still, yet, otherwise, on the
> contrary, of, although, however, not, despite, rather.

• Write the way you talk. Speak person-to-person: "talk on paper." Picture your reader sitting next to you, listening to what you say. Just talk to your reader clearly and simply, in a normal conversational style.

• Try to avoid -ing words (working, deciding, trying). They almost always cause you to use extra words, including "be" verbs. Instead, use the direct verb form: (work, decide, try.)

• Write with the "you" attitude—for your *reader's* benefit, not your own. That means you try to phrase your ideas in such a way that the reader finds them appealing. You try to look at things from the reader's viewpoint. This makes your writing more appealing and more acceptable.

• Use plenty of white space and short paragraphs. Even though you may use the more modern block style for letters and don't indent your paragraphs, you need lots of white space in the margins, between the paragraphs, and after the subheads you include in your copy. White space makes your letter or memo appear less formidable and more appealing to read. White space, which results when you indent your copy for lists of items, and typographic devices like dashes and leaders, help the reader to feel that reading the report isn't such a cumbersome task after all.

• Use graphic devices like bullets and dashes to attract the reader's attention. You can highlight lists of items with bullets by typing the letter "o," then filling it in with black ink: "•". Here's what some of the graphic devices look like. You can use your ingenuity to create more of your own.

Bullets
We need the new machine to:

• Maintain higher production
• Keep inventory levels high
• Reduce maintenance costs.

Dashes
We need this new machine to:

—Maintain higher production
—Keep inventory levels high
—Reduce maintenance costs.

Boxes
We need this new machine to:

■ Maintain higher production
■ Keep inventory levels high
■ Reduce maintenance costs.

Asterisks
We need this new machine to:

*Maintain higher production
*Keep inventory levels high
*Reduce maintenance costs.

USE LEADERS IN THE BODY COPY:

We need four new units:
. . . . 4B Battery
. . . . 30-Amp fuse
. . . . Acme 410 Header
. . . . 2″ lead casing.

• Choose specific, concrete words that draw vivid pictures in your reader's mind. Avoid general words like quality, nature, situation, effort, intent, course, condition. Instead, tell your reader the facts: Don't say, "The nature of the problem we're facing has caused a situation that, if not corrected in due course, will develop into a serious condition." What does that say? Nothing. It's better to say something like this: "The 10 percent absentee rate on Mondays in the Metal Stamping Department has plunged production quotas 15 percent below the norm. If this isn't corrected in one month, we'll have to fire three people and hire three more who will come to work every day.

• Be positive, not negative. Tell people what you *can* do for them, not what you *can't*. People want to do business with someone who says *yes*. Write in such a way that you sound *glad* to help them. Consider these examples:

Negative Statements	**Positive Statements**
To avoid losing your good credit rating ...	To preserve your good credit rating ...
We can't open an account for you until you send us your signature.	We'll gladly open an account for you as soon as you send us your signature.
You won't be sorry you did this.	You'll be glad you did this.

• Use plenty of personal nouns and pronouns. Put people into your writing. Whatever you write, no matter how technical, it's for another person, someone who may be very much like you. No matter how many people read what you write, only one person reads it at a time. The largest newspaper in the world is written to be read individually, by one person at a time. Use the simple *subject-verb-object* word pattern and plenty of personal pronouns: you, me, we, us, our, they—and use the reader's name whenever you can.

For example:

Look at this sentence:	Neither growth nor health can be sustained unless the daily foods provide various essentials that are called vitamins.
Isn't this one more interesting?	John, you need vitamins. We all do—young and old. You and I need them to build a healthy body and to keep ourselves strong and in good shape.

• Focus first on strong, colorful verbs, then the nouns, and only then the adjectives.

Here's a Sentence that Emphasizes the Nouns:

> The growth, development, and fortification of the body against viruses can be regulated by careful selection of foods and their vitamin content.

Now, Let's Emphasize the Verbs:

> You can help your body develop and grow while you fortify it against viruses. Select your foods and vitamins carefully.

• Write on just one side of the paper, double- or triple-spaced. Then you can revise easily and quickly. This also lets you cut up sections of your copy, rearrange them, and paste them together for retyping.

• Once you have a first draft, organize your ideas into a logical, natural order, into paragraphs that link similar ideas. Look at your subject matter and determine a common theme that ties the ideas together clearly. You can probably organize most reports, letters, and memos into one or more of these organizational patterns:

Chronological:	Events or processes in the order of the *time* in which they happen.
Spatial:	Physical relationships among persons places, or things. (East to west, small to big, up to down, inside to outside, etc.)
Criterion:	The measure or standard with which you consider something (sales volume, typing errors per page, scrap record).
Importance:	Present either the least important ideas first and build to the most important, or vice versa.
Familiarity:	Go from the simple, easy-to-understand and familiar, to the more complex, hard-to-understand and unfamiliar.
Details, examples, illustrations:	Just list as many related facts as you can.
Compare and contrast ideas:	You show the similarities when you compare things; you show the differences when you contract them.
Repeat and restate ideas:	Use different words, but try to explain the same idea many different ways, so there's no possibility of confusing your meaning.
Define your terms:	Let people know what words mean in the sense that you use them. If they have a specific meaning for you, say so.

Explain causes and effects, problems and solutions:	Tell why things are happening, or what will result because certain things are taking place.
Eliminate the alternatives:	List everything that won't work, and explain why it won't work. Then say what *will* work, and why.

• Before you begin, make a simple topic outline of your purpose for writing, your main point, and your subpoints.

• Review your first draft, cut out needless words, and make sure it's clear. If you could do just one thing to improve your writing, it probably would be to consider everything you write as needing at least one revision.

26. HOW TO PRESENT FACTS, FIGURES, AND STATISTICS EASILY

There's probably nothing more frustrating in putting a good business report together than deciding what to do about all the background data that led you to your conclusion. The temptation is to lump it all together at the end, in table after dreary table. But there are many other ways to deal with facts, figures, and statistics that will let you present them in interesting ways.

The first step is to get all your information together, in as concise a format as possible. Never mind about the logic or the order, just get it together, if for no other reason than to see what you have to deal with.

Next, find out what's common about each group of facts or statistics. Try to arrange them in an order that makes sense. Here are a few criteria to consider:

Size or volume.	Select your data by quantity. Arrange it by size, volume, or weight. For example, if you wanted to list the population of ten cities, you might list them from largest to smallest.
Common theme.	Look for similarities in the facts—they all took place about the same time; they caused similar results.
Chronology.	Arrange problems, issues, details, and causes in the order of time in which they took place.
Criteria.	Arrange the facts according to the standards by which you're measuring something, such as sales volume, scrap records, or typing errors.
Importance.	Present ideas from most important to least important, or start from the least important and move to the most important.
Space.	Arrange by geography or space relationship: inside to outside; big to little; lower to higher.

Checking the Facts

Before you start writing the report or decide how to present your facts, figures, and statistics, check to make sure you can count on the facts you have. You might ask yourself these questions:

- Do I have enough facts to draw a conclusion?
- Can I prove the facts? How? Can I depend on the data? Why?
- Are the facts relevant, or simply interesting?

- Why do I know the reader will accept them?
- What assumptions, if any, have I made concerning these facts?
- Have I clearly differentiated between the facts and assumptions?
- Have I included information on the criteria used to test the facts?
- Have I defined all the terms?

SIX WAYS TO ILLUSTRATE YOUR REPORT

Once you have your facts organized, you can decide how to present them. Ask yourself, "What's the clearest way to present these facts so the reader will easily see their importance?" Here are some suggestions:

Lists: You may simply want to list the details one after the other, perhaps alphabetically or chronologically. The important thing, however, is to leave enough white space around the list to make it stand out:

Additional Subjects:

Accounting
Advertising
Business Practice
Economics
Finance
Health

Tables: When you have more than one fact that's tied in with a larger fact or category, use a table that has the broader categories arranged in some vertical order, and the more specific, related facts arranged horizontally. Tables help you arrange similar data under the same headings so you can present ideas clearly.

TV Sets Sold by State

	Number Sold	Average Price	Color Sets	Black & White	Dealers Involved
Alabama	98,567	$245.	63,324	35,243	405
Alaska	49,789	$389.	34,987	14,802	118

Bar Charts: These let you show relationships at a glance, and help dramatize the differences between the facts. They help you to illustrate

344

Complete Handbook of Business English

periodic change, rather than continuous change. They catch the eye, and add interest to the page. Bar charts help you compare a few items, provided there are only two or three facts related to each one. And, if you can use color, you further dramatize the differences.

Gasoline Mileage Per Carburetor

Model A							
Model B							
Model C							
Model D							
	0	5	10	15	20	25	30

Miles Per Gallon

Line Charts: You can use either straight or curved lines to show trends in your facts. They help you to show a continuous change in values over a period of time. This is an excellent way to show what happens chronologically. Use graph paper to plot your points exactly, and don't use more than two or three sets of lines on the same chart:

Monthly Sales of TV Sets

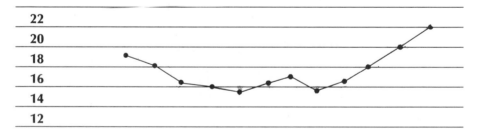

(In Thousands) Jan Feb Mar Apr May Jun Jul Aug Sep Oct Nov Dec

Circle Charts: Sometimes called pie charts, these help you see the relationship of the parts to the whole, usually shown in percentages.

Distribution of TV Set Sales by Sales Region

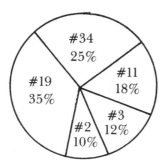

Flow
Charts: A final consideration would be to name the various stations at which some operation occurs, and arrange them in such a way that the reader can visualize the order.

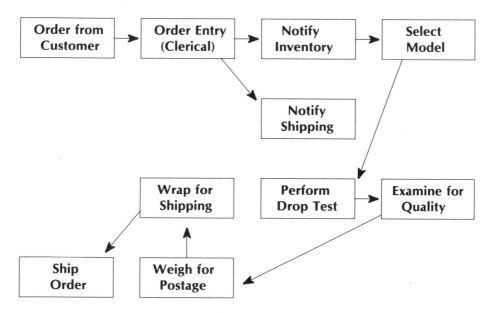

Pictograph: While you usually see this type of illustration in newspapers such as *The New York Times* and in color slide shows, there's no reason why you shouldn't use it to make your reports more interesting. They help clarify data by arranging it in colors or shades of black, in what appear to be three-dimensional pictures or shapes.

The Court's key decisions

Justice	Appointment	Oath taken
Warren E. Burger	Nixon	1969
William J. Brennan, Jr.	Eisenhower	1956
Potter Steward	Eisenhower	1959
Byron R. White	Kennedy	1962
Thurgood Marshall	Johnson	1967
Harry A. Blackmun	Nixon	1970
Lewis F. Powell, Jr.	Nixon	1972
William H. Rehnquist	Nixon	1972
John Paul Stevens	Ford	1975

Maps: With a map, you can show geographic areas—city, county, town, state, or country—as well as topographic information. You can probably use a copy of a map for a report that only one or two people will see, but if you expect wide distribution of your report outside your company, you should get copyright clearance for the map. Topographers are very protective of their artwork and can easily spot it, especially when it's published without authorization.

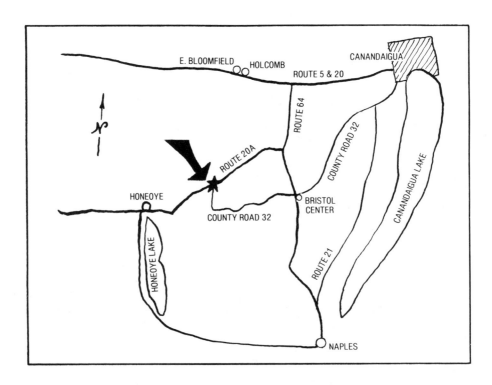

Regardless of what illustration technique you choose, keep these pointers in mind:

- *It should be accurate.*   Few things can jeopardize the credibility of your report more quickly than inaccurate illustrations. People spot them easily, and inaccuracies also make the body copy suspect.

- *Keep it simple.*   As in good writing, your illustrations should be simple to understand. The reader shouldn't have to hunt for the meaning.

- *Lable it carefully.*   All the data should be labeled properly so there's no misunderstanding. Again, clarity is the key.

- *It should complement the text.*   Your illustrations should blend in logically with the text, and help explain it. They're of little value if you group them together at the end and make the reader hunt for them. Try to place them as close as possible to the text they illustrate.

27. POINTERS ON BUSINESS LETTERS AND MEMOS

The style of your business letters and memos says as much about you and your business as what you say. Here are some pointers on writing effective business letters.

Paper

Choose a good bond paper with a rag content of at least 25 percent. You can't convince people yours is a first-class company if you use cheap paper for your letters. It costs you nearly $5.00 to write a business letter; the $.03 it may cost for your stationery and letterhead is money well spent.

What size paper? The usual is 8½" x 11", but you may want a smaller size as well for shorter, executive-level correspondence. Some companies use 7¼" x 10½" paper; others prefer half-size stationery at 5½" x 8½".

Color

White is still the most popular color, but many firms now use a more personal and warmer approach with soft pastel colors such as light grey, blue, tan, or buff.

Letterhead

You need a good letterhead. If you don't have one now, or if you haven't changed its design in several years, hire a commercial artist to design a new one for you. Keep it simple, use modern type, and keep the information as simple and as clear as possible. Your letterhead should include your name, address, zip code, and telephone number.

Parts of the Letter

Heading. Your letterhead and the date together form the heading that tells your reader where the letter comes from. That's another reason why a letterhead is desirable—it saves time. The correct forms for letters carried in this section will show you various places to locate the data, depending upon the letter style you choose.

Inside Address. Here you include the name and address of the person and organization you're writing to. This directs your message to the right person. That's another reason why you should include the executive or business title, either on the same line or, if the executive has a long name, on the next line.

Attention Line. When you address your letter to a company, you may want to include an attention line that will direct the letter to a specific person. This is usually considered a part of the inside address. It's usually placed between the inside address and the salutation, with a blank line before and after it. Example: Attention Promotion Director: Mr. Robbins.

Salutation. This is your personal greeting, and should include the person's name and courtesy title such as doctor, professor, superintendent, etc.

- Use Mr., Mrs., Miss, or Ms. when you're writing to a customer, to someone you don't know, or to a supplier, stockholder, prospect, or slight acquaintance;
- Use Gentlemen: when you're not sure who should be handling the situation. Use Ladies: if you know you are addressing women);
- Use Dear John: or Dear Mary: when you know the person's name and you'd normally use the first name if you were talking face-to-face.

Body. Keep the first and last paragraphs short. It's also a good idea to put your main message—your key idea—in the first or second paragraph, so your readers know exactly what the letter is about. Plan your letter with a short outline so that you, as well as your reader, know where your ideas are headed. Make no paragraph more than 10 lines long, and the average sentence should contain about 17 words. Mix longer paragraphs with shorter ones for variety.

Try to write a topic sentence for each paragraph. The topic sentence summarizes your main idea and makes it easy for the reader to understand the central issue of the entire paragraph. Type the letters single-spaced and double-space between paragraphs. Don't be afraid of white space in the letter—it makes your message easier to read. To provide more white space, you have to use shorter paragraphs, each built around a central idea. Use subheads to tell the reader the content of the paragraph; use graphic devices like bullets, dashes, asterisks, and periods to attract reader attention.

Complimentary Close. This should match your salutation in the tone of formality or informality. "Sincerely," "Sincerely yours," "Yours sincerely," are all good. "Yours truly" has become a cliche and many people don't like to use it. Some people like "Very truly yours" in its place. If you know the person you're writing to, "Best regards" is appropriate.

Reference Line. On the same line as your signature, but at the left margin, place your initials in capital letters as the sender of the letter. The typist's initials, in lower case, follow yours. *Example*: WTR:ab

Model Letters, Memos, and Invitations

Here are 15 models of the most frequent kinds of letters or memos you'll write in business. Of course, you'll want to include different information and approach things in a style that's comfortable and natural for you. But samples are presented here with the hope that you'll pick up the gist of their content and thus be able to write your own letters more easily.

REQUEST FOR INFORMATION

Gentlemen:

Introduce your request.
Tell why you're writing.

At the Widgets Convention in Chicago last month, I was quite impressed with your Model 10 Weeny Widget. It sounds perfect to help us launch our new line of Widgets. But before we make that decision, I need more information about your product.

Number your questions for easier reference later.

1. Is this the only model you carry? If there are others, will you send me technical literature about them?

Include specific details in your questions, not just generalities.

2. What major uses and in what major industries do people buy your product?

3. When you say the internal aluminum frammis is less than 2″ long, thus providing greater stability for fislong applications, do you mean you use other kinds of metals for other applications? If that's true, please tell me about those applications, and the various materials you use to make frammises.

Say what action you want your reader to take, and when you want it. Make action easy.

I need this information in two weeks to prepare for an engineering presentation, so I'd appreciate any help you can give me. If you like, please feel free to call me collect at (123) 456-7890 to provide the information. Or you can just drop it in the postage-paid envelope I've included with this letter. I really appreciate your help, and look forward to your earliest response in helping me include information on Weeny Widgets in this important presentation to management.

Say thanks, and include something that will move the reader to act on your request.

Sincerely yours,

REQUEST FOR HELP

Dear_____:

Arouse attention; state the problem.

If you weren't the best consultant available on plant site selection, I wouldn't be writing this letter. But we're a small food processing plant of about 200 employees and there's a good chance we can increase our business if we expand our facility or build a new plant. Each choice has certain advantages. And drawbacks.

Create reader interest.

Seems like a simple decision, doesn't it?But frankly, Mr._____, after thinking about what you said at a recent talk (or said in a recent article), I think my staff could use some advice from you. We've tried to look at the problem objectively, but we're completely divided as to which is the best route to take. I'd like to ask a great favor of you—even though I'm sure you have your hands full with your successful consulting business.

Call to action.

Could you come here for a few days and review the situation, and give me your opinion?

Stress reader benefit; make acceptance easy.

Of course, we'll pay all your travel and expenses, in addition to your usual fee. And frankly, I was so impressed with your ideas and the way you expressed them in the talk, I'd be flattered if you'd agree to stay with my wife and me. You might even consider it a short vacation. We have a tennis court and swimming pool, and my club has one of the best golf courses in the midwest.

Mr._____, I feel I need your help in this decision—one that can mean success or failure in my business.

Ask for a decision.

Can I roll out the red carpet for you?

Sincerely,

ASKING FOR A JOB

Dear_____:

Use a question for the opening; state the purpose of the letter.

Does General Engineering have an opening for an electrical engineer with three years' experience in microcircuitry?

Create interest; describe education and background.

I read General Engineering's Annual Report last year with great interest, especially the section which described your dramatic entry into the digital computer market. I believe my education in electrical engineering, and my solid background in microelectronics, would be strong assets as General Engineering continues to make inroads in this market.

Show your suitability for the position.

My resume shows, for example, the kinds of projects I've been involved in during the past three years. And the previous positions I've held in various mechanical engineering firms have been useful in helping me understand how the electrical circuitry is directly related to the mechanical components.

Ask for the interview; make action easy.

May I have an interview with you to discuss my qualifications further? I'd be glad to come to your office and, if you'd like further information, I can furnish it by return mail. You can call me collect at (123) 456-7890 if you'd like to discuss my background before you decide whether to interview me in person.

Thanks for considering my background for a position at General Engineering.

Sincerely,

REFUSING RESPONSIBILITY

Dear _____:

Begin on a friendly note.

We appreciate your letting us know about the problem you had with the 415 Super Wrench. We're always glad to hear from our customers.

Make the rejection clear; say why you are not responsible.

However, if you'll review our warranty (I've enclosed a copy for your convenience), you'll note that the adjustable wheel isn't warranteed for side impacts. From your letter, it's clear that someone used the wrench as a hammer—a wrong application, I'm sure you'll agree.

Offer to help another way.

But perhaps we can help another way. We can install a new wheel for you, for $2.95 plus shipping costs, and return your wrench to you about two weeks after we receive it. This would be a considerable saving over the $19.95 list price for a new wrench.

Make further action easy.

If you would like to take advantage of this service, simply return the wrench to our Customer Service Department, indicating the repair you'd like us to make. I hope you'll find this satisfactory. Thanks again for writing.

Sincerely,

REJECTING A BUSINESS OFFER

Dear_____:

Be polite.

Thank you for offering to provide packaging services for our Model AA Widget.

Be specific in the refusal.

Even though you could provide preprinted packages, and ship at a cheaper price than we asked for, we feel the Acme 60# paper is not suitable for our product.

Say why the offer is rejected.

We think the lighter weight will allow more damage to contents, and the potential decrease in customer satisfaction could be detrimental to our image. We also find we can buy the required paper from one of our other divisions, and handle the printing ourselves.

Don't criticize the firm or product because of possible legal problems.

I hope you'll understand that this in no way reflects on the continued good opinion we have of your company. We look forward to working with you in the future. But in this product consideration, we have decided to rely on other options.

If possible, let the firm know they still qualify for further business. End on a cordial note.

Thank you for your efforts. I'll let you know when we have another job you can quote on, because we have always enjoyed doing business with you and your firm.

Sincerely,

REFUSING LIABILITY

Dear_____:

Friendly opening.

Thank you for taking the time to write in about your experience with the Model A Bottle Warmer.

Refer to the customer's complaint.

I can certainly appreciate your concern about the possible danger of electric shock when you submerge the unit entirely in water.

Prove how you are not liable.

You'll note, however, on our warranty engraved on the bottom plate, that Acme is not liable for misuse of the product, "including submerging the unit in water."

Try to resell with other product or company features.

You may be interested to know that we've taken every manufacturing precaution possible to prevent shock: we rubber-coat all electrical circuits after thorough testing; we use shock-resistant ceramic and neoprene parts; we submerge each unit in water before it leaves the factory.

Offer possible reason to help the customer save face.

I think you'll agree that, once a unit leaves our factory, we have no control over its use. While we take every possible step to assure product dependability, a severe drop on a hard surface could cause a tiny crack that we can't control.

Close on a friendly note; offer some compensation as you continue to refuse liabiltiy.

However, we will be pleased to replace the unit at no cost if you'll mail it to us. While we can't claim liability for your experience with our unit, we would like to make up in a small way for your disappointment with our product. I'll look forward to hearing from you. Thanks again for writing.

Sincerely,

REFUSAL TO EXTEND CREDIT

Dear_____:

Use a buffer, a friendly note; show appreciation.

We appreciate the preference you've shown for Acme Products by your application for a charge account.

Explain the decision.

Give the decision.

Leave the customer a way out to save face or bring new facts to light.

As you know, our usual custom before we open a new account is to secure information that will help us decide whether credit is desirable. The information we've received is not adequate for us to grant your request at this time. If you feel we should know about other details that could favorably affect your credit, please call me so we can consider all the information.

Suggest alternative way to continue to do business.

Until then, we hope you'll let us continue to serve you on a cash basis. You have our assurance that we will continue to serve you well with friendly service and quality products.

End on a friendly note.

Please feel free to ask for consideration later, should conditions change.

Sincerely,

REFUSAL TO GIVE SOMEONE A JOB

Dear_____:

Open on a friendly note; use a buffer.

Express the rejection in positive terms; compliment the applicant.

Make your decision clearly known.

We appreciated the opportunity to review your background credentials for the position of_____with our firm. While we were favorably impressed, we feel that it would be wiser to choose a person whose employment experience more closely parallels the immediate situation we have in our organization right now, and have made a decision on that basis.

End on a friendly note.

We will keep your inquiry confidential and, with your approval, we would like to keep your resume and application on file for future employment opportunities.

Yours very truly,

REFUSAL TO ACCEPT A JOB OFFER

Dear_____:

Thank the company; compliment it.

Your offer of employment for the position of_____was especially well-received because I was so impressed with your fine organization.

Make your decision clearly known; don't blame the company.

Compliment someone specifically.

However, after much consideration, I've decided this position doesn't quite match the career direction I have in mind. I learned a great deal from the professionalism, courtesy, and friendliness everyone at (*firm name*) showed me, and Mr. _____was especially generous with his time.

Thank the company for considering you.

Thank you again for reviewing my qualifications, and discussing the position with me.

Sincerely,

PROMOTIONAL LETTERS

Any business letter that promotes a product, service, a special sale, or even an organization is really a letter designed to *persuade*. That means it should grab the reader's attention immediately, fire his interest, create a desire to buy, and then move the reader to action.

The guidelines: use specific references to the product or service that will *benefit* the reader in words that help people to visualize, vividly and dramatically, how the product or services will *help* them. Your opening line is probably the most important part of the letter, because if it doesn't grab the reader's attention immediately, he won't read the rest of the letter.

Here are only a few of the ways you can get the reader's attention:

- Refer to something important in the reader's life.
- Describe an actual problem the reader may encounter.
- Solve a problem the reader has.
- Tell a short story that will draw the reader into a larger message.
- Offer something special—at a real savings.
- Challenge the reader.

SELLING A PRODUCT

Dear_____:

Create attention with a startling statement.

It's a waste of time, but try to tear up the enclosed ID card that will help you improve plant security for only $.14 per employee.

Arouse your prospect's curiosity.

You can't tear the ID because we've printed it on special paper that won't rip, tear, or keep a permanent crease. Go ahead and try to tear it!

Relate product information to the reader personally.

Create a desire by stressing customer benefits.

Build benefit upon benefit.

Mr._____, as head of plant security, you know how important it is to keep employee ID cards from becoming damaged in the wash, the tool box, or at work stations. That's why you'll be interested to know that the Acme Plasticote Bond is perfect for your ID cards. You can buy this material for your employee ID cards at half the cost of the plastic-embossed cards most companies rely on. And, because the photo is automatically printed on the card as it is taken, each employee gets his or her ID in a matter of *minutes*, not *days*.

In fact, we're so convinced you'll like the Acme Plasticote Bond that we'll photograph each new employee of your company for one day—at no cost to you—just to prove how easy and effective this new system is.

Make it easy for the customer to take action.

Like to know more? Just call me collect, at (555) 123-4567, and I'll be glad to answer any questions. Or mail the postage-paid reply card to me and I'll send you more information by return mail.

You couldn't tear up the card, could you? Give me a call and I'll tell you why.

Sincerely,

CORRECTING AN ERROR

Dear Mr. Jones:

Write to a person, not a box number.

Don't lose your temper, and get to the point fast.

Give necessary background details.

Be specific; underline to clarify your key points.

Indicate the urgency, tell the person what you want.

I need your help in correcting a shipping error.

On September 1, 1979, we ordereds 12 No. A234 units, with 2" striker tabs.

Your invoice, #2345678, shows that you sent *2" striker tabs*, but what arrived were *3" striker tabs*.

We need the 2" units immediately, because they're an integral part of a larger unit we supply to our customers. Please ship the 2" units AIR EXPRESS immediately.

Indicate any action you've taken.

We are returning the 3" units for credit and shipped them via United Parcel on September 10, shipping label No. 567A.

We appreciate anything you can do to correct this error.

Yours truly,

28. HOW TO DICTATE LETTERS AND MEMOS

You can save a lot of time if you *dictate* your letters and memos rather than compose them yourself, whether it's in longhand or on your personal typewriter. But there are some secrets to dictating effectively, and if you don't know them and put them to use, you could make more work for yourself and your secretary. Some of these you can do automatically, or at least in your head. The others you may want to write down in the form of a personal checklist for yourself. Then you can refer to the checklist before, during, and after the dictation.

Know Your Objective

As in good writing, you need to know *why* you're writing before you actually begin. What's your purpose? What are you trying to accomplish? To put it another way, what do you want to happen as a result of your writing the letter or memo?

Get Your Act Together

Whether you dictate into a machine or you have a secretary waiting patiently, get all the information you need and have it on hand *before* you start dictating. If you don't do this, you'll waste time. And, if a secretary is involved, you'll waste his or hers, too. That's why you should have all the data you need right at your fingertips, ready to be quoted or summarized.

What's the Order?

If this is an especially long or involved memo or letter, take a few seconds to make a fast outline—a plan that tells you where you're going. Again, have the materials and facts ready, in the order in which you plan to present them.

Is Everything Ready?

If you're using a machine, make sure it's working properly. If you don't, you'll waste more time. And be sure you have plenty of belts or tapes on hand.

If you're dictating to a secretary, estimate the time you'll need and be sure you have enough to do the job at one sitting and that the secretary also has the time. It may upset you later if, half way through the dictation, the secretary has to remind you that you had agreed to giving him or her the rest of the morning off for a doctor's appointment.

361

What's It All About?

Especially if you're dictating into a machine, or your stenographer is someone from word processing or the typing pool who's not used to working with you, start with an overview:

Say who you are, what department you're in, and give your title if you want these facts worked into the memo or letter. This information will also help the stenographer trace the information and file it accurately for you later.

Indicate the priority. Do you want this letter in one hour? Mailed today? Out in three days?

Say what kind of document you're dictating: A letter, memo, business report, technical briefing, meeting outline, invitation, apology—whatever.

Specify the stationery. Letterhead? Plain bond? Memo? Personal letterhead? Envelope size? Is this a final draft or do you need just a rough draft?

Carbons or copies? Say at the start how many carbons or copies you'll need. Secretaries need to know this *before* they put the paper into the typewriter.

Filing instructions. Where should your file copy go? Under what category? How will you want to retrieve it? Should it be placed in more than one file because of the complexity of the subject? Let the secretary know this.

To Whom Are You Writing?

Clearly name the date, and carefully spell out the name of the person, company, and address you're writing to. A classic foul-up took place some years ago when an executive told his secretary to send the letter to Allis Chalmers and the final draft left his office addressed to "Miss Alice Chalmers." They say the folks at Allis Chalmers had the letter posted on their bulletin board for weeks. The executive obviously didn't proofread his letters. If it's your practice, identify the attention line—to whom the letter or memo is to be directed or, more commonly, the subject line—what the memo is all about. (It's also a good idea to limit the subject line to only four or five words. This makes it easier to read, and much easier to file. It may take a little extra thought on your part, but the savings in follow-up or memo retrieval time at a later date will be worth it.)

Spell It Out

As you dictate, spell out any unfamiliar or unusual words or proper names. And, if you want special puntuation such as dashes, quotation marks, underlining, ellipses, or capitals, spell that out, too.

Format Changes

If you change the margins, include lists of items, indent your paragraphs a different way, or do anything that's different from the way you usually send your letters, let the secretary or stenographer know. It's best if you do this in advance, but certainly you should make your wishes known as you dictate. It's easy to forget to do this, since we often tend to let our thoughts race ahead of our words. We assume that whoever is listening to us can keep up with us, but they can't, simply because a person can think at the rate of aboug 500 words per minute but can only speak (or understand a speaker) at about 120 words per minute.

Changing Your Mind?

If you change your mind in mid-sentence or mid-paragraph, simply excuse yourself politely with a "Please" or, "Excuse me, I'd like to change that. The sentence should read...." This not only shows courtesy towards the secretary, but it will help clarify changes you want to make. Incidentally, if you find yourself changing quite a lot of material and it becomes a pattern in your dictation, it may be because you haven't taken the time to plan your letter. A few minutes invested in some quiet thinking about your message will save you and your secretary many more minutes.

Some General Guidelines

Speak at a rate that's comfortable both for you and the secretary. If you find you have to repeat yourself fairly often to clarify your words, try pronouncing them more slowly and clearly. Many of us don't realize that we mumble or slur our words. This is especially the case with word endings. It can be hard for a secretary to understand whether you've said, "having" or "haven't." Ask the secretary or stenographer to read the entire draft to you before it's typed. If something doesn't sound right, correct it as it's being read.

Finally, ask the secretary to type the first draft double- or triple-spaced, so you can edit it properly. The best writers in the world write everything at least twice—even their letters. Editing the first draft of your letters and memos is probably the most important thing you can do to communicate clearly and produce effective letters and memos that reflect the thinking of a good executive.

29. WHEN TO DELEGATE LETTER WRITING

You can save much of your correspondence and handling time by delegating some of it to your secretary or administrative assistant. Especially if you've worked with this person for six months or more, he or she will know both your writing and your problem-solving style, and have a pretty good idea how you handle certain issues. This is also a good way to make your assistant's job more interesting and challenging: by including some creative work that will provide good balance for the day-to-day jobs that have to get done. Here are some guidelines to help you decide when you can delegate letter writing.

- *When the letters are routine.* When you find yourself saying the same thing in your letters to customers, suppliers, and people within the company, it's time to delegate your letter writing. With a little help from your assistant, you can probably sift out 20, 30, or 40 percent of the correspondence that tends to be routine or that falls into fairly distinct categories. Then it's simply a matter of providing a sample of how you solve the problem, and then indicating the guidelines you'd like followed in handling similar problems.
- *When your assistant shows initiative.* There are plenty of secretaries and administrative assistants who are smart enough to see that the way to get ahead in the organization is to ask for added responsibility, and then show how well they handle it. If you're lucky enough to have such a person, you can make a good investment in your own success by helping to bring him or her along. Delegating letter writing is a good way to do this, and it's an added opportunity to let the person know how much your appreciate the effort. Rewarding this kind of initiative with more creative work than usual is also a good way to stimulate more initiative; that says a lot for your leadership ability.
- *When the assistant can act independently.* The person who likes to act independently and think for herself or himself will usually find a way to let you know that—often during the job interview. Again, this employee is valuable and you'll do yourself a favor, as well as help the employee, by encouraging that kind of independent action. It means you'll have to have enough confidence in yourself to allow the person to make minor mistakes, but the investment in your time could well be worth the effort. An employee who is doing more than simply following the policy manual slavishly is a real asset to you and the organization—when you handle him or her right.
- *When the person has a commitment to the organization.* A person who wants to

get ahead in the company, *and who likes the company*, has plenty of opportunities to show talent simply through letter writing. But the commitment to the organization is important. Your goal in delegating letter-writing is to have confidence and security in the person that he or she can sign your letters for you and you know they'll be done well. That means the person should have the company's goals foremost in mind, and should not hesitate to look into better ways to approach a problem that will benefit the organization. It may even mean subordinating some personal goals so that the company will benefit; this, of course, means that a greater number of employees will also benefit, perhaps over a longer period of time.

- *When the person is committed to you.* Answering letters is an important part of an organization's business. What you, as a manager, say about your company helps determine its success. The person who writes letters for you has to support you and your goals enough to make you feel confident that he or she would solve the problem as you'd want it solved. If the person knows you are committed to her or his success, you'll be supported rather than undermined. But this requires that your relationship be on firm footing. The classic story of an employee who didn't support his boss involved the boss' sending him a note on how to handle a customer relations problem. The customer had complained about a hotel room and the manager had prepared several "form" replies that still sounded warm and personal. However, he didn't have the support of his assistant, and when he sent a note one day, clipped to the customer complaint, "Send this bitch letter #7," the assistant sent #7, and the note as well!

- *When the assistant wants job enrichment.* What better way could you find to develop a secretary than to allow him or her to compose the letters to be typed. You'll probably be pleasantly surprised to learn that your secretary knows nearly as much about certain subjects as you do—maybe even more. You can save yourself time and build in job enrichment by letting the secretary or administrative assistant write letters that may be less crucial than the ones you write. You may also find that the assistant will like the idea of writing the first draft of even the tough ones for you.

- *When the chance for advancement is possible or imminent.* You need to document someone's being ready for advancement, along with their ability to compose letters and memos, especially ones that deal with complicated or sensitive issues. This ability is a valuable trait—one usually associated with management-level people. When you find that the assistant wants to be considered for greater responsibility, try delegating some of the letter writing. How he or she handles this task should give you a good insight into their future management potential. And, if the chance for advancement is imminent, the assistant should have an even greater motivation to grab some different, extra work to prove his or her ability.

• *When they can take criticism as a growth opportunity.* An assistant who can't take criticism isn't the person who should be writing letters. The person needs to have strong self-confidence and to realize that any changes you make on letters, such as recommendations for style or content changes, need to be accepted as opportunities for growth. Your assistant needs to be the kind of person who takes risks and is willing to accept the consequences of mistakes because that's how growth occurs. If the assistant can't do that, then you'll have dreary, mechanical-sounding letters that won't do you or the organization any good.

30. HOW TO DEVELOP A TOPIC

It's easy to develop a topic once you organize your report or memo. First, determine what all your data have in common. What single thread or theme could you weave throughout all your material so that it can be identified logically as having a common character? Use the categories listed here as a checklist of what to look for in finding a common theme. Then, link your material to reflect that theme.

Causes/Effects

Here you show how one of the items was a cause for something, or the effect it had on some aspect of your business.

Examples

Situation	Effect
Sales people receive training only after they've been in the field for one month.	Customers complain that our sales people aren't familiar with our product or their problems.

Chronological Order

Organize your discussion in terms of the time in which events took place: hour by hour, day by day, month by month.

Examples

January 25, 1980	Widget X introduced into Region 10.
February 10	Quality Control begins receiving phone calls about Frammis B.
March 15	Sales personnel report growing resistance to discuss the product.

Compare

Show the similarities among all the facts.

Example

Employee A

Organizes material from customer information.

Plans monthly calendar for engineering department.

Analyzes work flow at the end of each week.

Employee B

Organizes material provided by the sales staff.

Plans weekly and monthly calendars for the department.

Analyzes sales traffic at the end of each month.

Contrast

Show the differences among all the facts.

Example

Product X

Weighs 26 pounds.
Costs $49.95 in retail stores.

Available in black or gray only.

Product Y

Weighs 19 pounds.
Costs $39.95 in both dealer and retail stores.

Available in black, gray, red, and yellow.

Criteria

Organize the information according to the standards by which you measured it, accepted it, or rejected it.

Example

	Previous Sales Experience	Highest Yearly Sales	Years in Field
Applicant A	10 years	$205,000	Six
Applicant B	5 years	$309,500	Two
Applicant C	14 years	$418,000	Nine

Definition

Define your terms, one after the other, either in the order in which they appear in the discussion, or in alphabetical order.

Example

In this report, we'll explain the 15 different aspects of the computer operation under discussion.

Absolute Address	An address permanently assigned to a storage location.
Address Modification	Change of address in a prescribed way by a stored program computer.
Alphanumeric	A character that includes both alphabetic characters (letters) and numeric characters (digits).

Details

List all the facts, examples, and illustrations that help explain your topic, then describe all the details specifically.

Examples

Product Research	This began with 10 scientists in 1979. $409,000 was put into the operation.
Market Analysis	This began by our reviewing target group indices from 1974-79, and was backed up with six focus group interviews each quarter.
Pilot Plant Start-up	Widget X went to pilot stage, using the CVB process modified to accept plastic molds.

Elimination

One by one, eliminate the alternatives. Show why each idea or option won't work, until you reach the final idea or option that will work.

Examples

Process 14	Required three more hours to start; experienced three shutdowns per hour.
Process 17	Efficiency dropped 14 percent at the end of four hours of operation.
Process 23	Delivered product quota projected within acceptable tolerances and scrap levels.

Problem/Solution

Show how each item in the data is a problem and explain the possible solutions.

Example

Problem		Solutions
Employees arrive late	Option 1	Decrease pay by 25 percent.
	Option 2	Give each offender a verbal warning.
	Option 3	Give employee one day off without pay.

Familiarity

Move from what the reader already knows and is probably familiar with, to what he or she doesn't know or isn't familiar with but needs to know. You build new facts and ideas on those already established.

Example

It is a known fact that a sterile bandage, applied to a flesh wound, helps it heal more easily. The same principle can be applied to eye infections. A sterile soft contact lens, used as a bandage over the cornea, can promote healing and lessen pain.

Importance

Proceed from the least important item to the most important, or from the most important to the least important, depending upon the topic.

Example

Here are the events described that led to the resignation of the president.

1/26/80	Employees asked for a review meeting.
1/18/80	President refused to discuss the issue.
1/29/80	Employee committee sent a letter of protest to the Board of Directors.

31. EFFECTIVE ENDINGS

One of the hardest skills to master in writing good letters and memos is to know how to stop writing—gracefully and effectively. But it's your closing that the reader will most likely remember best, because it's the last idea you present. That's why it pays to close your letter or memo effectively. Here are some suggestions.

Ask for Action

A frequent mistake in business correspondence is that we don't let people know what we're asking for. The good salesperson knows that you have to *ask* for the order or you probably won't get it.

Example

"May I have an interview with you within the next two weeks?"
"May I send you Widget 24 today, so you can take advantage of the discount?"

Make Action Easy

People hate to work, and will avoid anything that smacks of any effort on their part. When you ask for action, it has to be easy.

Example

"Just initial your address lable on the enclosed postage-paid business reply card and drop it in the mail. We'll do the rest."

Be Positive

Anything negative will weaken your argument and may force your reader to reject your proposal. Nearly anything you say can be expressed positively.

Example

Negative: "I'm sorry we couldn't be more helpful in answering your questions."

Positive:	"I'm glad we could help you answer the questions."
Negative:	"I hope this hasn't caused you any inconvenience."
Positive:	"Thanks for taking the time to tell us about your proposal."
Negative:	"We apologize for the mistake. It won't happen again."
Positive:	"We're glad you told us about your experience. We're now developing a new system to keep our quality at the high level we've always been so proud of."

Don't Use Trite Expressions

No one likes to hear cliches and over-used words and phrases. It makes you sound insincere.

Example

| *Trite:* | Thank you for your cooperation in this matter. |
| *Better:* | Thanks for your help. It'll make a big difference. |

Say Thanks

If "Please" is still the single most important word in the English language, "Thank you," is the most important phrase. Don't be afraid to say thanks and show your appreciation to your customers and associates.

Example

| *Poor:* | "Our employees will benefit greatly from your talk." |
| *Better:* | "Thank you for your generous offer to talk to our people. They'll gain much from the experience, and so will I." |

Be Friendly

There's no law, except stuffy old precendents, that says you have to be formal in business. Especially today, one of your biggest jobs is to convince people both inside and outside the organization that they *want* to cooperate with you and do business with you. People will also respond more easily when you keep things informal.

Example

| *Formal:* | "We are awaiting the receipt of your check in order to maintain your current credit standing." |

Friendly: "To keep your credit in good standing, Mr. Brown, just send us your check for $48.75 today. Thanks."

Add a Final Benefit

After you've made your request, close with a final benefit to the reader. People still don't take action unless they see some specific benefit to themselves.

Example

When you're ready to receive shipment, just give a call. Then you'll immediately qualify for the special insurance, the 90-day warranty, and the no-cost service agreement.

Add a Personal Note

Especially if you know your reader, you can add a final paragraph to remind the reader of your personal relationship or, even better, you can write in a personal comment or two.

Example

John, you and Flora will love the trip to the plant from the airport. The road is smooth and the route takes you by a row of dogwood trees that you both enjoy so much. They should be in perfect bloom in two weeks.

32. CORRECT TITLES FOR SPECIAL PEOPLE

Few things can embarrass an executive more easily in a business letter than to address an important person and use the wrong title or form of address. Special people merit special consideration in correspondence. We've included in this section the titles of special people that business executives are likely to contact frequently.

Person	Form of Address	Greeting (A) Business (B) Informal	Complimentary Close (A) Business (B) Informal	Personal Reference (1) For Speaking (2) For Writing
Educational Titles				
Chancellor (university)	Dr. John ⎱ Doe Dr. Jane ⎰ Chancellor	(A) Sir Madam (B) Dear Dr. Doe	(A) Very truly yours (B) Sincerely yours	(1) Dr. Doe (2) Dr. Doe or John ⎱ Doe Jane ⎰ Chancellor of ____ University
Chaplain (college or university)	The Reverend John ⎱ Doe Jane ⎰ Chaplain	Dear Chaplain Dear Mr. Miss ⎱ Doe Mrs. ⎰ Father	(A) Very truly yours (B) Sincerely yours	(1) and (2) Chaplain Doe or Mr., Miss, Mrs. Doe or Father
Dean (college university)	Dear John ⎱ Doe Jane ⎰ or Dr. John ⎱ Doe Jane ⎰ Dean (or Assistant Dean) School of ____	(A) Dear Sir Madam Dr. Doe (B) Dear Dean Doe	(A) Very truly yours (B) Sincerely yours	(1) Dean or Dr. Doe (2) Dean or Dr. Doe or Dr. Doe, Dean of…
Instructor	Mr., Dr. ⎱ John ⎱ Doe Ms., Miss ⎰ Jane ⎰ Mrs., Instructor	Dear Mr., Dr., Ms., Miss, Mrs., Doe	(A) Very truly yours (B) Sincerely yours	(1) and (2) Mr., Ms., Miss, Mrs., Dr. Doe

Person	Form of Address	Greeting (A) Business (B) Informal	Complimentary Close (A) Business (B) Informal	Personal Reference (1) For Speaking (2) For Writing
President	Mr., Miss, Mrs., Dr. John } Doe Jane President or President John } Doe Jane	(A) Sir Madam (B) Dear Dr. Doe Dear President Doe	(A) Very truly yours (B) Sincerely yours	(1) and (2) Dr. Doe or Dr. Doe, the President of ___
President/Priest	The Very Reverend John Doe, O.F.M. President	Sir Dear Father Doe	(A) Respectfully yours (B) Sincerely yours	(1) Father Doe (2) Father Doe, President of ___
Principal, school	Mr. Mrs. John } Doe Miss Jane Ms. Principal ___ School or (with doctorate) Dr. John } Doe Jane or John Jane Doe, Ph.D. Principal, ___ School	(A and B) Dear Mr. Mrs. Miss } Doe Ms. or Dear Dr. Doe	(A) Very truly yours (B) Sincerely yours	
Professor, assistant or associate	Mr., Dr., John } Doe Ms., Mrs., Jane Miss Assistant/Associate Professor of ___	(A) Dear Sir, Madam; Dear Professor Doe, Dear Dr. Doe or Dear Professor Doe	(A) Very truly yours (B) Sincerely yours	(1) Mr., Ms., Mrs., Miss, Dr. Doe (2) Professor Doe

Professor, full	Professor John ⎱ Doe ⎰ Jane *or* Dr. John ⎱ Doe ⎰ Jane Professor of ___	(A) Dear Professor Doe (B) Dear Dr. Doe	(A) Very truly yours (B) Sincerely yours	(1) and (2) Professor or Dr. Doe
Government Officials, Federal Attorney General	The Honorable John Doe The Attorney General	(A) Sir; Madam (B) Dear Mr., Madam Attorney General	(A) Very truly yours (B) Sincerely yours	(1) Mr., Mrs., Mr., Miss Attorney General Doe (2) the Attorney General, Mr. Doe or the Attorney General or Mr. Doe
Cabinet Officer addressed as "Secretary"	(A) The Honorable The Secretary of ___ (B) The Honorable John ⎱ Doe Mary ⎰ Secretary of ___ *or* The Secretary of ___	(A) Sir; Madam (B) Dear Mr. ⎱ Secretary Madam ⎰	(A) Very truly yours (B) Sincerely yours	(1) Mr., Madam Secretary Doe or Mr., Ms., Mrs., Miss, Dr. Doe (2) the Secretary of ___, John ⎱ Doe Mary ⎰ the Secretary or Mr., Ms., Mrs., Dr. Doe
Cabinet Officer, former	The Honorable John ⎱ Doe Mary ⎰	Dear Mr. Ms. ⎱ Doe Mrs. ⎰ Miss	(A) Very truly yours (B) Sincerely yours	(1) and (2) Mr., Ms., Mrs. Miss Doe

Person	Form of Address	Greeting (A) Business (B) Informal	Complimentary Close (A) Business (B) Informal	Personal Reference (1) For Speaking (2) For Writing
Chairman of a committee or subcomittee, U.S. Congress	The Honorable John / Mary } Doe Chairman Committee (or Subcommittee) on ____ United States Senate	(A) Dear Mr. / Madam } Chairman (B) Dear Senator Doe / Dear Representative Doe	(A) Very truly yours (B) Sincerely yours	(1) Mr., Madam, Chairman or Senator Doe or Senator (2) Senator (or Representative) Doe, the Chairman of the ____ Committee or Subcommittee on ____ or the Chairman or Senator Doe
Commissioner	The Honorable John / Mary } Doe Commissioner	(A) Sir; Madam (B) Dear Mr. / Ms / Mrs. / Miss } Doe	(A) Very truly yours (B) Sincerely yours	(1) Mr., Ms., Mrs., Miss Doe (2) Mr., Ms., Mrs., Miss Doe, the Commissioner or the Commissioner of ____
Director (federal agency)	The Honorable John / Mary } Doe Director ____ Agency	(A) Dear Sir / Dear Madam (B) Dear Mr. / Ms. / Mrs. / Miss } Doe	(A) Very truly yours (B) Sincerely yours	(1) Mr., Ms., Mrs., Miss Doe (2) John / Mary } Doe Director of ____ Agency or The Honorable Mr., Ms., Mrs., Miss Doe

District Attorney	The Honorable John ⎫ Mary ⎬ Doe District Attorney	(A) Dear Sir Dear Madam (B) Dear Mr. Ms. ⎫ Mrs. ⎬ Doe Miss	(A) Very truly yours (B) Sincerely yours	(1) Mr., Ms., Mrs., Miss Doe (2) District Attorney Doe or the District Attorney or Mr., Ms., Mrs., Miss Doe
Federal Judge	The Honorable John ⎫ Mary ⎬ Doe Judge of the United States District Court for the ____ District of ____	(A) Sir; Madam (B) My dear Judge Doe Dear Judge Doe	(A) Very truly yours (B) Very sincerely (1) Judge Doe (2) the Judge or Judge Doe	(1) Mr., Ms., Mrs., Miss Postmaster General or Postmaster General Doe (2) the Postmaster General, Mr. Doe or the Postmaster General or Mr. Doe
Postmaster General	The Honorable John Doe The Postmaster General	(A) Sir (B) Dear Mr. Postmaster General	(A) Very truly yours (B) Sincerely yours	(1) Mr., Ms., Mrs., Miss Postmaster General or Postmaster General Doe (2) the Postmaster General, Mr. Doe or the Postmaster General or Mr. Doe
Government Officials—Local Alderman, Councilman, Selectman	The Honorable John ⎫ Jane ⎬ Doe Alderman *or* Alderman John ⎫ Jane ⎬ Doe	Dear Mr. Ms. ⎫ Mrs. ⎬ Doe Miss Dear Alderman Doe Dear Alderman Doe Dear Mr. Ms. ⎫ Mrs. ⎬ Doe Miss	(A) Very truly yours (B) Sincerely yours	(1) and (2) Mr., Ms., Mrs., Miss Doe

Person	Form of Address	Greeting (A) Business (B) Informal	Complimentary Close (A) Business (B) Informal	Personal Reference (1) For Speaking (2) For Writing
City Attorney, Counsel, Corporate Counsel	The Honorable John } Jane } Doe (Title)	Dear Sir, Madam Dear Mr. } Ms. } Mrs. } Miss } Doe	(A) Very truly yours (B) Sincerely yours	(1) and (2) Mr., Ms., Mrs., Miss Doe
County Clerk, Treasurer	The Honorable John } Jane } Doe Clerk (Treasurer) of —— County	(A) Dear Sir, Madam (B) Dear Mr. } Ms. } Mrs. } Miss } Doe	(A) Very truly yours (B) Sincerely yours	(1) and (2) Mr., Ms., Mrs., Miss Doe
Judge	The Honorable John } Jane } Doe Judge of the ——Court of ——	(A) Sir, Madam (B) Dear Judge Doe	(A) Very truly yours (B) Sincerely yours	(1) and (2) Judge Doe
Mayor	The Honorable John } Jane } Doe Mayor of ——	(A) Sir, Madam (B) Dear Mayor Doe	(A) Very truly yours (B) Sincerely yours	(1) Mayor Doe (2) Mayor Doe or Doe, Mayor of
Government Officials— State Attorney (state), District Attorney	The Honorable John } Jane } Doe (title)	(A) Sir, Madam (B) Dear Mr. } Ms. } Mrs. } Miss } Doe	(A) Very truly yours (B) Sincerely yours	(1) and (2) Mr., Ms., Mrs., Miss Doe

380

	Envelope and Inside Address	Salutation	Complimentary Close	In Speaking, or Informal Introduction, and in Referring to
Attorney General	The Honorable John } Doe Jane Attorney General of the State of ____	(A) Sir, Madam (B) Dear Mr. Attorney Madam General	(A) Very truly yours (B) Sincerely yours	(1) Mr., Ms., Mrs., Miss Doe or Attorney General Doe (2) the Attorney General, Mr., Ms., Mrs., Miss Doe or the State Attorney General
Clerk of a court	John } Doe Jae Clerk of the Court of ____	(A) Sir, Madam (B) Dear Mr. Ms. } Doe Mrs. Miss	(A) Very truly yours (B) Sincerely yours	(1) and (2) Mr., Ms., Mrs., Miss Doe
Governor* *Adjust title to accommodate; Acting Governor; Governor-Elect; Former Governor; Lieutenant Governor;	The Honorable John } Doe Jane Governor of ____ * or His } Excellency Her	(A) Sir, Madam (B) Dear Governor Doe*	(A) Respectfully yours (B) Very sincerely	(1) Governor Doe* or Governor (2) Governor Doe* or the Governor* of ____ (used outside his or her state)
Judge, State Court	The Honorable John } Doe Jane Judge of the ____ Court	(A) Sir, Madam (B) Dear Judge Doe	(A) Very truly yours (B) Sincerely yours	(1) and (2) Judge Doe
Representative, Assemblyman, Delegate	The Honorable John } Doe Jane House of Representatives (The State Assembly; or the House of Delegates)	(A) Sir, Madam (B) Dear Mr. Ms. } Doe Mrs. Miss	(A) Very truly yours (B) Sincerely yours	(1) Mr., Ms., Mrs., Miss Doe (2) Mr., Ms., Mrs., Miss Doe or ____ Doe, the State Representative (Assemblyman, Delegate) from ____

Person	Form of Address	Greeting (A) Business (B) Informal	Complimentary Close (A) Business (B) Informal	Personal Reference (1) For Speaking (2) For Writing
Secretary of State	The Honorable John / Jane } Doe Secretary of State of ⎯⎯	(A) Sir, Madam (B) Dear Mr. / Madam } Secretary	(A) Very truly yours (B) Sincerely yours	(1) Mr., Ms., Mrs., Miss Doe or ⎯⎯ (2) Mr., Ms., Mrs., Miss Doe ⎯⎯ Secretary of State of ⎯⎯
Senate, President of	The Honorable John / Jane } Doe President of the Senate of the State (Commonwealth) of ⎯⎯	(A) Sir, Madam (B) Dear Mr. / Ms. / Mrs. / Miss } Doe Senator	(A) Very truly yours (B) Sincerely yours	(1) and (2) Senator, Mr., Ms., Mrs., Miss Doe
Senator, State	The Honorable John / Jane } Doe The Senate of ⎯⎯	(A) Sir, Madam (B) Dear Senator Doe	(A) Very truly yours (B) Sincerely yours	(1) Senator Doe or Senator (2) Senator Doe or ⎯⎯ Doe, the State Senator from ⎯⎯
Speaker (State Assembly, House of Delegates, or House of Representatives)	The Honorable John / Jane } Doe Speaker of ⎯⎯	(A) Sir, Madam (B) Dear Mr. / Ms. / Mrs. } Doe	(A) Very truly yours (B) Sincerely yours	(1) Mr., Ms., Mrs., Miss Doe (2) the Speaker of the ⎯⎯ or ⎯⎯ Doe, Speaker of the ⎯⎯
Supreme Court, State, Associate Justice	The Honorable John / Jane } Doe Associate Justice of the Supreme Court of ⎯⎯	(A) Sir, Madam (B) Dear Justice Doe	(A) Very truly yours (B) Sincerely yours	(1) Mr., Madam Justice Doe or Judge Doe or ⎯⎯ Doe, associate justice of the ⎯⎯ Supreme Court

Person	Address on Letter and Envelope	Salutation	Complimentary Close	Spoken Address
Supreme Court, State, Chief Justice	The Honorable John } Doe, Jane } Chief Justice of the Supreme Court of ___	(A) Sir, Madam (B) Dear Mr. } Chief Justice, Madam }	(A) Very truly yours (B) Sincerely yours	(1) Mr., Madam Chief Justice or Chief Justice Doe or Judge Doe (2) Chief Justice Doe or Doe, Chief Justice of the ___ Supreme Court
Supreme Court, State, Presiding Justice	The Honorable John } Doe, Jane } Presiding Justice ___ Division Supreme Court of ___	(A) Sir, Madam (B) Dear Mr. } Justice, Madam }	(A) Very truly yours (B) Sincerely yours	(1) Mr., Madam Justice Doe or Judge Doe (2) Mr., Madam Justice Doe or Judge Doe or ___ Doe, Presiding Justice of ___
Professionals				
Attorney	Mr. } John } Doe, Ms. } Jane } Mrs. } Miss } Attorney-at-Law	Dear Mr. } Doe Ms. } Mrs. } Miss }	Very truly yours	(1) Mr., Ms., Mrs, Miss Doe (2) Mr. Ms., Miss, Doe or Attorney (Atty.) Doe
Dentist	John } Doe, D.D.S. Jane } or Dr. John } Doe Jane }	Dear Mr. Doe	(A) Very truly yours (B) Sincerely yours	(1) and (2) Dr. Doe
Optometrist	John } Doe, O.D. Jane } or Dr. John } Doe Jane }	Dear Dr. Doe	(A) Very truly yours (B) Sincerely yours	(1) and (2) Dr. Doe

Person	Form of Address	Greeting (A) Business (B) Informal	Complimentary Close (A) Business (B) Informal	Personal Reference (1) For Speaking (2) For Writing
Physician	John ⎱ Doe, M.D. Jane ⎰ or Dr. John ⎱ Doe Jane ⎰	Dear Dr. Doe	(A) Very truly yours (B) Sincerely yours	(1) and (2) Dr. Doe
Veterinarian	John ⎱ Doe, D.V.M. Jane ⎰ or Dr. John ⎱ Doe Jane ⎰	Dear Dr. Doe	(A) Very truly yours (B) Sincerely yours	(1) and (2) Dr. Doe
Religious/Clerical Abbot	The Right Reverend John Doe, O.C.S.O. Abbot of _____	(A) Dear Father Abbot (B) Dear Father	(A) Respectfully yours (B) Sincerely yours	(1) Father Abbot (2) Father Doe
Apostolic Delegate	His Excellency, The Most Reverend John Doe Archbishop of _____ The Apostolic Delegate	(A) Your Excellency (B) My Dear Archbishop	(A) Respectfully yours (B) Respectfully	
Archbishop	The Most Reverend Archbishop of _____ John Doe or the Most Reverend John Doe Archbishop of _____	(A) Your Excellency (B) Dear Archbishop Doe	(A) Respectfully yours (B) Sincerely yours	(1) Your Excellency (2) the Archbishop of _____ or (1) and (2) Archbishop Doe
Archbishop, Episcopal	To His Grace The Lord Archbishop of Canterbury Canterbury, England	(A) Your Grace or My Lord Archbishop (B) My Dear Archbishop	(A) Respectfully yours (B) Sincerely yours	(1) Your Grace (2) The Lord Archbishop

Position	Address	Salutation	Complimentary Close	Informal Address
Archdeacon, Anglican or Episcopal (Apiscopal)	The Venerable The Archdeacon of ___ or the Venerable John Doe	(A) Venerable Sir (B) Venerable Sir My dear Archdeacon	(A) Respectfully yours (B) Sincerely yours	(1) Archdeacon Doe (2) The Archdeacon of ___ (with a doctorate: Dr. Doe)
Bishop, Anglican	The Right Reverend The Lord Bishop of ___	(A and B) My Lord Bishop	(A) Respectfully yours (B) Sincerely yours	(1) Bishop Doe (2) The Lord Bishop of ___
Bishop, Catholic	The Most Reverend John Doe Bishop of ___	(A) Your Excellency (B) Dear Bishop Doe	(A) Respectfully yours (B) Sincerely yours	(1) and (2) Bishop Doe
Bishop, Episcopal Presiding	The Most Reverend John Doe Presiding Bishop of ___	(A) Most Reverend Sir (B) Dear Bishop	(A) Respectfully yours (B) Sincerely yours	(1) Bishop Smith (2) Bishop Smith
Bishop, Episcopal	The Right Reverend The Bishop of ___ or The Right Reverend John Doe Bishop of ___	(A) Right Reverend Sir (B) Dear Bishop Doe	(A) Respectfully yours (B) Respectfully	(1) Bishop Doe (2) the Episcopal Bishop of ___
Bishop, Methodist	The Reverend John Doe Methodist Bishop	(A) Reverend Sir (B) Dear Bishop Smith	(A) Respectfully yours (B) Sincerely yours	(1) Bishop Doe (2) Bishop Doe
Brotherhood, member of	Brother John, O.F.M.	Dear Brother John	(A) Respectfully yours (B) Sincerely yours	(1) Bishop John (2) Brother John, O.F.M.
Brotherhood, superior of	Brother John, O.F.M. Superior	Dear Brother John	(A) Respectfully yours (B) Sincerely yours	(1) Brother John (2) Brother John, O.F.M. Superior of ___
Canon	The Reverend John Doe Canon of ___ Cathedral	Dear Canon Doe	(A) Respectfully yours (B) Sincerely yours	(1) and (2) Canon Doe

Person	Form of Address	Greeting (A) Business (B) Informal	Complimentary Close (A) Business (B) Informal	Personal Reference (1) For Speaking (2) For Writing
Cardinal	His Eminence John Cardinal Doe Archbishop of _____ or His Eminence Cardinal Doe Archbishop of _____	(A) Your Eminence (B) Dear Cardinal Doe	(A) Respectfully yours (B) Sincerely yours	(1) Your Eminence or Cardinal Doe (2) His Eminence Cardinal Doe or Cardinal Doe
Clergyman, Protestant (not Episcopal)	The Reverend John Doe with a doctorate: The Reverend Dr. John R. Smith	Dear Mr. Doe Dear Dr. Doe	(A) Respectfully yours (B) Sincerely yours	(1) Mr. Doe (2) the Reverend Mr. Doe or The Reverend John Doe or Mr. Doe (1) Dr. Doe (2) The Reverend Dr. Doe or Dr. Doe
Dean (of a cathedral)	The Very Reverend John Doe _____ Cathedral or Dean John Doe _____ Cathedral	(A) Very Reverend Sir (B) Dear Dean Doe	(A) Respectfully yours (B) Sincerely yours	(1) Dean Doe (2) Dean Doe with a doctorate: Dr. Doe
Moderator, Presbyterian	The Moderator of _____ or The Reverend John Doe with a doctorate: Dr. John Doe	(A) Reverend Sir (B) Dear Mr. Moderator	(A) Respectfully yours (B) Sincerely yours	(1) and (2) the Moderator of _____ or Mr Doe (1) and (2) Dr. Doe

Personage	Envelope and Inside Address	Salutation	Complimentary Close	Speaking To / Referring To
Monsignor Domestic Prelate	The Right Reverend Monsignor John } Doe or The Rt. Rev. Msgr. John Doe	(A) Right Reverend and Dear Monsignor Doe (B) Dear Monsignor Doe	(A) Respectfully yours (B) Sincerely yours	(1) and (2) Monsignor Doe
Papal Chamberlain	The Very Reverend Monsignor Joe Doe or The Very Rev. Msgr. John Doe			
Patriarch (of an Eastern Orthodox Church)	His Beatitude the Patriarch of ____	Most Reverend Lord	Respectfully yours	(1) Your Beatitude (2) John Doe, the Patriarch of ____ or The Patriarch
Pope	His Holiness the Pope or His Holiness Pope ____	(A and B) Your Holiness	Respectfully yours	(1) Your Holiness (2) His Holiness the Pope or His Holiness, Pope ____, or The Pope
President, Mormon	The President Church of Jesus Christ of Latter-Day Saints	(A) My dear President (B) Dear President Doe	(A) Respectfully yours (B) Sincerely yours	(1) Mr. Doe (2) Mr. Doe
Priest, Catholic	The Reverend John Doe with a doctorate: The Reverend John Doe	(A and B) Dear Father Doe	(A) Respectfully yours (B) Sincerely yours	(1) Father Doe (2) Father Doe
Priest, Episcopal	The Reverend John Doe with a doctorate: The Reverend Dr. John Doe	(A) Dear Mr. Doe (B) Dear Father Doe	(A) Respectfully yours (B) Sincerely yours	(1) Mr. (or Father) Doe (2) Mr. (or Father) Doe (1) Dr. (or Father) Doe (2) Dr. (or Father) Doe

Person	Form of Address	Greeting (A) Business (B) Informal	Complimentary Close (A) Business (B) Informal	Personal Reference (1) For Speaking (2) For Writing
Rabbi	Rabbi John Doe *with a doctorate:* Rabbi John Doe, D.D.	(A) Dear Rabbi Doe (B) Dear Dr. Doe	(A) Respectfully (B) Sincerely yours	(1) and (2) Rabbi Doe (1) and (2) Dr. (or Rabbi) Doe
Sisterhood, member of	Sister Mary Joan, S.J.	(A) Dear Sister (B) Dear Sister Mary Joan	(A) Respectfully yours (B) Sincerely yours	(1) and (2) Sister Mary Joan Sister Mary Joan
Sisterhood, Mother Superior of	The Reverend Mother Superior, S.J.	(A) Reverend Mother (B) Dear Reverend Mother	(A) Respectfully yours (B) Sincerely yours	(1) Reverend Mother (2) The Reverend Mother Superior or The Reverend Mother
Sisterhood, Sister Superior of	The Reverend Sister Superior, S.J.	(A and B) Dear Sister Superior	(A and B) Respectfully	(1) Sister Superior (2) The Sister Superior
United Nations Officials				
Representative, American (with ambassadorial rank)	The Honorable John } Doe Jane United States Permanent Representative to the United Nations	(A) Sir; Madam (B) Dear Mr. Madam } Ambassador	(A) Respectfully (B) Sincerely yours	(1) Mr., Madam Ambassador or Mr., Ms., Mrs., Miss Doe (2) Mr., Ms., Mrs., Doe or the United States Representative to the United Nations or the United States Representative to the United Nations or UN Representative _____ Doe

388

		(1) Mr., Madam Ambassador or Mr., Ms., Mrs., Miss Doe (2) Mr., Ms., Mrs., Miss Doe or the Representative of … to the United Nations or UN Representative _____ Doe
Representative Foreign, (with ambassadorial rank)	His } Her } Excellency John } Jane } Doe	(A) Excellency (B) Dear Mr. Madam } Doe
General		
Two or more men/ same surname	Mr. John Doe Mr. William Doe or Messrs. J. and W. Doe	(A) Gentlemen (B) Dear Messrs. Doe
Two or more men/ different surname	Mr. John Doe Mr. William Black or Messrs. J. Doe and W. Black or Messrs. Doe and Black	(A) Gentlemen (B) Dear Mr. Doe and Mr. Black
Two or more married women/same surname	Mrs. John Doe Mrs. William Doe or Mesdames J. Doe and W. Black or The Mesdames Doe	(A) Mesdames (B) Dear Mesdames Doe

Complimentary close (Representative Foreign): (A) Respectfully (B) Sincerely yours

(Two or more men/same surname): (A) Very truly yours (B) Sincerely yours

(Two or more men/different surname): (A) Very truly yours (B) Sincerely yours

(Two or more married women/same surname): (A) Very truly yours (B) Sincerely yours

Person	Form of Address	Greeting (A) Business (B) Informal	Complimentary Close (A) Business (B) Informal	Personal Reference (1) For Speaking (2) For Writing
Two or more unmarried women/same surname	Miss Jane T. Doe Miss Mary N. Doe or Misses Jane and Mary Doe or the Misses Doe	(A) Ladies (B) Dear Misses Doe	(A) Very truly yours (B) Sincerely yours	
Two or more women/same surname/marital status unknown	Ms. Jane T. Doe Ms. Mary N. Doe	(A) and (B) Dear Ms. Jane and Mary Doe	(A) Very truly yours (B) Sincerely yours	
Two or more married women/different surnames	Mrs. John Doe Mrs. James Black or Mesdames Doe and Black	(A) Dear Mesdames Doe and Black (B) Dear Mrs. Doe and Mrs. Black	(A) Very truly yours (B) Sincerely yours	
Two or more unmarried women/different surnames	Miss Jane Doe Miss Mary Black or Misses J. Doe and M. Black	(A) Ladies (B) Dear Miss Doe and Miss Black	(A) Very truly yours (B) Sincerely yours	
Two or more women with different surname/marital status unknown	Ms. Jane Doe Ms. Mary Black	(A and B) Dear Ms. Doe and Ms. Black	(A) Very truly yours (B) Sincerely yours	
Divorced woman	Mrs. Jane Doe Black (maiden name plus former husband's surname)	Dear Mrs. Black	(A) Very truly yours (B) Sincerely yours	
Widow	Mrs. John Doe	Dear Mrs. Doe	(A) Very truly yours (B) Sincerely yours	

PART IV

Managing
The Numbers in
Your Life

33. METRICS MADE EASY

Congress passed the Metric Conversion Act in 1975. It allows voluntary conversion of our traditional measuring units to this decimal system by 1985.

With metrics, there's only one unit for measuring a quantity such as length or volume. All other units relate to it, and to each other, in multiples of 10.

We measure quantity in five ways, and only one—time—won't be affected by the change. Here are the other metric units:

Quantity	Metric Measuring Unit
Length	meter (m)
Weight	gram (g)
Temperature	Celsius (°C)
Volume	liter (l)

Use Prefixes for Multiples

With metrics, we use prefixes to show which multiple of 10 the unit represents:

Prefix	Multiple
kilo (k)	1000 X
hecto (h)	100 X
deka (da)	10 X
deci (d)	1/10 X
centi (c)	1/100 X
milli (m)	1/1000 X

Since it takes 1000 millimeters to make 1 meter, and 1 millimeter equals .001 meter, you can determine similar relationships:

LENGTH

Traditional	Metric
3 feet = 1 yard	1000 millimeters = 1 meter
36 inches = 1 yard	100 centimeters = 1 meter
5280 feet = 1 mile	1000 meters = 1 kilometer

(A meter is about 3 inches longer than a yard)

393

WEIGHT

Traditional	Metric
438 grains = 1 ounce	1000 milligrams = 1 gram
16 ounces = 1 pound	100 centigrams = 1 gram
2000 pounds = 1 short ton	1000 grams = 1 kilogram
1000 kilograms = 1 ton	

(A kilogram weighs a little more than 2 pounds)

VOLUME

Traditional	Metric
2 cups = 1 pint	1000 milliliters = 1 liter
2 pints = 1 quart	100 centiliters = 1 liter
4 quarts = 1 gallon	
8 pints = 1 gallon	

(A liter contains a little more than a quart)

Metric Conversion Table

Conversion To Metric: Multiply By	Conversion From Metric: Multiply by

LENGTH

inches	2.54	centimeters	millimeters	0.04	inches
feet	30.0	centimeters	centimeters	0.4	inches
yards	0.91	meters	meters	3.3	feet
miles	1.6	kilometers	kilometers	0.62	miles

AREA

sq. inches	6.5	sq. centimers	sq. centimeters	0.16	sq inches
sq. feet	0.09	sq. meters	sq. meters	1.2	sq. yards
sq. yards	0.8	sq. meters	sq. kilometers	0.4	sq. miles
sq. miles	2.6	sq. kilometers	hectares	2.47	acres
acres	0.4	hectares			

MASS (Weight)

ounces	28.0	grams	grams	0.035	ounces
pounds	0.45	kilograms	kilograms	2.2	pounds
short ton	0.9	metric ton	metric tons	1.1	short tons

VOLUME

teaspoons	5.0	milliliters
tablespoons	15.0	milliliters
fluid ounces	30.0	milliliters
cups	0.24	liters
pints	0.47	liters
quarts	0.95	liters
gallons	3.8	liters
cubic feet	0.03	cubic meters
cubic yards	0.76	cubic meters

VOLUME

milliliters	0.03	fluid ounces
liters	2.1	pints
liters	1.06	quarts
liters	0.26	gallons
cubic meters	35.0	cubic feet
cubic meters	1.3	cubic yards

TEMPERATURE

Fahreinheit $\begin{cases} \text{Subtract 32} \\ \text{then multiply} \\ \text{9/5ths, then} \\ \text{by 5/9ths} \end{cases}$

TEMPERATURE

Celsius $\begin{cases} \text{Multiply Fahrenheit} \\ \text{by Celsius, then} \\ \text{add 32} \end{cases}$

Equivalent Units of Length

Inches	Centimeters	Centimeters	Inches
Inches	cm.	cm.	Inches
1	2.54	1	0.39
2	5.08	2	0.79
3	7.62	3	1.18
4	10.16	4	1.57
5	12.70	5	1.97
6	15.24	6	2.36
7	17.78	7	2.76
8	20.32	8	3.15
9	22.86	9	3.54
10	25.40	10	3.94

Feet	Meters	Meters	Feet
ft.	m.	m.	ft.
1	0.30	1	3.28
2	0.61	2	6.56
3	0.91	3	9.84
4	1.22	4	13.12
5	1.52	5	16.40
6	1.83	6	19.68
7	2.13	7	22.97
8	2.44	8	26.25
9	2.74	9	29.53
10	3.05	10	32.81

Yards	Meters	Meters	Yard
yd.	m.	m.	yd.
1	0.91	1	1.09
2	1.83	2	2.19
3	2.74	3	3.28
4	3.66	4	4.37
5	4.57	5	5.47
6	5.49	6	6.56
7	6.40	7	7.66
8	7.32	8	8.75
9	8.23	9	9.84
10	9.14	10	10.94

Miles	Kilometers	Kilometers	Miles
miles	km.	km.	miles
1.0	1.61	1	0.62
1.5	2.41	2	1.24
2.0	3.22	3	1.86
2.5	4.02	4	2.49
3.0	4.83	5	3.11
3.5	5.63	6	3.73
4.0	6.44	7	4.35
4.5	7.24	8	4.97
5.0	8.05	9	5.59
		10	6.21

Equivalent Units of Volume

Ounces	Milliliters	Milliliters	Ounces
liq. oz.	ml.	ml.	liq. oz.
1	29.57	10	0.34
2	59.15	20	0.68
3	88.72	30	1.01
4	118.29	40	1.35
5	147.87	50	1.69

Quarts	Liters	Liters	Quarts
liq. qt.	l.	l.	liq. qt.
1	0.95	0.5	0.53
2	1.89	1.0	1.06
3	2.84	1.5	1.59
4	3.79	2.0	2.11
		2.5	2.64
		3.0	3.17

Gallons	Liters	Liters	Gallons
gal.	l.	l.	gal.
0.5	1.89	1	0.26
1.0	3.79	2	0.53
1.5	5.68	3	0.79
2.0	7.57	4	1.06
2.5	9.46		
3.0	11.36		
3.5	13.25		
4.0	15.14		

Equivalent Units of Weight

Ounces	Grams	Grams	Ounces
oz.	g.	g.	oz.
1	28.3	1	0.4
2	56.7	2	0.07
3	85.0	3	0.11
4	113.4	4	0.14
5	141.7	5	0.18
6	170.1	6	0.21
7	198.4	7	0.25
8	226.8	8	0.28
9	255.1	9	0.32
10	283.5	10	0.35

Pounds	Kilograms	Kilograms	Pounds
lb.	kg.	kg.	lb.
1	0.45	1	2.20
2	0.91	2	4.41
3	1.36	3	6.61
4	1.81	4	8.82
5	2.27	5	11.02
6	2.72	6	13.23
7	3.18	7	15.43
8	3.63	8	17.64
9	4.08	9	19.84
10	4.54	10	22.05

Equivalent Units of Temperature

Fahrenheit	Celsius	Celsius	Fahrenheit
°F	°C	°C	°F
− 10	− 23.33	− 30	− 22.00
0	− 17.78	− 20	− 4.00
10	− 12.22	− 10	14.00
20	− 6.67	0	32.00
30	− 1.11	10	50.00
40	4.44	20	68.00
50	10.00	30	86.00
60	15.56	40	104.00
70	21.11	50	122.00
80	26.67	60	140.00
90	32.22	70	158.00
98.6	37.00	80	176.00
100	37.78	90	194.00
212	100.00	100	212.00

Equivalent Fractions

Inches	Millimeters
1/64	.39688
1/32	.79375
1/16	1.58750
1/8	3.17500
1/4	6.35000
1/2	12.70000

Metrics For the Home

SPOONFULS
¼ tsp. . . . . 1.25 milliliters
½ tsp. . . . . 2.5 milliliters
¾ tsp. . . . . 3.75 milliliters
1 tsp. 5   milliliters
¼ tbls. . . . . 3.75 milliliters
½ tbls. . . . . 7.5 milliliters
¾ tbls. . . . . 11.25 milliliters
1 tbls. 15   milliliters

OUNCES
¼ oz. . . . . 7.5 milliliters
½ oz. 15   milliliters
¾ oz. . . . . 22.5 milliliters
1 oz. 30   milliliters

CUPS
¼ cup. . . . . 59 milliliters
⅓ cup. . . . . 79 milliliters
½ cup. . . . . 118 milliliters
⅔ cup. . . . . 157 milliliters
¾ cup. . . . . 177 milliliters
1 cup . . . . 236 milliliters

PINTS-QUARTS-GALLONS
½ pint 237   milliliters
1 pint 473   milliliters
1 quart . . . . 946.3 milliliters
1 gallon 3785   milliliters

WEIGHT IN OUNCES

¼ oz. . . . . 7.09 grams
½ oz. . . . . 14.17 grams
¾ oz. . . . . 21.26 grams
1 oz. . . . . 28.35 grams

POUNDS-KILOGRAMS

¼ lb. . . . . .113 kilograms
½ lb. . . . . .227 kilograms
¾ lb. . . . . .340 kilograms
1 lb. . . . . .454 kilograms
2.205 lbs. . . . . 1 kilogram

LENGTH

1 inch . . . . 2.54 centimeters
1 foot . . . . 30.48 centimeters
1 yard . . . . 91.44 centimeters
100 feet . . . . 30.48 meters
1 mile . . . . 1,609.00 kilometers
50 mph. . . . . 80.47 kilometers/hr.

TEMPERATURE

32°F. . . . . 0° Celsius
68°F. . . . . 20° Celsius
212°F. . . . . 100° Celsius

SQUARE MEASURE

1 sq. in. . . . . . 6,452 square centimeters
1 sq. ft. . . . . . . 929 square centimeters
1 sq. yd. . . . . 8,321 square centimeters
1 acre . . . . . . 4,047 square meters

34. TABLE OF WEIGHTS AND MEASURES

Linear Measure

12 inches (in.)	= 1 foot (ft.)
3 feet	= 1 yard (yd.)
5½ yards	= 1 rod (rd.), pole, or perch (16½ feet)
40 rods	= 1 furlong (fur.) = 220 yards = 660 feet
8 furlongs	= 1 statute mile (mi.) = 1,760 yards = 5,280 feet
3 miles	= 1 league = 5,280 yards = 15,840 feet
6076.11549 feet	= 1 International Nautical Mile

Liquid Measure

4 gills	= 1 pint (pt.) = 28,875 cubic inches
2 pints	= 1 quart (qt.) = 57.75 cubic inches
4 quarts	= 1 gallon (gal.) = 231 cubic inches = 8 pts = 32 gills

Area Measure

144 square inches	= 1 square foot (ft.)
9 square feet	= 1 square yard (yd.) = 1296 square inches
30¼ square yards	= 1 square rod (rd.) = 272¼ square feet
160 square rods	= 1 acre = 840 square yards = 43,560 square feet
640 acres	= 1 square mile (mi.)
1 mile square	= 1 section (land)
6 miles square	= 1 township = 36 sections = 36 square miles

Cubic Measure

30¼ square yards	= 1 square rod (rd.^{2}) = 262¼ (in.^{2})
1 cubic foot (ft)	= 1,728 cubic inches (in.^{3})
27 cubic feet	= 1 cubic yards (yd.^{3})

Surveyors' Chain Measure

7.92 inches (in)	= 1 link
100 links	= 1 chain (ch.) = 4 rods = 66 feet
80 chains	= 1 statute mile (mi.) = 320 rods = 5780 feet

Troy Weight

24 grains	= 1 pennyweight (dwt.)
20 pennyweights	= 1 ounce troy (oz. t.) = 480 grains
12 ounces troy	= 1 pound troy (lb. t.) = 240 pennyweight = 5760 grains

Dry Measure

2 pints (pt)	= 1 quart (qt.) = (67.2006 cubic inches)	
8 quarts	= 1 peck (pk.) = (537.605 cubic inches) = 16 pints
4 pecks	= 1 bushel (bu.) = (2,150.42 cubic inches) = 32 quarts

Avoirdupois Weight
(The "grain" is the same in avoirdupois and troy weight.)

27^{11}⁄₃₂ grains	= 1 dram (dr)
16 drams	= 1 ounce (oz = 437½ grains)
16 ounces	= 1 point (lb) = 256 drams = 7,000 grains
100 pounds	= 1 hundredweight (cwt)*
20 hundred weights	= 1 ton = 2,000 pounds*

In "gross" or "long" measure, the following values are recognized.

112 pounds	= 1 gross or long hundredweight*
20 gross or long hundredweights	= 1 gross or long ton = 2,240 pounds*

*The terms "hundredweight" and "ton" mean the 100-pound hundredweight and the 2,000 pound ton, respectively: these units may be termed "net" or "short" when necessary to distinguish them from corresponding units in gross or long measure.

EQUIVALENTS

Lengths

Angstrom (A)	=	0.1 nanometer (exactly)
	=	0.0001 micron (exactly)
	=	0.00000006 inch
1 cable's length	=	120 fathom
	=	720 feet
	=	219.456 meters (exactly)
1 centimeter (cm.)	=	0.3937 inch
1 chain (ch.)	=	66 feet
(Gunter's or surveyors)	=	20.1168 meters (exactly)
1 decimeter (dm.)	=	3.937 inches
1 degree (geographical)	=	364,566.929 feet
	=	69.047 miles (avg.)
	=	111.123 kilometer (avg.)
of latitude	=	68.078 miles at equator
	=	69.043 miles at poles
of longtitude	=	69.171 miles

1 dekameter (dm.)	=	**32.808 feet**
1 fathom	=	**6 feet**
	=	**1.8288 meters (exactly)**
1 foot (ft.)	=	**0.3048 meters exactly**
1 furlong (fur.)	=	**10 chains (surveyors)**
	=	**660 feet**
	=	**220 yards**
	=	**⅛ statute mile**
	=	**201.168 meters**
1 hand (height measure for horses from ground to top of shoulders	=	**4 inches**
1 inch (in.)	=	**2.54 centimeters (exactly)**
1 kilometer (km.)	=	**0.631 mile**
	=	**3,280.8 feet**
1 league (land)	=	**3 statute miles**
	=	**4.828 kilometers**
1 link (Gunter's or surveyors)	=	**7.92 inches**
	=	**0.201 meter**
1 link (engineers)	=	**1 foot**
	=	**0.305 meter**
1 meter (m)	=	**39.37 inches**
	=	**1.904 yards**
1 micron (μ) (the Greek letter mu)	=	**0.001 millimeter (exactly)**
	=	**0.00003937 inch**
1 mil	=	**0.001 inch (exactly)**
	=	**0.0254 millimeter (exactly)**
1 mile (mi.) (statue or land)	=	**5,280 feet**
	=	**1.609 kilometers**
1 international nautical mile (INM)	=	**1.852 kilometers (exactly)**
	=	**1.150779 statute miles**
	=	**6,076.11549 feet**
1 millimeter (mm.)	=	**0.039.37 inch**
1 nanometer (nm.)	=	**0.001 micron (exactly)**
	=	**0.00000003937 inch (exactly)**
1 pica (typography)	=	**12 points**
1 point (typography)	=	**0.013837 inch (exactly)**
	=	**0.351 millimeter**
1 rod (rd.), pole, or perch	=	**16½ feet**
	=	**5½ yards**
	=	**5.029 meters**
1 yard (yd.)	=	**0.9144 meter (exactly)**

Areas of Surfaces

1 acre	=	43,560 square feet
	=	4,840 square yards
	=	0.405 hectare
1 are (a.)	=	119.599 square yards
	=	0.25 acre
1 bolt (cloth measure)	=	100 yards (on modern looms)
length	=	42 inches (usually, for cotton)
width	=	60 inches (usually, for wool)
1 hectare (ha.)	=	2.471 acres
1 square (building)	=	100 square feet
1 square centimeter (cm²)	=	0.155 square inch
1 square decimeter (dm.²)	=	15.500 square inches
1 square foot (ft.²)	=	929.030 square centimeters
1 square inch (in.²)	=	6.452 square centimeters
1 square kilometer (km.²)	=	247.105 acres
	=	0.386 square mile
	=	1.197 square yards
1 square meter (m.²)	=	10.764 square feet
1 square mile (mi.²)	=	258.999 hectares
1 square millimeter (mm.²)	=	0.002 square inch
1 square rod (rd.²) sq. pole, or sq. perch	=	25.293 square meters
1 square yard (yd.²)	=	0.836 square meter
1 barrel (bbl.), standard,	=	7,056 cubic inches
for fruits, vegetables,	=	105 dry quarts
and other dry commodities except dry cranberries	=	3.281 bushels, struck measure
1 barrel (bbl.), standard,	=	5,826 cubic inches
cranberry	=	86⁴⁵⁄₆₄ dry quarts
	=	2.709 bushels, struck measure
1 board foot (lumber measure)	=	1 foot-square board 1 inch thick
1 bushel (bu.) (U.S.)	=	2,150.42 cubic inches (exactly)
(struck measure)	=	35.238 liters
1 bushel, heaped (U.S.)	=	2,747.715 cubic inches
	=	1.278 bushels, struck measure*
1 bushel (bu. (British Imperial)	=	1.032 U.S. bushels struck measure
(struck measure)	=	2,219.36 cubic inches
1 cord (cd.) firewood	=	128 cubic feet

*Often recognized as 1¼ bushels, struck measure.

1 cubic centimeter (cm.³)	=	0.061 cubic inch
1 cubic decimeter (dm.³)	=	61.024 cubic inches
1 cubic inch (in.³)	=	0.554 fluid ounce
	=	4.433 fluid drams
	=	16.387 cubic centimeters
1 cubic foot (ft.)³)	=	7.481 gallons
	=	28.317 cubic decimeters
1 cubic meter (m.)³)	=	1.308 cubic yards
1 cubic yard (yd.³)	=	0.765 cubic meter
1 cup, measuring	=	8 fluid ounces
	=	½ liquid pint
1 dram, fluid (fl. dr.)	=	0.961 U.S. fluid dram
(British)	=	0.217 cubic inch
	=	3.552 milliliters
1 dekaliter (dal.)	=	2.642 gallons
	=	1.135 pecks
1 gallon (gal.) (U.S.)	=	231 cubic inches
	=	3.785 liters
	=	0.833 British gallon
	=	128 U.S. fluid-ounces
1 gallon (gal.)	=	277.42 cubic inches
British Imperial	=	1.201 U.S. gallons
	=	4.546 liters
	=	160 British fluid ounces
1 gill	=	7.219 cubic inches
	=	4 fluid ounces
	=	0.118 liter
1 hecoliter (h.)	=	26.417 gallons
	=	2.838 bushels
1 liter (l.)	=	1.057 liquid quarts
	=	0.908 dry quart
	=	61.024 cubic inches
1 milliliter (ml.)	=	0.271 fluid dram
(1 cu. cm. exactly)	=	16.231 minims
	=	0.061 cubic inch
1 ounce, liquid (U.S.)	=	1.805 cubic inches
	=	29.573 milliliters
	=	1.041 British fluid ounces
1 ounce, fluid (fl. oz.)	=	0.961 British fluid ounces
(British)	=	1.734 cubic inches
	=	28.412 milliliters
1 peck (pk.)	=	8.810 liters
1 pint (pt.), dry	=	33.600 cubic inches
	=	0.551 liter

1 pint (pt.), liquid	=	**28.875 cubic inches (exactly)**
	=	**0.473 liter**
1 quart (qt.) dry (U.S.)	=	**67.201 cubic inches**
	=	**1.101 liters**
	=	**0.969 British quart**
1 quart (qt.) liquid (U.S.)	=	**57.75 cubic in (exactly)**
	=	**0.946 liter**
	=	**0.833 British quart**
1 quart (qt.) (British)	=	**69.354 cubic inches**
	=	**1.032 U.S. dry quarts**
	=	**1.201 U.S. liquid quarts**
1 tablespoon	=	**3 teaspoons**
1 fluid drams	=	**½ fluid ounce**
1 teaspoon	=	**⅓ tablespoon**
	=	**1⅓ fluid drams**

Weights or Masses

1 assay ton (AT)	=	**29.167 grams**
1 bale (cotton measure)	=	**500 pounds in U.S.**
	=	**750 pounds in Egypt**
1 carat (c)	=	**200 milligrams**
	=	**3.086 grams**
1 dram avoirdupois (dr. avdp.)	=	**$27^{11}/_{32}$ = 27.344 grams)**
	=	**1,722 grams**
1 grain	=	**64.799 milligrams**
1 gram	=	**15.432 grains**
	=	**0.035 ounce, avoirdupois**
1 hundredweight, gross or long (gross cwt.)	=	**112 pounds**
	=	**50.802 kilograms**
1 hundredweight, net or short (Cwt. or net cwt.)	=	**100 pounds**
	=	**45.359 kilograms**
1 kilogram (kg.)	=	**2.205 pounds**
1 microgram (γ) (the Greek letter gamma)	=	**0.000001 gram (exactly)**
1 milligram (mg.)	=	**0.015 gram**
1 ounce avoirdupois (oz. avdp.)	=	**437.5 grains (exactly)**
	=	**0.911 troy ounce**
		28.350 grams
1 ounce troy (oz. t.)	=	**480 grains**
	=	**1.097 avoirdupois ounces**
	=	**31.103 grams**

1 pennyweight (dwt.)	=	1.555 grams
1 pound, avoirdupois	=	7,000 grains
(lb. avdp.)	=	1,215 troy pounds
	=	453.59237 grams (exactly)
1 pound, troy (lb. t.)	=	5,760 grains
	=	0.823 avoirdupois pound
	=	373.242 grams
1 ton, gross or long	=	2,240 pounds
(gross ton)	=	1.12 net tons (exactly)
	=	1.016 metric tons
1 ton, metric (t.)	=	2,204.623 pounds
	=	0.984 gross ton
	=	1.102 net tons
1 ton, net or short (sh. ton)	=	2,000 pounds
	=	0.893 gross ton
	=	0.907 metric ton

Spirits Measures

Pony	=	0.5 jigger
Shot	=	0.666 jigger
	=	1.0 ounce
Jigger	=	1.5 shot
Pint	=	16 shots
	=	0.625 fifth
Fifth	=	25.6 shots
	=	1.6 pints
	=	0.8 quart
	=	0.75706 liter
Quart	=	32 shots
	=	1.25 fifth
Magnum	=	2 quarts
	=	2.49797 bottles (wine)
For champagne and brandy only:		
Jeroboam	=	6.4 pints
	=	1.6 magnum
	=	0.8 gallon
For champagne only:		
Rehoboam	=	3 magnums
Methuselah	=	4 magnums
Salmanazar	=	6 magnums
Balthazar	=	8 magnums
Nebushadnezzar	=	10 magnums

| Wine Bottle (standard): | = | 0.800633 quart |
| | = | 0.7576778 liter |

Weight of Water

1 cubic inch	=	.0360 pound
12 cubic inches	=	.433 pound
1 cubic foot	=	62.4 pounds
1 cubic foot	=	7.48052 U.S. gal
1.8 cubic feet	=	112.0 pounds
35.96 cubic feet	=	2240.0 pounds
1 imperial gallon	=	10.0 pounds
1 U.S. gallon	=	8.33 pounds

35. SHOULD YOU USE FIGURES OR WORDS?

Today, we write most numerals in figures, although all numbers below 100 can be written as words. The numbers one to nine, in written copy, are usually written as words.

Whichever style you use, be consistent. If you decide to use a figure in one section of your report, don't write it in words in another section of the report. Here are some guidelines that show optional styles.

Compounds

If two numbers make up one unit, express one in words and the other in figures.

two 8-file cabinets
35 ten-file cabinets

Adjacent Figures

Don't place two figures next to each other unless they are in a series.

Correct
By 1981, two hundred people will be ...
Incorrect
By 1981, 200 people will be ...

Dates

Use figures to show dates in business letters.

November 29, 1981

Numbered Lists

Whether they're within a paragraph or listed vertically, put enumerations in figures.

Your job is to:
1. Plan for results
2. Set goals
3. Motivate people

Exact Amounts

Express exact amounts in figures unless they begin sentences (you don't need to use both, side by side.

We've sent 300 copies of the *Deskbook* for your training session.

Three-hundred copies have been sent.

Figures

Use figures to show numbers of contracts, policies, catalogs, rooms, streets, shares, percentages, measures, sizes, and fractions.

Agreement 24; Policy A-100; Catalog 24; Room 126; 9 Sterling Square; 10 shares; 10 percent; 175 pounds; size 7; $17\frac{3}{8}$

Footnotes

Use figures to show pages cited, and superscript figures to refer to text footnotes.

... he reads well."[2]
[3]Ibid., p. 10.

Four or More Digits

Any number of four or more digits uses figures with each set of three digits separated by commas. Exceptions: to show contracts, policies, checks, streets, rooms, or page numbers.

12,000 items
14,000 profit
2,414,000 people
4,100 words
page 1241
contact 14616
name 2214

Fractions

Put single fractions and fractions with whole numbers into words if they are in a running text; put fractions in series and tabulations into figures.

one-third of the budget ...
the pot weighs two and one-half pounds.

Model A	$2\frac{1}{4}$ lb.
Model B	$2\frac{3}{4}$ lb.
Model C	$4\frac{1}{3}$ lb.

Market Quotes

Put market quotes in figures.   24 bid—28 asked.

Weights and Measures

Use figures if you abbreviate the   21 cu. ft.
unit. If you don't abbreviate the   twenty-one cubic feet
units, express the number in
words.

Money

Use figures and decimal point plus   The set of books cost $8.95.
two ciphers for even dollar   The bids were $50, $75, and $100.
amounts; repeat the $ before each   The pen cost 29 cents.
unit. Units less that one dollar in
running test are written as the figure plus the word *cents*.

Percentages

Use the figure plus the word *per-*   ... said 26 percent of the people ...
cent. In tabulations, use the figure   alcohol 15%
with the % sign.   water 30%

Ordinals

Express ordinals in words if used   The fourteenth employee to come
in a running text; use them in   in late ...
combination for some street ad-   188 East 69th Street
dresses.

Round Numbers

Express these in words, usually,   ... twenty to thirty people applied.
but use figures for more emphasis   We didn't expect that 30 people
if you like.   would quit.

Series

Use figures in most series.   We need 5 drawers, 10 desks, and
                                                   3 blotters.

Small Numbers

Generally, the numbers one to   two new desks
nine are written out; use figures   12 new desks
for 10 and above.

Time

Express time in words if the word   She left at four o'clock.
o'clock is understood. When the   He came at ten forty-five.
time is followed by a.m. or p.m.,   She left at 4 p.m.
use figures.   He came at 10:45 a.m.

PART V.

Applying English in Executive Meetings

---

36. DUTIES OF THE CONFERENCE LEADER

One of the best ways an executive can get results is to conduct an effective, productive meeting of key people involved in a problem or project. That may mean giving directions, securing valuable information, or facilitating the combined thinking and energy of the group. Effective meetings can be excellent, efficient ways to get things done through people.

Besides letting people know the agenda in advance, starting the meeting in time and keeping it on the topic, you as the manager of the meeting, can be extremely productive by directing and controlling the meeting so that everyone feels a sense of accomplishment and purpose when the meeting is over. Here are your major duties as a conference leader.

Why the Meeting?

Before any other business, state the purpose of the meeting in a stimulating, thought-provoking way. Do this in a way that will help you arouse interest, motivate thinking, and create a desire and commitment to help solve the problem or provide information.

EXAMPLES

- "We're meeting today to try to solve a problem that's costing our company over $250,000 each year—absenteeism."
- "This meeting has two key goals: to develop ideas for a new packaging system, and to outline possible ways to market Product X."
- "We've asked you to meet to day to help develop guidelines for relocating our employees to the new facility."

Stimulate to Action

It's important that everyone in the group participate in the discussion. That's why each person was invited. If there is someone in the room who is *not* expected to participate, then why is he or she there? You need to secure participation from everyone in attendance.

Ask Key Questions

An excellent way to keep the discussion moving, and to get results, is to use questions for control and direction. Why questions? Because each question requires an answer. You can't ignore a question without appearing to be rude, inattentive or stupid. Using the right question at the right time is an excellent way to accomplish the results you want.

Stay on Target

It's your job to help people stay on the topic. Especially if they get excited about a topic, people tend to digress. The free mind knows no limits and wants to explore all sides of an issue—wants to outline even the subtle relationships between the major topic and minor issues. That's where you come in. You have to direct people's thinking on the subject at hand. That's the only way you can get results within the time alloted for the meeting.

Don't Dominate

It's a real temptation for a manager to call a meeting and then lecture to those present. If you're the boss and your subordinates are at the meeting, you'll have to work extra hard to get them to offer differing opinions, alternate views, critical comments. Their first inclination is to stay on your good side ... to agree with you and make you feel comfortable. Many employees think such an approach represents *job security* when, in fact, just the opposite may be true. Maybe the job will be most secure when innovative ideas are respected and sought after—even ideas that may threaten the status quo. For this reason, you as the meeting manager can't dominate the discussion, and you can't allow anyone else to do so, either. As soon as a dominant person is allowed free rein, he or she will intimidate or stifle the others. This point is so important that if you find someone dominating the meeting, and you simply can't get him or her to stop it, you should stop the meeting and schedule it for another time. Then find a way to deal with that person. Until you get this issue resolved, you'll have limited participation from the others.

Summarize

Especially in longer meetings, you need to summarize what's gone on so far, to help people know what's been accomplished and where the discussion should be headed. You also need to summarize at the end of the meeting. What should you summarize? Accomplishments, results, agreements, disagreements, problems, issues—anything that will clarify the action of the meeting so people can understand the key issues simply and clearly.

End the Meeting

You also need to draw the meeting to a logical close. When the discussion is over and people begin to digress, it's time to end the meeting. Once you've met your objectives, you're simply wasting people's time and the company's money by prolonging the discussion. Summarize what's been accomplished, what the next step is, and thank everyone for being so helpful. The meeting is over.

37. TEN WAYS TO USE QUESTIONS FOR CONTROL

You can control a meeting almost entirely by the use of good questions. Questions are better than statements because they require answers. It's nearly impossible for someone, after you've asked a question, to look at you and say absolutely nothing. Here's how to use questions to get good results at a meeting.

Get People Talking

You can get the discussion started and help keep it going by asking questions like these:

- "John, what do you think about the situation?"
- "Mary, what are your views?"
- "Tom, we haven't heard from you lately—any ideas?"

Stimulate Interest

As a meeting leader, you may have to motivate people to participate more. You may need to whip up their interest enough to get the ideas flowing freely. Try using questions like these:

- "What is the single most important way to save money ... so we can all expect more money in our paychecks?"
- "What's the most likely way our competition can hurt us badly?"
- "Why do you think upper management isn't listening to us?"

Provoke Thinking

There are times when the discussion becomes so bland and predictable that you have to make people think more critically and probe deeper. Plan to use questions like these:

- "If you were told you had to come up with a totally new product that would reverse our situation—or lose your job—what would that product be?"
- "In what ways does our product merely imitate the features of competitive products?"
- "What can we do to return more money to employees and still lower the cost of the product?"

418

Accumulate Facts

Sometimes you need to gather data at a meeting—secure important facts and figures from those present. You may want to ask questions like these:

- "John, how many units does the Acme Company sell each month?"
- "Theresa, what did you find out about the packaging requirements?"
- "Tom, what's the per-unit R & D cost?"

Distribute Discussion

Someone who is talking too much does just as much damage as someone who says too little. Everyone needs to participate to the extent they're able to. That means you'll probably have to step in from time to time to make sure everyone is equally involved. You can do that with questions like these:

- "Those are good ideas Jim, and I think it will also help us to get some differing opinions. Ted, what's your opinion?"
- "Jerry, you seem a little quiet. How about sharing some of the things you told me earlier?"
- "Jim, the point Alice just made seems to conflict with what you said earlier. What do you think?"

Develop a Subject

Sometimes you'll want to expand the topic and explore new opportunities on a subject. The right question can stimulate people to develop a subject more thoroughly, see it in a new and different light, and develop some new insights related to it. To make this happen, consider questions like these:

- "We've been talking about the economic aspects. But how will this affect employees?"
- "What other concerns should we have that relate to this issue?"
- "Jim, that's interesting. Can you tell us more?"

Check People's Understanding

Sometimes it's important to establish whether people at the meeting really understand the issue, and whether the information they have is accurate. Use questions like these to find out:

- "Tom, what's the source of the information you just gave us?"

- "Jack, just to be sure we all understand the problem from the same perspective, would you summarize what we've discussed so far?"
- "Mary, will you tell Tom what you think he said? That'll help us check the accuracy of the message up to this point."

Get Back to the Topic

It's easy for people to digress from a topic, especially if they're enthusiastic— or bored. A good conference leader can use questions to guide people back to the topic and keep the meeting productive. Think about using questions like these:

- "That's an interesting observation, but a little off the topic. Can we stay on the subject of employment?"
- "Jim, would you mind rephrasing that observation, but relate it more to the topic of employment?"
- "Do we really want to discuss sale forecasts? Our subject right now is really employment."

Change Discussion Direction

Sometimes a group will complete discussion on one aspect of a topic and need to consider the subject from another viewpoint. This may also be necessary when the discussion gets bogged down. To help change the direction of the discussion, ask questions such as these:

- "It looks like we've pretty much covered the topic of employment needs. But how do you think they'll relate to the sales forecast?"
- "Can we change the topic and discuss employment now?"
- "We seem to be getting bogged down. Can we switch to another aspect? What about employment needs?"

Arrive at Conclusions

A major role of the conference leader is to help people reach conclusions as a result of the discussion, and make decisions. Questions can help you direct the group's thinking toward important conclusions. Examples:

- "On the basis of what we've discussed so far, what are your conclusions?"
- "What do you think should be done now?"
- "Now that we've looked at the topic from a number of viewpoints, what's your conclusion? Tom?"

38. TYPES OF QUESTIONS AND HOW TO ASK THEM

There are really four different kinds of questions you can ask to control a conference. Each one has a specific purpose and can help you accomplish certain objectives.

Overhead

You may have heard this kind of question called "rhetorical," but with today's fast pace of business, we don't have much justification for asking questions just for the sake of rhetoric. However, when you don't want to appear threatening, when you want to set a non-directive tone for that part of the meeting and you don't want anyone in particular to reply, use the overhead question. It can start the discussion and get the group's attention.

Examples:

- "Why is it that sales volume is so unpredictable in Region 10?"
- "How can we make people more productive?"
- "How can we build sales more easily?"

Direct

Questions you direct to a specific person, for a specific purpose, can help you get answers fast, although they're more threatening (there's no place for the person to hide). But if you ask the question in a friendly, cooperative, supportive manner, you can get some fast results, as below.

Examples:

- "John, can you tell us what you found out about the crop record?"
- "Eleanor, will you please tell the group what your department projects for February sales?"
- "John, why don't you agree with this proposal?"

Reverse

A common trap you can easily get into is to *answer* questions from the group, instead of *asking* the questions yourself. If you let this happen, you'll lose control of the meeting, and take on the role of peacher and oracle instead of the role of conference leader, in which you facilitate group interaction so that the ideas come from the group. Here are some reverse questions you can use to ask the person to answer his or her own question:

- "Why do you say that?"
- "What do you think about it?"
- "How would you handle it?"

Follow-Up

Sometimes a person will bring up a question that can't be answered immediately—perhaps because someone isn't at the meeting or because not all the facts are in. When that happens, write the question down and bring it up for discussion later in the meeting. Use questions like these to do this:

- "John, what do you think about the March forecast now, after hearing what we've just heard?"
- "Earlier someone asked about the tardiness problem. Jack, what's your opinion now?"
- "We never really discussed Ann's question about sales figures earlier in the meeting. Tom, can you provide some information now?"

39. HOW TO ASK QUESTIONS TO GET THE BEST RESULTS

Simply asking questions won't guarantee your success as a conference leader. It's *how* you ask the question that will make the difference. Here are 11 tips that will help guarantee your success in using questions to control a meeting.

Propose the Question

It takes a lot of planning for a successful meeting—that's why there are so many poor ones. Often, the conference leader hasn't done his or her job. As you prepare for the meeting, determining what you want to accomplish, write down the key questions that need to be answered. Alongside each, job down the name of the person you think is best qualified to answer it.

Don't Bias Your Wording

One good reason for writing down the question in advance is that it can help you to keep your biases out of the wording. You probably don't think you'd make such an obvious mistake as saying, "Bob, you agree that the price is too much, don't you?"

The more authority you have in the organization, the greater the tendency will be to set up a question so that everyone will see things *your* way. Check the wording of the questions to see if you aren't hinting at the answer you want, or whether you're revealing your own prejudices or opinions.

Avoid Difficult Questions

If the question is too complicated, (for example, there may really actually be two or three questions packed into one), people will not be able to answer it easily, and your meeting will be bogged down. Here are examples of complicated questions you should avoid:

- "Should we consider pricing the key factor, or should packaging, advertising, and sales promotion costs be added to research and development costs for a total sales cost?"
- "How can we cut our labor costs—by decreasing tardiness, cutting employees, automating more, or should we think about new work methods?"

Don't Be Vague

Good questions are specific. Those that are too vague or general will be confusing and people are likely to misinterpret them. Then, valuable time will be wasted as they respond to what they *think* you said. This question is too broad:

"What do you know about employee morale?"

Here's a better one:

"What things break down employee morale?"

Avoid YES or NO Questions

Asking questions that allow a simple yes or no answer may make for a short meeting, but you won't accomplish much because you'll only skim the surface of the issue. Use how, what, why, who, when, and where questions that will deliver more information.

Use a Conversational Style

By their nature, questions are threatening, so it's good to ask them in a normal, conversational tone. You may even want to practice asking the question aloud to see how it sounds, especially if the issue you're discussing is sensitive. A warm, friendly, supportive manner will go a long way in helping you get the results you want.

Pause

Don't spit out one question after another, and don't jump on one person right away for an answer. Give people time enough to think about the question. Then, when they've had a reasonable amount of time, ask for the answer:

• "How do you think we can raise employee productivity?" (wait 3-5 seconds.)
Now say,
• "Tom, what do you think? You've had some success in this area already."

Call on Someone

Asking questions to the group in general may be all right for the overhead style, but you'll get more results and maintain better control if you call on someone directly, using his or her name. This has the added advantage of allowing you to give everyone a chance to talk and share ideas. You can easily direct your questions to the quieter people if necessary, and you can direct the discussion away from those who tend to dominate it.

Acknowledge the Answer

You'll keep the meeting going more smoothly if you acknowledge each answer. This lets each person know you appreciate the contribution and prepares the group for the next question. It also stimulates other people to contribute more to the discussion. Here are some ways you can acknowledge the answer:

- "Those are good observations, Mary. Thanks for the work you've done."
- "Good point, Bill. I think that's worth pursuing. Can anyone add to this?"
- "That's an important point we should keep in mind. Any other comments?"

Don't Let Someone Flounder

Who needs embarrassment? Certainly not the folks at *your* meeting. So don't make people agonize when they obviously don't know the answer to a question, have come unprepared, or simply can't participate. Give them a face-saving break by moving on to someone else. Here are three good responses to help someone who's floundering.

- "Jim, this question may have caught you off guard. We'll come back a little later."
- "Mary, right now may not be the best time for you to respond to this question. We'll come back later on."
- "John, maybe we don't have enough information for you to respond right now. Let's hear from someone else first. Jack?"

Don't Repeat Questions

One good way to encourage people *not* to listen to you is to repeat every question more than once. As soon as people get the message that daydreaming is all right and that they don't have to pay close attention, they probably *won't*. *Solution*: Ask your questions just once. That way, people will learn to listen more carefully. You'll waste less time and the meeting will be less boring to everyone.

40. WHAT AN EXECUTIVE CONFERENCE LEADER SHOULD AVOID

Anything can happen at a meeting, no matter how well you prepare for it. Consider:

The group won't talk:	Clarify your objective or the point under discussion; ask direct questions.
Arguments break out:	Step in and redirect the discussion; a light or humorous remark may help; let the other members break up the argument.
Silent members:	Invite the silent people to talk more. Ask questions people can answer easily. You may have to talk privately with people who have a reputation for being quiet.
Talkative members:	When they pause for a breath, break in and direct the conversation to someone else.
Know-it-alls:	People who appear to have all the answers may well intimidate others. Ask him or her for specific reasons, but don't criticize them openly. These people *must* be subdued or the group will fail.
Side discussions:	Good planning will avoid most of these, but they'll still occur from time to time. Deal with each situation individually as it happens, but don't let them continue.

There are also other traps you need to avoid if you want to run an effective meeting. Watch out for these personal mannerisms that can limit your success:

1. *Arguing.* It's your job to *facilitate* an open flow of ideas, rather than decide in advance which ideas are acceptable and which aren't. If you question the wisdom of some of the ideas, reply on good questions that are well directed to focus on the validity of the idea. Don't say, "I disagree with that viewpoint," (you're automatically throwing down the gauntlet for a win-lose battle.) Instead, ask: "That's an interesting viewpoint. How do you others feel about it?"

2. *Sarcasm.* Sharp, caustic remarks that are designed to position you as critic and judge of someone's ideas will stifle any free flow of ideas. No one likes to be on the receiving end of a sarcastic, biting remark. If sarcasm is

part of your personality, consider taking steps to curb it. (Better yet, spend some quiet time with yourself, honestly trying to discover why you enjoy slicing up other people.)

3. *Ridicule.* In any good meeting, even some of the best thinkers can come up with some mediocre or even fairly stupid ideas. An open discussion means people feel comfortable enough to say whatever is on their minds, and, incidentally, it's only in this kind of environment that good ideas can blossom. The first indications of ridicule from the conference leader will immediately stifle further openness. People will automatically protect their self-images and put up defenses. When that happens, you can forget about candor.

4. *Distracting Mannerisms.* Don't fidget, twiddle your ring, play with your glasses, touch your nose, say things like, "Oh … Ah …" and so on. Any peculiar mannerism will be picked up and draw attention *away* from the discussion. You say you don't *have* any such mannerisms? Consider your former teachers. Did you know even *one* who didn't have some personal mannerism you remember even today? Of course not. We all have pecularities as human beings. The trick is to know what they are and play them down. Or use our positive traits to focus attention on more positive, more important issues. Try to get in front of a TV monitor as you give a presentation or conduct a meeting. Then watch yourself afterwards—ideally with a trained communications specialist who is willing to point out where you need improvement.

5. *Forcing Your Own Opinion.* If you're so convinced that your viewpoint is preferrable to all others … that it alone holds the best solution to the problem at hand, then you don't need a conference to discuss it and get the views of other people. Simply call a meeting, tell people what you've decided, and discuss how best to implement your idea.

   But, if you want a wide range of ideas, want to hear what others think, want sometimes conflicting views, don't force your opinion. As soon as you do, people will sense that they're supposed to rubber-stamp your ideas and not make waves. Forcing your ideas on other people probably won't make them change their minds. You'll simply drive their true feelings underground and face a group of docile, mindless, obedient-appearing employees who, deep inside, are building serious resentment against you.

6. *Manipulate the Meeting.* You hate being a puppet of another person. So do other people. If you consciously decide that you're going to manipulate the meeting, control the discussion to your advantage and push people into accepting your position, you'll offend a lot of people, because they'll immediately sense what you're doing. If you don't like being controlled by someone else, you can be sure that many people you're trying to manipulate don't like being controlled, either.

7. *Violating Confidence.* If you've had discussions with people outside a meeting that was personal or confidential, you have an obligation to protect these confidences. If you reveal something that someone else considers confidential, you will immediately lose all credibility with that person. You also can be sure that, almost minutes after the meeting is over, word will spread that you violated the confidence and that you're not to be trusted. When that happens, you will probably *never* regain the trust of people you work with, and your value to the organization will be considerably lessened.

   Learn to keep a secret, or at least tell people you don't *want* to hear anything that can't be discussed openly. However, this is an unrealistic viewpoint that will cut you off from the mainstream of action in the organization.

8. *Discussing Personalities.* Keep personal habits, traits and peculiarities *out* of your meetings. When you begin discussing the bad points about people who aren't present at the meeting—gossiping, backbiting, or simply discussing the *person* instead of his or her actions or decisions—you're in trouble. People will automatically assume, and rightly so, that you'll discuss *them* at the next meeting in which they're not present. Again, people won't trust you.

9. *Emotionalism.* Getting emotional means you're so upset with a situation that you can't relate the facts clearly. This is a behavior that is simply *not* condoned in business. You can attend all the encounter groups you like, all of which will convince you of the value of sharing your feelings openly, but it will destroy you in business.

   The fact is that most people have been conditioned to look down their noses at people who are "emotional." We are taught that emotion gets in the way of facts and decision-making. Another fact of life is that only people toward the top of the organization are allowed more freedom in sharing their emotions openly, directly in proportion to people *below* them on the organizational ladder.

   When you, as a discussion leader, become angry over an issue, few people will say, "This problem is so serious that Tom was unusually upset; we'd better consider it carefully." Most will say, "Tom is clearly out of control. We'd better take what he says with a grain of salt."

10. *Quibbling.* Don't let the discussion degenerate to the point where you nit-pick tiny details of a person's remarks. Once this happens, you can say good-bye to any real discussion of the key issues. In fact, some people will deliberately try to bait you into quibbling to avoid the real issue. When you find yourself moving into this superficial mode, simply say, "Maybe we'd better stop and evaluate this discussion. We seem to be quibbling over relatively minor points. I'd like to move on to the real issue:_____."

11. *Interrupting Others.* If you continually interrupt other people when they pause for a breath, you'll soon have a battle on your hands, or else people will simply let you air your own views and not share theirs. When you interrupt, you automatically say, "What I have to say is more important than what you have to say, so please be quiet." If you have this tendency, and many bright, upper-level executives do, practice holding back. If there are people at your meeting who really can't keep up with you, then ask yourself why they're there in the first place—and deal with that issue *outside* the meeting.

12. *Pressuring the Group.* Pressure at a meetings can come from several sources such as not allowing enough time, the indecisiveness of group members, and a lack of adequate information to make a decision on deadline, among others. Allow enough time, make sure the people at the meeting can handle a fast-paced session, and don't expect good decisions based on inadequate information.

    Realize, too, that when you put pressure on people at a meeting, some will respond beautifully since they require outside pressure to do their best. Yet many others will retreat and give you superficial agreement simply to get away from the pressure. There is probably far too much pressure in business today anyway, and it's often put there because executives made poor decisions at some stage and then require their subordinates to run twice as fast to make up for it.

    Make no mistake, however; if you're putting pressure on people at a meeting because of a previous foul-up—your own or someone else's—people will know about it and resent it. If you have to pressure people at a meeting, lep them know you realize it and make it as palatable as possible.

13. *Posing As an Expert.* Like the problem of forcing your own opinion, posing as an expert will give you leadership problems in a conference. If you're really the expert, then why are you holding the meeting? And even if the purpose of the meeting is to inform people about your information and your decisions, it's a good idea to do this in a way that suggests humility. You can't lord things over others, because there is always someone around who knows just enough to make you look foolish. Furthermore, many people will simply stop participating in the discussion, and allow you to make your own decisions—and your own mistakes.

14. *Talking Over Their Heads.* This mistake is in the same category as posing as an expert—you'll turn people off and not get their cooperation. People are quick to sense when you try to show how superior you are by using technical words they're not likely to know, when you refer to upper-level decisions they obviously couldn't know about, or make similar mistakes.

Good conference leaders have the ability to make people like them and make people feel they're all part of the same community of interests. If you talk in such a way that people won't understand you, you cut yourself off from that community and lose much of the benefits you might have received from it.

PART VI

How to Give Powerful Presentations

41. GUIDELINES FOR SPEAKING EFFECTIVELY

Few people are *born* speakers ... *born* presenters. Successful speakers *make themselves* successful by learning and practicing a few important techniques. This section of the book will give you all you need to know in order to deliver powerful, effective presentations.

Be Prepared

You need to have enough material so you won't have to worry about what to say. When you know your subject matter well, it makes you confident, because it usually means you know more about the topic than anyone else in the room. And why not? You've spent weeks preparing for your talk ... checked library sources on recent articles ... interviewed experts ... and contributed a lot of your own thinking. When you know your topic, your audience, and your objectives; when you've practiced your talk, thought about it, discussed it with people who are interested in you and the topic; when you've organized your ideas, practiced your introduction, worked in good stories to illustrate key ideas *you prepared*, then you are ready to deliver your talk with confidence.

Make Sure They Can Hear You

Talk loudly enough to be heard. Speakers who mumble, don't speak up, or don't use a microphone well can be really annoying. Speak up. Open your mouth. (If you're speaking in a large hall with no microphone, your mouth should be open enough to insert two fingers). Practice breathing from your diaphragm, rather than forcing air out of your throat. You shouldn't have to force your voice excessively to be heard. You should feel resonance in your face, especially around your nose, when you're projecting your voice properly.

Stay on the Topic

Especially when you've prepared a lot of material, or when you're well versed in your subject, it's easy to wander from the topic. But this annoys an audience and can be confusing. Develop a simple outline you can remember, and try to stay with it.

It's also a good idea to have a topic sentence in mind before you begin your talk. That helps clarify your theme, not only for your audience, but also for yourself. As you develop your talk, you can recall the theme and ask yourself, "Is what I'm saying really on the topic?" If you're not sure that what you're saying is related to your topic, your audience won't be sure, either.

Use Examples

People remember things they hear when they're expressed in concrete terms. A good way to make ideas concrete and vivid is to use examples from real life to reinforce your point.

Stories or anecdotes based on your personal experiences, along with humorous illustrations and specific examples, will dramatize your message and help people remember your message. You are communicating primarily through the ears, so you have to make your ideas become memorable pictures in the minds of your listeners. If you can say to yourself, "Whoever is listening to me can easily *see* the picture I'm drawing ... can easily *imagine* what I'm saying," you can be pretty sure they'll get your message and *remember* it for a long time.

Watch the Audience

The only way you can establish rapport with your audience is to look at people directly—not at your notes. This may be difficult at first, but it's worth the effort. Practice your talk often enough so you can speak from an outline. Use overheads, a flip chart or slides to help you cover key points, but amplify them as you look at your listeners. A good presentation is really a good conversation with many people at the same time. Just as you look at your listener in a two-person conversation, you should look at your listeners who may number 10, 50, 100 or more. By watching how people react to your talk, you can modify what you say and that assures your message is being well received.

Don't Use Notes

You may need to refer to a few key ideas from a basic outline from time to time, but you shouldn't read your talk from notes. It dispracts the audience, keeps you from paying attention to the speaker/audience interaction that's so crucial in a good presentation, and makes your talk seem dull. A good point to remember is this: if you can't remember what you want to say, how can you expect your listeners to? They can't and they won't.

Realize that Fear is Natural

It's perfectly normal to be afraid to get up and speak before others. It's the single most common fear that people have. But consider this: the reason you're afraid is that you *want* to do a good job, and you're afraid you might not. That's really a *positive* attitude.

A speaker, teacher, actor, preacher who isn't just a *little* afraid of getting up to speak probably won't do a good job. It's that drive to be accepted and well received by the audience that makes good speakers. Fear is you body's natural reaction to a strange and threatening situation, but the only way you can overcome this fear is to practice speaking in front of groups as often as possible.

Talk before groups as often as you can—at work, in church committees, at club meetings, at PTA meetings. Don't miss an opportunity to get on your feet and say a few words. You say you'll dread it? Of course you will! But each time you do this, you'll feel just that much more confident and more ready to speak at the next opportunity.

Concentrate on Beginnings and Endings

People will form their strongest and most lasting impressions of what you say from what you say first and last. First impressions count, and they last. Make your topic statement at the beginning. Let people know who you are by the ease and friendliness with which you begin your talk. Then let them know what you have to say right at the beginning.

Use the middle of the talk to develop your ideas more fully. Then, use the conclusion to summarize key points and dramatize them in a memorable way. Begin and end your talk with a startling statement, a strong quote, a personal reference, an exhibit, a specific example, or an illustration that will appeal to the audience's self-interest. If you don't give them something to remember, what's the point of doing all the work to prepare the talk?

Use Gestures

Gestures help you keep your audience's attention and dramatize your ideas. Reinforce your main points with gestures such as pointing; moving the hands to show giving, receiving, or rejecting; clenching the fist; facing your palm to the audience to show caution; moving one hand against the other to show dividing or separating.

Use your face also, to show emotion and to reinforce your talk: move your eyebrows, grit your teeth, open your lips, show a broad smile. Even use pantomime or impersonation if they'll help drive home a point. You feel that's acting? Of course it is, and that's part of any good presentation.

Five-Step Format for a Good Presentation

Here are five simple steps to guide you to a successful presentation, and you can use them for either long or short talks.

WAKE THEM UP

Your first job as a successful speaker is to get people interested in you and your message. You have to wake them up ... take their minds off their own thoughts and get their attention. Your listeners aren't necessarily open-minded or automatically interested. How to do it? Use some showmanship: try a dramatic story; show a model or photograph or a broken machine part; use a tape recording or color slide—anything that will spark an interest.

SAY WHY THEY SHOULD BE INTERESTED

Pick something that will motivate your audience (See page____for a list of the most common motivators) and build a portion of your talk around it. Paint a verbal picture of the benefits of accepting your idea or viewpoint. In short, make sure the audience knows why your topic is relevant. Each listener is asking the question, "So what?" Tell them *why* they should pay attention, and show what your talk will do for them.

SUMMARIZE THE MAIN POINT

You must be able to state the point of your speech precisely, and you must make sure your audience gets this point. If you can't state the main idea in one sentence, it's probably not clear enough in your own mind (and won't be clear in anyone else's either). Your topic statement should be mentioned several times, in different ways, to make sure people get the message.

PROVE YOUR POINT WITH EXAMPLES

Keep using example after example, until there's no doubt in anyone's mind what your idea is and why people should accept it. You're better off with a presentation that uses one main idea people can understand and accept, than with a talk.

SUMMARIZE

There's an old saying about speeches: "Say what you're going to say: say it; say what you said." The audience has to be made to remember and understand clearly the point of your talk—what you were driving at. Restate your topic statement or rephrase it, but tell the audience the key points in your talk. They'll be psychologically conditioned to remember the summary, if you make it clear you're summarizing your talk. Begin your summary with a statement such as:

- "Now, let's summarize."
- "Let me sum up."
- "What have I been saying? Simply this."
- "Here's what all this means to you."

Eight Ways to Control Your Fears

Fear is natural—it's the body's natural reaction to a strange, new, threatening situation. And the fear of speaking in front of a group is the top fear named in *The Book of Lists*. But you *can* control your fear, and even turn the energy that comes with fear to your advantage.

1. *By-Pass Your Fears*

    Keep your mind on the talk and communicating with your audience, rather than on your fears. When you concentrate on your fears, you're focusing on yourself instead of your audience.

    Keep your mind where it belongs, on what you have to say, rather than on yourself and the possibility of failing. Stay positive and think of the good things you have to offer the audience. Remember, "There's nothing to fear but fear itself."

2. *Be Prepared*

    When you know your subject thoroughly, there's little to fear, because you probably know more about the topic than anyone else in the room. This will make you more confident about the presentation and make it easier to answer questions.

3. *Use Humor*

    Whenever you can make people laugh, it will put both you and them at ease. It's also easier to laugh about your mistakes, too. When you use humor, people feel more comfortable with you, and you'll feel more comfortable with them. Laughter is good medicine for fear.

    Get in the habit of telling humorous stories. Practice telling them so you can adapt them to different situations. People will enjoy you more and you'll enjoy yourself. If you think humor isn't a highly valued talent in our culture, ask yourself, "Who's more popular at parties, dinners, and outings—humorous or serious people?" Comedians are nearly always well received; philosophers, rarely.

4. *Be Confident*

    When you're confident, you communicate it, and it puts your audience at ease. You can show your confidence by using a strong voice that doesn't falter; by speaking slowly enough so you don't have to grope for words; by smiling frequently, if appropriate, with good humor injected into your talk; by using firm, definite gestures; by not putting your hands to your face as you talk, and not fidgeting with rings, pencils, your lapels, or whatever.

5. *Speak Slowly, with Short Sentences*

    Talking too fast will make you feel even *more* nervous, because you know you're on the brink of losing control. We tend to speak quickly when we're nervous, almost as if we're rushing to finish the talk, just to get it over with. A good way to establish control is to speak more slowly and deliberately, especially in the beginning. It may sound forced to you, but your listeners won't know the difference. They'll simply hear a careful, deliberate speaker who is in obvious control of the group. The slower speed can actually have a reverse effect on you. It will help you to relax more and you'll almost feel your nervousness subside.

Shorter sentences help you keep track of ideas and give you more time to breathe. Long sentences bore your audience and are terrible traps. They allow you to begin one idea and invite you to explore sub-topics of the idea. Before you know it, you're exploring other subjects and are off the topic you were supposed to speak on. Long sentences are also easy for you to forget, and that would make any speaker nervous. Stay with short sentences. They give you good, consistent control of your ideas.

6. *Watch Your Audience*

Think of your talk as a one-to-one conversation with someone in the audience. Pick one person and look at him directly and talk directly to that person. After a few sentences, pick another person and talk directly to her. Do that for your entire talk, and you'll take your mind off your fears. Concentrate on your audience, not on yourself. Watch for the usual cues people will send you about your message. That's the only way you'll learn their reaction. Try to be sensitive to the body signals of the audience and you'll be better able to forget your fears.

7. *Use Plenty of Pauses*

Pauses help you use shorter, clearer sentences. They help you establish control, speak more slowly, deliberately, and carefully, and with controlled emphasis. Pauses help you to choose your words more care-fully, and to use words with greater accuracy. Also, because you're in better control of your delivery, you're more confident and relaxed. Pauses help you to think ahead, to plan your gestures, to "read" the audience better and, in general, to be in control of your talk. When you're in control, what's there to fear?

8. *Turn Fear into Enthusiasm*

Fear can stir up a lot of negative energy inside you. Your body produces adrenalin, your heart beats faster, and your sweat glands begin to work overtime. In some people, all this can even cause the bowels to signal a need to evacuate.

But, you can channel all this energy by turning the negative emo-tional energy, your fear is generating into positive energy that can *help* your presentation. Do it by being enthusiastic. Raise your volume and tone; use gestures, show the excitement you feel about your ideas. You can sell practically *anything* with enthusiasm, (and without enthusiasm, you can't sell a thing.) When you concentrate on being enthusiastic, your heart will continue to beat with the exhilaration that comes from a positive, responsive audience; the adrenalin will lend more power to your voice and give you physical stamina; your sweat glands may continue to operate freely, but you won't even notice them; and by turning fear into enthusiasm, even your bowels will relax.

Now, go ahead and give your talk—without fear.

Secrets of Convincing an Audience

Here are five secrets of convincing an audience to buy your ideas—to persuade people to accept your viewpoint.

1. *Appeal to their dominant motives.*

Turn to page—and you'll see a list of what motivates people—their needs. Pick one or two of those needs and show the audience how your idea or proposal will meet those needs. Show them specifically and graphically how, for example, they can save money: how much money, when they'll save it, what they can do with the money saved, and how they'll get the money.

2. *Present your ideas in terms of what people already believe.*

People accept new ideas only when they "fit in" with what they already believe. It's rare when we are convinced to do something—believe something—that doesn't already conform to our present value system. That's why we tend to choose books on topics we already like, watch TV programs that don't threaten our opinions, and choose people as friends who pretty well agree with our basic values.

To convince your audience, whether it's one person or 500, find out the existing beliefs (what people already think about the topic). Then phrase everything you say in such a way to show that your idea really confirms what they already believe.

Once people believe you and trust you, you may be able to change their opinion *slightly*, and make them say, "Oh, I see ... isn't that interesting." But, for the most part, people will accept only what they already believe.

3. *Use the "Yes" response method.*

Begin your talk with a series of propositions that people easily agree with and accept most easily—something to which they'll automatically say yes. Keep making statements that cause people to say yes to you. Then, show how they can easily continue to say yes to your idea.

Smart salespeople do this all the time. Think about the opening statements you heard from a car salesperson, a real estate broker. They probably said something like this: "Isn't this a beautiful car (home)?" And you said, "Yes." If you said no, they probed for what you wanted until you began to say yes. If you said, "No, the kitchen is too small," the salesperson would have been foolish to say, "You're wrong, it's a big kitchen." She may have said, "It certainly looks that way at first glance, doesn't it? But let me show you how compact everything is."

As long as you can put your proposals in terms that people will say yes to, you can convince them of your idea. As soon as you hear a no, you've got to stop and meet that objection. When you're sure you have the yes response (people will signal it immediately—even by smiling or nodding their heads), then go on to your next point.

4. *Use the "this-or-nothing" approach.*

Show people how they must accept your idea or else it will conflict with what they already believe in, or else their basic needs won't be met, or else the alternative will be unpleasant to live with. Show what it will be like if they *don't* accept what you propose.

If you're presenting plans for buying new equipment, show what will happen if you *don't* get it—how sales will go down, how employee turnover will increase because of added frustration, how the scrap record will continue to drain profits, or how customers will continue to be disappointed.

5. *Use concrete facts, and vivid illustrations.*

People don't buy abstract ideas such as economy, beauty, comfort. They buy a proposed saving of $500 (they can buy a new color TV set with that). They're interested in a beautiful car because it has long, graceful lines, and is painted in their favorite shade of blue or silver. They buy a chair because their backsides feel good when they sit on *this* cushion and not on *that* cushion; because their legs seem to fit the seat contours so well that there's no question as to exactly why *this* chair is comfortable.

So, tell stories that will illustrate your idea. Help people visualize what you have to say. Describe your idea in concrete terms—what people can see, touch, feel, smell, or taste. For example, don't just say the new calculators are fast and attractive. Say, "The Model D will let us do 10 more calculations than other models will, and we can perform them 40 percent faster. The units are dark brown, and will match our walnut desktops. Because of their special circuitry, normal operator error is cut by at least 60 percent."

Sell Your Ideas with Showmanship!

Every successful person knows the value of selling his or her ideas, and selling them more effectively than someone else. That takes showmanship, and a dramatizing of ideas by putting them in the best light possible.

No matter what you do, you make a powerful, lasting effect on people whenever you use showmanship. Why? Because people can understand your ideas more easily, and remember them. For example, it's pretty well accepted that the best teacher is also a good actor. Actually, it's the same with anyone who presents ideas well, whether it's during a business discussion, a sermon, or a sales call. You can use showmanship to good advantage, whenever you have an idea to share.

Consider just some of the ways people present ideas:

- A salesperson calls on a customer who has previously bought a competitor's product;

- An executive presents a new organization plan to the executive committee;
- A minister talks to his congregation to suggest a new way to look at moral values;
- A product manager explains to the divisional vice president why he wants to allocate $1.5 million for research;
- A school board presents the yearly budget to a community that is already pressured by money demands;
- An advertising manager proposes an ad campaign;
- A marketing vice president wants agreement that his strategy will produce the best sales results—*two years* away;
- An English teacher introduces a new unit on poetry—to the toughest gang of boys in the school;
- A lawyer presents evidence to convince a jury that his client is innocent;
- A small businessman explains his new business idea to a bank to get financing.
- The new president of a local club wants to stir up more interest in her organization.

Every day, in every walk of life, in nearly every position of responsibility, people present their ideas to other people.

Here are some good showmanship techniques you can use when you present an idea to either just one other person, or to a large group.

- Each year, one of the country's most successful doctors lectures on good practice management at major conventions.
- A sales manager in Chicago won approval to reorganize the staff and add new people by placing on the vice president's desk a six-inch-high stack of orders that couldn't be handled because he didn't have the staff. When he told the boss that these inquiries represented $500,000 in possible orders, which could be filled in just three months if he could add two people to his staff for five percent of that amount, he got his approval.
- A saleswoman keeps her customer's attention riveted on her presentation by writing the key points upside down as she talks to her customer. Customers literally can't take their eyes off the paper as she summarizes product benefits: "Warranty Service ... Cost Savings ... Long Service Life" all written perfectly, but upside down, so the customer can read them easily.

You're probably on the lookout for ways to show off your ideas in your next talk. Here are some to consider:

One of the most important things you do in making any presentation is to have a good beginning. It's really true that first impressions count. If you can convince your audience, whether it's one person such as our boss, or a whole roomful of people, that you've got something special to say, you're in. People will easily filter everything you do or say through the successful image you established at the outset. They'll tend to see everything you do as successful!

So consider ways you can use showmanship right from the start. That will give you a head start in using other showmanship techniques throughout your presentation.

APPEAL TO PEOPLE'S SELF-INTEREST

We're all a little selfish. Of course, we can compromise from time to time, by simply putting aside some of our own needs so people we are trying to relate to can achieve what *they* want in terms of *their* needs. But, when you think about it, we sometimes only *appear* to sublimate our own needs. Actually, we simply change our behavior.

Before you begin to sell your ideas, try to find out what motivates the person you are talking to, and use some showmanship to dramatize the fact that you really *are* interested in his own self-interest. Consider these samples, for starters:

SERMON OR HOMILY

There isn't a person living who doesn't want peace in his life. That is one reason we go to church—to bring peace into our souls. A good way to begin a talk or homily would be to say to the congregation, "I have something very special to share with you this morning ... and it is sealed in this envelope." Then you hold the envelope in the air for everyone to see. Don't hurry. Pause. Turn around so everyone can see you.

Next, say something like this: "What is inside this envelope is guaranteed to bring peace into your life. *Absolutely guaranteed.* And in just 10 minutes from now, I am going to open this envelope and tell you what it is."

What you have put inside the envelope could be nearly anything appropriate: a passage from scripture that tells people to love one another; the word "Love" written in the center of the page; an admonition for people to share their talents.

Then you can easily take 10 full minutes to tell why people want peace today ... why it is more needed than ever before ... how difficult it is to achieve ... the list goes on. What you are really doing is building toward that time when you open that envelope—with a flair, of course. You appealed to their self-interest: the desire for peace and contentment, and you can hold people spellbound for a long time.

BUSINESS MEETING

You can also bring a stack of reports into a business meeting and place them on the desk. Before you begin your presentation, say something like this: "Ladies and Gentlemen. This stack of reports represents all the customer complaints we've received in the last three weeks, and they all center around only one topic. I am betting that no one in this room can guess what they're complaining about."

SALES CALL

Here's still another idea from a sales manager in Cincinnati, Ohio. Suppose you're planning to talk to a sales propsect about the new line of widgets, and they're the most durable on the market. You know the prospect is interested in durability, so you begin by saying, "If I could show you a material that is so durable it carries a moneyback guarantee for five years that it won't break, would you want to know more about it?" (The answer has to be, "Yes!") "Well, I do have that material to show you, and the name of the *one* product made from it is in this envelope. I'll tell you the name in just five minutes, because first I'd like you to have the opportunity to test this material, which I have in my hand, in any way you like. Go ahead ... try to damage it."

As soon as the prospect is convinced, you hand him the envelope and let his discover the name of your product. Then you discuss other benefits.

While we're on the topic of sales calls, why not show a prospect a new $100 bill and say, "This $100 will be yours just one week after you buy our product, because that it how much you'll save in one week." You might even open the presentation with the question, "How would you like this $100 bill in your pocket next week?"

CLASSROOM

Grab the interest of the class the minute it begins. Instead of saying, "Today we'll review the material you can expect on next week's test," show them your envelope and wave it in the air. Let them all see it. Then tease them. Say, "I'll tell you exactly how to get an "A" on the test next week. I have it written down for you and I'll share it with you in just 10 minutes. But first, let me tell you why this test is so important ... " You'll have their attention and they'll love you for it.

CONVENTION WORKSHOP

Each year, one of the country's most successful eye doctors lectures at major conventions on the topic of good practice management. The Bellaire, Texas doctor has his audience spellbound for three hours at a time and his lectures are always packed—sometimes there's not even standing room. Yet, the ideas he talks about have been around for years. They've been published in just about every book written on the topic of practice management and people motivation. But his attraction is that he's a speaker who shows off his ideas in a lively, entertaining manner. For example, whenever he has an important idea to emphasize, or when someone in the audience raises an important point, he rings a little bell for everyone to hear.

And he does it with a flourish. It's not uncommon for him to be in the middle of the audience (he rarely stays behind the lectern), hear a question and respond, "What a great question! That's a ringer!" Then he nearly runs to the lecturn, grab the bell, holds it high over his head and rings it for all it's worth. Then he says, "Listen ... let me tell you why that question is so important."

SALES TRAINING/POSITIVE ATTITUDES

A sales trainer in Rochester, New York wanted to prove to new salespeople that we all tend to overlook the good things about people and focus only on their flaws. He wanted to dramatize the importance of having a positive attitude about people. He went to the front of the room, erased everything on the chalkboard, and told the class, "Look ... I want to show you something." He drew a small dot in the middle of the chalkboard, but large enough for everyone to see. Then he stepped back and said, "Tell me, what do you see up there?"

He got all kinds of answers: a dot, a speck, a mark, a scribble. Then he said, "Doesn't anyone see the chalkboard? Why did you look at just the speck? Isn't the entire chalkboard more impressive, more important than the tiny dot I drew? That's what I mean about the problems we create for ourselves in dealing with people. We pick out their faults—the tiny specks—and overlook the more obvious good qualities, which usually far surpass the bad one." He would finish up that introduction by saying, "Now, let's find out how we can build *good* customer attitudes."

CLASSROOM DISC JOCKEY

An English teacher in Rochester, New York who wanted to show his class how to read a literary passage with enthusiasm, taped a three-minute broadcast of one of the nation's top disc jockeys who has a syndicated program featuring the week's top hit records.

He got them interested in the subject by announcing, at the start of the class, "I'm going to let you hear one of the country's top speakers." Then he turned on the tape.

Most of the kids were familiar with the DJ, so he knew they'd value anything that positioned him as an expert. He transcribed the two or three minutes of his patter, and duplicated enough copies for the entire class. Then he asked for volunteers to read the script and record how they emphasized their words. After taping three or four student samples, he played them back to the class, then played the DJ's version again. Of course, the DJ's technique had all the polish they lacked.

Then the teacher said, "Now I'm going to show you how to put that same feeling into what you read so people will pay attention to *you* and remember what *you* say. It's easy when you know how."

Try a little showmanship in your next presentation. You might feel embarrassed at first, but chances are your audience will love you for it!

How to Handle Questions and Objections

The real job of selling—of convincing people—doesn't begin until you have to handle an objection and do it successfully. That means you need a plan so you can answer any question or meet any objection with confidence. Here's how to do that.

    A. *Provide information.*

        Assuming you know your topic thoroughly, nothing can be a stronger argument than your presenting concrete facts. Fact, after fact, after fact. Answer with information that will prove the correctness of your position beyond all doubt.

    B. *Use comparisons.*

        Show the similarity of what you've said with something else the audience is familiar with. In class, for example, to show the foolishness of an attitude based purely on negative feelings, or showing power for the sake of power, I've used this comparison: "Your saying that is like the man who said, 'I'm going home now, and if dinner isn't ready, I am going to raise hell. And if it is ready, I'm not going to eat it.'"

    C. *Argue the point.*

        You may have to hold your ground and defend your position by arguing the point, but don't use this tactic unless you're sure you're right. You can best argue your position in two ways:

        I. *Attack the line of reasoning.*

            Show the opposite idea is illogical. Show how the conclusion is unacceptable and would actually be harmful.

        II. *Confront a personal motive or established belief.*

            Focus on the person's apparent motive for holding an opposing position. Show how it really serves only that person, and no one else. Show how the belief, which you are opposed to, is not in the best interests of everyone. For example, students often say, "You shouldn't make class attendance and participation mandatory." Well, if you don't make it mandatory, here are some likely results:

            • People miss important additional material you cover and aren't able to find out which sections of the text the instructor thinks should be emphasized.

            • Students miss the vital interaction and exchange of ideas with fellow students.

            • If students have to ask the instructor what material was covered, it wastes the instructor's time.

- When students miss class or come in late, it disturbs the smooth organization of the class and distracts the other students.

The conclusion? Except for absence because of illness or occasional personal reasons, it's important for students to attend every class and be there promptly when it begins.

D. *Ask a question.*

Ask the person to explain further the who, what, when, where, why, and how of his position. If he has trouble answering easily, you'll be able to demonstrate the weakness of his argument. As soon as you see him waver or stall for the answer, probe further. Eventually, the person will have to give you facts or admit the weakness of his position.

E. *Use humor.*

Many times you can meet an objection and get the other person to back off by using humor. A funny story or comment will relieve tension and give the person a face-saving way to back off. Especially if you can make fun of the situation, without ridiculing the other person, you can often ease the tension and motivate the person to withdraw his objection.

F. *Use prestige.*

Refer either to your extensive background, your published articles, or the experience or published ideas of other people. Again, you have to use facts. For a person to take a position that is opposed by every major expert in the field; that lacks support from a wide body of published data; that is clearly inconsistent from what others have shown to be true, is clearly absurd.

G. *Admit ignorance.*

It's just possible that you don't have all the facts. If you don't know, say so immediately. The worst thing you could do would be to try to fool an audience—they'll see through you immediately. Simply say you don't know, and if you can, offer to find the information and get back to the other person. No one can possibly know *all* the answers to *every* question, so it's no shame to say you don't know an answer.

42. PROVEN GUIDELINES FOR A SUCCESSFUL PRESENTATION

Knowing how to give a successful talk is no mystery, and there *are* sure-fire ways to be successful, provided you stick to the guidelines. They're not difficult, but they're vitally important. I've found these particular ones work well for me.

Define Your Terms

Knowing your audience is one of the first rules of good speaking. That means you choose your language carefully. If you deliberately use words people won't understand, believing that it's their job to find out what you mean, you're really making a decision *not* to be understood clearly and easily. *You* may understand what a reverse convoluted widget is and be able to talk about it easily with your peers, but if there are stockholders in your audience who don't know what it is, you need to tell them. So, make sure people know the meaning of the words you use.

Get Rid of Words You Don't Need

You need to spend all the energy you have just to keep people paying attention to you. So why risk losing your audience just for the sake of using a few pet words you like, or keeping words in your talk that you really don't need? If the words you use really don't work, carve them out—they're dead wood you don't need. One reason people tend to daydream is that some speakers take five minutes to say something they could say better in less than a minute. Unless a word is critical to your audience's understanding of your talk, get rid of it.

Don't Use Pretentious Terms

People soon learn when you're trying to impress them just for the sake of showing off. For example, don't say "purchase" when the word "buy" will do just as well. Don't say "appropriation" for "money." Be yourself. (If you wouldn't use a certain term when you were explaining something to your spouse or a friend, don't use it in a talk.) An aide to Pope John XXIII was carried away by his own rhetoric when he referred to a statement of the Pope in this way: "These are the words of the Holy Father as they fell from his august lips." Pope John told him, "Just say, 'The Pope said....'"

447

And consider this—the most important words in life have just one syllable: God, smile, health, joy, birth, death, warmth, peace, sex, love. Here's another example of the effect you can have by using big words instead of words of one syllable:

> Consistent with the desirability of establishing reasonable brevity as a prerequisite of adequate communication, the accompanying reproduction from an international publication is posited as prima facie evidence that polysyllabic verbosity is neither per se nor per accident a concomitant of linguistic ability.

Now look at this sample:

WORDS OF ONE SYLLABLE

When you come right down to it, there is no law that says you *have* to use big words when you write or talk.

There are lots of good, small words that can be made to say all the things you want to say, quite as well as the big ones. It may take a bit more time to find them at first, but it can be well worth it, for all of us know what they mean. Some small words, more than you might think, are rich with just the right feel and taste, as if made to help you say a thing the way it should be said.

Small words can be crisp, brief, terse—go to the point, like a knife. They have a charm all their own. They dance, twist, turn, sing. Like sparks in the night, they light the way for the eyes of those who read. They are the grace notes of prose. You know what they say the way you know a day is bright and fair—at first sight. And you find, as you read, that you like the way they say it. Small words are gay, and they can catch large thoughts and hold them up for all to see, like rare stones in rings of gold, or joy in the eyes of a child. Some make you feel, as well as see: The cold, deep dark of night, the hot, salt sting of tears.

Small words move with ease where big words stand still—or, worse, bog down and get in the way of what you want to say. There is not much, in all truth, that small words will not say—and say quite well.

Joseph A. Ecclesine
Printer's Ink

Treat People's Feelings Carefully

Just a few years ago, a famous politician learned the hard way that it was inappropriate to use the word "Jap" instead of the word "Japanese." Public indignation was overwhelming. Another politician of national reputation lived to regret *his* poor joke about birth control and the Pope: "You no playa da game, you no maka da rules." His apologies were never enough, and eventually, his tendency to be crude in public, consistently ignoring the sensitivity of people, forced him out of office.

So, watch your're words. Ask yourself, "Will anyone be offended by what I'm saying?" If there's any question about injuring people's feelings, rephrase your statements. Consider the different effect each of these two men had on their girlfriends, while saying essentially the same thing:

> "Honey, you've got a face that would stop a clock."
>
> "Honey, when I look at you, time stands still.

Welcome Questions from the Audience—Anytime

The more questions you get during your talk, the more you know you're stimulating the audience. Questions help keep your presentation lively, and establish ongoing relationships with the audience. Today, people bring a lot more to presentations they attend: they often have questions beforehand; they have problems and issues they want to deal with; they have job-related situations they want answers to; they have personal experience and ideas of their own that they want to share and test with you.

So, invite questions, right from the start. Many people will want to ask anyway, so it might be a good idea to say at the beginning, "I'd like you to feel free to interrupt me at anytime and ask questions. As long as the questions are on the topic, I'll be glad to answer them." (You might even consider placing portable microphones throughout the audience to help people ask questions.

If one person has a question, it's likely that others have it too, so you might as well answer the question immediately and put their minds at rest. Of course, if you find that the questions are keeping you from meeting your presentation objectives, you might have to say, "That's something we can't deal with here, because of its complexity, (or it's not really relevant right now). But see me after the meeting and I'll try to answer it for you."

Make Your Ideas Personal, Specific, Interesting

Few people like to hear about theories. No one really likes to hear an analysis of someone else's analysis. You have to talk specifics. Put things in terms of what people can see, feel, hear, touch, taste. Relate the ideas as you experienced them, by telling short stories of what happened to you that illustrates your point. Don't talk about employee tardiness, for example, without telling about Monday morning when you came in late, or the $258 in profits that were lost when Ruth, Sam, and Joe walked in at 9:30 instead of 8 a.m.

Colorful stories will make the talk lively, too. People love to hear a good ancedote. Many of the major lessons of scripture have stayed with us for hundreds of years because they were told in story form. Look at the impact of this statement: "A rich person and a poor person pray differently and, as a consequence, they may not have their prayers answered."

Now look what happens when it's said this way: "Two men went down ot the temple to pray...the one a rich, the other a poor. The rich man said,..."

If you can, phrase your major points in terms of what would happen to people in your audience. From time to time, use the technique that evangelistic preachers use: look at your audience, smile and say, "Hasn't that happened to you? Let me see, raise your hands if that happened to you." You'll get good audience participation and good rapport...and often a good laugh from the audience.

Put Sparkle into Your Talk

Make your talk sing with liveliness. Show your enthusiasm with strong, forceful gestures. Keep your voice strong and expressive. With enthusiasm, you can sell almost anything because it's so catching. Without enthusiasm, you can't sell a thing, including an idea. Watch your audience constantly through good eye contact. Keep a pleasant look on your face, and smile as often as you can. A sincere smile as you talk will really please your listeners. If your life is full of zest, put that zest into your talk. It'll catch on and you'll establish a reputation as an interesting speaker.

Keep Your Eye Contact Strong

As you talk to people and try to get them to accept your ideas, watch them. Look them in the eye. You're trying to establish a good relationship with them, and you can't do that without good eye contact. Know your talk well enough to be able to deliver it with only brief glances at your notes. Look from one person to another, even if your audience is as large as 200 or more. You won't be able to see people's reactions as clearly as you would in a room of, say, five or ten people; but people will feel your personal touch because you're looking at *them*, not your notes.

Make Your Gestures Spontaneous

Your gestures should be natural, lively, and come from the heart. If you try to fake them, people will notice them immediately. If you haven't used gestures in your talks, try using just one until it becomes natural. The gesture of pointing is a good one to begin with. (For some reason, business people, unless they're in marketing, seem to think that making a presentation means talking from a lectern, with both hands gripping the sides as color slides light up a screen behind them.)

But a good business presentation stimulates an audience to action. Marketing people usually know how to do this, because they're used to selling their ideas. Use the gestures of pointing, dividing, or clenching the fist, for example, to lend more forcefulness to your talk. Try gestures, and watch how people pay more attention to you.

Check Annoying Personal Mannerisms

You'll annoy people if you distract them as you speak by constantly clearing your throat, fidgeting with your tie or favorite ring, or twitching your head. Remember how your classmates used to count the mannerisms of certain teachers? I once had an English teacher who kept taking off his glasses and putting them back on again whenever he wanted to make a point. At least five of us kept score during each class and the high count for eyeglass distractions during one class was 54 times. We didn't learn much English in that class. A good way to discover your pet mannerisms is to watch yourself give a two-minute presentation on closed-circuit TV. You'll see quickly how you come across to other people. Watch what you do with your hands. If you keep touching your nose or earlobe, for example, or shuffle your notes around constantly, you've got a mannerism that should be eliminated. If you want to do something with your hands, use gestures, or hold a pencil or piece of chalk to keep your hands quiet.

Have a Neat Personal Appearance

A sloppy appearance is as distracting as an annoying mannerism. People usually dislike speakers who stand up to give what is assumed to be their best ideas and show up with a dirty shirt or blouse, messy hair, a rumpled shirt, or a tie that looks like a leftover from a garage sale. Take a good look in a mirror before you leave the house to give your talk and ask yourself if your appearance is good enough to make a positive impression.

Be Sure People Can Hear You

A speaker who doesn't talk loud enough to be heard is insulting the audience and wasting both his and their time. It's a mark of an inexperienced speaker to mumble quietly instead of projecting the voice loudly. If there's a question in your mind whether you can be heard or not, ask people if they can hear you. Even better, practice speaking loudly. Take advantage of opportunities to speak up at PTA or Scout meeting—if only to practice your vocal projection. Open your mouth large enough to allow two fingers to slide between the teeth easily. Try to feel your voice vibrating through the facial bones and cavities, and bring your breath up from your diaphragm, rather than your throat.

Make Your Beginning and Ending Memorable

First impressions count—especially when you make a speech. People tend to judge you on the basis of what they think when you first start to speak. If you sound unprepared, or aren't sure of yourself, your audience will tend to filter everything you say through that impression, even though the rest of your talk is right on target.

It's the same for the end of your talk. Once you begin your conclusion, people tend to perk up their ears and pay more attention to what you say. (Some of your audience will have daydreamed during part of the time you spoke, and they want to catch up on what you've said. That's one reason why you need to summarize your main points at the end.)

The last picture people have of you as you finish your presentation will be the one that they remember most easily. So plan your beginnings and endings. They should be dramatic and memorable. Use strong quotes, vivid illustrations, or whatever will help people remember what you say.

I once taught public speaking to high school students and told them to make their talk so memorable that people would remember it for twenty years or more. (Boy, was that an ideal!) I still remember Jim Doig's talk on fingerpainting. He showed us all how to fingerpaint and emphasized all during his talk that using plenty of water was the key to fingerpainting success. As he spoke, he continually dipped his hand into a pail of water and splashed it on the paper mounted on the chalkboard at the front of the class. When he finished his talk he said, "But remember, the most important thing to remember about fingerpainting is to use plenty of water." With that, he picked up the pail of water and threw the entire contents at the blackboard. I doubt whether any one of the students in that class—some 16 years ago—has forgotten that talk.

Change the Pace and Pitch

Good writers know they must mix long and short sentences. Some sentences have to lumber along slowly and carefully so they won't lose the reader. Other sentences have to "sing"—the ideas they reveal seem to bounce off the page. It's the same with a good speaker.

You know how dreary it is to listen to someone's monotonous voice drone on and on. Like the chanting of the Divine Office in a monastery, or the repetition of a mantra in transcendental meditation, a presentation given at the same speed from beginning to end will put people to sleep for sure.

So, every few minutes, change the pace. Talk faster ... or slower ... than normal. Raise and lower your voice for dramatic effect. This is especially easy if you're using a microphone. For example, you can bring it closer to your mouth and lower the pitch and speed of your voice as you say something like this, "Now listen to something important... " or "What I'm going to tell you in the next few minutes can make you famous." Put variety into your talk, through changes in word speed and tone, and you'll keep people interested in your talk.

Stick to your Plan

A good speaker plans a talk just as a traveler plans a trip. You wouldn't dream of planning a trip to Toronto, and then, half way there, change direction for New York City. It's the same with a good talk. You plan it carefully, with good reasons. Also, the more you know about your topic, the bigger the temptation to veer off in different directions and discuss related subjects. So, plan your talk, and talk your plan.

Set a Time Limit

Haven't you been annoyed as you listened to what was supposed to be a twenty-minute talk, only to sit through thirty, forty, even fifty minutes? That's another mark of a poor speaker. A good speaker never goes over a time limit, unless audience reactions are so persistent and enthusiastic that people won't let the speaker go. And that doesn't happen too often.

Build your talk around your plan, manage your time effectively and stick to it. Your audience will be grateful for your consideration and will be more receptive to you. And, as a practical matter, once you go beyond the planned time limit, people focus their attention on their watches, not on you. So don't kid yourself into thinking people are hanging on your every word; they're not.

Keep Notes on Small Cards

When you give a formal talk in which you're legally, politically, or financially liable for every word you say, you probably will have to read a prepared speech. (But even a prepared speech can sound interesting, with personal words and short, interesting sentences.) When you can, try to speak extemporaneously. Know your subject well enough so that you only need to refer to a few 3″ x 5″ cards from time to time. Don't read the cards—that's as bad as reading from a prepared text. After all, if *you* can't remember what you want to say, how can you expect your listeners to?

Put your outline on cards, using letters large enough to be read easily. Refer to your cards when you need to, but try to keep your attention on the audience.

43. HOW TO INFORM AN AUDIENCE AND GET RESULTS

The purpose of the informative presentation or speech is to secure understanding from the audience. To accomplish this, talk slowly enough to be understood, but fast enough to hold their interest. Watch the audience carefully to gauge this. If you see people looking bored, or whose attention is wandering, you're speaking too slowly. When they start asking each other questions and motioning toward you, you're losing them.

Here are suggestions for content that will help you inform people effectively:

Make Your Plan Clear

1. Organize your talk so you don't have too many main points. Three key points for a talk are plenty. Any more and you'll lose the audience. Of course, you may well have subpoints that reinforce what you want to say, but each subpoint should clearly relate to the main point. Reinforce it, and drive it home.

2. Clarify the logical relationship between your main points. What may seem clear and perfectly reasonable to you may be a hopeless muddle to your audience. For example, make sure you outline the details of each step in your conclusion, leading the audience along with you at each step of the way. Good sales people know the importance of this, and constantly develop each point with information that says "which means...." For example, it's not enough to say that a mattress is soft. Add the "which means...." "This mattress is so soft you could put a tennis ball under it, and you wouldn't feel the bulge. This means you'll get a full night's sleep, without interruption because of unwanted lumps. And that means you'll wake up rested, ready to tackle the day's work enthusiastically. That means you'll work better, with greater satisfaction and success." See the difference? You could almost go on and on indefinitely.

3. Make your transitions clear. *You* may know where your speech is headed, but your audience doesn't. You have to tell them...with transitional words. They're like signposts along the way—pointing out the direction your ideas are taking.

Here are transitional words to help guide your listeners:

"Go-Ahead" Words	These help you tell your reader to keep on reading. They say, "More of the ideas coming. Get ready!" For example:

And, more, moreover, more than that, furthermore, also.

Some go-ahead words mark the start of a more important idea, like a summary or a result of earlier ideas:

Thus, so, and so, therefore, consequently, accordingly.

Other go-ahead words tell you to keep reading, but also say you're about to come to a stop:

As a result, finally, concluding, in conclusion.

"Change-Idea" Words

Other transitional words tell your reader you're changing the direction of thought. They say, "Stop thinking this way; here's another, different idea to consider." Examples:

But, yet, nevertheless, otherwise, although, despite, in spite of, not, on the contrary, however, rather, still.

See how transitions help this paragraph:

A fashionable wardrobe can't make a plain person beautiful. *But* it's amazing how you can improve your appearance with good-looking clothes. *And,* you often feel better about yourself when you're well dressed. *Moreover,* when you feel good about yourself, you feel good about other people. *So* it makes sense to be well dressed.

Be Specific, Not Abstract

Don't sacrifice clarity for accuracy of detail. Too many details can muddle a reader. Nevertheless, facts and details make a talk interesting, and abstract words are dull. We learn through our senses, so facts need to be presented in terms of what we see, hear, smell, taste, and touch.

Vague, general, and abstract words say very little. Try to use the exact word you need to describe your idea. Here are typical abstract nouns you should avoid: *quality, nature, problem, reason, situation, method, effort, intent, course, condition.*

Here are typical wordy, awkward, vague phrases you should drop from sentences: *by means of, due to the fact that, for the purpose of, in order to, on the basis of, to the extent that, with respect to, in connection with.*

For example, the sentence:

"The nature of mercury is such that it is a liquid at room temperature."

This is better written:

"Mercury is a liquid at room temperature."

Here's another:

"This computer prepares sales promotion letters quickly."

This sentence reads better when written:

"The IBM 400 computer types 1,000 personalizes sales promotion letters in one hour."

Use charts and graphs whenever possible. These days, nearly all lecture rooms have access to an overhead projector. If you can use colored slides, even better. Look at how dull this information is:

"Three salespeople from Region C produced widely different results:

No. 1 Achieved sales of $1200—an increase of 200—20% over the previous month.

No. 2 Achieved sales of $800—an increase of 400—50% over the previous month.

No. 3 Had sales of $1600—a decrease of 400% over the previous month."

Look how easy it is to illustrate these facts with a single graph:

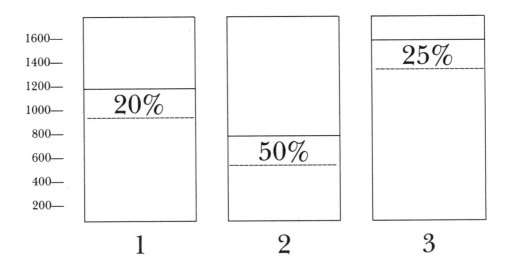

Don't Be Dull

This is an age of instant entertainment, thanks largely to TV. Even a 60-second commercial can cost over $100,000 to produce, just to make it entertaining. That's the kind of competition you face as a speaker. Good teachers know the importance of acting, and entertaining the class from time to time. Use figures of speech like, "He was a tiger at the sales meeting." And use plenty of humor. The world is deadly serious as it is, and people will be grateful for your humor. It can relieve tension and help people understand, and remember, your message.

Use Terms People Understand

A presentation to inform is not the time to confuse people with strange words. If your audience understands and appreciates technical words that help clarify your meaning, fine. But why use words like obfuscate, concatenate, and ratiocinate when confuse, link, and reason can do just as well? Talk *with* people, converse with them. Don't talk *to* them. You may just find someone in the audience who know as much or more about the topic than you do, and who will talk *back* to you.

44. THE DEADLY SINS OF DEADLY SPEAKERS

Get ready for some soul-searching. You really can't be an effective or persuasive speaker if you're one of these:

1. *The Elocutionist*
He's carried away by the sound of his own voice. He loves to hear it resonate and vibrate through the microphone, then bounce around the room. You can spot this speaker when you hear exaggerated pronunciations, phoney words, and pompous phrases. Another tip-off is that you'll hear lots of words, but little meaning. Twenty words are used when ten could do the job. Trying to get solid meaning from an elocutionist is like trying to get a nourishing meal from cotton candy.

2. *The Verbal Gymnast*
This bird likes to display his verbal plummage. He shows off with poly-syllabic words, technical terms, jargon, and antiquated words like peruse (instead of read). You soon turn him off, and people will turn you off if you try to show off how many words you know.

3. *The Oracle*
This person knows everything, or thinks he does. There was a know-it-all in my high school class. He walked around whistling a song only he could hear. He never asked a question out of curiosity—only to show what he knew, or to test what someone else knew. No one liked him. As far as I know, he didn't have any friends. You may be an expert in your field, but if you sound like you think there's nothing more to learn about a topic, you'll lose people. And it's only a matter of time before someone will make a fool of you. This can be a serious problem for a chief executive who is used to sending information downward, but who seldom gets self-critical feed-back upward.However, you can be sure that people are laughing at you and think you are really a fool if you come across as "the Oracle."

4. *The Hermit*
This person mumbles to himself. You have to ask yourself, "Why in the world would someone get up to talk, and then mumble so that few people could hear him?" It's true some hermits aren't aware of the problem. Others are simply too insensitive to be aware that they have a problem. A nationally famous authority on English literature once showed up to speak at an exclusive prep school. He walked on the stage, sat down at a table, buried his face in the book he had brought along and mumbled his observations for his entire talk. Hardly anyone heard him. The man who told me the story was there and recalled how one articulate student said, "Wasn't he refreshingly arrogant!" My friend said, simply, "I thought he was a boor."

5. *"Ole Mouthy"*

This person spits out a continuous stream of words with little or no thought behind them. He's not interested in his voice, or the effect it's having on the audience. But he's scared stiff of a few seconds of silence. So, word after word, phrase after phrase spew forth, often riddled with useless cliches. Sometimes you wonder when he breathes. And if he can take the time to think about what he is saying, why should his listeners?

45. EIGHT GESTURES THAT ADD PUNCH TO YOUR TALK

Gestures help you communicate more easily and clearly. They also make your talk more forceful and memorable. Good gestures are given in a relaxed, rather than tense, manner. They're *vigorous*, so there's no doubt about their usefulness. They're definite. with no misunderstanding as to what they mean, and they're timed so that they reinforce your meaning exactly when you need it. (You may have to practice in front of a mirror.)

Here are eight kinds of gestures you can use to fortify your talk:

Pointing

You can point to your hand, to a book, to something your audience can imagine, or to your audience. Pointing draws audience attention to a specific idea, and helps you, the speaker, to control their attention.

Giving and Receiving

Moving your hands outward in a gesture of giving, can make you look generous, reluctant, or enthusiastic, and can have a whole variety of meanings. It's the same when you use a receiving gesture you can also communicate many fine shades of meaning.

Rejecting

Hold your palm toward the audience, cross your arms, close your eyes, and push your hands outward ... all these can help you dramatize your rejection of an idea.

Clenching the Fist

You can show determination, anger, frustration, and many other strong feelings by clenching the fist.

Cautioning

Whether you use your index finger pointing outward, a cautioning gesture tells your audience to slow down its thinking, to proceed carefully, to consider all the aspects of what you're saying. A caution gesture also helps you establish control by letting your audience realize you've thought of the hidden problems they may have overlooked.

Dividing

You can show division by using one hand to chop against the other; by slicing up the air in front of you into sections. This gesture helps your audience see the complexity of your idea.

Facial Expressions

Here you have a tremendous variety to draw from. A turned up nose, raised eyebrows, or a scowl can draw emotions in ways that words can't. Body language accounts for as much as 80 percent of what we communicate, and much of that comes from facial expressions.

Pantomime and Impersonations

One of the best ways to keep an audience interested is to dramatize what you're saying. Act out your meaning, move around the lectern, and show people what you mean. Imitate speech and actions; make the audience visualize the person or situation you're referring to, and you'll have a captive audience in the palm of your hand.

46. THIRTEEN POWERFUL WAYS TO BEGIN YOUR TALK

First impressions count, especially with speakers. The first image you create in the minds of your listeners are you begin your talk is the one they're most likely to remember. Begin successfully, with confidence, and you'll probably end up with a successful talk.

After many years of teaching and giving presentations, I've discovered 13 secrets of a good beginning and will share them with you. But first, there are four things you have to remember to get the talk going. You need to wake people up, hold their attention, establish their willingness to listen to you, and then lead smoothly into the body of the talk. Now, here are the 13 secrets:

Use a Startling Statement

People need to be jolted now and then, but not violently. They're so busy with their own affairs they sometimes find it hard to settle down and pay attention to a speaker. So it's your job to start off with a statement that will question their values, challenge their established beliefs, and give them a minor shock. Here are some examples:

"Real charity doesn't care whether it's tax deductible or not."

"The world is full of willing people: some are willing to make fools of themselves; some are willing to let them."

"Everyone who comes here brings happiness: some when they arrive; some when they leave."

Use Suspense

Give your audience only a hint of what's coming—something they'll like or benefit from. It's like saying to a child, "Wait a few minutes for what I have to tell you and I'll give you a chocolate cookie."

For example, within the next 200 words of this chapter, I'll give you a secret to involving your audience. I don't care how big the audience is, or where it's located, or the topic of your talk. This secret to involving your audience personally won't cost you any money, and, once you use it frequently, people will say how interesting your talks are.

Use suspense. People love a little excitement in their lives and if you can give them a little tingle when you speak, so much the better. How do you create suspense? Don't give away all your key points at once. Let people know, for example, that you have *three* suggestions; that you found out something extremely strange about the little town you visited last summer; that you have finally discovered why your boss is so successful. Then talk around the problem, explaining the background and the relevant details. Say how the discovery helped you and why you want to pass on this information. Only then should you reveal your key point—only when your audience is drooling to know about it.

Ask a Question

The secret to involving your audience? Ask questions—important questions that make people come up with answers, even if the answers are only in their own mind. Every question demands an answer. That means your audience will have to respond to your question, even if it's only internally, and that means involvement. Here are some relevant questions to answer, depending upon your audience:

For business people:	"Would you like to know how you can increase your profits by 23 percent?"
For students:	"Would you like to know how to pass the next test—easily?"
For salespeople:	"Why would a simple revision in our standard presentation practically guarantee a sales close?"
For consumers:	"What three kinds of meat give you the best food buy, dollar for dollar?"

Open With a Strong Quote

People love to hear quotable quotes. Look at these, for example:

"Progressive education? Tell me about it! The teacher is afraid of the principal; the principal is afraid of the superintendent; the superintendent is afraid of the school board; the school board is afraid of the parents; the parents are afraid of the children. And the children? They're not afraid of anybody."

"It takes some 3,000 bolts to hold a car together, but only one nut to scatter it all over the countryside."

"When I think of the men who were my teachers, I realize that most of them were slightly mad. ... I have the most unpleasant recollections of the teachers who taught me. ... They were distinguished by unparalleled ignorance. ... " From *Hitler's Secret Confessions* (1941-44)

Old Arkansas lawyer Senator John McClellan once said: "I found out a long time ago that no matter how scared you are, you're a damn sight better if nobody knows it."

Make a Personal Reference

No one likes to listen to a "canned" talk and there's no reason for a talk to sound "canned," unless you stop working to make yourself interesting. Refer to your audience. Say how pleased you are to speak to salespeople from Brown's store because you've had many pleasant experiences shopping there. Tell why you like to talk to these teachers especially, because you met so many ahead of time who told you so many good things. Say you're glad to have the opportunity to talk to the Buffalo barbers, because they seem to be so well informed about the latest cutting techniques and hair styles.

You may have to dig a little to find the right personal reference, but you can often get the background material simply by talking to the program chairperson ahead of time and asking some personal questions about the group:

"What are they like? What issues concern them right now? What are their goals? What don't they like?"

A 10- or 15-minute conversation with someone who knows the group will give you all the information you need.

Tell an Anecdote or Make a Humorous Reference

People love humor. A good laugh is the grease that helps human relationships fit together more easily. Anecdotes don't need to be funny, but they do have to help you emphasize a point. An anecdote is a story with a point, and it's often one of the best ways to help you win your point with your audience. If you can come up with something humorous yourself, and tie it in with the audience or the other speakers, that's even better. But it usually takes a seasoned speaker to do this.

Get a book of anecdotes, stories for speakers, famous quips, or whatever source you like, and prepare a few anecdotes before you give your talk. By the way, it's a good idea never to go to a meeting or a banquet without one or two stories you can tell. You *never* know when you'll be asked to say a few words.

Here's a sample anecdote I use whenever I want to stress the point of breaking news gently to people. I call it my "Cat Story."

A man had a cat he was really fond of. When he had to go to Europe for six weeks he asked his brother to take care of his cat while he was away.

He was gone about two weeks and decided to call his brother to see how things were going. He asked his brother, "How's the cat?"

The brother said, "The cat's dead."

The man was so shocked that he simply hung up the phone, and didn't contact his brother again until the trip was over. When he came home he called his brother and said, "Why did you do that to me?"

"Do what to you?"

"You know—about the cat—the way you treated me when I called to ask you how the cat was."

His brother said, "What did I do? I just told you the cat was dead, and that was the truth."

The man said, "But you know how much that cat meant to me. Couldn't you have broken the news to me a lot more gently?"

His brother said, "What do you mean?"

He said, "Well, if I called you and said, 'How's the cat?' you could have said something like, 'She went up on the roof ... but there's no problem and we're just getting her down now.'

"And if I called you the next day and said, 'How's the cat?' you could have said, 'We got her down from the roof, but she scratched her paw a little so we've taken her to the vet. But really, there's no problem and the cat is fine.'

"If I called you again and said, 'How's the cat?' you could have said, 'The cat's fine. The vet did say she had developed a slight infection from the scratch, but he's given her some medication and she's sleeping fine.'

"And if when I called again and asked, 'How's the cat?' you could have said, simply: 'The cat passed away in its sleep, but there was no pain at all ... it was very peaceful. I'm sorry.'"

The brother thought for a minute and said, "Okay, I see your point. I'm sorry, I guess I was a little hard." The man said, "That's all right, it's over. Let's forget it. By the way, 'How's Mom?'"

His brother said, "She went up on the roof ... "

So sprinkle your talk with anecdotes, especially at the beginning. And if you can begin your presentation with your own "Cat Story," you'll have the audience in the palm of your hand.

Plunge Into Your Topic Immediately

There are many advantages to beginning your talk by jumping right into the topic. Especially with busy, impatient people in the audience, you might do well to get started right away—no delays. Simply begin your talk like this:

"Good morning. Profits at Acme Thread are an important topic these days, especially as we continue revising our plans for next year. This morning I want to show you why our profits have been falling, and what we can do about it in the next three to six months."

Then proceed to give them all the facts, up front, no wasted time or words. You can explain later on ... answer questions, provide background information if people seem to want it. But, basically, you should give your key points in the first few minutes of your talk.

State Your Purpose

People often like to know what your angle is, even if they've been told the purpose of your talk well in advance. They like to know where you're coming from, as it were, so they can form their ideas accordingly.

In this kind of opening, you tell people what you hope to accomplish—why you're talking to them. If you're talking to the Acme Thread sales group, for example, you might say something like this:

> "The reason we're here this morning is to find out how we can boost sales by 15 percent in the next six months, consolidate our territories, and make better use of our time.
>
> "Why is this important? Because we need a better market share to retain our current position. We need to cut down on the duplicated efforts that can result in having more territories than we need. And if we make better use of our time, we can make better, more profitable sales calls, with less effort, and with a greater return. That means money in our pockets—yours and the company's.
>
> "So our purpose this morning is clear—how to improve sales and work more effectively—with greater rewards for us all."

Refer to the Occasion

A good way to begin a talk, which is especially appropriate for luncheon or after-dinner presentations or special meetings, is to refer to the reason why everyone is together at the meeting. Mention the organization, the purpose of the meeting, and then show how your talk fits in with that purpose.

With this opening, you might say something like:

> "It's remarkable to see so many shoe store managers like yourselves meeting to see how you can improve your sales by improving customer relations. You know, you're in the business of making people feel comfortable—not only about the way they feel physically, but the way they feel about themselves when they walk out of your store with your shoes. This evening, I'd like to suggest some ideas that will help you make people comfortable in other ways as well—about your store, the people who work for you, and the products you sell."

Use an Exhibit

People love toys. Maybe it's from our early days in school when we loved "Show and Tell" sessions, but we all love to see something physical, specific, or graphic, especially at the beginning of a talk.

To open your talk, why not bring an exhibit you've built? Think about the fascination you've felt as you walked through a shopping mall and saw special exhibit tables:

- An insulation company has some cutaway partition samples with before-and-after examples of how their insulation works.
- An artist who sells chalk portraits has 10 or 15 samples of her work on display so you can see the results up close—easily and dramatically. You quickly visualize how you or a close friend or relative would look in such a portrait.
- A supermarket has a charming person cooking a new kind of meat dish in an electric fry pan—right there in the mall. She invites you to sample the dish for yourself, holding out the meat on a toothpick or in a small cup. Free food! Cooked right there! Of course you'll try some.
- Teachers know the value of exhibits. English teachers who talk about Shakespeare's special theatre try to get a model of it for everyone to see; math teachers who explain the formulas derived from various conic sections often bring in models of the sections to show how the curves of the parabola, ellipse, and hyperbola are generated.

People are fascinated by something physical, and you can capitalize on this fascination by starting your talk with an explanation of the exhibit.

Appeal to Their Self-Interest

Every group wants something. Talk to the program chairman and find out the group's goals, then build your talk around them. For example, a group of teachers may want information on how to be more effective in securing their benefits from the administration or the school board. Salespeople may want to know new ways to make a close more easily. A group of farmers may want to know new marketing ideas to get top dollar for their products.

Find the hot button for each group and talk to it. Build everything you say around the goal of helping them achieve that goal. And, of course, your opening sentence, your first few minutes, should stress that theme loud and clear. Here are some openers:

- "Tonight let's talk about how you, as modern farmers, can market your products to get top market dollars without a lot of extra work on your part."
- "Good benefits are important to teachers today—teachers like you, who want to provide security for your families. In the next 15 or 20 minutes I'll show you some of the ways you can get those benefits and the security you want."
- "As salespeople, you want to make as few unproductive calls as possible, and close on more of them. Give me just one-half hour of your time ... with

an open mind … without distractions … and I'll show you how to double your closing rate."

Issue a Challenge

People like a goal. And they like a specific challenge to do something that's possible, but is perhaps a little difficult. It's kind of a test we use to confirm our own self-worth.

You can begin a speech by challenging people to achieve something that's important to them by inviting them to reach beyond their ordinary performance to excel. You might start out your talk with something like this:

"A 15 percent drop in absenteeism will bring our profits back into line, and keep everyone working for the next six months. I'd like to challenge you supervisors to make our absenteeism rate drop at least that much. The Executive Committee doesn't think you can do it. I believe you can, and I'll show you how. I think it's a challenge worth fighting for."

"We *can* improve the math scores of our students. We *can* improve their reading skills. We *can* help them write better. And we *can* measure our improvement. The school board has challenged us to prove that we can do this even though, quite frankly, they don't see how it's possible without a tremendous outlay of money. I believe you people have the skills, the talent and the experience to make this happen … at little or no cost to the district. Think about it. If you can accept this challenge, we can prove our value to our students even more than we have in the past."

"This evening I'm going to offer you a challenge … a challenge so important that, if you can meet it successfully, will mean a better life for all of us, including you and your families. Here's the challenge…."

Some Other Ideas

Just a few more hints about a good opening. Memorize your opening sentence, so you start off confidently and smoothly. Get to the point of your talk quickly. People will give you only about two or three minutes of their attention before they make a decision to let their mind wander.

The most important thing is … *believe in yourself*. If you're confident that you can give a successful talk, if you feel good about yourself, you'll probably give a great talk, Think about the successful things you already do. Think about the fine preparation you've made to give the talk. You've got many past successes going for you!

Open with short, forceful sentences—ideas that will jolt the listener into tuning in to *you alone*. Short sentences are like little punches: they keep jabbing away at the reader's mind until you've pushed it gently into the position where you want it.

Finally, make your opening inviting. It's your job, during the first few minutes of any talk, to make people like you and like what you have to say. You do that with smiles, with words that are pleasant, and with an attitude that you like the people you're talking to, and that you have something interesting and exciting to share with them. You're really inviting them to listen to you. And that's something you can't force.

47. EIGHT WAYS TO END YOUR TALK MEMORABLY

Now it's time to end your talk. How can you do it so people will remember what you said? First, don't bore your audience with a long conclusion. Be brief. You've probably heard speakers who said, "In conclusion ... " and went on for another 15 minutes. Of course, don't stop so abruptly that you surprise the audience, leaving them uncomfortable. But make your closing short and to the point. It's a good idea, too, not to introduce new material in the conclusion, and don't use long, involved sentences. Your audience may be naturally tired (yes, even of you!) and may be looking for some relief.

Another point: don't try to save a lost cause—a speech you know has been a failure—by dragging out the ending. If you weren't successful this time, for whatever the reason, chalk it off and get your closing over with. Finally, don't forget to plan the final sentence of every talk. Your last sentence is something people will remember for a long time, so plan it carefully and make it memorable.

Now for the eight special ways to end your talk:

Summarize Key Points

This is by far the easiest way to end a talk, and may, in fact, be the most popular. You simply review your key points to make sure people understand them clearly. You might say something like this:

> "Before we leave, let me just mention the key points discussed. First, it's important that we cut costs by 15 percent in the next three months. Second. ... "

Summarize Your Theme Generally

If you merely want to leave people with a general impression of your theme, rather than review the details of your talk, you can reiterate your theme or summarize it generally. Say it in a different way, perhaps from a different viewpoint. But your objective, in using this kind of close, is to make sure people know what your position is. To do this, you may say something like this:

> "This morning, we've talked about absenteeism—what causes it and how to control it. We could sum it all up this way: people miss work because they don't like it, either because of the organization, their supervisor, or themselves. We need to find out what the reason is. Then we can control it by counseling, by discipline, by policy, or by training."

Use the Same Method Used in the Introduction

If you opened with a quote, end with that same quote. Opened with a startling statement? Close with the same one. Did you give the audience a challenge? Repeat the challenge again. Whatever method you used to begin your talk, use that same method again. It'll bring your talk full circle and reinforce the impact you had at the beginning.

Visualize the Future

Help the audience picture what the future would be like if they accept your ideas. Draw verbal pictures so vividly that they can almost taste your ideas. Here's a sample:

> "Imagine what would happen if the new ordering system I propose were put into effect tomorrow: Purchasing would send the requisition to accounting. Within two days, the order would be placed. We could expect delivery one month later and products would be on stream just two days after that. We'd improve customer turn-around time by 50 percent. That means we'd handle orders in six weeks or less, not eight weeks, as we do now. And that means. ... "

Appeal to Their Emotions

Use your ending to leave people with a feeling of warmth, pride, fear, or lightheartedness—whatever is appropriate for your subject. For example, suppose you were giving a talk on teaching. Your theme: teachers too often waste time and opportunities by staying with the traditional course of study, instead of developing material that students want and need. You might end your talk this way:

> "If there's a question in your mind whether teachers are forced to waste their time on the traditional curriculum, think about this: I have taught in high school for 10 years.
> During that time, I have given assignments to a murderer, an evangelist, a fighter, a thief, and an imbecile. The murderer was a quiet little boy who sat in the front row and regarded me with pale blue eyes. The evangelist, easily the most popular boy in the school, had the lead in the junior play. The fighter lounged by the window and let fly with raucous laughs at times I least expected. The thief was a light-hearted romantic with a song on his lips, and the imbecile was a soft-eyed little animal seeking the shadows.
> Today, the murder awaits death in the state penitentiary; the evangelist has been dead a year; the fighter lost an eye in a brawl in

Hong Kong; the thief, by standing on tiptoe, can just see the windows of my room from the county jail; and the once gentle-eyed little moron now beats his head against a padded wall in the state asylum. All these pupils once sat in my class, sat and looked at me gravely across worn desks. I must have been a great help to these people—I taught them the rhyming scheme of the Elizabethan sonnet and how to diagram a complex sentence."

Suggest Definite Action

Tell your audience exactly what you recommend ... tell them what to do. If you want people to prepare monthly work plans, tell them that; if you want people to join a community service group, suggest which ones they could consider; if you want people to put their money into real estate instead of stocks, tell them how to go about it.

In this kind of closing, you can't weigh your words and you can't hold back. You need to make the action absolutely clear. You want people to talk in such a way that there's no doubt in their minds. Be specific and concrete. People should be able to picture exactly what you say so there will be no doubt as to what they should do and what will happen if they do what you want.

Use an Appropriate Quote

Pick a quotation that sums up your main theme—something memorable that people will think about for a long time. When your talk is finished, you might end by saying something like this:

"We've been talking about the importance of training people in today's industrial setting. Let me leave you with a quote from a person I worked with and who has more than 20 years' experience training people:

'Ignorance is not the problem. The problem is not knowing *when* we are ignorant.'

"Ladies and gentlemen, it is our job to help people realize *when* they don't know something. Thank you."

Here are two more quotes you can close on:

STRENGTH

"Gentleness is a divine trait: nothing is so strong as gentleness, and nothing is so gentle as real strength."

LOVE

"The person who believes in nothing still needs someone to believe in him or her."

Use an Illustration, Tell a Story

A final way to end your talk with a bang is to tell a story or anecdote, or use a personal reference to dramatize your theme. Just as stories build interest throughout the talk, a good story at the end can help people remember your main point.

You might use a story about something interesting that happened to you, or you might choose a story that you know your audience will relate to. For example, if your talk centers on education, you could relate something like this:

"You know, students have changed. Ten years ago, when a student slept in my class I could say, "Hey, somebody wake that guy up." A student would poke him and say, "Hey, stupid wants you to wake up." Today I have to think twice before I say that, because the answer I'm likely to get back is, "Why should I? You put him to sleep!"

Here's another:

"It's easy to tell the difference between graduate and undergraduate students. If you walk into the classroom and say, "Good morning," and the students greet you in return, they're undergraduates. If they write it down, they're graduate students."

48. SAMPLE OUTLINE YOU CAN USE FOR ANY TALK

It's true, you have to gear your talk to your audience, and that means planing your talk to meet their needs. But here's a sample outline you can use for practically any presentation. It'll help you to keep you key points to a minimum, and to develop each point specifically.

I. *Introduction:*
   A. Opening: ask a relevant question, or present a story, quotation, or other interest-arousing material.
   B. Reveal the purpose of your talk.
   C. Show how your subject will concern the audience.
   D. State your main points.
II. *Body:*
   A. First point
      1. Say what supports your main point.
         a. Elaborate or explain what supports the main point.
         b. Further elaborate.
      2. Second point
         (Repeat as above)
      3. Third point
         (Repeat as above.) Continue with as many main points as are necessary. However, the more points you include will make it that much more difficult for people to remember what you say.
III. *Conclusion:*
   A. Summarize main points for clarity.
   B. Remind the audience of your central idea or message.
   C. Closing: use an impressive statement, question, quotation, story, or some similar device to end on a powerful, memorable note.

INDEX

477